Jeffrey Robinson is a bestselling American author who has lived in Europe for the past 19 years. Born and raised in New York, he was educated at Temple University in Philadelphia. After serving four years as an officer in the United States Air Force, he moved to the South of France. Using that as his base, he spent the next dozen years vagabonding around the world, writing articles and short stories. He moved to London in 1982 and is married, with two children.

Other Books By Jeffrey Robinson

FICTION:

Pietrov and Other Games

The Ginger Jar

NON-FICTION:

Bette Davis – Her Stage and Film Career

Teamwork – Comedy Teams in the Movies

The Risk Takers

Minus Millionaires

Yamani – The Inside Story

Rainier and Grace

THE RISK TAKERS
– FIVE YEARS ON

Mandarin

A Mandarin Paperback
THE RISK TAKERS: FIVE YEARS ON

First published in Great Britain 1990
Reprinted 1990
by Mandarin Paperbacks
Michelin House, 81 Fulham Road, London SW3 6RB

Mandarin is an imprint of the Octopus Publishing Group

A CIP catalogue record for this title
is available from the British Library
ISBN 0 7493 0455 3

Printed and bound in Great Britain
by Cox & Wyman Ltd, Reading, Berks

For SJR *with love*

Contents

Many thanks for immeasurable help to my agent Leslie Gardner, my editor Jane Carr and my pal, La Benayoun.

I am, of course, extremely grateful to the scores of people I spoke with – some of whom appear in this book, many of whom don't. They include deputies and assistants, financial journalists and City analysts, co-workers and competitors. They also include all those secretaries who put up with my badgering for information and appointments, and who somehow overlooked my usual impatience and ill temper to arrange appointments with their boss.

I would also like to express my gratitude to Dialog Information Services, of Palo Alto, California, for access to their unrivalled sources of business and technical information. Dialog is the world's largest on-line database service and has proven to be an invaluable research tool. I don't know what I would have done without them. Actually, yes I do. I would have spent twice as much time to come up with half as much information.

Most importantly, I wish to say thank you to the risk takers who are portrayed here, all of whom at one point or another gave me some of their time. I trust they will understand that, while the chips have fallen where they may, at least they have fallen honestly and without malice.

Five years on I am still convinced that you guys are much more fascinating than movie stars and football players.

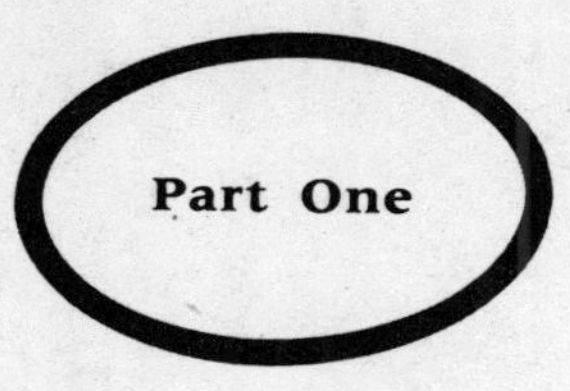

The Risk Takers

Introduction

The airlines have a lot to answer for.

I'm convinced they do it on purpose.

Every time I fly, no matter what airline, no matter what country, the seat next to mine gets assigned to the local variation of a skinny, bald-headed man in a green-striped polyester tie who, within six minutes of take-off, insists on asking, 'So, what do you do?'

My stock reply is, 'I'm in scaffolding.'

Most of the time I get a momentary blank stare followed by a polite smile, something like, 'How interesting,' and that's the end of that. After all, what kind of meaningful conversation can two total strangers possibly have about scaffolding?

But beware of skinny, bald-headed men in green-striped polyester ties flying to Cleveland, Ohio.

'No kidding.' His face lit up and his bony hand extended across the arm rest. 'Thurgood Frong,' . . . or something like that . . . 'I'm in fasteners.'

There could be no doubt that the airlines were out to get me. 'Fasteners?' Did he mean bra hooks? 'Er . . . no kidding.'

'Yeah, screws and bolts. We do a lot of stuff for scaffolds.'

'Oh, those kinds of fasteners.' Too bad.

'So what's new in your end of the business?'

'Not a helluva lot,' I shrugged. 'Nice tie. What's new in your end of the business?'

'Well,' he said with great pride, leaning closer to let me in on his best-kept secret, 'we're very long on dry wall screws.'

Why shouldn't we all be? 'Sounds terribly exciting.'

'Let me tell you something.' He grabbed my sleeve. 'When I

say we're long on DWS . . .' dry wall screws, as we refer to them in the biz . . . 'I mean we've just invented a screw that will go right into a wall. No mollies. No plugs. No filler. Straight into the wall and the sucker grips.' He waved a triumphant fist. 'Mollies are dead. We're going to own the world!'

Alas, poor Molly.

'Read my lips.' He repeated, 'WE ARE GOING TO OWN THE WORLD.'

For the only time in my life I suddenly had something good to say about Cleveland.

I mean, if enthusiasm counts for anything, this guy will undoubtedly own the world long before Molly even knows what screwed her (figure of speech!).

But then, I readily admit that I like these types of characters and in fact have been collecting them for a very long time.

The first one I can recall bumping into was back at the end of the '60s.

Through no fault of my own, I found myself stuck for a couple of weeks in a dusty, sage-brushed West Texas town called Lubbock. As the old joke goes, it was second prize. (First prize meant you didn't have to go to Lubbock at all.)

Plunked down in the middle of flat, hot, cattle country, Lubbock was – and almost certainly still is today – a cowpoke town where young men walked through the main street wearing cowboy hats, jeans and with spurs on their boots. They'd probably have worn chaps as well, except it isn't easy climbing in and out of a pick-up truck without spilling your beer can while dressed like that.

The motel where I stayed was owned by and named for a local hero called Donny Anderson. He grew up there, went to Texas Tech University there, and eventually turned into a big-deal professional football star. He wore Number 44 for Dallas or Green Bay, or some team like that over several seasons. Memory fails. But, just so that no one would miss the point, the swimming pool in the lobby of the Donny Anderson Motel was shaped like an American football helmet with the number 44 painted across the bottom.

In those days there were no such things as bars in Texas. The State licensing laws prohibited them. Instead there were private clubs – except they were open to anyone willing to pay the $1 one-night entry fee. You walked into the club at the Donny Anderson Motel and the smiling girl at the door asked you to sign the guest book. She said, 'Hi, my name is Wilma and you'll be my guest at the club tonight. You'll have to pay for your own drinks, but you are welcome to use my drink locker.' Her drink locker turned out to be the club's bar. She and the bartender might well have been the only legitimate members of this club – although I suspect the manager and owner were members too. Maybe Donny Anderson was also. I never asked.

Signing in one night, I followed a guy who wrote his name in the guest book as Frank something. I can't remember his last name. I have no idea what happened to him. I never saw him again. He may be, by this time, one of the best-heeled guys in America. Or he may be broke. But I'd bet that he struck it rich.

He was in his 30s, well dressed, with a salesman's handshake and a salesman's grin. His particularly easy drawl gave him away as being from Georgia – it's a very different accent from what you hear in Texas. As it was early, and as the place was dead empty, we shared a table. I seem to recall that eventually other people came along and sat with us. But I don't remember who they were, although if memory serves, one was a flashy young woman whom he introduced as his secretary. That's what you had to do in America in the late '60s. Especially in places like Lubbock, Texas. Separate rooms, please.

After the usual amount of small talk, coupled with a few Margueritas – besides beer that's what they like to drink in that part of the world – he mentioned that he was in town on business.

And his business was chasing tornadoes.

Just one week before, Lubbock had suffered the wrath of the gods as a tornado ripped through the town. Seems they built the place in the wrong spot – tornadoes happened there with nasty regularity. And the tornado that smashed through Lubbock, Texas, in the early summer of 1969 had been one of the most devastating ever. Entire buildings were uprooted. The roads had flooded. Destruction was everywhere. Lubbock looked like Berlin at the end of 1945.

Frank was one of the first to reach the town. He was, in the purest sense, an asset stripper. He heard about the tornado, grabbed his chequebook, and got on to the next flight. He moved into the Donny Anderson Motel for as long as it would take him to buy up the town. A wrecked bridge. Steel girders. Iron fencing. The remains of a gas station. Junked cars. Twisted buses. He grabbed whatever scrap and junk he could lay his hands on. The insurance adjusters, who came through at about the same time, paid off claims and found themselves owning the spoils. In turn, Frank was willing to pay for everything the insurance companies didn't want. And they didn't want almost all of what they had paid for. Anyone who wasn't insured was also an obvious seller. Within a day or two word got around that some guy named Frank was in town with his pockets full of money. The motel switchboard lit up like a Christmas tree. Whatever anybody in the fallen city of Lubbock wanted to sell, Frank was willing to buy. If he had to pay 10 cents on the dollar that was fine. If he could get it for 5 cents on the dollar, that was even better.

In between buying sprees, which he did from the back of a rented car with a line of credit at a local bank, a clipboard and pre-printed contracts, he stopped at what few phone booths were still standing to ring his office in Georgia and list the new inventory. His game was simple. Buy cheap, then sell fast to someone, anyone, for more than he paid. The trick was to find someone, anyone, who would know what to do with contorted steel bridge girders.

It was your basic cash and carry – a big-money business, he claimed, as long as he got all the ingredients right. But it could easily be financial disaster if he didn't. The last thing he wanted to do was get stuck with a bunch of battered telephone poles that he couldn't sell, wouldn't want to store, and didn't have the slightest intention of ever using. Added to that, he was also facing the competition – who knows how many other Franks were staying at other motels along the tornado's path, flooding the market with dollars to buy, and scrap to unload.

His particular type of risk taking relied heavily on instant turnover. Sure, he had regular clients on whom he could count to take a certain amount of snarled aluminium siding. And sure, much of what he bought was probably pre-sold. Much of what he bought that summer might even have changed hands several times before anyone came to take it away. Ideally, he wanted to sell before he bought, using the banks' money to purchase the scrap based on the contract to sell. The difference was pure profit. If he got his timing wrong, the difference was a flat loss. Then again, his business was built around so-called 'Acts of God', which meant he had to rely on just the right number of natural disasters and just the right amount of destruction every year to keep him in silk suits and blonde secretaries. Too few twisters meant scrap-buying prices would be high and the cost of getting in the game perhaps prohibitive. Too many earthquakes would flood the sellers' market and diminish his profits.

It struck me, as he talked, that his act was a pretty exciting one. That his kind of wheeling and dealing was a terrific way to earn a living. Looking back, I guess the idea for *The Risk Takers* had already begun to germinate.

It was eight or nine years later when I met my second risk-taker. I was living in the South of France by then, writing short stories for the slick magazine market but relying heavily on the *International Herald Tribune* to buy my non-fiction features, which helped to pay the rent. I don't remember exactly how I met Marty Ackerman, but he and his wife Diane were in France that summer, having rented a gigantic villa on Cap Ferrat.

In 1960, Ackerman was a New York lawyer with an office on Park Avenue. He was 28 years old, married, with young children, living in suburbia. But he was also a man burdened with an unnerving feeling that his life was a treadmill. One morning, he simply decided to change all of that. He walked out of his office and stepped into the nearest bank. With very little effort he was able to negotiate a relatively small $10,000 personal loan. Because the United States happens to be a lawyer-oriented society – the government is run by lawyers and so are a huge number of major corporations, including banks – Ackerman had no trouble getting in to see the loan manager, convincing him that he needed the money to fix up his office, and signing the proper papers. They wrote him a cheque right away.

With that in hand, he headed for the next bank on the block where he opened a deposit account for $10,000. The total time involved was less than an hour. Having nothing else to do before lunch, he repeated the procedure with another pair of banks. The interest on the $20,000 in term deposits was nearly enough to offset the interest accrued on the $20,000 loans. In other words, the cost of all this was relatively low – a couple of points per year.

Except he didn't wait a year.

Within a few months he paid off the loans and cleared his accounts. Now he had a proven line of credit with four banks. So he borrowed more, saved more, and paid off those loans. Then he started all over again. By moving increasingly larger sums of money, he established a working relationship and credit record with so many banks that, within twelve months of his first loan, he was able to borrow, solely on his signature, over $100,000. That was the money he put down to purchase a struggling company in Philadelphia.

The climate was right for such things in America in the '60s. If you knew what you were doing, one company could get you two, and two could get you four. All you had to understand was that a pyramid can only stand when the base is flat and the top is pointed. Upside-down it is guaranteed to topple. Throughout the '60s there were stories of upside-down pyramids that came crashing down. But Ackerman's was built right and within eight years that ailing Philadelphia company was a $150 million conglomerate. He owned a private jet, a bank in Beverly Hills, and the once-mighty Curtis Publishing Company.

By the time the '60s ended, Ackerman was thinking of opting

out. What he did was what many risk-takers always promise to do but never get around to. He decided that he'd now lived all the ego trips of success in America, and went in search of something else. He divested himself of several homes – including a nine-storey Park Avenue townhouse which he sold to the East German government – packed up his art collection and with Diane, his second wife, and their new baby, he moved to London.

As he said at the time, 'In those days, if I didn't work from 7 a.m. until 11 or 12 at night, I had guilt pangs. I was exhausted, too heavy and out of shape. My first marriage went bad. I had a permanent sore on my ear from the telephone receiver. I looked at myself one day and realized I was getting old. I had to get off the treadmill.'

Speaking as someone who knew first hand, he believed that the kind of money he made in the '60s could still be made now. 'But only by young people who are willing to take massive risks. It can only be done by young people who have no money and therefore nothing to lose. When you have money you become too conservative.'

Almost predictably, after a few sedentary years in Europe, Ackerman and family headed back to New York. When last heard from he was practising law – with a little bit of risk taking on the side, just to keep his hand in.

In many ways, the start of Sam Cummings's career as a risk taker is the same. In 1950 he had nothing to lose. Today he is the largest and single most important arms dealer in the world. His company, Interarms, is said to own so much hardware that, had he the soldiers to go along with it, he would be the fourth or fifth largest army on earth.

Cummings is a likeable man who tries, at every turn, to play down the idea that war is good for his business. 'As soon as there is any trouble in the world, the governments themselves get into the arms business and force the private dealers out. We've never supplied any nation, anywhere in the world, during a time of real or potential hostilities. But then, yes, you'd be quite accurate in saying that my business, like war, is based totally on human folly and not on human wisdom.'

Born in Philadelphia in 1927, he landed a job during the Korean War with the Central Intelligence Agency as a weapons expert. Strictly overt, he insists. Absolutely nothing spooky. 'You could even reach me on the phone there.' For three years he sat in an office looking at pictures of captured weapons, writing reports, explaining what those weapons were and where they came from. 'It didn't take too long before I grew very tired of looking at those same pictures.' So in 1953 he decided to go into business for himself. But the only business he knew was guns. He settled on the name International Arms Corporation simply because that had the right ring to it. His address was a post office box in Washington DC and his stationery listed him as Vice-President. 'I couldn't afford an office and I figured I'd only be Vice-President so that anyone I dealt with would think there was at least one other person in the company, and maybe a secretary.'

He wrote to governments all over the world offering to buy any surplus arms they had. His only response came from the police chief of Panama. 'That was especially fortunate because in those days Panama was one of the cheapest places you could fly to. The police chief had a stock of 5000 – 6000 weapons for sale. Forty years' worth of stuff they had taken off revolutionaries, bank robbers and drunken sailors. I offered him $25,000, he accepted, and then I was faced with the problem of where to get the money because I didn't have a nickel.'

Returning to the States, he started ringing gun dealers around the country. He wanted $60,000 for the lot. One dealer in California said sure. Cummings used the dealer's acceptance to get credit at the bank. That paid for the guns. The Californian's cheque for $60,000 paid for the overdraft and expenses, and left him with a $15,000 profit. He then rushed back to Central America where his pal the Panamanian police chief put him in touch with other people who had guns for sale. As his business grew, military people started asking him where they could buy quality arms. He knew the manufacturers, thanks to contacts he had developed during his CIA years, and he found himself acting as a broker. 'This was during the years of the rearmament of Europe. The timing was right. There has always been a huge collectors' market, but the surplus arms market had never really been exploited in quite the way I was doing it. However, brains had nothing to do with my success. I fell into it. Dumb luck and serendipity.'

Dumb luck and serendipity is certainly an over-simplification. A better word might be control.

The gambler bets on the horse. The risk taker owns the horse, owns the race course, owns the parking lot concession and probably also owns the nearest hot dog stand. True, there is a risk element with both. But with the punter, luck is in control. With the risk taker, he must control.

Throughout the 1980s a Texan named T. Boone Pickens was living proof of that.

Chairman of Mesa Petroleum Co., he is a tall, slender 62-year-old who looks more like an investment banker than a ruthlessly tough, oil baron who's constantly found success in failure. Almost every time since 1973 that he's gone into the market looking to take over a company with a hostile bid, somebody else winds up winning the company. Yet it's the damnedest thing, that every time he lost he wound up making a lot of money.

Most people called that game 'greenmail'.

Pickens has always insisted that wasn't what he had in mind, and is even on the record as being against greenmail – that is, going in for a take-over, running up the share price, and then bailing out with a substantial profit. It was a particularly faddish trick of the junk bond decade. As long as you could get someone to pick up your high-risk paper, you didn't even need real money to scare certain companies.

But there was a lot more to his act than IOUs and Lone Star bravado.

What Pickens always did so very well was to control the market in which he was a buyer. In some cases his mere presence was enough. At least that's what it looked like in the autumn of 1983 when he went after Gulf Oil. Pickens and seven partners started buying Gulf shares at $45. They'd acquired some 21.7 million shares by the time Pickens announced his plans to revamp Gulf. And that sent Gulf's board into a frenzy. Obviously there was no place in the Pickens plan for them. So the guys on top – the ones whose jobs were at stake along with their egos – panicked. A fierce take-over battle ensued. Pickens kept the heat on and at one point campaigned for uncommitted shares as if he was running for office. When everything including name-calling failed, the Gulf board went in search of a white knight, a suitor who'd be willing to save them from Pickens. Standard Oil of California arrived on the scene to merge with Gulf and the war was over. Beaten once more, Pickens relinquished control of the battle by selling those 21.7 million shares at $80 per and limped all the way to the bank, a battered and beaten man, with a $760 million profit.

Not bad for a few weeks' work.

Controlling the game and therefore being able to minimize your risks is only one element. The high-flyers whose names have become household words in the City and along Wall Street have all made money by combining control with other factors. Much like the football player who controls the ball, controls his opponent and helps his team control the game, he also needs speed, know-how, the right mental attitude, the best physical condition and maybe even the luck of a dry pitch. Also like the football player, he will almost definitely lose by doing nothing more than losing control.

Freddie Laker is the perfect example.

He began life in the airline business in 1938. He was just 16. Jokingly he says he used to sweep out the hangars. His biography says he was in training as an engineer. It wasn't until after World War II that he actually began making some money. He got into the buying and selling of planes and parts, and when the Berlin Airlift came along in 1948 his planes were in the air. In 1951, when the Divided City was blockaded again,

Laker was there flying cargo in and out. Also flying refugees out. A quarter of a million of them.

Twenty-five years later, Laker took aim at what he knew could be the aviation world's most lucrative market. He wanted to do for transatlantic travel what McDonalds had done for hamburgers. At its peak, Laker Airways had revenues of about $500 million. Shareholders' equity was a tenth of that. As he put it, 'My company made a profit every year except 1981/2. In fact, on 31 March 1981, we were in the black to the tune of £3 million. But in this business you only need to make one loss if it's big enough.'

By 5 February 1982, the loss was indeed big enough and Laker was out of business.

A tall, pleasant man, Laker sounds something like Stan Laurel. He's got that same kind of accent. A folk hero and larger-than-life optimist, he became Sir Freddie in the days when he was champion knight of the skies. He had all the trappings of a wealthy man – expensive cars, a yacht, a farm – plus a face and name almost as recognizable as any pop star's. When the airline went under, he lost the cars, the yacht and the farm. He had to take the FLY I numberplate off the Rolls and transfer it to a Volkswagen. A travel firm paid the liquidator to use the name Laker on a holiday company, so the best he could do was remortgage his home to get up another stake and try again with a company called Skytrain Holidays. He got Tiny Rowland of Lonrho to go into partnership with him, and at least for a while it seemed as if he could make a comeback.

Whether Laker lost control of his airline or others took it away from him, became the object of several lawsuits. The liquidators claimed there'd been a conspiracy by a consortium of 12 companies, in direct violation of US anti-trust laws. They wanted $1.1 billion to make everything right again. The consortium, which included British Airways, Pan Am, TWA and British Caledonian, denied the charges. But the liquidators had enough cards to play that, in the summer of 1985, British Airways, on behalf of the consortium, negotiated a 'no admission of guilt' settlement. The 'not guilty' parties paid $48 million to see the case off. That included rebates for all of the Laker customers who were left holding useless tickets and an $8 million payment to Sir Freddie.

Conspiracy or not, Laker was already plagued with serious problems.

Looking back, he says that, at least in the beginning, he wanted to produce a one-class airplane. 'DC-10s run with 380 people. Maximum seating on our DC-10s was 345, all economy.' He eventually did create another class on his planes, and now he admits that might have been an error.

'It probably was a mistake going into the other class of service the way we did at the end. We shouldn't have tried to fight the other airlines at the front of the plane, except they started to fight us in the back of the plane with their low standby fares. I felt that, by fighting them upfront, I might be able to get them out of the standby business.'

He didn't.

Another part of the problem was his commitment to buy more planes. 'I bought two A-300 airbuses. In hindsight, it might have been better had I not.'

Suddenly he could no longer control the fight with the major transatlantic airlines. They'd forced him to defend himself on their turf. Nor could he maintain control of his debt situation because he was in over his head on those two A-300s. His problems compounded themselves when sterling took a nosedive and he lost control of his foreign currency exposure. 'The pound fell 26% and that cost us $50 million. We survived the oil crisis and two groundings of the DC-10s. So it's kind of ironic, isn't it.'

By not having hedged properly in foreign exchange, his profits turned into debt. Instead of minimizing his risks with financial futures and options – a mistake Richard Branson purposely tried to avoid when he started Virgin Atlantic – Laker become a sitting duck target to the whims and fancies of the dollar–sterling ratio.

*

When it comes to currencies, control means timing, and timing is everything. You find that out by spending one very hectic hour with another type of risk taker, a guy named Derek Tullett.

His company is called Tullett and Tokyo. And his business is foreign exchange.

The room in the City where Tullett does his thing is filled with men in shirtsleeves, more than a hundred of them, shouting at each other, then into telephones, and then at each other again. They sit around ten-sided tables, their neckties pulled down and their collars open, juggling three and four telephones while also trying to keep an eye on panels of flashing lights that mean more calls are coming in.

A man with a beard calls out, '86 I sell.' A colleague across the table answers, '81 I give.' Others at the table scream into their phones, '81 offered,' repeating it as they push buttons to open direct telephone links to banks all over the City. '81 offered . . . 81 offered . . . 81 offered . . .'

Then a man with two phones to his ears announces, 'Munich wants a quid.' The man with the beard lunges for his telephones, shouting, '74–86 overseas.' A man with glasses yells, '77 we bid a pound.' The Beard stabs a finger towards him, '77 you pay.' Glasses nods, 'B of A, London.' The Beard nods, 'Yours. Done. County Bank.' At the same time, someone calls out, '73–85,' and someone else yells, '89 I sell,' and someone yet again barks, 'Munich wants a quid.'

Fifteen seconds have gone by.

And somewhere in the confusion £1 million has changed hands.

'The excitement generated in this industry is quite special,' Tullett says. He's a short, muscular man in his early 60s, a former rally driver, and around the City still known as a tough opponent on the squash courts. 'With so much money changing hands so very quickly, this is a high-stress industry.'

High stress is an understatement. Guys at the dealing tables burn out in their 30s. With so much money floating around, it takes a minimum of two years' training before Tullett will turn any of his brokers loose on a small handful of banks. Just as a side note, basic pilot training with the RAF is only 42 weeks.

'The minimum for a dollar/sterling deal is £1 million. And deals of £50 million–£100 million are common. It all happens at lightning speed. The broker is asked by a bank to sell some currencies for the highest price. But a broker on the other side of the table has been asked by another bank to buy some currencies for the lowest price. And timing is one of the major skills of broking. If you grab too fast, the bank you're dealing for may wind up paying more than they would have by waiting for the next deal one minute later. But if you wait 60 seconds too long, as other deals come in, as bids and offers change the market prices, then the bank you're broking for might wind up with less.'

Banks need to go back and forth between large sums of currencies, either speculating on their own account or buying and selling for clients. They come into a market – like the dealing room at Tullett and Tokyo – and expose themselves to the powers of supply and demand. That is the very backbone of foreign exchange rates. Heavy buying raises the price, heavy selling lowers it. It's no more complicated than that. Because the brokers and bankers know they're always talking in millions, they never actually say the word 'million'. They talk about a quid or ten pounds or twenty dollars. When the value of the pound is quoted in relation to dollars, the exact rate is carried out to four decimal places. As everybody in the marketplace knows that the pound is being traded at $1.65-something, they merely have to announce '75–85' to indicate that the spread for a pound is $1.6575–85. That's 10/10,000ths. On £1 million it represents $1000. On £90 million you're talking about $90,000.

In this case it's the banks taking the risks for their clients. The brokers at Tullett's place are merely the conduit for those risks. But Tullett is in his own right very much a risk taker. And a sense of timing was the talent that got him into the game.

London is the world's leading money-broking market

because there are so many foreign banks in the City. But the market is relatively young, only going back to 1953 when the Bank of England literally 'denationalized' foreign exchange dealings. Tullett came on to the scene in 1956, joining the currency brokerage house Savage and Heath. Within a few years he was a partner. Ten years later he was Managing Director. He always wanted to go out on his own however, but until 1971 the timing never seemed quite right. You don't really need anything to become a foreign-exchange broker besides the skill of the trading business and a couple of telephones. Plus, of course, the confidence of your clients. Tullett had all of that. He had a reputation for being one of the best in the business. And, with hindsight, those who prophesied doom for Tullett now have to admit that he was the last entrepreneur who could have created a broking house to compete on the international scene. The trouble was, at the time, the pundits figured there were already too many well-established brokers in the market.

Tullett wouldn't take their advice. With immaculate timing he'd spotted a window and crawled right through. 'It was a very difficult thing to do because by that time there were already a number of well established brokerage houses in London. Getting a share of the market meant offering services to banks that other dealers weren't. In those days most of the broking houses concentrated on the Eurodollar markets. That's where the money was. So we decided there might be room for us if we emphasized the foreign-exchange side of the business, while also providing dealing tables for Eurodollars and Certificates of Deposit.'

The day he went into business, the firm of Tullett and Riley – as it was then called – consisted of 15 people. Five years ago he employed 750. Today there are 2500 employees in 15 offices around the world. They deal in Forex, the money markets, leasing finance and financial futures. The product is money. The specific currency is irrelevant. The important thing is to put buyers with sellers and borrowers with lenders faster than his competitors. In return for arranging the deals, he takes a small commission – sometimes as low as 0.02%. But the volume is enormous. He won't disclose the Tullett and Tokyo figures, yet one recent estimate has it that in any given 24-hour period, $600 billion is 'recycled' around the world. A fairly good guess is that perhaps as much as 10% of that comes through Tullett's offices.

Looking at it closely, Tullett really only took a minimal risk when he went into business because he knew the market and the market knew him. He had the patience to wait for his moment and the expertise to recognize it when it came. But there was certainly more at stake than just his money. In this case he had his reputation to think of as well. As reputation can at times be considered a commodity, some risk takers are very willing to use that as their stake.

By definition 'the company man' is not overly entrepreneurial. All too many employees spend more of their time keeping their job than doing their job.

On the other hand, if the employee was extremely entrepreneur-motivated, he wouldn't be working for the company, he'd be owning it.

There are, of course, 'intrepreneurs', as they're now called, because without forward-thinkers and corporate risk takers, there would be no profits. But the Chief Executive at major public corporations like ICI or Unilever has decidedly less room for flamboyance. Many such companies, and Unilever is the perfect example, tend to promote from within, bringing management up through their own system. In the end they wind up with competent, albeit extremely dull, executives. Occasionally, however, a corporate man will seize an opportunity and become a kind of personal risk taker. John Harvey-Jones formerly at ICI always stood head and shoulders above his peers.

So has Lee Iacocca.

He made himself a multi-millionaire by saving Chrysler against all odds. Like Laker, he found himself being cast in the role of the folk hero. Unlike Laker, he's still on top.

An engineer by profession, Iacocca's first job was as a trainee with the Ford Motor Company. Public as it may be, Ford is still run by the Ford family, so even the most ambitious guy can only go so far up the totem pole. Iacocca was the most ambitious of men, is known in the industry as the father of the Mustang – one of the most successful automobile lines ever – and wound up two dozen years after his debut as President of the company. He was there eight years until Henry Ford II gave him the boot. Just like that, Iacocca found himself on the dole. It was at a precarious time in his life – in his 50s, too old to start again, too young to call it quits.

There are few species more pathetic in the cut-throat world of American business than the unemployed corporate president. But Iacocca had a reputation and within a few weeks of getting thrown out at Ford – the Chairman's explanation to him was, 'It's just one of those things' – he turned up at Chrysler.

However this wasn't exactly a promotion. Chrysler was in debt to the tune of $1.2 billion. Their cash flow was disappearing into the black hole of interest payments. The management was, as Iacocca puts it, 'in a state of anarchy. The company consisted of a cluster of little duchies, each one run by a prima donna'.

In a real sense, he had nothing to lose. Tbe ship was sinking and nobody in America really expected he could save it. Five years later he had cleaned up the company, replaced almost all of its upper management with old pals from Ford who knew his style, and paid off the debt. He took the risk of sure failure and turned it into the biggest success story in the history of American industry.

Some people even say that he was born to the job, named Iacocca because it stands for 'I am Chairman of Chrysler Corporation (of) America'.

More recently, Howard Macdonald tried to do the same thing at Dome.

The game he played might even be called 'no-lose'.

Any number of executives working for the 'Seven Sisters' – the major oil companies – might have fantasized about solving the problems of Canada's Dome Petroleum, but it took Macdonald to accept the challenge. And in the back of his mind he must have realized that this was a golden risk-taking opportunity. 'I wouldn't use the term no-lose. But I think it's fair to say that going into this job one is fire-proof, at least for a while.'

Macdonald was a company man at Royal Dutch/Shell for 23 years – although he never liked to be thought of as a company man. 'Shell happens to be the most free-thinking and decentralized of all the oil majors.' He arrived in London from Scotland in 1958 as a founder of KCA, one of the original British drilling contractors. But money for drilling was hard to come by in those days – the North Sea bonanza was yet to happen – so after two years he joined Shell and rose through the accounting side of the business. He became Controller in 1974 and Treasurer in 1977.

While Macdonald was courting bankers in the City, a fellow named Jack Gallagher was making a reputation for himself in Calgary, Canada, as the risk taker who was Dome Petroleum.

Canada is of course an enormously wealthy country. Unfortunately, many of the resources are buried under snow and permafrost. Gallagher had been a whiz-kid at Standard Oil of New Jersey, a geologist by profession, who at the age of 33 in 1950 was approached by a group of investors to manage Dome, then a very insignificant company. Gallagher didn't just join Dome, he became Dome. With Gallagher, Dome was the first oil company to drill an exploratory well in Canada's Arctic. Dome was considered the leader in High Arctic oil technology. As the '60s became the '70s, Dome participated in 11 wildcat wells in the Arctic islands, and made three important gas discoveries. That was also about the time they began preparing to drill in the Beaufort Sea, north of the Yukon territory and west of Victoria Island. By the polar route it is almost exactly half-way between Montreal and Yokohama. It's so far north that the ice only begins to clear in mid-July. There is, these days, little doubt that the Beaufort will one day fulfil its promise. But Gallagher and Dome found out the hard way that the day was further off than they had led their bankers to believe. By 1981, Dome's oil exploration operation was so huge that it included the largest corporately owned marine fleet in the world and the biggest private air force in Canada.

Gallagher was personally worth a few hundred million dollars. He was a wheeler-dealer of the old school, with all the flamboyance imaginable. It would be a tough act for anyone to follow, under any circumstance.

It was especially tough for Macdonald because by the time he got to Dome the company was nearly broke. The Gallagher smile was no longer enough for the bankers. It was like Burmah Oil, but three or four times worse. Their long-term debt stood at $6.3 billion (then £4.4 billion). Mining and ship-building costs had skyrocketed by more than 12 times in under five years. Finance charges and interest had expanded nearly 14 times. Gallagher found himself on the outside, his personal wealth down by almost 90%, his ego in tatters.

The story that went around Canada at the time – some swear it's true – is of Gallagher's right-hand man coming to see him, with good news and bad news. Gallagher said, 'What's the good news?' The answer was, 'We can buy Gulf Oil for $200 million.' Now Gallagher asked, 'What's the bad news?' And he was told, 'They want $50 down.'

The bankers who found themselves owning Dome needed someone to put the company back together. But there weren't exactly long queues of applicants for the job. One financial writer likened it to flying kamikaze planes. Another said the head hunters had to look for someone in Europe because no Canadian would be crazy enough. That's not exactly the way Macdonald saw it. In the back of his mind was a simple outline: if I win, I'm a hero – if I lose, they'll say, too bad but no one could have saved Dome anyway.

He started talking to Dome and their Canadian bankers in the spring of 1983. They offered him the Chief Executive's desk, and he took over that autumn. In between the initial meeting and his first day on the job, he had to think about problems on two fronts. First was Dome. He believed that the company was caught in a financial timing vice. There was an extremely strong asset base, but the mountain of debt was getting close to insurmountable. He had to get that down. Being able to talk the banks into rescheduling would help. He managed that to some degree. Selling off some assets would be necessary. He also managed that. Finally he would have to 'unfrock and eliminate the distrust factor'. Coming into Calgary clean, with his Shell reputation to back him up, was a big step in that direction.

Second, he had to establish for himself a minimal-risk contract. After all, if he was going to put his reputation on the line it had to be worth his while. So he negotiated a five-year deal, with a clause to renew if both parties agreed. It also contained a 'break clause' at the three-year mark, giving him the chance to reassess his own risks during 1986 – a lifeboat clause just in case the ship was taking on too much water. Dome offered him $500,000 a year. It was decent by North American standards but in those days it was enormous by British standards. On top of that came a $4 million share option fund, which was set aside, out of any creditor's reach, just in case Dome did go broke. Of course, if he somehow managed to raise Dome from the near-dead, then he'd become an Iacocca-style hero. In both cases his future was assured. And only in the event of failure was his ego at risk.

As it turned out, he managed the impossible.

He somehow made Dome attractive enough that three oil companies were willing to bid for the company. The winner, in a $4.2 billion deal that was finalized with only one month left to run on his five-year contract, was Amoco Canada. The sale not only satisfied Dome's bankers, it also put something into the shareholders' pockets.

If they haven't yet erected a statue to Howard Macdonald in Calgary, they should. Then again, success breeds success. National Westminster Bank has since brought him back to the UK as Chairman and Chief Executive Officer of the ailing Nat West Investment Bank, where Macdonald is well on the way to repeating his Dome success.

A similar type of personal risk was Richard Giordano's when he agreed to become Chief Executive Officer at the BOC Group in 1979.

Not that BOC was another Dome. Just the opposite. It's always been one of Britain's most solid companies. But Giordano put his reputation on the line and knowingly exposed his ego to enormous risk because from the moment he arrived in London he was a star. The press was ready to put him under a microscope, the City fathers were sceptical, and not a few British industrialists were jealous. He was, at the time, Britain's highest-salaried executive.

The first-generation American son of Italian immigrants to New Jersey, Giordano, now 57, was educated at Harvard University and Columbia Law School. He worked as a Wall Street attorney until 1963 when he was hired by an industrial gases company called Airco. It was near his home in New Jersey. It seemed like a good idea. And eight years later he was President of Airco.

Then along came BOC (formerly the British Oxygen Company) under the direction of Sir Leslie Smith, and they tried to take over Airco. Giordano fought hard but lost. However, Smith liked the way Giordano operated, and hired him to be Chief Executive Officer and heir apparent. The idea was that Smith would be the boss in the boardroom, while Giordano would run things outside. But the American said right from the beginning that he wasn't going to come to the UK on a British salary. So Smith – who'd worked all his life for a British salary – convinced the BOC board to pay Giordano $479,000, more than twice what he himself was making.

'Being an American running a major British company', Giordano explained at the time, 'has sometimes meant walking a very fine line. BOC today is clearly less British. But not less British and more American. It's more international. A lot of people thought the first thing I'd do was turn BOC into an American company. And that was bound to be a source of resentment in this country.'

As a matter of fact, it wasn't.

He is constantly rated among the most respected industrialists in the country and still very much a star as far as the City is concerned. He's no longer the highest-paid man in the kingdom – that title swings back and forth between James Hanson and Tiny Rowland – although tears need not be shed as he's still among the top ten. In 1985 when Smith retired, Giordano added Chairman to his title as CEO and saw home a decade of unprecedented success. Under his stewardship, BOC's share price has increased nearly 900%.

In many cases, risk takers don't see themselves as taking risks. At least the Reichmann brothers of Toronto, Canada certainly didn't think they were taking a risk when they bought most of Manhattan.

Albert, Paul and Ralph Reichmann have always been portrayed as the great mystery men of Canadian business. They don't socialize the way many other businessmen do. They aren't seen at all the right spots. They don't hand out photos and press kits every time a journalist calls. In fact, a good many journalists who write about them often complain that they can't ever get beyond the extra-tight security which surrounds the family. The problem turns out to be that many of those journalists are either too lazy to try, or the Reichmanns know in advance those journalists are not going to play straight.

In this case getting an interview with Albert Reichmann was no more difficult than picking up the phone one Sunday afternoon and ringing his office. He works on Sundays and he personally answered. A meeting was arranged without any fuss.

So much for great mystery.

President of Olympia and York (O&Y), the family's privately held company, Albert Reichmann's office is on the 32nd floor of the First Canadian Place building in the very heart of downtown Toronto. It's a large corner room, with a round table near the windows where guests are served coffee – he always drinks tea – and treated to a magnificent view of Lake Ontario.

What makes the vantage point truly unusual is that this vista is perhaps the only one of Toronto where you can't see any office blocks built, owned and managed by the Reichmanns.

The family arrived in Canada via Tangiers during the 1950s, refugees from the Holocaust. Forced to flee Vienna in 1938 where Samuel Reichmann had been a merchant, they'd gone first to Morocco and established themselves as bankers. In 1956 Reichmann *père* sent Paul and Ralph to North America. They started in the carpet and floor tile business, and became so successful that the rest of the family quickly followed.

In 1964, sensing that a major property boom was on its way, the Reichmanns set up a group called O&Y Investments, comprised of O&Y Developments, O&Y Floor and Wall Tiles and Domus Engineering. For the next 13 years they went about their business unobtrusively, developing small properties, making a reputation for themselves as solid players in the Canadian market and generally flourishing in the new world.

Then came 1977.

The City of New York was teetering on the edge of bankruptcy. Debt was mounting and for a while there appeared to be little anyone could do but sit by and watch the Big Apple go broke. However, the Reichmanns refused to believe that New York could sink. So they flew down there one morning and by the end of the afternoon they'd bought eight buildings in prime locations for $320 million.

That deal put them in the major leagues.

'New York is the centre of the world,' Albert says. 'And we believed that would never change. We went into New York and found properties that were renting at $9–12 per square foot. We knew that if we could buy good locations and good-quality buildings, it would pay off when the demand came back.'

It has.

These days it's not unheard of for New York property to rent at 10 times what they paid for it.

Albert is 62. His brother Paul is 60. The two of them jointly manage the real estate side of their business. Ralph, 58, handles the family's other interests. Together they reportedly own 92% of O&Y, with the rest 'almost certainly' divided among the clan. One says 'almost certainly' because when you ask Albert who owns what, he answers in an embarrassed way, 'It's not important.'

That's his way of saying, it's none of your business.

Because they are so private, and good intelligence about their affairs is so hard to come by, at least one Toronto real estate analyst has literally made a career out of being the Reichmann expert – even though he admits to never having met them. But Albert says he doesn't care about that sort of thing. He says, any information anyone truly needs to know about them can be gotten. In other words, serious players can always find out about other serious players. The rest of the world is irrelevant.

'We make all our own decisions,' Albert insists, stressing the fact that O&Y is more efficient for being private. Decisions can be made quickly because there's no need to worry about boards or shareholders. Whatever Albert says, or whatever Paul says, or whatever Ralph says, goes. Some people consider Albert the financial expert and Paul the strategist, but Albert claims it's even simpler than that. 'We are brothers who share a common interest and a common trust. We work well together because we think alike. We always come satisfactorily to the same unanimous conclusion.'

They stand by each other's decisions and the tradition of the handshake is honoured. Their word, they say proudly, is their bond. When the Reichmanns built the Shell Center in Calgary, the project was three-quarters finished before the final contracts were signed. The problem was that, by the time it came to sign those contracts, the markets had gone against the Reichmanns and they actually stood to lose money under the original agreement. It goes without saying that they signed it as they'd originally promised they would. 'When we make an agreement we proceed with it as if it were signed. Even if the economy has changed, we stick by our handshake. We were trained as bankers in Morocco and we learned that you have to live up to your word. The first time you don't honour a handshake is the last time anyone will shake hands with you.'

Because they are who they are, raising money when they need it is hardly a problem. Thanks to a continuing stream of innovations in the North American capital markets, they've been able to raise money publicly while still maintaining their publicity-shy aura. In late 1985, for instance, the brothers created O&Y Enterprises as a subsidiary of their main company. With that title on the stationery, and C$3.5 billion in the bank, they went to the market with the largest preferred share issue to that point in Canadian history – an even C$1 billion.

When they went into the New York market in 1977 they secured mortgages from a single lender covering a single building. But with large increases in recent years in both the size and price of commercial properties, the Reichmanns discovered that their field of potential lenders was more and more restricted to the largest banks, insurance companies and pension funds. So a couple of years ago, when they were considering an $875 million refinancing of three New York office towers, they actually had to go to Salomon Brothers on Wall Street to put together a mortgage pool.

Next they embarked on the development of Battery Park City along the tip of Lower Manhattan. Encompassing the World Financial Center, the area is a combination of space for business, retail shops, and residential houses for up to 25,000 people.

Today they own 30 major buildings in 14 American cities, including 12 skyscrapers in New York. They have also developed a dozen world-class shopping centres in 11 cities, including Faneuil Hall in Boston, South Street Seaport in New York, Harton Plaza in San Diego and Union Station in St Louis.

Having created a real estate empire which easily ranked among the top three in North America, they proceeded to get into the oil business. In 1985 they bought a controlling stake in Gulf Canada for C$2.8 billion. A year later, they used Gulf to buy Hiram Walker Resources, the liquor and spirits group for C$3.3 billion.

There is always one Reichmann brother spearheading every significant project which gives O&Y very much of a family feel to it. And Paul Reichmann is the brother who's come to London to oversee their interests in Canary Wharf, on the Isle of Dogs in London's docklands.

The biggest planned commercial property development in Europe, it represents an investment of close to £3 billion. The idea is to build an entire mini-city on a derelict site on the Isle of Dogs which will include office space to suit the expanding City, shopping and leisure complexes, parking for 8000 cars and two 400-bed hotels.

The Reichmanns came into the deal in July 1987 when the American who'd orginally conceived the scheme ran into financial difficulties. It made sense to the Reichmanns because they could pick up the pieces cheaply enough and were prepared to sit on it as long as necessary to make money with it. They are long-term thinkers who almost never get involved in anything unless they are convinced they can do it well and make money at the same time.

Occasionally, however, they get it wrong.

In 1981 they took a heavy position in natural resource stocks at the very time when those kinds of shares were peaking. They also went a little too far in backing the ubiquitous Robert Campeau.

A French-Canadian developer, the Reichmanns first ran across him in 1980 when they purchased a 9% share in Royal Trust which just happened to have been a Campeau take-over target. In 1987, just after Campeau bought Allied Stores for $3.5 billion, the Reichmanns helped bolster his cash-flow situation by purchasing from him a half share in one of his buildings. In 1989, when Campeau collapsed, the Reichmanns found themselves holding 5.2 million shares of his stock which they had paid $60 million for. It might have been worse, had they not already declined to give him an $800 million bridging loan to help him save his Federated Stores chain which owns Bloomingdale's. On the other hand, the Reichmanns didn't take IOUs for their loans. One is secured with a half interest in a Toronto skyscraper, another is secured with a southern California supermarket chain Campeau had owned.

But then a few hundred million here or there is really small potatoes for the Reichmanns.

As one Canadian journalist points out, they have a finger in just about every economic pie. From the morning's newsprint to the office block, from the drink with lunch to the bank which cashes your checks, from the petrol pump to the flat you live in, the Reichmanns are turning Canada into a one-company town.

They control, either directly or indirectly, an estimated but still staggering $45–50 billion in assets.

Said one usually caustic Canadian magazine, 'In an era when you can't trust your banker, they're the exception. Budding entrepreneurs should use them as role models, because sometimes, the biggest are the best.'

With the Reichmanns it's a question of knowing what opportunity looks like and what to do about it when you find it staring you in the face.

Irvin Feld is one of the few people in America who ever managed the same trick, to the extent that millions of children will forever be grateful.

We met in the mid-1970s, in Monte Carlo, in the early days of the annual Monaco Circus Festival. Feld was there because he was a modern-day P. T. Barnum, the man *Time* Magazine once called 'the greatest showman on earth'.

A kind and gentle man, with a receding hairline, and glasses that he constantly re-adjusted even though they weren't falling off the end of his nose, Irvin Feld was raised in Maryland and once spent time as a young boy hawking snake oil at carnivals.

By the end of the 1930s, Feld went into snake oil merchandising on a much grander scale by opening a store in Washington DC. As racial prejudice was running rampant in the America of those days, and as Washington has long been a major black population centre, Feld was approached by the

NAACP (the National Association for the Advancement of Colored People) with an offer to back him in a drugstore/soda fountain where blacks could congregate and feel at home. Feld argued that he wasn't a pharmacist but the NAACP said that was no problem. They agreed to help him hire a black pharmacist. All they wanted was a store conducive to a primarily black trade. So Feld said fine.

Early on he saw a market among his black customers for music. Because in the States the customer is always right, he cleared out a corner of the store and opened his own record department. It was an immediate success. 'This was during the '50s,' he explained over breakfast in Monaco that first time we met. 'I wanted to bring more customers in and I thought that the way to do it was to let them know what kind of music they'd find if they came inside. I put speakers on to the street in front of the shop and played loud music to attract business. Now every record store in the world does that. But nobody was doing it in those days. It worked so well that I decided perhaps the next step was to get the singer himself. I started booking acts. It helped to sell records.'

The drugstore became a record shop and the record shop became the Super Music City chain. Then he started his own recording label, Super Discs. Getting to know his artists, he quickly discovered that most of them were in need of personal management. He signed them up, then booked them on concert tours.

'I think the fancy word is impresario. I produced concerts with Paul Anka, Fats Domino, The Platters, Frankie Avalon, Fabian, Bill Haley and the Comets, and James Brown. When the Big Bopper, Buddy Holly and Richie Vallens were killed in a plane crash, they were on a tour for me. I produced Errol Gardners's first recording. I bought Nina Simone her first gown for a concert she did for me. It was a very good education in show business.'

He booked his acts wherever he could, in whatever facility a city could provide. By the mid-1950s that meant large seating-capacity arenas. Little did he know then just how good an education he was getting.

At the same time, the Ringling Brothers and Barnum and Bailey circus was in trouble. It was July 1956. The 'Greatest Show on Earth' was playing Pittsburgh, and when they struck the circus tent that summer, it could have been for the last time ever.

Feld heard the circus was closing and within 24 hours he managed to contact the man who owned and ran it, John Ringling North. When they met, Feld persuaded him that the circus should be promoted much the same way Feld was promoting rock and roll. North was willing to give it a try and within three months Feld had the circus back on the road. But now, instead of playing in a tent, Feld moved the circus indoors to those arenas where he had been booking concerts.

By 1962 the world's largest circus was firmly on its feet again.

Then John Ringling North moved to Europe. Before long Feld grew tired of commuting to Switzerland or Spain to confer with North. He knew that changes were necessary to bring the show into the late-'60s and the '70s. And he wanted to make those changes. But North was of the old school where changes came slowly. The menagerie was de-emphasized because most cities had their own zoos. The side-shows of 700-pound ladies and two-headed tattooed giants were discontinued. The fire-eaters and knife-throwers were put to work in large production numbers. But still more had to be done.

'I woke up on the morning of 1 January 1967 and made myself a New Year's resolution. I said, either I buy the circus or I quit.'

The next evening, Feld and North sat down to dinner together in Switzerland. Feld said he wanted to buy the circus. North said it wasn't for sale. Feld refused to take no for an answer. North kept saying no. Feld said he couldn't continue running the circus unless he owned it. North said he wouldn't sell. And there they sat until six or seven the next morning when one of them finally broke. It was North.

'He finally agreed to sell the circus to me for $7.5 million. But he had a long list of conditions for the sale. First of all, the sale had to be for cash. No credit. No time payments. Money in the bank on the closing day. Then he said I had to buy it as it was, which meant including a few lawsuits. Then he said he wanted to be able to change his mind right up to the last second.'

Feld came back to the States, put a group together who could finance the project, and offed to Europe with his backers. North was willing, until suddenly, out of the blue, one of the backers announced that the group would pay only $6.5 million. Feld was stunned. North was furious. The deal was ripped up and North threw them all out. It took months for Feld to convince North that he knew nothing of the counter-offer. When North finally said okay I believe you, he upped the price to $8 million.

By September 1967 Feld had new backers. On 22 November, Feld, with his son Kenneth and daughter Karen, met John Ringling North in Rome's Colosseum and handed him a cheque for $8 million. For the first time in 96 years the 'Greatest Show on Earth' didn't belong to anyone named Barnum or Bailey or Ringling.

While North took his $8 million and bought gold at $32 an ounce, Feld set about creating a circus that would rival any spectacle in the world. He put together a second unit. Each unit tours for two years, alternating cities every year. Because each of them is a totally different show, every city gets a brand new circus every year. He sought young performers, lowering the average age from 46 to half that, assuring a future mine of talent. He created Clown College so that aspiring clowns could learn their trade. Then he filled his shows with clowns, more than five times as many as they used to have. He put acts in all three rings, and put performers in the air and along the tracks too. What had been a circus of 83 performers became a circus of more than 160. He even worked out a way to get children from the audience into the show.

In 1979, with Kenneth now his partner, Feld decided to branch out to other forms of show business. Father and son took over the management of two ice shows – 'The Ice Follies' and 'Holiday on Ice' – then combined the shows into the greatest ice extravaganza ever. Two years later, Feld Sr. hit upon the idea of using Walt Disney characters to bring plot and story lines into the ice shows. The result was 'Walt Disney's World on Ice', then 'Walt Disney's Great Ice Odyssey' and 'Walt Disney's Magic Kingdom on Ice'. At the same time they became associate producers of the smash-hit *Barnum*. After conquering Broadway they aimed their sights towards Las Vegas and created 'Beyond Belief', a standing-room-only magic show at the Frontier Hotel that has broken all Las Vegas box office records since 1981.

Irvin Feld died in Florida in September 1984 at the age of 66. He had come a long way from the snake oil and soda fountain days. But he knew what he was doing and he took his risks accordingly. The legacy he left is a world filled with children of all ages who will gasp and marvel for generations at just how wonderful life is when you're sitting in a seat at the circus.

This was not a business book five years ago.

It is not a business book now.

Basically, it is a book about people.

What makes these people special is that they are stars, much the same way that Redford and Newman and Sinatra are stars. They are also, in many cases, a mass of contradictions. As charming as some of them can be, that's also how tough and nasty they can be. As refined as some of them have become, that's how basic they are at times. As open and frank as some of them honestly are, that's how tight they can hold their cards, how close to the line they're willing to go.

These men are in the business of creating wealth.

Except they don't do it for the money.

No, what drives them is something else. It's the game. That's what really counts. Winning and losing. And money is simply the way they keep score.

In describing a handful of men who also appear in this book, Kenneth Fleet, as Executive Editor of *The Times*, wrote, 'All have established high reputations for their business acumen;

they have built up very large corporate empires with considerable power in their industrial spheres; they are strong personalities; they have amassed personal wealth as well as created financial strength within their companies; they remain ambitious; and by virtue of all these shared qualities, they have the power of decision that few, if any, around them are likely to question.'

In addition to that, I would suggest that, to a man, they exhibit an above-average intelligence, a startling sense of individuality, remarkable memories, unnerving stamina, an uncanny ability to smell a deal, a certain kind of personal presence that tastes like money and tends to ensure confidence, and a native talent to spot the real risks, which they then proceed to minimize.

The sole criterion I used in selecting the portraits in this book was my own fascination. I can't really define the qualities that attracted me, but I know them when I see them. Nor do I mean this to be a definitive listing of great international risk-takers. I simply present these portraits for what they are – stories of and insights into men who do for real what so many people merely dream of.

Conspicuous by their absence are women.

There were none in the book five years ago.

There are none in the book now.

In both instances I would have been more than delighted to include as many female risk takers as I could find.

Come to think of it, that's precisely what I've done.

I looked. I rang people. I wrote letters. I searched the City. But I couldn't find a single lady wheeler-dealer to match with the men in this book. Sure, there are women in business doing interesting things. And, yes, inroads have been made by women in some of the usual male-chauvinist worlds, such as investment banking. All too often, though, their presence around the Executive Suite is token. Begrudging concessions to changing times. Reluctant concessions by pin-striped, grey-templed men who believe that to give a little now will avoid having to give anything at all later on. Come on, they say, aren't we to be complimented for being liberated enough to consider a woman as our equal, to consider a woman capable of being able to keep up with us, to allow a woman use of the Executive Loo, and anyway the girl's got great legs!

I considered the late Laura Ashley, but felt she hadn't been adventurous enough. She most certainly created a business with great skill. She is definitely part of the 'designer vogue' that will for ever symbolize part of the '80s. She has, without any doubt, left a proud legacy. However, since her untimely death, her husband has had his difficulties making the business work. Perhaps her style has had its day. Styles do, after all, change. Or perhaps her presence was the glue that held it all together. Whatever. I simply couldn't find in her story that certain panache that makes some businessmen just that much more special.

I thought of Debbie Moore and her success with Pineapple Dance Studios. But she ran into a less than overwhelming reception when she tried to expand into New York and has since also had her problems in London. She was a big star when Pineapple went on to the Unlisted Securities Market. Yet when she tried to finance her American adventure she had trouble finding backers. New York is a city filled with dance studios because Broadway is where dancers go to make their fortune. It's *A Chorus Line* and all that. I'm sorry but Debbie Moore didn't seem right five years ago and is even less right now.

Then I thought about Jennifer d'Abo. There's no denying her success with Rymans, the stationery and office equipment chain. She bought it in 1981 when it was losing money and turned it into a profit maker. She has however since sold it and taken up interests in other areas, notably as chairman of Moyses Stevens Florists.

One of the big success stories of the '80s was Sophie Mirman and the Sock Shop. At least for a couple of years. She started at Marks and Spencer, learned retailing there and left to help start the Tie Rack, a chain of very small, specialist shops where location was the key. Airports. Train stations. Tube stations.

Shopping malls. She met a young accountant named Richard Ross who also worked at Tie Rack, they fell in love, got married and decided to apply the Tie Rack formula to socks and tights. At the height of their success they had 108 shops and something like 80% of a company worth £72 million. When they went public on the USM in 1987, they were 53-times oversubscribed. Two years later they were fighting to stay in business. They'd overpaid for sites in Britain, overextended themselves in the United States, and got caught in the crunch with increasing interest rates and decreasing sales. Oh well, at least she tried.

The woman who probably came the closest is Anita Roddick. She and her husband Gordon created The Body Shop, an up-market bath-oil and soap emporium with creams, lotions and potions all geared for the 'green' revolution of the '90s. Where women entrepreneurs are concerned, she is, without a doubt, the great survivor of the '80s.

In 1977, when she came up with the Body Shop concept and needed less than £20,000 to get the idea off the ground, the banks wouldn't give her the time of day. Of course, when she came to the USM in 1984, valuing her company at £2.3 million, every bank manager in Britain was inviting her to lunch. (That old adage about bank managers and umbrellas is so right. As soon as the sun is shining, there they are with hundreds of them. But try to find one in the rain!) Today her business is worth £500 million, putting her in the league with Dixons and W. H. Smith. There's no taking her success away from her. The City loves her and for the moment the Fund Managers are even willing to overlook the fact that she's a woman – as long as her shares keep out-performing the market.

So why isn't Anita Roddick a risk taker? Well, she is. But one store does not an empire make. And in a funny way this book is as much about empires as it is about the people who make them.

In the meantime, my sincerest apologies to the women of this world. Indeed, there are women in Britain successfully running companies. Unfortunately, none of them are doing their thing on a very grand scale. None of them have credibility on the international scene. Sadder still, this is primarily a man's world and it isn't going to change very soon. A woman on her own, wheeling and dealing, simply can't get very far with the City. The City won't allow it. The City was built by men. The City is run by men. The City is a club exclusive to men. The only real chance she's got is if her husband – or any man – puts himself staunchly behind her. Then the response becomes, sure, we men in the City are liberated enough to let the lady take the glory but we'll do the real heavy business with her old man because men know how to talk to each other and anyway, if God wanted men and women to be equal, He would have given women a better understanding of Current Cost EPS.

Maybe television and the movies, and the bare-chested fantasies of after-shave ads have done more damage than anyone suspects. We accept the sexy image of a man running around the globe, playing for millions. However, there is something slightly discomforting, in an unflattering and aggressive way, when a woman does the same thing.

A man can be tough. That's a compliment. Being referred to as a 'tough bird' is anything but.

There are women on corporate boards these days, but they're generally 'safe' women in 'safe' boardroom seats. Lady Grantchester is a non-executive director at Littlewoods, the company founded by her father Sir John Moore. Olga Polizzi is an executive director at Trust House Forte, but her maiden name is Forte. Baroness Oppenheim Barnes, a former Consumer Affairs Minister, is a non-executive director of Boots and Baroness Young is a non-executive director at Marks and Spencer, but none of this has anything to do with equality, none of this has anything to do with women making a breakthrough in a man's world.

The Institute of Directors says that 5% of their members are women. A survey of the CBI is hardly any more encouraging. The Hansard Society recently commissioned a study called 'Women At The Top', and polled 180 CBI members. Those companies reported 795 male executive directors on their main boards but only four women.

It is possible, of course, that business, like war, is simply not something most women are psychologically prepared for. Success in business, like success in war, may be too enmeshed with the killer instinct. Sure, a woman may fight to defend her offspring, but it is just possible that natural female instincts – whatever they may be about – are not about corporate takeovers, mergers and acquisitions.

It could also have everything to do with male approval. That's one of the areas where the sexes are alike. Men want male approval, which could be what football, beer, bragging about sexual conquests and entrepreneurship is all about. Successful men are heroes. Women also want male approval, which is what lipstick is all about. Of course, brains and identity count. Please don't get me wrong. But it's a rare woman who could, or even would want to, win male approval with football, beer and bragging.

Perhaps it's just as rare a woman who would do it by becoming an entrepreneur.

Women can inspire. But the world we know today, at least in the West where businessmen can rise to stardom, is all about men who control.

That's another point against women.

Women have made colossal strides running countries. To get that far, a lot of people have to believe in them. Nobody has to believe in a wheeler-dealer except himself. So maybe men are more easily satisfied than women and making a great success of herself in business simply isn't enough.

At the general election of 1979, 19 women were elected to the Commons. Four years later there were 27. Four years after that there were 41. One would imagine the world was progressing.

Hardly.

Just because Britain has elected a woman as Prime Minister does not mean that British society has come very far. It was a fluke. The very fact that Parliament still meets at hours designed to coincide with the business life of men in the City – conflicting quite blatantly with the hours a woman with children would have to keep – makes Mrs Thatcher the exception.

The real test is not the first woman at Number 10.

The real test is, how long will it be before there is a second woman at Number 10?

Or, what would the City say to a woman as Governor of the Bank of England? Or as Chancellor of the Exchequer? Or Chairman of the Rota Committee at Lloyds? Or Chief Executive Officer of a major international merchant bank?

Even better, name one woman with some power around the City who isn't referred to by her male colleagues as 'a really bright girl'.

Very little has changed in five years.

Too many men still feel women are meant to be pregnant, barefoot and in the kitchen.

I'm sorry to say that it will take a long time before a woman is ever permitted to find her way into a book like this.

1

'I've just returned from Barbados,' he said, as the rain teemed down on to the terrace of his London hotel suite. 'I played golf 40 days on the run. I was feeling so fit. I'm back here a week and I've got a sore throat and feel knackered.'

He sighed.

'Why aren't we doing this in France? I bought a house in the South of France so that I could spend time golfing there. We should be in Mougins at one of those cafés with red-checkered tablecloths, sitting outside with a bottle of wine.'

I said I could be packed in fifteen minutes.

He said he was always packed. 'I'm probably in airplanes four days a week.'

So, came the remark, sounds like nothing's changed in five years.

'A lot has changed,' he said. 'I hit 50 and everything changed.'

Robert Sangster's stamina for travel remains legendary.

Take for example a bank holiday weekend a few years ago.

He had house guests at his estate on the Isle of Man – ten friends who'd come to play golf and go to the races. But that was also the weekend he had a horse running after a million-dollar prize in Chicago. So at eight on Sunday morning, while his guests were still asleep, he flew from the Isle of Man to Heathrow to catch the ten o'clock Concorde to New York. At JFK he changed for a flight to O'Hare and, at 1 p.m. local time, he was lunching with friends and watching the race. His horse finished second. At seven that evening he boarded a Chicago-to-London flight, which brought him into Heathrow at dawn. He then got his plane back to the Isle of Man and arrived home in time for a morning's round of golf.

'I suppose I still think of myself as a travelling salesman. Someone once wrote that I fly 100,000 miles a year. But I figure they're way off. If they said a million, that would be fine. I don't tot them up.'

Being in airplanes as much as he is, he reckons he's got globe-trotting down to a fine art. 'I only have a little bag. I've stopped using the terminals. I only get there about a quarter of an hour before. I suppose if I miss the plane I miss it. You can take more of a risk if you travel lightly. You can be in Los Angeles going to London and if Pan Am is delayed for three hours you can jump on TWA. But if you put yourself in the system, if you have luggage checked in, you're stuck. You know how you get those boarding passes with your ticket inside? The trick is to take the ticket out and put it inside the original ticket and then get on standby for somebody else.'

A few years ago, to make life easier getting to and from the Isle of Man, he bought a small charter airline, and one of those planes is always available for him when he needs it. He doesn't, however, fly himself. And the reason why might well sum up his philosophy of life: 'I tend to leave everything to professionals. I think I once said that the most important people in our lives were the pilot and the jockey. If you have a bad pilot, why have a jockey? And if you have a bad jockey, why train the horse? I tend to stick to the best.'

Practising what he preaches, he has always surrounded himself with the best horses, the best trainers and the best jockeys, the best breeders, the best vets and the best stable boys. Within a dozen years of getting into racing, he earned his place in thoroughbred racing history as the best in his business, sort of like what De Beers has always been to diamonds – what Sinatra has always been to saloon singing.

You can easily tell just how important he became by the enormous amount of jealousy that appeared hand in hand with his success. He is disliked by people who've never met him and frequently misquoted by journalists who've never interviewed him. But he is revered by the people who work with him and know how skilfully he's managed his affairs.

Slightly stocky at about 5′ 8″, he has always been an avid golfer . . . 'I play now to a 14 handicap which is good commercial golf' . . . and, in spite of what the gossip columnists profess, really quite shy. His late father owned and ran Vernons Pools – of football fame – so Sangster grew up never having to worry about his next meal, considerably more comfortable than most, working at Vernons until 1973 when he persuaded his father the company should go public.

It was that 'mistake' that brought him into the horse business.

'I was inheriting the company then. I had a trust and when I was 30 I inherited a third. When I was 35 I inherited a third. When I was 40 I inherited a third. So now I'm 38. I owe the bank for inheriting share certificates, Vernons' paper, and I'm now owing capital gains tax of something like £5 million. We'd had Labour governments – Wilson – and we've just got Heath in – you know, the three-day week – and I could see that when I hit 40 and inherited the third tranche, I'd be owing the bank £8 million plus. I'd own the shares and might be even worse off. So I persuaded my old man to go public.'

But Ted Heath called an election for the very day Vernons was to hit the market. It proved a fateful day for both of them. Sangster then had to spend a year in the City attempting to pull off a reverse take-over. He tried to get together with Corals, the bookmakers. When that didn't work he went to see the Sears Group and Charley Clore. He courted the Rank Organization and Hanson Trust. The market was falling. And he was getting nearer to 40. He finally put a deal together with Cyril Stein at Ladbroke, valuing the Vernons Group – which included the pools company and four main Ford agencies – at £18 million. It would have made Sangster the largest shareholder in Ladbroke. But when he went home to Liverpool and said, right, it's done now, and we're getting so much cash, we own this and that, and I'll be able to stay in England and pay off the capital gains tax, his father said he didn't want to know about Ladbroke.

'So I said, well, it's now March and I've got three weeks to get out of the country. I left and went down to Spain, to Marbella. It was my year out. I thought a lot about a business because I wasn't going to play golf with [Sean] Connery all my life. Then I went to Australia, trying to get football pools in there and saw the terrific market potential for horse racing. I'm very glad I didn't stay in the country because I wouldn't be in the horse business. I'd probably be slogging away in Vernons Pools trying to keep that going.'

To over-simplify, Sangster's business used to come in two parts. There were the races. And there was bloodstock. He'd buy bloodstock to win races and when he won races he'd breed for bloodstock.

'The key to it is that you've got to win races. It's no good having the blood if you're not winning. You've got to be successful. It's a slippery slope. And yet to be successful, as you know, in any walk of life, you're unpopular to a certain degree through jealousy. But to make the business work, you've got to win the races.'

When that was still his business, the idea was to keep coming up with horses like Northern Dancer who'd done it all. Unfortunately, Sangster adds, it was not one of his horses. But Northern Dancer is the perfect example of how money is made with a horse. Bred in Canada, by Nearctic – son of Nearco – and out of Natalma – daughter of Native Dancer – he won the 1964 Kentucky Derby in record time, and followed that with a win in the Preakness. Although he lost the Triple Crown that year by failing to go the distance in the Belmont Stakes – Quadrangle beat him – he was put out to stud, having been syndicated at the then spectacular sum of $2.4 million. He proved to be the ultimate investment in bloodstock, being named UK Champion Sire in 1970 and again in 1977, an unheard of feat for a foreign horse that had never stood in the UK. However, he was responsible for two Derby-winners,

Nijinsky and The Minstrel, and also fathered Try My Best. Some 22 years after his racing career ended, long past the point when most normal stallions have dropped back, Prince Abdullah of Saudi Arabia was still willing to pay $1.2 million for a share of him.

Northern Dancer is, of course, the exception.

Anyway, Sangster admits, breeding is hardly a sure thing. 'Seattle Slew and Spectacular Bid were Kentucky Derby-winners and they were both bought for less than $50,000. So you do get the odd freak. Breeding isn't a guarantee. But it goes a hell of a long way towards it. Statistically, Northern Dancer got 22% stakes-winners to foals. So if you were getting a quarter of his crop you knew you were cutting the risks, eliminating a lot of errors. Percentage-wise you were going to come up with four or five stakes-winners.'

When that business was good it was great.

Then the market changed.

And Sangster turned 50.

Suddenly everything started to look very different.

His first horse was a gelding who won five races.

He figured he had the game knocked.

But his next horse didn't win any races. In fact, he didn't see the winner's circle again for nearly two years.

'The first year I started a stud, before I left England, I lost £800,000. I remember seeing the figures and thinking, crikey, what the hell am I up to now. Obviously getting good horses has helped. But it's always been very hard to explain the business to accountants and bank managers. Say you start with 20 horses and come up with two superstars, two very good horses, six fair horses that win an odd race, and ten bums that can't get out of their own way. Well, it's very easy to make a profit. Sell your best and keep your worst. What I've done all the time is to sell my worst, those ten that couldn't get out of their own way. Of course that means your books show a loss. Say you average £10,000 a horse and you bought 20. That's £200,000. But your ten bottom ones could be worth only

£2000 each. By selling them you're taking losses on paper. But the two top ones, which you keep, could be worth £200,000. It was always a struggle to explain that.'

He doesn't necessarily have to bother with such explanations any more because accountants and bank managers know very well who he is. And that these days he owns more than 1200 horses.

'I got that figure off a computer. But they're having foals every day so the figure changes. If I say I haven't got a clue, I sound so dreadful. You sound so blasé if you say you don't know. But honestly, I've never totalled them up. I really don't know.'

In theory, as a racehorse owner, he's worth whatever his horses and the land under them are worth. But the racing game is based on the concept that winners are where the money is. To come up with a winner worth a fortune, you might have to begin by investing a fortune. Even then there are no certainties. Where racing and bloodstock are concerned, it's easy to throw good money after bad. Although, if you can get just one great horse, you can pay for it all.

Sangster proved that with a horse he bought in the States for under $250,000 called The Minstrel.

'We were having a bad year. We went to America in 1975 to buy yearlings, and say, just to take a figure out of the air, I invested a million dollars. By July 1976, they're just babies, two-year-olds and they haven't run. So you've got to invest another million on yearlings before you've seen how your wine has matured. In '77 we came up with what we thought was a good colt and a good filly, The Minstrel and Cloonlara. She was a 6–4 favourite first time out and finished third. First time out The Minstrel also finished third. We then took The Minstrel to Ireland for the Irish 2000 and we got stuffed. The Derby was in June and we had the yearling sales coming up again in July and it looked as though we'd have to invest another one or two million. That's when The Minstrel won the Derby. That horse pulled the Derby off, and we recouped everything we spent. That one horse. But it's very lucky to win a Derby.'

When prices reached the top, The Minstrel stood at about $400,000 a service and earned $16 million a year.

Traditionally, thoroughbred horses are shared out in fortieths. Although, because broodmares can produce only one foal a year, Sangster keeps them down to three or four partners simply to avoid all the complications that can arise when 40 partners each want to go with a different stallion. Much like shares in mines or oil wells, horse flesh is a very active commodity, traded worldwide. For the first half of the last decade, he was buying horses at the average rate of about $9 million per year. In 1979–80, Sangster bought two-thirds of a dam from E. P. Taylor in the States for about $800,000. The dam was bred with Taylor's Northern Dancer and the result was El Gran Senor. In 1984 that horse won the Irish 2000 and everything else, and was unbeaten going into the Derby. He lost there by a short head. Still, the horse came to be worth $40–60 million because he was the likely heir to his father's throne. It was much the same story with a mare called Fairy Bridge, an unbeaten champion in Ireland. Sangster paid under $100,000 for her. He bred her to produce Sadler's Wells who, after winning the Irish 2000 Eclipse and the Irish Derby, was valued at $24 million, or $600,000 a share.

'I get fun out of racing, but there isn't a lot of room for mistakes. Between the wars, or even just after the war, before crippling taxation hit the big racing empires, you had the Dukes of Norfolk, Rosebery, Derby, and they all had terrific stables. They probably had 30–40 horses and a lot of fun no matter what the prize money was. Of course taxation crippled them. Today perhaps they could only afford to keep one or two horses in training out of earned income. It all costs so much. It's a very expensive luxury.'

As long as bloodstock prices were high, the way they were at the beginning of the '80s, racing was a relatively popular alternative investment, especially along Wall Street. But most syndicates eventually lose money and Sangster tends to regard such schemes as nothing more than another way to gamble. 'It's a very special field. I'll give you an example. If we lose a race, I talk with the trainers and we try to analyse what went wrong. I might say, remember when a similar thing happened with a horse and we tied its tongue down, maybe that will work. By seeing so many races around the world, by talking to all the leading trainers, one learns the business. So the success of a syndicate depends on who's managing the syndicate. They've really got to know what they're doing, otherwise you can get your fingers burnt.'

To keep from getting his own fingers burnt, Sangster travels the world, meeting people, talking about horses, getting to know his sales outlets.

'I have to travel. To meet the stud masters. To get to know buyers. By travelling around, somebody might tap you on the shoulder and say, our stallion is getting to 18, have you anything in the pipeline coming up. I say, I've got just the one for you, or I ask what kind of blood are you looking for? Are you looking for Northern Dancer blood? Or the Seattle Slew? Whatever. I can then produce the article. Maybe they can't afford El Gran Senor so I say, well, this one down the line in training met with an accident but he was a bloody good horse. And I can categorically assure you, because you're going to see me again and again, that he was a very good horse on the gallops but he broke down and never hit a racecourse. So therefore we'll take $100,000 for him. You've got to know where your market is.'

You've also got to know what the market will bear.

In the early '80s the top price an Australian stud could pay was about $4–5 million for a highly rated stallion. In those days they couldn't sell their yearlings because they didn't have the kinds of entrepreneurial buyers who'd pay bigger prices. The Americans got up to $60 million, which is what the bid was for El Gran Senor before the Derby. Although in those days Seattle Slew was probably worth $80–100 million for stud purposes. In Ireland they could do a horse for about $30 million. In South Africa they got up to $3 million.

In England, Newmarket is the major market. But the centre of the bloodstock world is the Blue Grass State of Kentucky. And when the bloodstock business was good, prices at auction in Kentucky were unreal.

'I remember one night when they sold something like 60 or 70 yearlings and averaged over $800,000 a head. I said to my father, you could buy four main Ford motor agencies in the North of England for one yearling and know you'd have a successful production line. Or you could buy a chain of greengrocer stores for the price of one yearling. To average over $800,000 that evening – it was frightening really.'

That horse flesh as an international commodity has become a fact of life does not always please everyone in the business. And here Sangster has often been criticized. But in a very real sense the making of a worldwide market was an idea whose time had come. Sangster might have been one factor. Jets and communication were decidedly another.

'Fifteen or 20 years ago there were probably only two or three breeders who went from Europe to America. We knew probably the top 10 stallions there. The Americans knew probably one of ours. Now I should think we know the top 200 in America and they know our top 100. It's become a world business rather than a little insular business. I'm sure Lord Rosebery would never ever have dreamt of importing an American jockey or using American stallions. You know there's an awful lot of jingoism talked about wonderful British stallions, but to keep a stallion in England, in this day and age – I mean, as of today, your air fare is costing $5000. To go to Northern Dancer, to get a nomination, just to get your mare covered, cost nearly $1 million. So what's a $5000 air fare?'

Simply by virtue of having been the biggest in the business, Sangster would have a major influence on that business. But he's also one of racing's more knowledgeable spokesmen, and there can't be any denying that he's always put his money where his mouth is.

'Because people are more informed, stallions coming to America are being picked out of South Africa and Australia.

I've probably helped that. Or pushed it. Fifteen years ago, I took eight or nine fillies to race in Florida. Our season ends in October, November, and theirs was just beginning. We learned an awful lot even though we couldn't get on the course because it was trial and error adapting them to the climatic change. If you can run them five days from when they arrive in America, they'll run terrifically well. Then they'll lose their form. But we were I think the first to take a big team. Nowadays there are probably something like 200 horses that come from Europe to race in America. And every day you open the trade magazines, the *Blood Horse* or *Thoroughbred Record*, there's a horse that used to race here in Europe that is now in America. I suppose that's a major contribution, that Americans come over here and buy our racehorses off the course. There's a great interchange of horses.'

Just as there is a great interchange of jockeys.

In 1979 Sangster convinced a 19-year-old Steve Cauthen to come to England. Cauthen had been riding steadily in the States for two-and-a-half years and in his first full year on the American tracks had 487 winners worth $6 million in prize money. His first year in England he brought in a mere 52 winners. His second year there were 61. In the end it took him five years to win the English jockey's title – the first American to do it since 1913. Convinced that foreign jockeys mature more quickly in Europe, Sangster then brought a 25-year-old Brent Thomson to England.

'I brought him to race here in 1984 because I felt he needed a serious challenge to help him improve on what was already a winning career. I paid him a retainer of £10,000, plus air fares, plus accommodation, plus a car. On top of that he got the usual 10% of winner's and jockey's fees for riding. The risk for me was minimal. He rode 30 winners that year and we probably covered the whole cost of the exercise right there. But that's not the point. Even if he hadn't had any winners, it still would have broadened his outlook. It made him a better jockey when he rode for me in Australia. You see, jockeyship is confidence. I knew if I could get him to think like Muhammad Ali he'd get on those horses and have the confidence of Muhammad Ali. You might leave Australia as the champion jockey but you come back as a real man.'

However, Robert Sangster will for ever be remembered as the man who brought the Arabs into racing.

'I courted them because they had money to spend and I believed that an influx of money would stimualte the markets. It was money that could have gone into the theatre or into making films. Instead it came into the horse business. Years ago, when I first went to America, you didn't get many English trainers there. Now Concorde's jammed with English trainers. By that money coming into the racing industry, everyone benefited. From the stable lads to the jockeys. Listen, jockey retainers are probably ten times higher than they were ten years ago because the Arabs made the business so much more competitive.'

In the end, ironically, the Arab-dominated bloodstock business turned out to be a monster that keeps coming back to haunt him.

'They didn't drive me out of the business but I think they've probably driven a lot of other people out because they couldn't compete. I didn't know when I brought them in just how big they were going to become. I thought at the time it was good that they did come in. But nobody ever realized what a monopoly they'd achieve in racing.'

And now he quietly confesses to a little regret. 'I suppose if I hadn't brought them in I'd still have something of a monopoly. But then I think they'd have come in anyhow. Although if I had the chance to do it all over again, knowing what I know now, I probably wouldn't do it again. After all, you can't compete in the purchasing market with them. Nor can you race against them. I suppose I saw it a few years after they came in and that's why I diversified. I switched from buying to breeding and selling.'

He had to.

Because in the last five years he stopped winning races, the market turned against him and he hit the half-century mark.

*

Sangster's fiftieth birthday party in May 1986 was the Manx bash of the year. More than 600 people descended on his island estate to help him celebrate. But all the king's horses and all the king's men couldn't quiet the uneasy feeling in the pit of his stomach that everything was going sour.

'We'd had a disastrous run in 1985–6 where we didn't have a top winner. So rather than putting more of my money in, we devised a company called Classic Thoroughbreds. I took 6% of it. But that's not been successful. It shakes one's confidence.'

Breeding fees had tumbled from their all-time highs and in some cases were down as much as 50%.

On top of that he was having trouble at Manton, his stud farm in the hills of Wiltshire.

He bought the 2330-acre estate in 1985 for £6 million and quickly sank another £5 million into improvements. With seven different gallops, it's the largest thoroughbred training facility in Britain and arguably the most luxurious in Europe. He stocked it with a team of home-bred horses but only managed to come up with four winners the first year. Even though he changed trainers the following year and had 100 winners, Manton has never proven itself to be the investment he'd originally hoped it would.

'The place is beautiful and up to standard. Don't get me wrong. But because of my Isle of Man domicile, I'm not allowed to spend the night there. I have to go to a local hotel. I've got 60 horses training there and even though I own it I still have to pay full fees, which is about £230 per horse a week. That adds up. I pay the same fees as Sheikh Abdullah and the Maktoums (Sheikh Mohammed) who train there as well. Then I also have to spend £300,000 a year on security and make all the improvements. So it seems rather financially pointless of me to have the place any more. The media has for some time been speculating that I want to sell Manton because I need the money. But that's not it at all. It's worth, probably, £15–18 million to a Japanese or a Saudi. I want to sell it because I can't use it properly and I keep thinking to myself that if I could put £15–18 million on deposit I could pay for all my horses and still have a nice bit of change left over. I want to sell because selling it makes good financial sense.'

At about the same time he was burdened with the worry of what to do about Vernons. His father had been getting on . . . he died a few years ago . . . and Vernons was a business that didn't much interest Sangster.

It was Irish financier Michael Smurfit who inadvertently helped Sangster come to a decision.

On Ascot Friday 1988, Sangster was entertaining some 60 guests in his box at the racecourse when Smurfit came up to him and, almost out of the blue, wondered if he wanted to sell Vernons. Sangster explained he hadn't considered it since the hassle in the '70s when he tried to go public. Smurfit volunteered that he had a client who could be interested. So just like that Sangster said okay, let's talk. The following Saturday, early on the morning of the Irish Derby, Sangster and his two finance directors helicoptered to Smurfit's office in Dublin. Smurfit eventually revealed that his client was Gerald Ronson and that together they'd valued the company at £40 million. By noon Sangster had them up to £46 million.

With an hour or so to spare before helicoptering on to the races, Sangster and his two finance directors walked across the street to a local pub. Over a pint of Guinness they decided there was still plenty of room left in Ronson's offer and convinced themselves that he might go as high as £55–7 million. In the end Ronson said no, but the idea of selling Vernons was now firmly implanted in Sangster's mind.

While all this was going on, Sangster's oldest son, Guy, had left a brokerage house in the City of London to take up a post at a company called Thompson T-Line. They'd once been in the circus van business but had long since evolved into timber. As it turned out, they happened to be looking for acquisitions.

Not realizing that the answer to selling Vernons was almost as close as his son's nose, Sangster went to see Jimmy Goldsmith with the idea of merging Vernons, Aspinall's and the Hard Rock Café into a group. The two met in Paris. Goldsmith liked the idea. But two days later he rang Sangster to say that

Peter de Savary had just bought Aspinall's so the idea wouldn't work. Undaunted, Sangster went to see de Savary. But before they could fully discuss the idea, Guy Sangster discovered that Thompson T-Line was in fact very interested in Vernons. Sangster Sr. met with them and negotiations proceeded rapidly.

They bought Vernons for £95 million.

'I wasn't interested in running the business and frankly I felt it was almost immoral, or at least unacceptable, that two Liverpool families should virtually control the pools. That's the Moores of Littlewoods and the Sangsters of Vernons. You also have to understand that the pools is the worst bet in the world. The government takes 42.5% and the companies running them take at least 32.5%. The leaves the punter with 25% tops and usually less. What's more, I had it on very good authority that people were being head-hunted in Australia to start Loto in the UK. The reason why Loto should be successful here is because you can run it at just over 4% over turnover. In other words, more goes back to the punter. It's a much better bet. In fact, wherever Loto has appeared to compete with football pools, football pools disappear. In Belgium, Loto wiped out the pools in under three months. It happened in every state in Australia. Wherever I built up football pools, as soon as Loto came in, that was the end. I knew that if Loto ever came into England, football pools would be wiped out. So here was someone willing to give me £95 million. The price was right. The time was right. It made a lot of sense to sell.'

The large influx of cash helped clear all Sangster's borrowings, which left him sitting on about £60 million.

Soon after Thompson bought Vernons, Ladbroke bought Thompson. In 1989 Guy Sangster and a few of the others from Thompson got out and formed their own venture capital company, Grantcheston Holdings, in which Robert Sangster took an £8-million stake.

'However, with interest rates at 15%, I've left most of the Vernons money in the bank. I formed a company called Sangster Group to invest in property. I'm not yet earning as much in property as I do in horses, but there are certainly a lot of interesting investments to be made in property. It's the safe switch since reaching 50. I've been misquoted that I was selling Vernons to concentrate on the racehorse business. But that's nonsense. I'm now thinking more of family and family investments than I ever did before. I've even promised my three eldest sons that not one more penny would go into the racehorse business than is in it now. And I'm keeping to that. Hitting 50 sure in hell woke me up. When you get to 50 you probably don't have the balls to gamble as much as you did when you were younger. I've changed a lot. I've gone safe.'

Safe, perhaps. Dull, never.

With his oldest son Guy in venture capital, his second son Ben looking after the stud side of the family thoroughbred business and his third son Adam in banking in Hong Kong, Sangster and his third wife, Sue, have now started a new family. Their son Sam was born on his old man's birthday in 1987.

'I'm doing all the things now that I missed when I was 25 – 26 – 27. Being a father again is wonderful. The little one comes into my study and talks and pinches everything. It's incredible. I'm loving it.'

Sangster attends race meetings whenever he can – usually three or four days a week. Normally he likes to go to Phoenix Park in Dublin every Saturday – he owns 40% of the track – and then to France for races on Sunday.

'Ireland could definitely use Sunday racing. We tried to get it at Phoenix Park and actually came very close. Funnily enough, it's not the church who is fighting it. After all, France is the biggest Catholic country and they've got it. Ireland would be a natural. It would also be very good for England. Maybe it's never worked in England because we get such good racing midweek. We have the best horses in the world racing in the UK, purely because of the Arab influence. Of the top hundred yearlings sold in the world, most of those are sold in America. But probably 90% race here. What you're also finding now is that your Kentucky Derby-winners and Preakness-winners are not the best bred because, apart from the private studs, most of the best animals come in through the sale ring. The best of the American horses are being bought by the Arabs specifically to race over here. So you're getting a very high competitive standard. I suppose it's like boxers. I mean, if you have all the best coloured fighters from Detroit fighting in Europe, then the standard will be much higher here, whereas the competition in America is so strong that whenever some British heavyweight goes over he gets his name written on the soles of his feet.'

English racing may be the top of the league, but he is personally partial to Irish racing. 'I suppose they're natural horsemen. They're natural tinkers. They're certainly the best judges. And like New Zealand, they have the best climate. They also have a lot of good tax concessions.'

However, not everyone in the Irish racing community thinks as highly of him. For the past several years he's found himself the centre of a *brouhaha* over his intentions to one day close Phoenix Park. The local punters want to keep it open for ever. Sangster and Vincent O'Brien would, if they could, close it this afternoon.

'Yes, if we could get planning permission, we'd close it. Vincent and I both own 40%. We've leased it for two years for a peppercorn. But there's a lot of money tied up there. Now, if we could get planning permission it would probably be worth £15–20 million for property development. It's in central Dublin. And it's not making money as a racecourse. The average gate is probably 4–5000 people. We'd have to be fools if we didn't apply for planning permission.'

That said, there are a few changes he'd also like to make in UK racing, beginning with the prize money.

'Most of the time, winnings simply go back to the horses, to cover their expenses. Anyway, in America it's a much more major factor than it is in Europe. You get million-dollar races there. You get 2000-guinea races here. In America, with the paramutual system, the prize money is better. I win much more pro rata in America than I do here. Although in America

I miss the bookmakers. I like their noise. I like the colour they add to racing. But the problem here is that the money you bet with the bookmakers doesn't come back into racing. Australia has the best system in the world. They have bookmakers on the course, with their satchel and just one pencil, and the Tote off course in the cities. You can't bet with a bookmaker in the cities. So they funnel all that money through the Tote and back to racing. And their prize money makes ours laughable. I mean, second prize in the Melbourne Cup is worth more than our Ascot Gold Cup, which is the feature race at Royal Ascot. You've got to get the prize money to match. Our Derby's worth quarter of a million pounds, or so. In Australia and the US the prizes are going up all the time and there are lots of races worth two, three, four times our Derby.'

Another thing he'd like to see changed is the way racing is taxed.

'The government has now got a tax of 10% which they'll never let go. No government in England will ever say, we'll give 5% back to racing. But look at Australia. Their tax is 3%. The government gets 1.5% and racing gets 1.5%. I don't think any government, Conservative or Labour, will ever say, okay, we'll reduce the rax in England to 4% and give racing half. But what they don't realize is the law of diminishing returns. In Australia the turnover per head is so much greater that probably they get more for their 1.5% than the British government gets from their 10%. There are many more winners that reinvest in Australia. Everyone bets there. And you only have to be half-smart to win in Australia. If you're getting 93% return, if they're only taking 7%, you're betting against the pin-prickers who pick the horse with a pin. If you know a little bit more you tend to win money. Here you're betting against 23%. It's very hard to win any money. If I could change anything I'd change the betting format. But people a lot more able than I have tried and you're just banging your head against the brick wall.'

Until those changes happen, if they ever do . . . and the way things look at the moment they probably won't . . . he just goes about his business, which these days seems to be keeping in front of the competition.

'It's just like racing. You've got to stay in front. It doesn't really matter what the race is. All races are great if you win them. So now I've branched out to National Hunt racing but only with stallions. I won't race geldings because geldings can't be bred. The Arabs haven't come into National Hunt racing. I guess it's too cold for them. The Japanese are coming back into racing very strongly, especially in Australia so I suppose it won't be long before they come to England. Stud prices dropped considerably in the past five years although the market has come back by about 50% since 1985. And we're still in front of the Arabs on the breeding side. They don't have a good stallion yet. I'd give them five years to catch up, so by then we might be in the Quarter Horse game. Why not? Whatever it takes to keep a step ahead of them.'

2

David Thieme

As far as David Thieme was concerned, he was simply inviting a few friends to dinner.

Nine hundred friends.

Every February in London, just before the Institute of Petroleum held their annual banquet, Thieme would host a black-tie affair at the Royal Albert Hall. And the 1981 event was probably the best ever. He decorated the place with the colours of his Essex Overseas Petroleum Corporation – blue, red and silver. He hired Roger Verge to cook the meal (he's the three-star owner/chef of the Moulin de Mougins near Cannes in the South of France), while the Roux Brothers made the dessert. Because Thieme and Essex were, in those days, sponsoring Colin Chapman's Lotus racing team through the Formula One Grand Prix circuit, he figured it was only natural that the evening's door prize should be a Lotus Essex Turbo Esprit – then about £22,000-worth of automobile. And, just to make the evening complete, he hired Ray Charles to sing.

Less than six weeks later David Thieme was arrested in the boardroom of the Credit Suisse Bank in Zurich. The charges were fraud and embezzlement of $4.5 million. On top of that, the bank said Thieme and Essex owed them another $40 million. Thieme said the charges were false and malicious.

And he aimed to prove them wrong.

David Charles Thieme was born in 1941, in Minneapolis, Minnesota, but was raised in New York. His grandparents had come to the States from Heidelberg, Germany, just before the turn of the century. His father was an aeronautical engineer and at one point worked on the CG–4A and CG–13 gliders used during World War II. Thieme himself trained as an industrial designer. During the '60s he glossed and glittered trade shows for Mercedes, and jet-interiors for the Lear Corporation. 'I started my own design firm when I was 19. You don't need much to do that. One drawing board, one chair, one room, two pencils and no money.'

He made his first fortune before he was 30.

'I was sitting in a saloon in Dallas, Texas. After you spend any amount of time in Texas you can't help but smell oil everywhere. A friend told me about an opportunity, about a bunch of cowboys who drove pick-up trucks and who were looking for some backing in a small operation. They had a well they wanted to drill. Now you know what the chances are that anything like that actually works. Most of the time you kiss your money goodbye. Well, I sank $25,000 into this and, believe it or not, they hit. It was dumb, blind luck. Of course it was fun for a gringo, but I knew I had been lucky once and that's where the fun ended. I sold out for more than my original $25,000. Considerably more. And then I went back to my design business.'

But the oil bug had bitten.

A tall, thin man, Thieme sports a goatee, square sun glasses and clothes in dark midnight-blue. At first glance he appears mysterious. But he's an obsessively polite man whose only visible passions are music, motor racing and the oil business.

In the good old days his address was a hotel suite in Monte Carlo. A table was always waiting for him in the bar of the Hotel de Paris. If peroxide blondes who camp-follow the jet set ever interested him, he certainly doesn't show them off. His lady friends tend to be very young, albeit quiet women who stay with him for long periods of time.

'It was in August 1973 when I sold my design firm because I wanted to take a leap into the commercial end of the oil business. I compiled whatever I could on the so-called spot market, because I wanted to know everything there was to know before sinking my money into it. Less than two months later war broke out in the Middle East. The fertilizer hit the windmill. There wasn't anything else to do but jump on a plane and go to Arabia. When you don't know anything about the oil business, the only way to learn is to get down on your knees and crawl around until you find out what you can. It doesn't take long though because it happens to be a simple business.'

What he learned about this 'simple business' was how to operate an independent oil company.

He called his company Essex Overseas Petroleum – although he never bothered to give himself a title. The scope of his business was the transportation, refining and marketing of petroleum products with leased shipping and refining capacity. In other words, he'd sit in his office in Monte Carlo with computers and telephones buying crude at the lowest possible rate and either selling it to someone else, or refining it himself and then selling the refined product to someone else. His game was one of percentages. He'd try to get a small percentage somewhere in the middle of what amounts to a colossal sum. A mere half percent of two million barrels at $26 a barrel comes to $260,000.

In the beginning his deals were modest. Most of them were nothing more than putting the supplier in contact with the receiver. As he grew more confident, he started financing his own deals, mostly joint ventures with first- and second-level independents. What eventually came about was an Essex network of a dozen or so trading companies, scattered around the world – although even in the best of times he never employed more than three dozen people.

In 1976 business was good and he began what he hoped would be a long-term relationship with the head office of the Credit Suisse Bank, at 8 Paradeplatz, Zurich. He was making money, and so were they. He invited them to his parties. He got them reserved seats at the Grand Prix races. They saw him making money, a lot of money. But they also saw him spending money, a lot of money.

'Some people guessed I shelled out as much as $1.5 million for the party in 1981 at the Royal Albert Hall. And I've heard people tell me that the Lotus team must have cost me as much as $15 million a year. Frankly, I hope it looked like it cost me that much. I wanted it all to look expensive. But in all honesty, without saying how much it did cost, it was nowhere near that kind of money.'

The way he saw it, the parties and the racing cars were just his way of advertising to the people with whom he was doing business.

'If I took them out to dinner twice a year, separately, it would have cost me a fortune and taken up all my time. So I simply invited everyone to dinner on the same night. Look at it this way. If Proctor and Gamble could get all of the housewives who buy their soap together under one roof, they wouldn't need to advertise on television. As for the car races, I've always said that in Formula One only two things can happen. You can spend money and you can lose races. But the name Essex was everywhere.'

1979 was the year kings were made in the oil business. But Thieme insists he wasn't a king. At best he admits to having become a demi-baron.

'Oil is the last frontier. After being in the oil business, there can be no more fun anywhere else. Oil is like nothing else in the world. It's a game where you get in fast and get out fast. Fortunes are made on volume and velocity. But it's an extremely volatile game because fortunes are lost that way too. The market can reverse itself instantly with one gunshot or a few politically harsh words. To operate in the oil business you need chutzpah and luck and raw nerves steadied with Jack Daniels.'

Then came 1980. 'It was a tough year.'

And that was followed by 1981. 'That year was almost suicidal. It made the bubonic plague look mild.'

To understand what happened you've got to get deeper into the nature of the oil business – much deeper than Thieme's explanation of it being merely 'a simple business'. On paper it might be. In reality it is anything but.

The major oil companies – the Exxons, BPs, Shells and Mobils of this world – control 80–85% of the business. The rest is divided among 50–60 independents, except that the top 25 independents divide up nearly 15% of the market, leaving very little room for anyone else. Depending on consumption levels, those independents could be vying for anywhere from one to three million barrels a day. The oil-producing nations, under the OPEC umbrella, try to set an official price. But that doesn't really mean much because everything is open to negotiation. Almost every standing contract or term-supply can come under discussion, revision or renegotiation if one of the partners smells a better deal somewhere else.

When prices drop, as they did in 1980 and have continued to do with the oil glut, some companies find themselves sitting on oil for which there is suddenly no market at their committed price. It's known as a 'distressed cargo'. Some company chief goes to bed at night thinking he's made money but when he wakes up the next morning he finds that the price has dropped and he's facing a huge loss. It happens just that quickly.

At the same time, there's some independent trader like Thieme, willing to pick up that cargo. While it's impossible to say how much distressed cargo there is in the world at any given period, suffice it to say that in a soft market there are millions of barrels available for the trader who knows how to buy them and where to unload them. For the shrewd operator, they say, it's like hunting goldfish with a machine gun. The cargo itself can change hands any number of times between producer and eventual buyer, with prices going up or down at every step. If the last guy who gets it or delivers it is to make money, he's got to have sold it or optioned it before he ever sees it. In a slow slide of prices, or even in a slow climb of prices, everyone involved with the cargo is very careful. But in a rapid chute or a ferocious climb (which is what 1979 was all about) there is big money to be made. The trick is to be short in a slide and long in a climb. If you are, you get rich quick. If you're not, you go bust even quicker.

The prices for refined petroleum products are determined

minute by minute in five major world markets: Rotterdam, Houston, New York, Singapore and Tokyo.

They're the spot markets.

In good years, the price of a barrel's-worth of refined products was more than the cost of a barrel of crude plus the various premiums the Arab producers sometimes taxed on top. The difference was profit. What happened in that 1980–1 period was that the price for one barrel of refined products was actually less than the price of a barrel of crude. The difference was loss. Exxon and Texaco, BP and Shell can always cushion their losses by raising their prices at the petrol pumps. The public complains, but the major oil companies own the game and can pretty much make up the rules as they go along.

In spite of their pretensions, the majors have done little more than give lip service to public attitudes.

However, independents, such as Thieme's Essex, had no pumps and no public. They had no way of pawning their losses off on anyone. A super-tanker riding the seas carries as many as two million barrels. In the good days, that could mean profits for an independent in the $1–4-million range. In 1980–1, when the dice turned, the $1–4-million range fell into the loss column. Although Thieme never divulged how big he was winning in 1979, one fairly good guess puts him over the $100 million mark. Perhaps as much as $120 million. But when the market turned sour, it quickly evaporated. Again, he won't say to what extent. He refuses to talk about such things. The same way he won't say how much he spent on the big parties and the race cars. Because he is such a private person, the element of mystery is heightened. 'So what,' he likes to say. 'A little mystery never hurt anyone.'

Except that little bit of mystery was one of the reasons he was arrested.

10 April 1981.

An article about David Thieme appeared that Friday morning in the *International Herald Tribune*. It was a feature story titled 'David Thieme: Mixes Oil and Racing'.

In the article he spoke about his lifestyle, about all the gloss and all the glitter, about the oil business, and about the upcoming Formula One season. There was a race scheduled that weekend in Argentina and as the Lotus sponsor, Thieme attended all the races, running around the globe to entertain clients on Grand Prix weekends.

So there he was in print saying how much he was looking forward to being in Buenos Aires and there were the gnomes at Credit Suisse thinking, not with our money!

They knew the oil business was in a pretty awful state. Having financed an enormous number of deals with Thieme, it looked as if his bad luck could also be their bad luck. And now here he was in the *International Herald Tribune*, pictured wearing his square sun glasses, looking mysterious, talking about big parties and race cars and South America.

Throughout that spring he'd been meeting regularly with Credit Suisse to reschedule and restructure his debt. He thought that, while the negotiations were tough, everything would eventually sort itself out. On 30 March 1981 the quarterly agreement between Essex and Credit Suisse ended. The Essex debt was reportedly $20 million. According to documents later filed with the Swiss courts, the bank officials were already arranging Thieme's arrest. That's probably why they did not call in the quarterly loan agreement when it ended. Perhaps they needed some way to lure him back to the bank. Thieme, of course, wanted to extend the agreement. The bank demanded a show of good faith and got him to sign over to them a $5 million guarantee in his own name towards the Essex debt. Then they demanded more. They got him to put his signature on papers allowing the bank ownership of certain Essex assets – aircraft, specific commercial receivables, real estate and various vehicles, including the three-storey Essex bus that Thieme used as a hospitality suite at the Grand Prix races. The total, by Thieme's count, came to nearly $15 million.

When Credit Suisse and Thieme joined forces in 1976, the Essex line of credit was $5 million. Over the years it grew to as much as $100 million. And both parties agree that between 1976 and 1981 Essex had borrowed and paid back with interest nearly $1 billion. But none of that mattered to Credit Suisse that April. Typical of most banks, they liked him when he was flush, but the romance ended when they saw he wasn't.

Making matters worse, Credit Suisse had suffered through the likes of Bernie Cornfeld and the Investors Overseas Services scandal. They'd followed that by fumbling their way through a £543-million embezzlement by some of their own employees at their branch in Chiasso.

Now, they decided, they had to worry about David Thieme.

Taking charge for Credit Suisse was a short, fat, somewhat offensive character named Joseph Muller. As Executive Vice-President for 'Special Assignments', he was head of the bank's private CIA. He and Thieme met in a conference room one floor above the Paradeplatz, on the Bahnhofstrasse side of the bank's headquarters. Thieme believed the meeting would go on all day, although he assumed there'd be a break for lunch. But, as lunchtime neared, Muller showed no signs of adjourning. Thieme remembers that Muller seemed to be dragging out the morning session, as if he was waiting for something to happen. Muller kept leaving the room, coming back and then going out again. For most of the morning he was in shirt-sleeves. Then, suddenly, he reappeared with his jacket on. With him was a group of men Thieme didn't know. They turned out to be the police. The officer in charge told Thieme in English that he was being arrested on charges of fraud and embezzlement.

When the shock of that wore off, Thieme asked, 'Is manslaughter included?'

The officer in charge looked puzzled, and mumbled, 'No.'

Thieme asked, 'Do you want it to be?'

The officer in charge said, 'Of course not.'

'So,' Thieme pointed to Muller and shouted in his anger, 'then get that motherfucker out of here!!!'

Muller left the conference room smugly convinced he was on top.

The police seized whatever assets Thieme had on his person. In Switzerland it's known as a 'pocket arrest' and it's often used in cases of debt so that those assets can be put towards the debt. They got some cash. Then the police escorted him to his hotel suite where they confiscated whatever else they could find. Finally, he was led off to jail.

Word immediately went out to the press that Thieme had been stopped on his way to South America. It was totally untrue. Whether anyone at the bank deliberately released false information or if some confusion evolved because of the South American reference in the *IHT* article is unclear. But certain journalists were told that Thieme had been arrested at the airport heading for Buenos Aires. That could have played some part in the judge's decision to refuse bail. Ironically enough, the fact that Thieme was refused bail played straight into Muller's hands. He needed to be absolutely certain that Thieme would be immobile for several days. His entire case was riding on it.

Muller had built his reputation at the bank on being able to get something on anybody. While planning his battle with Thieme, he quite skilfully managed to unearth an employee at Essex who was susceptible to manipulation. Muller convinced her to come to Zurich, using the ploy that the welfare of the entire Essex staff depended on her. She agreed. On Monday 6 April, a Credit Suisse representative in Monaco drove her to Genoa, Italy – more than 90 minutes away – to meet a plane for Switzerland. The international airport at Nice is 20 minutes from the Principality by car, and only five minutes by regularly scheduled helicopter. Air France and Swissair provide daily services from Nice to Switzerland. Yet Credit Suisse flew her out of Genoa. Then, Muller wouldn't see her that day. She was told he was too busy. It was the same story on Tuesday. She waited for him five hours until he cancelled the meeting. On Wednesday they did speak, but only very briefly, discussing Essex finances for 5–10 minutues before Muller made an excuse to cut the meeting short. They did not meet on Thursday. And on Friday, while still hoping to see Muller, the woman was told about Thieme's arrest.

By Saturday morning she was in a panic, absolutely terrified of Muller.

That's when he announced that they were going to Monaco. Joining them were Dr Thomas Lehner, one of the bank's in-house attorneys, Dr Michael Werder, a Zurich-based attorney representing the bank, Patrick Lahusen, a Credit Suisse Vice-President who'd handled the Essex loan account, and a minor Credit Suisse employee who in the end had very little to do with any of this.

The party checked into six adjoining rooms at the Loews Hotel Monte Carlo – literally a five-minute walk from Thieme's offices. All of the rooms were booked in the name of Michael Werder and paid for by him with a credit card. At no time did the name Credit Suisse appear on the reservations, registrations or room-service bills. Lehner, speaking for the bank, later claimed that the group had been invited to enter the Essex offices, escorted there legally by an authorized employee. He insisted that no papers were ever removed from those offices. He did however admit that photocopies were made of the papers found in David Thieme's desk, but added that this too was at the invitation of the woman employee. Werder would not make any comments. Lahusen has since met a less than cheerful fate at the hands of his former employers, being forced to resign. And Muller, quite purposely and consistently, has made himself unavailable for comment.

Yet, in a sworn statement before the Monégasque Prosecutor's Office, that woman employee paints another version of the events of that weekend.

She says that the contingent arrived in Monaco on Saturday afternoon but did not go to the Essex offices until well after dark. She puts the time at about 10 p.m. when Muller ordered her and Lahusen to go with him. She says the two men already had a list of documents they were looking for. She swears that Muller insisted on waiting outside, in the gardens facing the offices, until she and Lahusen had gone into Thieme's office, then raised and lowered the blinds twice to tell him the coast was clear. She says that the three of them spent about two hours in the Essex offices, with Muller and Lahusen rummaging through desks and files. It was midnight when they got back to the hotel where Muller showed the bounty to Lehner and Werder. It's a curious point that neither Lehner nor Werder went along to Thieme's offices. Both are attorneys. Both are officers of the court. Neither would ever be foolish enough to take any risk that might be confused with breaking the law. And both remained at the hotel.

The following morning, Muller told her that certain papers he'd been hoping to find were not among the cache, and he ordered her back to the offices to find them. It was daylight. Lahusen went with her. Muller did not. But the two found nothing and, as they were both frightened that they'd be caught, they returned to the hotel empty-handed. Muller was furious. He was by now, according to the woman, showing signs of his own anxieties. He said they would check out of the hotel immediately and go to Nice. There they piled into the office of a French lawyer where, the woman claims, she was forced to sign over to Credit Suisse certain Essex assets for which she had control. Asked in an interview to confirm that this particular agreement was indeed signed in Nice on Sunday 12 April, Thomas Lehner, who was present, recalled that it was. The only problem here is that the agreement the bank later presented in their case against Thieme bears the dateline Zurich, 10 April.

'I spent 13 days in jail. When I was finally released on bail, the bank officials were quite obviously upset. They were worried. They expected me to jump bail and run for my life. Instead I spent the next seven months co-operating fully with the Swiss authorities who were investigating the case. I don't think Herr Muller counted on me doing that. But I did because it was vital for me to prove to the Swiss authorities that I was not guilty of any wrong-doings.'

In presenting their case, Credit Suisse set out to prove that Thieme had defrauded them of $3.8 million in a fuel oil sale, misappropriated some $490,000 of their funds, and embezzled a further 180,000 Swiss francs. While the Swiss authorities were studying the Credit Suisse evidence, the bank was moving against Thieme in the Cayman Islands, trying to wrap up the part of the Essex empire registered there. They also filed suit against Thieme and Essex in New York.

Releasing Thieme on bail was the first indication Muller and the bank had to suggest the tide could possibly turn.

A little more than one month later, on 29 May, Thieme produced evidence to prove that the fuel oil deal had nothing to do with Credit Suisse, having been financed through the Banque de Paris et des Pays-Bas in Geneva. Furthermore, the allegedly misappropriated and embezzled funds were sitting snugly in an Essex account with yet another bank, where they'd been all along. Now Essex filed suit against Credit Suisse in New York to the tune of $125 million – supposedly the largest single lawsuit to date ever brought against a foreign bank in the United States. He also filed against them in Switzerland and Monaco on behalf of Essex, including criminal charges against Muller, Lehner and Werder for what he claimed was the 'Watergate-style break-in' of his offices. The worldwide claims totalled about 400 million Swiss francs (then somewhere close to £100 million).

The bank, in an effort to collect some of the money on the assets they'd managed to seize, put the Essex plane up for auction. No one bought it. Then, a lower court in Zurich ruled that the pocket arrest of Thieme's personal property in the bank's conference room on 10 April was illegal.

And exactly eight months after his arrest, the Swiss authorities announced that they were dropping all charges.

The next morning Thieme held a press conference in Zurich. 'Eight months ago to the day, I was falsely arrested in the conference room of Credit Suisse, main branch, Paradeplatz, in a desperate and malicious act of irresponsibility by my former banking partners. Today, I am pleased to inform you that by decision of Dr Gianpiero Antognazza, state's attorney of the Canton of Zurich, dated 8 December 1981, all proceedings against me based on the obviously unfounded charges by Credit Suisse have been terminated. Both district attorney Dr Bruno Schadler and state's attorney Dr G. Antognazza have spent seven months thoroughly investigating and have concluded, as I have always believed they would, that there are no grounds for the Credit Suisse charges. I have therefore instructed my attorneys to investigate the question of false arrest and malicious prosecution on the part of Credit Suisse. Additionally, authorities in other countries continue their investigations and proceedings against specific officers of Credit Suisse for criminal behaviour. Furthermore, we are continuing a number of civil actions in various jurisdictions. In particular, our New York attorneys are vigorously pursuing claims against Credit Suisse in excess of $125 million.'

Many of the journalists present knew Thieme through his Formula One connections, had reported his arrest and were quite familiar with the bank's claims against him.

One of them expressed the bank's side of the story, claiming the charges had been dropped due to a lack of jurisdiction. Thieme answered: 'The charges were dropped because there was simply no evidence to support the bank's charges. I was arrested in Switzerland after the bank's lawyers and Herr Muller had plenty of time to plan their case against me. It's obvious they knew very well when they made their move where the jurisdiction lay. Had there been jurisdictional problems, their legal staff would have seen that immediately. Had it only been a question of jurisdiction, the Swiss state's attorney's office would have handed down that ruling at the very beginning. No, the ruling they handed down is one of complete vindication.'

It went on like that for the better part of an hour. When the press conference ended, three rather burly men who had been sitting in the rear of the room, unnoticed by Thieme, came forward and introduced themselves as bailiffs of the court. They had with them a warrant for a pocket arrest. They said they were there on behalf of the bank to seize whatever assets Thieme had on his person and in his hotel suite. But this last-minute bit of histrionics proved fruitless. They found nothing. And Thieme was quoted in the Swiss papers the next day: 'Credit Suisse certainly is a bunch of poor losers.'

Six days after the Swiss dropped charges against him, the Supreme Court of the Canton of Zurich upheld the lower court decision in favour of Thieme concerning the first pocket arrest. The court wrote that seizing his assets inside the bank's conference room was 'in bad faith', adding that Credit Suisse had 'violated the trust created by its own conduct. Such methods contradict the principle of good faith in business relationships and accordingly are not deserving of legal protection'.

For a Swiss court to say that about one of the country's major banking institutions was a slap in the face. Yet more was to come. The bank had 30 days to appeal against the Swiss prosecutor's decision to drop all charges, but they didn't. Instead, Credit Suisse filed an appeal against the Essex suit aimed at them in New York, while at the same time withdrawing their New York suit against Essex and Thieme. They now claimed there was no jurisdiction there for the suit against them. However, the New York courts felt differently, ruling that the Essex suit could indeed be heard there. Over the next year the bank appealed that decision twice, rising to higher courts each time, and they lost twice. Obviously frustrated, they finally moved against one of their own. Patrick Lahusen was charged with disloyal management and fired. The official line was that Lahusen had over-extended Thieme's line of credit. Lahusen's 'liquidation' brought on such severe depressions that he was virtually eliminated from the case.

Thieme's feeling is that Lahusen was the scapegoat, slaughtered to cover up for others.

'Anyone who knows how a bank conducts business knows very well that Patrick Lahusen could never have acted by himself to approve whatever huge loans came across his desk. When requests for additional credit were sent to the bank, those requests had to go up the ladder. We're not speaking of a $3000 car loan. We're talking about a line of credit upwards of $100 million. That sort of business can only be approved at the very top. Don't think for a minute that the highest ranks of Credit Suisse didn't know what was going on. It was their job to know. On the other hand, if the top levels didn't know, with such huge sums involved, as the bank now claims, then the crucifixion of Mr Lahusen is just as immoral because it means that the top-ranking men of Credit Suisse are totally incompetent.'

At Credit Suisse they've never been too keen to answer questions about Thieme's case. The official spokesman is the lawyer, Thomas Lehner. A tall, thin, German Swiss, then probably somewhere in his mid-to-late 30s, he pounded loudly on his desk to demand that questions aimed at him be made softer. He answered direct questions with long-winded and well rehearsed speeches about the bank's responsibilities. When he wasn't banging on his desk or threatening to end the interview, he was laughing and shaking his head, insinuating that the questions being asked were stupid, irrelevant and based entirely on fallacies.

When asked if Credit Suisse filed charges against Mr Thieme and/or Essex in New York and then withdrew those charges, he spent five minutes emphatically denying that to be true, saying it showed an ignorance of the case. What actually happened, he explained, was that, after charges were filed in New York, they were not withdrawn but rather moved to Switzerland where it would be more convenient for officers of the bank to testify.

Yet when asked why Thieme had been vindicated by the Swiss courts, Lehner took the stance that it was only a matter of jurisdiction, which directly contradicted the bank's argument for moving the civil case from New York to Switzerland.

Then, to further support the bank's contentions against Thieme, Lehner pointed out that the Swiss authorities had not in fact let him off scot-free. Thieme, he said, had been ordered to pay costs. Oddly enough, those costs after seven months of investigations amounted to a mere 3000 Swiss francs (something like £750).

The way Thieme saw it, charging him such a sum was just a gesture. 'After all, I came to their town, to fight them in their language, with their own laws and in their own courts. And I won. Can you blame them for trying to save some face?'

Disregarding that, Lehner maintained he could easily prove Thieme wrong, and would be quite willing to do so, except that Swiss banking laws prevented him from speaking out. In fact, throughout a three-hour interview, Lehner spent an inordinate amount of time hiding behind Swiss banking laws. At one point he said that, if only Thieme would release him from liability under the banking secrets act, he would happily make public a copy of the Credit Suisse criminal charges against Thieme. 'It's very revealing,' he promised. But Thieme himself willingly provided a copy of those charges, and, anyway, they were the same ones that the Swiss prosecutors had studied, investigated and eventually dismissed.

When asked about the entry into the Essex offices, Lehner said there was nothing at all illegal about that. When asked why it took place at night, Lehner said it was to avoid alarming any employees who might have been working there. When asked why, if it was a legal entry, neither he nor Dr Werder went along – after all, couldn't attorneys be subject to sanctions for taking part in any sort of illegal action – he said it was because they were otherwise busy. Doing what? He wouldn't say. When asked if the scenario of the Essex employee was correct, especially her description of Muller waiting outside for the all clear signal, Lehner said that was ridiculous, in spite of the fact that he'd sworn he wasn't there.

The bank tried, Lehner went on, to get Thieme to slow down when the oil market went soft in 1980. But, to their horror, Thieme seemed to prefer large parties and racing cars to 'good business sense'. And Lehner did not want anyone to forget that Thieme and Essex still owed the bank tens of millions of dollars, with the interest accruing daily.

Thieme never denied that there was a debt. He just saw it

differently. 'A commercial dispute does exist with the bank. But, by our calculations, the Essex debt is considerably less than the figure the bank continues to use. You must also understand that a great deal changed in our relationship with the bank when they had me slapped in a cell. That's why we have consistently maintained that, before anyone from Essex sits down with our former banking partners to discuss our obligations to them, they have several explanations to make about their own behaviour.'

About a year after Thieme's arrest, a BBC television crew from 'The Money Programme' tried to ask for some of those explanations. They were refused entry to the bank. When they started filming on the Paradeplatz – a public square – bank guards threatened to have them arrested if they didn't move away from the bank's front door.

The BBC crew were surprised.

Thieme was not. 'I think the bank must realize that they've worked themselves into an awkward position. The last thing they want is anyone looking too closely at the way they've treated me. But if you study the records in Zurich, you can see how Credit Suisse has dealt heavy-handedly with a number of their clients. In a lot of cases the clients haven't been able to fight back. This is not the case with me.'

For the next four years, David Thieme continued running around the world flogging oil. Only a little of the gloss and glitter had changed. But his wheeling and dealing inevitably slowed down. The market was awful and, admittedly, he'd been commercially hurt by the arrest. No, he used to tell friends, the game just isn't as good as it used to be. Eventually he left Monaco and headed for Paris. When last seen he was living there, with a very beautiful young brunette.

After a while the bank wrote off the debt, while the lawsuits and the counter-suits just fizzled away. They're probably still on the books in various courts somewhere, but when money isn't coming in fast and furiously, lawyers move on to greener pastures too.

It took Credit Suisse several years to sell the Essex plane.

They also wound up one of the Essex companies, although it was just an empty shell. At the end of the day, for all of their efforts against Thieme and Essex – and after who knows how many millions of pounds in legal fees – the biggest victory they could honestly claim was the seizure and sale of a cache of 800 Cuban cigars which they found in Thieme's name, sitting in a rented humidor in Zurich, exactly one block from their own front door.

3

Michel wrote the scripts.

Albert came along as the hired co-star.

And together, over seven Mondays in Cardiff, for 12 hours every day, they cooked and bantered in front of the cameras to put 13 shows on tape for the BBC.

Each taping began at 7 a.m.

Michel would be early, meeting with the director, setting up, preparing everything so that each recipe could be made three or four times.

At exactly seven Albert would swagger in – the way Clint Eastwood walks on to his sets – and Michel would hand him the day's script.

'Who's this for?' Albert would ask.

Michel would look around. 'There are only two of us, who do you think it's for?'

Albert would read his script, his half-glasses falling off the end of his nose, and invariably he'd mumble, 'You're not expecting me to cook this, are you?'

'Why not?' Michel would want to know. 'You make that dish better than anyone.'

'Yes, yes,' Albert would now agree. 'A piece of cake, brother. A piece of cake.'

So Michel would stand behind the stove and start to explain a sauce and Albert would stand next to him saying the sauce was all right but stir it more and don't add so much cream and watch out for the flame, don't let it get too high. Then it would be Albert's turn. One day he was demonstrating how to bone a huge slice of meat and did it so fast that they needed a retake.

In fact, he did it so fast the second and third times that the camera simply couldn't pick it up and Michel had to keep yelling, 'Slow down.'

And when the seven weeks were over, someone said, let's do another series.

Albert said, okay, yes, why not.

Michel merely raised his eyebrows.

'Making television shows with brother', Michel now admits, 'takes a great deal of diplomacy. I would happily do it again because I love challenges. But let me put it this way, it's much easier to cook with him than to be on television with him.'

Albert shrugs, 'When left alone I work wonders.'

Albert Henri Roux owns Le Gavroche on Upper Brook Street in London's Mayfair. It was the first restaurant in the UK to be awarded three stars by the Michelin Guide.

Michel André Roux owns The Waterside Inn, on the Thames in the small Berkshire village of Bray. In 1985 it became only the second restaurant in Britain to win the three stars award.

With just 25 three-star restaurants in the world, Michelin therefore rates the Roux brothers among the world's finest chefs.

The funny thing about them is that they don't look like brothers. But they're both quick to assure anyone who asks that they are. In fact, they hardly ever refer to each other by name. They really do call each other 'Brother'.

Raised in the French region of Saône-et-Loire, Albert was born in Semur-en-Brionnais in 1935. He's shorter, with grey-speckled hair. Michel was born in the neighbouring village of Charolles in 1941. He's taller, with blond hair and a French schoolboy look in his eyes. Their father, and his father before him, were both charcutiers. At the age of 14, Albert began an apprenticeship as a pastry chef, spending five years to learn his trade before accepting a post in London to cook for Lady Astor. At about the same time, Michel began his apprenticeship, also in pastry. He spent two years before being appointed pastry chef at the British Embassy in Paris. Then Albert went off to do his military service with the French Army. And eventually Michel was called for his service. By the time they were both back to cooking again, Albert was head chef for Major Peter Cazalet at his stately home in Kent, and Michel was Chef de Cuisine for Miss Cecile de Rothschild in Paris. But the two of them had always wanted to go into business together. So Albert told Michel to come to London, that they could find a backer and open a restaurant.

Michel arrived in 1967.

And the original Le Gavroche, on Lower Sloane Street in Chelsea, was only the start of their empire.

'In a very real sense,' says Michel, 'our risks are a nightly affair. After all, we would not put our names on a product which we didn't create. And every night we put our name on our product. In our case, we've got to win every game. But it goes further than that because cooking is our daily oxygen. It's got to be done in a grand place. Cooking is a day to day work. We couldn't go for long periods of time out of Gavroche or Waterside. It's a very personalized business. Like any show that's done every day, if the maestro is sick, he might be replaced for a day or two. But not for very long. So basically all of the things happening in our group get right back to what the two brothers are doing in the kitchen.'

Albert moved Le Gavroche to Mayfair in 1981, taking the basement of a building on the corner of Park and Upper Brook Streets. And it must be said that the first two years there were a disaster. The place was full. The first year's turnover was £1 million. But the cost of the move was £750,000 and that first year's profit in Mayfair was under £50,000. It took a lot of work to make it a success. Albert began taking orders later at night. Then he managed to fill the private dining-rooms upstairs three, four, five times a week. That alone boosted turnover by at least one day more a week.

Michel believes that moving Le Gavroche came very close to being a mistake.

'It was a very bad move for the first two years. I don't think we should have gone for Upper Brook Street where the rates are so expensive. Although it shows now we did the right thing since we're managing 47 Park Street, above the restaurant. But who knew at the time? Who knew that the fellow who owns 47 Park Street would suddenly realize that in his building he had people who were able to run and fill up the place?'

It was nearly a year after they moved to Mayfair that the gentleman who owned 47 Park Street realized what it could mean to have the Roux brothers in the building. Until they came along, 47 Park Street was a tired bunch of service flats. Albert discovered over lunch one day that the man was most anxious to bring the brothers into his business. But Albert explained that the first thing he'd need was a guarantee that money would be spent redecorating to their standards. The owner agreed to shell out more than £1 million just to redecorate. In the end he spent closer to £2 million. Today Albert manages the most discreet hotel in London offering 54 suites, each with a kitchen.

The brothers' empire extends to several restaurants and into various aspects of food service.

There's Le Poulbot in the City and Gavvers at Le Gavroche's old address. There used to be a restaurant called Gamin, near the Law Courts, but they sold that a few years ago.

One of the areas where they've concentrated a lot of effort in the past five years has been in outside catering. That began when the brothers realized that not everyone in the City could get out for lunch and that the quality of food being cooked in some 'executive canteens' was pretty terrible. In a few cases, they supply pre-cooked dishes. In other cases, they've actually taken over the running of those canteen kitchens. They've installed chefs full-time in bank head offices around the City, cooking strictly to Roux Brothers recipes. Among their clients are Kleinwort Benson, Credit Lyonais and the BAFTA Club in Piccadilly. Outside catering has been so successful that the Banque de Paris et des Pays-Bas hired the Rouxs to do all the planning for the kitchen and food service in their new headquarters building.

In 1973 they set up a *pâtisserie* in Wandsworth because they needed to supply their own group with pastry, bread, croissants, *brioches, pains au chocolat,* and cakes. When they saw the potential of that business, they started taking in clients from the outside. These days you can buy Roux Brothers products at Harrods, the Meridien and even at two Waitrose supermarkets – one on the Kings Road, the other in Barnes.

Nine years later they applied the same theory to their own butcher shop. Opened at the end of 1982, La Boucherie Lamartine on Ebury Street in London represented an investment of £150,000. This year, with half their business wholesale and the other half retail, they're expecting turnover to reach £1.3 million. Albert controls the butcher shop with his partner, a former Roux Brothers employee, Marc Beaujeu. The two also recently bought the Mayfair poulterers, Bailey's, opposite the Connaught.

There have, however, been a few failures. In 1973 they opened a charcuterie in Henley. But it didn't work. Michel thinks it might have been a little too sophisticated for the area and that kept people away. So after a year they closed it and swallowed a £50,000 loss. A few years ago they lost again with a charcuterie. One of their sisters had been running Le Cochon Rose, near Gavvers, with her husband but she decided to go back to France.

'It was just as well,' Michel says. 'We've got a sister who is so dreadful with people. She got rid of the clientele so beautifully that we found ourselves with a shop that was clean, with a great line of products and nobody wanted to buy from us. We're in a country where people like to be looked after nicely, and certainly not ignored. She turned the Cochon Rose from a profit-maker into a loss-maker. So, when she left, we didn't feel like going to find another charcutier. If she hadn't been our sister, we would have sacked her.'

The most spectacular success of the past several years has been in the brothers' development of a new cooking process.

'It's not a complicated process,' Albert explains, 'but we've put many years of research work into it and have now begun to produce. It's based on the idea that food can be cooked in a vacuum. Now, vacuum-packing of food has been around for a long time. You know, cooking in the bag. I simply took it a step further.'

The idea is to cook a dish under very high pressure, then vacuum-pack it immediately. That keeps both the taste and texture of the product fresh. The rest of the secret lies in the bag that's used.

'I wouldn't call this fast food. I would call it good bourgeois cooking. Some of the dishes are worthy of a two-star Michelin restaurant. We didn't have to create special dishes for vacuum-cooking. We followed Escoffier. We tested it by serving some of this food in the City with our outside catering and it's been a great success. We tested it with merchant bankers and they liked it.'

They had an offer of £250,000 for the vacuum-cooking method while it was still in the experimental stage. They turned down the offer, and instead opened a restaurant in the City called Rouxl Britannia which features this vacuum-cooking method. They hope someday to turn it into a chain but so far they've stuck with just one place. Not long ago they set up a factory near Heathrow where they produce these vacuum-cooked dishes, and through a company that's now four years old, called Home Rouxl, they distribute these dishes to their outside catering unit and certain specialty shops such as Harrods and Selfridges.

The main problem with expansion is obvious. There are only two brothers and if they want to keep their reputation intact, they've got to personally assure that anything bearing their name meets with their own high standards.

Adds Michel, 'We can't expand without having the quality of our restaurants suffer. But we can expand by using our skills to create recipes which we cook sealed into those plastic bags and then sell into appropriate markets. We want to popularize cooking which is called cuisine bourgeoise.'

These days the Roux Restaurant Group – including the two independent units, Gavroche and Waterside Inn – employs 500 people and turns over in excess of £10 million.

*

When Albert is in the kitchen, it's like Olivier playing Hamlet.

In the centre of his stage are four large ovens, surrounded by the various stations – sauce, vegetables, fish, hors d'œuvres, salad and pastry. Facing the doors to the dining-room is the service bar where waiters hand in orders and collect highly decorated plates of food on silver trays. Every night there are three different kinds of canapé, and 130 of each kind. Tonight it's quail's eggs and foie gras and salmon mousse with chives. Albert stops to inspect the hors d'œuvres station, nods and walks on. He stops to look at someone preparing a *petit pâté de bécasse* – a woodcock paté. 'Bien,' he smiles. Then he asks loudly in French, 'How many pheasant pies are there tonight?' Someone answers in English, 'Fourteen.' No one seems to realize they're working in two different languages.

Dozens of copper pans in varying shapes and sizes sit on the stoves. Some with sauces. Some with boiling water. Some with vegetables. Two large frying pans have meat in them. A couple of smaller ones await ingredients. Albert inspects them all, just as the first orders begin to come in. One chef takes the orders from the waiters. And calls out loudly to everyone in the kitchen, 'Huit foies gras. Huit toast. Deux papillotes. Deux menus exceptionels.' And like a Greek chorus, each cook at his station shouts back, 'Oui, chef.'

As the evening progresses, the kitchen gets hotter.

Albert claims it isn't hot. But it is. Very hot. He insists it's much cooler in his kitchen than most others. Some corners of the kitchen are less hot than others, but where it's hot – in spite of what Albert thinks – it is very hot.

A dish of scallops with creamy scrambled eggs is being made at the fish station when Albert says, 'Non, mes enfants. Mais non.' Heads turn. 'It must be done like this.' He moves the dish aside and starts to make another.

The chef at the meat station calls out orders non-stop.

In the middle of his *ad hoc* cooking school, Albert looks just long enough to ask, 'OK for that pheasant pie?' The clock in his head told him one of the orders was ready. Then, without missing a beat, he continues with the scallops, showing everyone what the dish should look like. 'You see it, my children?' He hands it to the fish chef and goes to look at a plate being decorated with watercress. 'Put some ice on that watercress.'

And all the time one chef is calling out, 'Canapés, huit. Scallopes, deux. Quatre menus.' And all the time the others shout back, 'Oui, chef. Oui, chef. Oui, chef.'

There are two private parties in suites at 47 Park Street. Albert has already checked their menus, but now he goes upstairs to speak with the head waiters assigned to those parties. 'Make sure we've got a carving board here.' Later he will return to carve the roasts at the table. Public appearances are part of being a star.

An order for a table of six comes in. Albert tries to speed things along because people are waiting for tables and it's not moving as quickly as he wants. Then a dessert order comes in. Soufflé for two. And coming up is a chocolate roll filled with fresh raspberries and liqueured coffee beans, covered with a Melba sauce. Albert pokes his head around a corner and asks, 'Ready?' The English pastry chef says, 'OK for la rouleau.' Albert takes the tray with the chocolate roll. 'Le rouleau,' he corrects. The pastry chef shakes his head. 'La. Le. La. Le. Who cares?'

Some cheese soufflés are taking too long to get out, so Albert moves in to help. A waiter tells him that two clients want to visit the kitchen. Albert wonders if they're both pretty women. The waiter says no. Albert seems disappointed but perks up when he hears that one is a French chef. He finishes with the soufflés then goes into the dining-room to meet his guests. A few minutes later he brings them into the kitchen, making no attempt at all to hide his enormous pride. The tour lasts only a few minutes, but for those few minutes this is Alain Proust showing Nigel Mansell his winning Formula One.

As paperwork is now piling up, Albert goes into his tiny office to check bills and make up his shopping list for the next day. This is the first time in nearly three hours that he's had the chance to sit down.

Twenty minutes later the last of the evening's orders is in.

Twenty minutes after that, the last of the main courses is out.

The hors d'œuvres chef is starting to clean up. The pastry chef will work at full speed for another hour. Albert checks that the washing up has begun – the kitchen must be made absolutely spotless for the next morning – and then looks at the orders remaining on the hooks above the service bar. A few salads. And some desserts.

Content that the war is being won, the 'General' is now going home. He cooked 67 lunches and now 91 dinners. Except for a little siesta after lunch, Albert has worked a 15-hour day.

But just as he's ready to leave, the room-service phone rings from one of the suites at 47 Park Street. Everyone else is too busy. Albert takes the order. A silver tray is brought over. So is a plate. So is a silver bell to cover the plate on the tray. The plate is decorated with watercress and one radish, which has been carved into a flower. And then, the man who is considered one of the two best chefs in the UK makes a room-service ham sandwich.

Their first book, *New Classic Cuisine*, was a profitable venture in more ways than one.

Written by Michel, but with both their names on the cover, it helped to reinforce the idea that the Roux brothers were the foremost chefs in Britain.

It sold 35,000 copies in hardback in less than a year and is still selling, has been translated into French, and also appeared in the United States. There's no doubt that the book helped in some small way to fill up tables in the restaurants during the winter, especially among American clients. But, more importantly, the book documented their skills and ingenuity. And business offers have come in because of it. Michel Roux assists British Airways in supplying meals from their own recipes, acts as consultant to assess food served on board – especially first-class meals on jumbos out of Heathrow – and has created menus for Concorde. Albert is a consultant to Marks and

Spencer, rating existing products and helping them come up with new ideas. He's also done consulting work for Procter and Gamble in the States, and is an adviser to The Point at Saranac Lake, in upper New York State, a hotel-restaurant that had once been the Rockefeller family's winter shooting lodge.

Their second book was all about pastry. Their third was called *The Roux Brothers At Home*, which tied into their television series. Their fourth was a definitive tome on French country cooking.

Many of their recipes are, for the lack of a better expression, extraordinary.

For instance, there's a dish that's called 'Scrambled eggs with eggs'. All you need is 12 hen's eggs, 12 quail's eggs, white wine vinegar, white bread, clarified butter, snipped chives, double cream, salt, pepper and four ounces of Beluga caviare. There's another they do, which is a Swiss cheese soufflé that anybody can make at home, as long as you've got an oven that isn't off the recommended temperature by even a couple of degrees, otherwise it won't work.

One afternoon, in a Chinese restaurant, Michel ordered a lobster, which was brought to the table for inspection, still alive. Immediately Michel said, 'Canadian.' I asked, 'Did you hear an accent?' He shook his head, 'You can always tell by the colour.'

On another occasion he was tasting a steak and kidney pie, guaranteed to have been made fresh. But he complained the kidneys had been frozen. The waiter insisted they hadn't. Michel opened one and explained to him how you could tell that a piping hot kidney had once been frozen by the texture of the inside. The manager finally admitted that it had.

The point is, their business is food and they know their subject about as well as anyone can possibly know any subject.

There's a recipe in one of their books for a *pâté sablée* – a shortbread dough. The reader is advised, while making the dough, to 'work the mixture with your fingertips until the ingredients are thoroughly blended'.

It sounded like a minor point to Michel's wife Robyn the first time she tried it. So, when she got to the part where she was supposed to use the palm of her hand, she figured the hell with this, and reached for her food processor. This is why, she thought, God invented the Magimix. As far as she was concerned, the dough was perfect. She shaped it into shells, added a pear filling and tossed them into the oven. She was just taking the finished dessert out when Michel came into the kitchen, glanced, then mumbled as he walked by, 'You shouldn't have used the food processor.'

Her mouth dropped. 'How could you possibly tell?'

He didn't have to answer.

Noblesse oblige.

One of the things the brothers have done, almost since the beginning, is help to establish their own competition.

Through their efforts, former Roux chefs have been encouraged and even assisted financially in setting up their own restaurants – top-quality, well acclaimed places like Tante Claire, Interlude de Tabaillau, Le Mazarin and Paris House at Woburn Abbey.

They refer to these joint ventures as 'the children', and the way it works is simple. The employee must have been with the Rouxs for a minimum of five years. Then he must have demonstrated great ability, confidence, trust, skill and ambition. But they don't go to him and suggest he should start his own business. If one of the staff thinks he's ready, he must approach them. If they agree, the Rouxs line up banks, bank managers, lawyers and locations. Albert and Michel try to help them decide what kind of place they can best handle – 30 covers, 60 covers – the grading of their cooking, how many people they should have on the staff, and which area of London they should be in. As soon as plans begin to gel, Albert and Michel invite a few of their best clients to become shareholders, to put some money into the restaurant.

In the spring of 1982, they undertook their first foreign joint venture. Christian Germain, a former chef at The Waterside Inn, wanted to return to France. So the brothers helped him set up the Château de Montreuil, a hotel-restaurant near Le Touquet.

There were for a time thoughts of expanding into the States. One of their former chefs wanted to start his own place in Santa Barbara, California, so the Rouxs helped him launch The Waterside Inn there. It began as a joint venture but Albert eventually bought out Michel. But it's never really taken off. The food is terrific, it's just not the right kind of food for Santa Barbara. As Albert puts it, 'People there prefer three martinis, grilled prawns and a salad. It's the wrong place for a restaurant like ours.'

He's holding on however, because when he first came to London, people said the same thing about England. In those days, if you wanted a good meal in London you went to Victoria Station and caught the first train to Paris. The Rouxs changed all that. They brought a style of cooking to London that most people didn't understand. Today that's not the case.

At the same time, since they've been in England, they've also come to understand a few things about English food.

'English food is under-rated,' Michel says, adding that at one point a few years ago he and Albert thought about opening an English restaurant in Paris. 'We had an offer which would have been fantastic. It was on the Champs-Elysées and it wound up that Jimmy Goldsmith bought it for another £30,000 more than we were willing to pay. We would have called it The English House, and offered the best of Britain. Traditional English cooking with care, love and dedication.'

There are, he concedes, even certain traditional English dishes that are as good, if not better, than some regional French dishes.

'Such as steak and kidney pie with oysters. There are beautiful joints and roast beef. There's also chicken with bread sauce, grouse with bread sauce as well, loin of pork with crackling and apple sauce, and redcurrant jelly with nicely marinaded and roasted game. Shepherd's pie is a lovely dish, simple and nice. Then there's black pudding from Scotland.

And haggis is excellent. Serving English food to the French is still something I believe I some day want to do.'

The problem with English cooking, as Albert sees it, has simply to do with the people eating it.

'I think the English definitely have an inferiority complex when it comes to talking about food. It's a question of education, of understanding, of growing up with food as part of the culture. The English should talk about food with pride because there are some wonderful dishes in this country. They really know how to roast. I love shepherd's pie, especially if it's good and sloppy. Or steak and kidney pud. What could be better than that when it's done right. The next thing is that the English must learn how to eat. They gobble their food. They don't take enough time to enoy it. And as long as that inferiority complex is there, they won't progress. However, if things change as much in the next 20 years as they have in the last 20 years, they'll be up with the French.'

Up with the French? Coming from one of the 25 most acclaimed chefs in the world – who happens to be French – that sounds like heresy.

'You think so? Let me tell you that in France people are starting to eat conventional foods. And that's a shame because the French have always known that cooking good food is easy. What the English can learn from the French is that it all begins with the produce. People in this country don't spend enough time buying the right produce. They don't criticize their suppliers. They don't insist on the finest produce. They settle for second-rate. When you go shopping for produce, you've got to say no, I don't want this one I want that better piece. The French do it all the time. The English are too polite. It's very important to buy your salad where it is best and if that place doesn't have good leeks, then you must go somewhere else for that and somewhere else yet again for tomatoes.'

In May 1988 the Westminster City Council filed 20 charges against Albert Roux, 15 under the Food and Drinks Act and five under the Health and Safety Act. They claimed that inspectors had found a host of violations, alleging poor hygiene and unsafe work conditions. They claimed that the kitchens at Le Gavroche were filthy.

Albert nearly went berserk.

He contested all 20 charges.

At one point – 'shortly after the charges came at me out of the blue', as Roux puts it – the Council's inspector, Alexander Parker-Brown allegedly promised Roux that if he pleaded guilty there would be no publicity. Roux's answer was a stern, 'If you think Albert Roux is going to do that, then you have another thought coming. I will take it to the highest court in the land to prove that I am not guilty and to ensure there is not a stain on my reputation.'

In the event he didn't have to go much further than magistrate's court.

The case was heard in early 1989. During the opening stages, several curious points were raised. To begin with, the charges were filed a full nine and a half months after Parker-Brown visited the kitchens. None of the allegations against Roux were currently viable. It was revealed that during his inspection, Parker-Brown asked Roux to autograph a cookbook for his wife. Roux alleged that Parker-Brown had also hinted he might like to bring his wife to the restaurant for dinner, although Parker-Brown denied it. Next, Parker-Brown admitted he'd never read the regulations and codes of practice relating to the way he was supposed to do his job. Furthermore, he could not recall if he ever cautioned Roux that he was entitled to seek legal advice and that anything said could be used in prosecution. As it turned out, Albert Roux voluntarily supplied certain documents to Parker-Brown, believing he was being helpful. Parker-Brown remembered warning Roux about the pending prosecution, although there was no reference to that in his notes. Nor could he suitably explain why the charges were filed more than nine months after the inspection. After all, if they were serious enough for prosecution, having presented a health hazard, shouldn't they have been lodged immediately? Nor could Parker-Brown explain how an independent survey by the *London Illustrated News* had named Le Gavroche as the second-cleanest kitchen in London, at about the same time that the Council found it the filthiest in Mayfair. Parker-Brown introduced photographs into evidence that did not show specific violations, explaining them away by complaining of a faulty camera. In one specific instance, pigeon droppings on an outside shed turned out to be paint splashes. Parker-Brown's technical assistant made two sworn statements about the kitchen, claiming he was still employed by the council, several months after he had in fact left the council's employment. The technical assistant also swore he took refrigerator temperatures, something which Parker-Brown had to admit never happened as their thermometer was broken. Parker-Brown and his technical assistant also disagreed on the route they took through the kitchen on their tour of inspection.

Before the first two weeks of the case were out, the magistrate dropped five of the 20 charges. At the end of the hearing he cleared Roux of the remaining 15.

The City Council had suffered its worst defeat ever.

Oddly, in September 1983 they went after the Café Royal with 44 charges. The restaurant successfully defended 32 of them and were fined £675 for the remaining 12. At the time, the Head of Environmental Services for the City Council, Brian Denyer said, 'We prosecute those who show a deplorable lack of care in complying with the regulations.' However at the same time, the magistrate hearing the Café Royal case was provoked to berate Denyer's office, 'Cases involving premises which enjoy public prestige should not be prosecuted just to show an example.'

The council's health inspectors of course deny they go after important restaurants just for the sake of publicity. Although it's obvious that they get a lot more points in the public's esteem when they can nab a Gavroche. Closing down the corner Tandoori take-out doesn't make the papers.

Losing the Roux case, on the other hand, was a major

embarrassment for the Council's Chief Environmental Health Officer, Robert Crozier.

'We prosecute about 30 cases a year and each of those cases involves quite a number of violations. I don't think we've ever been thrown out of court on every count before. Not in quite such publicized circumstances. Very embarrassing. Very disappointed, obviously.'

One of the strange things about the Roux case was that long before it got to court, the restaurant had put its house in order.

Crozier concedes that is true, but adds, 'Our view was that conditions were sufficiently bad to warrant prosecution at the time.'

Obviously the court disagreed.

As stated in court, 'Mr Parker-Brown came into Mr Roux's life with a thermometer that didn't work, a defective camera, inadequate notes and a technical assistant whose imagination bordered on the phantasmagorical.'

Here Crozier laughs. 'I think that's exaggerated.'

He claims Parker-Brown's biggest mistake was not in taking Roux to court, but in asking Roux to autograph that book for him. 'It was a very unfortunate mistake.'

The insinuation is that if Parker-Brown hadn't done that, Westminster might well have won their case.

It is, of course, nonsense.

Crozier goes on, 'Well, we could have withdrawn the prosecution at one stage but we felt it was a matter of principle. Wrongly as it turned out. We felt the conditions were sufficiently bad and the risk to the customers was sufficiently serious that we were obliged to use the law.'

Had there been customer complaints?

'No. But then that's often the case. Customers are often unaware of the conditions under which food is prepared.'

Except that this is an open kitchen. Roux proudly invites customers in. You'd think the last thing a chef would do with a filthy kitchen is invite his customers along to see it.

'But', he points out,' if a customer goes into a restaurant and buys a meal, they don't expect to be poisoned.'

Except, you just said there were never any customer complaints.

'No.'

Again, if the problem was solved by action on Roux's part, why go to court and waste tax-payers' money? What did you have to win? The only thing going to court could do is get good publicity for your department which comes in handy every year at budget time.

'That's one point of view. The real threat of court proceedings usually results in either the business ceasing to trade or major improvements are carried out.'

Anyway, there's got to be some truth in the statement by one of Albert's expert witnesses who said, 'If you look hard enough in any restaurant you can always find something.'

Crozier shrugs that off as 'one of those throw-away remarks'.

But is it true?

He says, 'Yes, of course it is. That's why we have a discretion to prosecute. We're not obliged to prosecute. It's up to us to use our discretion fairly. We only prosecute what we regard as the worst cases.'

Or the most famous cases?

'I've explained all of that to you. The law requires people to . . . it's not . . . he didn't comply with the law until he was involved with this department. When we visited on a routine inspection, we found that he was, in our view, breaking the law.'

Roux claims his costs add up to £130,000. Crozier says the City's costs are less than half that, at about £60,000. And he notes that 'the court decided not to award prosecution costs against our local council. A little bit of saving grace. They could have decided that we pay the defence costs'.

In Crozier's mind that's a partial victory.

But how did the council take losing the case?

He acknowledges that a report was written for the council who obviously wanted to know what went wrong. But the report is confidential and he would not release a copy.

'It said that the case was taken in good faith and properly

administered but several things went wrong as the case progressed. The council was supportive of its officers. We have a very good track record of prosecutions. We lose one case in a hundred. Unfortunately that's how the system works, we're accountable to the court.'

As a matter of fact, the confidential report was not nearly as supportive as Crozier would have one believe.

And after confronting Crozier with a copy of it, he backed down a bit. 'It was critical in the sense that we lost the case. But the council decided there was no need for any further action.'

In other words, no one got fired.

'Well, if you'd like to put it that way, yeah.'

It wasn't very flattering, was it?

'No.'

The fact is the council questioned why the case was even brought to court in the first place.

'Well, I mean . . . that . . . as you know, with the legal process, once you get entangled with the legal process . . . you have to make a decision at some stage, at a very important stage, as to whether you are going to prosecute and set those wheels in motion.'

And that, in fact, should not have been done.

'Obviously not . . . in retrospect.'

Again, the report isn't very flattering.

'Neither should it be. We're not in the business of losing cases.'

Funny, most people would have thought they were in the business of seeing that kitchens were kept clean.

Albert says he's semi-retired these days.

His own son Michel now cooks at Le Gavroche, although Albert is there every day, keeping an eye on everything. Yet Albert insists that his son is in charge.

'I want to become a country squire with my dogs.' He has a big home near Chichester where he and his wife Monique plan on spending the rest of their days. 'Since I am not cooking so much now here, I have the urge to cook at home on the weekends. But Monique says I'm messy. Frankly, she's right. At Gavroche there are people to clean up after me. At home there's only Monique to tell me, don't put it there, clean it up now.'

Michel and Robyn live in Bray – 'above the store' – in a cottage they just bought next to The Waterside Inn. A few years ago he applied to the city council for a change of use for the venue so that he could use the huge sitting-room in the cottage as a private dining-room for the restaurant. It was a very frustrating experience because certain people in the village objected. They wouldn't even listen to his argument. They felt that he was enlarging the restaurant and that would bring more traffic into the village.

'All I ever intended was to create a private dining-room which could seat eight people. It literally took me two years and I finally won. It's amazing how much of a storm in a teacup some people made of it. If they think there's a lot of traffic in the village with my restaurant there, imagine what it must have been like before I came here, when the building was a pub.'

Michel's son is cooking in France and expects to join his father in Bray in a few years. Five years from now Michel sees himself spending more and more time with Robyn at a small farm they bought in the South of France. They go there whenever they can. He writes there, produces his own wine there and thinks there.

And when he thinks, it's usually about food.

Something like the way a great composer knows music, knows what something will sound like just by reading the notes, without hearing it played, great chefs compose dishes in their head and can taste them long before they ever cook them.

On one trip to the farm, Michel acquired a kilo of black truffles. Worth their weight in gold, he dreamed up a dish that was basically nothing more than truffles, egg, cream and a little Emmental cheese sprinkled over the top.

He then cooked the dish one evening for friends. It took nearly half an hour and cut a good chunk into the kilo.

Needless to say it was magnificent.

So why, came the question, don't you serve this at the Waterside Inn?

'There are just two reasons,' he explained. 'The first is that it would take my chefs too long to prepare. I cannot tie up my kitchen for that long. The second is, I'm afraid my customers couldn't afford it.'

4

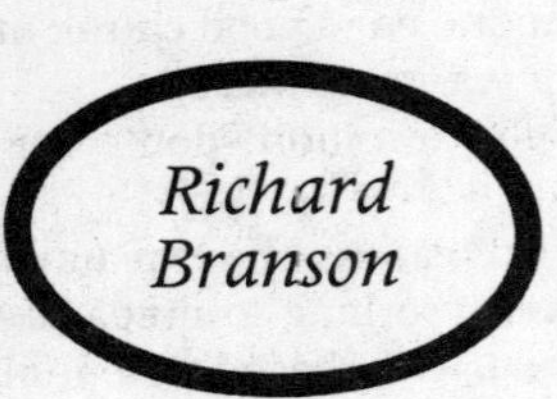

Five years ago Richard Branson was only just beginning to tread where no one but Freddie Laker had dared to go.

And at the time he admitted that running an airline had never been one of his life-long passions.

'I only thought about it for the first time when the idea was proposed. Originally I was sceptical. I spent two weeks going over the figures and finally decided that just because Freddie Laker went down, it's no reason why we shouldn't have a go. I figured we could learn from his mistakes.'

Those mistakes, he felt, were fairly obvious, especially with the benefit of hindsight.

'Laker didn't lose because he didn't have any passengers for the North Atlantic run. No, he was selling seats. When he went under he was flying at 83% capacity. He lost because he bought too many planes and found himself swamped by massive currency problems. The dollar swung and he suddenly found himself facing huge debts. The other problem is all that business about possible interference from the major airlines. Depending on how much of it you believe, whether or not it's true, I think it's unlikely that they would try anything like it with us. If they did it at all, I don't think they'd do it twice.'

Five years ago this chapter ended with the idea that Branson would either succeed, or those would go down as famous last words, alongside 'Hey, General Custer, where'd all them Indians come from?'

Consider this as my public apology to Richard Branson.

He has not only succeeded where Laker failed, he keeps on

beating the big airlines, British Airways included, at their own game.

Branson's career began in a phone booth when he was just 15.

Twenty-six years later – he is no longer thirtysomething – Branson remains a most unlikely tycoon. Founder and by far the largest single owner of the Virgin Group, he's nearly £1 billion-worth of record companies, book publishers, gay discos, straight pubs, cable TV, satellite TV, record shops, film production companies, recording studios and an airline. He likes to have his picture taken in the bathtub, do TV adverts, race speedboats across one ocean, fly balloons across two oceans, and even when he gets plucked out of the middle of either ocean by a rescue helicopter, he comes up looking happy and boyish.

Richard Branson has become extremely good at being Richard Branson.

'I never actually set out to see how I could make the most cash. I've always merely tried to make the figures fit the ideas I've had rather than the other way around. I guess that's doing it backwards.'

The house that Branson built employs about 5000 people, most of them young, most of them fiercely loyal to him. Because he likes to promote from within, today's record-shop cashier knows he or she could be tomorrow's group accountant. That sort of two-way dialogue between employee and benevolent monarch is, he believes, one of the reasons his business keeps growing. Because he feels high-rise office blocks defeat the purpose, there are never more than 50 people in any one of the Virgin offices, which are usually converted houses spread throughout North London. It may mean lots of switchboards and lots of messengers back and forth. It may also mean lots of rent. But he's comfortable that way and he says his employees are comfortable that way too.

The world according to Branson is loose, relaxed, and filled with perks – come up with a great idea and you get a slice of the pie, do your job and you get a week in Portugal, no wives, no husbands, no friends permitted. Just 600 fellow workers alone together for the first time, off for a romp in the sunshine. Whatever goes on, goes on. It's like an annual class trip. It's the 'one big happy family' style of Godfathering. Maybe IBM doesn't work this way. But Virgin does.

He himself used to work at home, which was a houseboat in a canal near a decrepit cement bridge that says 'Borough of Paddington, 1914' in raised letters, and all sorts of other things in spray-can orange. But five or six years ago, during a bout of pneumonia, his doctor advised less damp accommodation. So he moved – live-in lady and their daughter in tow – to a nearby flat. But he kept the floating office. Since then he married his live-in lady friend and took their two children to a £4.5-million mansion in Holland Park. They also share a country estate in Oxfordshire and their own island in the Virgin Islands. But the houseboat is his office. His desk – a round table cluttered by papers, notes and four telephones – is in the centre of what would otherwise have been the wheelhouse. Two secretaries run up and down the gangway to find their captain on the bridge. The uniform here is jeans and sweaters.

'I don't change my style of dress when I go to lunch with my bankers. One of the special things about being successful is that you can afford the luxury of not worrying what money can buy. You can dress the way you feel comfortable. You can afford to drive a practical car rather than an ostentatious car. Sometimes I write out a cheque for something reasonably extreme like a couple of million pounds, and I chuckle. It seems unreal.'

Maybe that's partially because it wasn't all that long ago when those cheques didn't have as many zeros.

'I was a kid and I kept our company account at Coutts. Well, I had an overdraft facility of, I think, £350, and one day it went to £375. The bank manager called me into a small room and sat me down and gave me a lecture. I mean, you should have seen how they looked at us when some of my people would come into the bank to deposit money barefoot. Anyway, he said to me, "Look after your bank and your bank will look after you."'

For nearly 18 years he did look after his bank but when the crunch came, they didn't look after him.

Add this to the collection of yet-again-another-brilliant-banker-to-the-rescue stories: in June 1984, the night before Virgin Atlantic was to make its maiden run to New York, the airline's only 747 lost an engine. A replacement cost £600,000, which Branson didn't happen to have handy. The easiest place to get it, of course, was Coutts. It only took him about £250,000 beyond Virgin's overdraft limit. That didn't seem like a lot to him, especially when Coutts used to tell him that he was their single largest client – although he always suspected the Queen had more assets than Virgin did. Yet the bank saw it differently. They'd graciously extended a £3-million line of credit to him – in spite of the fact that the group was turning £98 million and making £10 million profit – but £3 million didn't mean £3.25 million! Branson came home from the inaugural flight to find the bank manager at his front door, threatening to bounce Virgin's cheques if £250,000 wasn't deposited by morning. Branson exploded and showed the bank manager the door. (The PS to the story is that when he tried to take his business to Barclays, the board turned him down. Third time lucky, Citibank offered him a £30-million line of credit in a matter of days, based on exactly the same accounts that had been submitted to Coutts and Barclays. That credit line has since been multiplied nearly 10 times and Branson and Citibank seem to be living happily ever after.)

Anyway, Branson left school – he went to Stowe and hated it – and came to London in the middle of the swinging '60s. Having been a student he saw the need for some sort of national student magazine, so just like that he decided to start one.

'I called it *Student*. I needed £5000 in advertising to put out the first issue, but I didn't have an office or anything like that, so I found a phone booth and opened the yellow pages and started selling.'

The magazine came out whenever he could raise the money for it over the next four years. At the same time he started a student advice service, which survives today in a slightly changed form.

'We had all sorts of people coming to us looking for help. In those early days my office was in the crypt of a church. My desk was a slab of marble above two coffins.' He makes a face. 'Actually I think I was very lucky when I started. I had absolutely nothing to lose.'

Not quite. *Student* Magazine managed to lose enough money that its days were eventually numbered. In what would be the final issue he printed an ad offering cut-price records. It was a last-ditch effort to somehow raise a stake. It proved an overwhelming success.

So Branson became the first record-discounter in the UK.

From selling records he branched out to making them.

'Mike Oldfield came to us and wanted to record some songs he did when he was a kid, but we didn't have any money. We gave him a list with the names of every music publisher in town and sent him to see them. They all turned him down. A year later we had some money and decided to give record-producing a try, so we made our first album with him.'

It was called *Tubular Bells*, and has sold more copies than any album since *The Sound of Music*.

Despite appearances, it hasn't always been high times for Branson.

In 1971 he ran up against HM Customs and Excise.

His discount record business was only just making it but he soon figured out a scheme to help it along. By declaring records for export at Dover, claiming purchase tax rebates and driving around the port a few times, he could head back to his discount store in London and offer cut-price records on the back of the taxman. It worked the first night. It worked the second night. It didn't work the third night. He spent that one in jail. His mother bailed him out. Having a grandfather who was a judge and a father who was a barrister and magistrate probably didn't hurt his case. The courts settled on a £60,000 fine and gave him enough time to pay it. When his debt was paid, Branson wrote to the authorities thanking them for their understanding. No one had to remind him that, had he been a poor black kid from Brixton, the story might not have had the same happy ending.

A few years ago he was reminded again that everything he touches doesn't automatically turn to gold. He tried to launch a 'what's happening' kind of magazine in London and failed within a very short time. This time he did have something to lose. It cost him £500,000.

But both those incidents pale by comparison to his flirtation with the stock market.

Looking to fund expansion in the US, Branson announced in 1986 that he was going public. He hoped to raise £70 million. But instead of setting a fixed price for the offering, he chose to put the shares out to tender. He said he'd issue as many as 50 million shares at a minimum price of £1.40, or 27.6% of the company. Speculation was that over-subscription could drive the opening price as high as £1.90.

When the big day came, the City's interest in Branson fell short of expectations.

Virgin's shares opened at the striking price and immediately started to slip.

The offer raised £55 million, valuing the company at just over £240 million.

Branson said that he was disappointed.

Two years later he conceded the whole thing had been a mistake.

He and the City simply couldn't see eye to eye on what the Virgin Group – and in particular what Richard Branson – were all about. He accused fund managers of being short-sighted, more interested in their quarterly growth charts than in what might be happening with a company three or four years down the line. At the same time the City saw Branson making the front page every time he grinned – or vice versa – cavorting through one publicity stunt after another. They saw him as a self-publicist and the more staid City-folk, especially the ones who control the more staid institutional funds, tend to be suspicious of self-publicists. The problem has been compounded by Branson's innate shyness. The fun-loving, extrovert image is just a façade, hiding a personality that is so shy, especially when asked to make a speech to investment bankers, that he borders on the inarticulate.

With his shares in the 85–95p range, Branson said if the City didn't want to own his shares, he did and offered to buy them back. He put together a management buy-out, but one the likes of which the City had never seen before. Branson said he felt a sense of commitment to the 600,000 shareholders who'd come into the game at £1.40, and even if no one else thought they were still worth £1.40 a share, he did so he was going to buy them back at the same price. He put together a company called Glowtrack with some of the other Virgin directors, found four banks to back them, and gave everybody their money back.

As one editorial summed it up, 'Richard Branson might never have convinced the City of London of his abilities as a businessman, but admiration for other of his qualities survives. Even hardened cynics in the market are describing his offer to buy back shares in Virgin Group as the actions of an honourable man.'

In April 1990, the *Sunday Times* Magazine listed him the seventeenth wealthiest man in the nation. He was behind Gerald Ronson, Jimmy Goldsmith and Robert Maxwell. But he was well ahead of Tiny Rowland and Asil Nadir. In fact, the magazine had him worth more than the two of them put together.

Branson's gimmick, if there is one, is understanding that stardom means access and access puts him towards the front of the queue when someone's looking to make a deal. So part of his job is maintaining his stardom. That's what the speedboat race across the Atlantic was all about. That's what the balloon adventures were all about. People he's never met take his calls because, after all, it's Richard Branson on the line. Mrs

Thatcher appealed to him in June 1986 to help clean up Britain because she knew he could do what mere actors or singers couldn't – recruit a work-force of 5000 unemployed teenagers and organize them into an effective nationwide campaign. The streets of Britain's major cities are still filthy but at least for a while it seemed like a good idea.

Branson used his name, grin and access again a year or so later to champion a safe-sex campaign. His Virgin Healthcare Foundation marketed Mates condoms, in an effort to help educate young Britain in the battle against AIDS. At the same time he opened talks with the Soviet Union to send Mates condoms to Russia. It helped establish a certain image for him there which he eventually translated into a Moscow stop on Virgin Atlantic's London–Tokyo route. He also used his access with the Soviets to do a joint venture with Intourist – tour packages to the USSR. The Russians liked him so much they put him on Intourist Ltd's board of directors.

And that's where he's very different from most people who are simply famous for being famous. Once in the front door, he has the sixth sense for a profitable deal which he then maximizes by cutting Virgin in along every step of the way. For instance, some years ago when he footed the bill for the film *Electric Dreams*, Virgin recording star Boy George did the soundtrack, which was released as a Virgin album. Virgin Books did the book. Virgin Film Distributions did the distribution. Virgin's video game company is doing the video game, while Virgin's video operation is putting out the video.

Branson got into satellite television at a time when the analysts still had high hopes for such things. He bought into British Satellite Broadcasting, began to have second thoughts and decided to get out. He offered his 11.2% share of BSB to Michael Green at Carlton. When Green said no, he went to Alan Bond and unloaded his stake there, chalking up a £1-million profit for his efforts. Bond has come to regret the purchase and Branson remains the only one yet to make any money out of satellite television in the UK. He also bought into, sold out of and bought back into Super Channel, the European satellite.

Yet for all of Branson's skills and boyish charm, there is another side of him.

When Virgin agreed to produce the film version of Orwell's *1984,* Branson knew that the score should be done by a musician whose music could also sell albums. Producer Simon Perry and director Michael Radford said, fine, but insisted that the music must be good for the film as well as for selling records. In April 1984 David Bowie was suggested by Virgin, but it turned out that he was too busy to meet the film's deadline. To make certain that they would have a score at all, Perry and Radford convinced Virgin to let them commission Dominic Muldowney, an experienced film composer. He wrote the score that August and it was recorded at the beginning of September.

That's when Branson announced he'd signed the job over to a rock group called The Eurythmics. Perry and Radford were horrified. First, they felt The Eurythmics were quite wrong for the film. Second, they were worried about the time-scale. The Eurythmics said they would deliver their music by 28 September, which was only one week before the first press viewing. Perry tried to make Branson understand that the risks were absolutely enormous. The Eurythmics had never composed a score before. He asked Branson to promise that, if the music didn't work, they wouldn't be obliged to use it on the film. Branson said, yes, I quite understand and oh, by the way, they can't come to London because they have tax problems so they want to do this in the Bahamas.

As far as Perry was concerned, the notion of a couple of film composers, especially as raw as The Eurythmics were, not even being able to come to London to work with the director, was outlandish. To top it off, they were on an American tour and wouldn't even be able to start work until 11 September. Radford phoned them in the Bahamas, briefed them, sent them a video cassette, and thought this hasn't got a hope in hell. But Branson was quite impervious. He said he was paying them a

great deal of money and mentioned the figure of $600,000 – more than everybody of serious consequence on the film put together was going to be paid. Richard Burton had been contracted with a small fee and a percentage of the picture. The original budget was £3.7 million. Then the budget was revised during shooting and went up to £5.5 million. The actual cash cost to put it on the screen was £4.8 million.

'Richard Branson is a very strange person,' Perry says. 'He has a great deal of charm. He's slightly extravagant, kind of mercurial, a rather appealing character because he's very unexpected. But he doesn't appear to have a solid, personal, heart-felt opinion about anything. It's very difficult to deal with that. He has no real passion. He's desperately shy, terrified of being caught out. A film is a complex artistic object. If the man who's got the purse strings – and in this country that means he's got all the power – doesn't have a firm opinion himself about what you're doing, you can't really have a dialogue.'

The Eurythmics delivered the music a day before schedule. Radford laid it roughly on the film that night, and had a showing for the Virgin execs the following day.

Perry continues, 'The music was quite horrendous. It was totally inappropriate. We thought it was prima facie inappropriate and that no one would be taking it seriously. But we realized as the viewing went on that, actually, the guys from the record company were very pleased with the results, that they thought it was very good.'

The Eurythmics' music was not used at the première. The Muldowney version was the one that got the good reviews across most of Europe. Then a combined version was prepared by Radford using a little of The Eurythmics' music so that Branson could keep his rights to the soundtrack album. But The Eurythmics, or their management, changed their minds and said it would be all their music or nothing. That meant Branson had to re-soundtrack prints of the film around the world with the all-Eurythmics' version. Complicating matters, The Eurythmics' music was mixed on to the film in one night by some Virgin executives who, Perry says, had very little idea of what they were doing. He points out that there is camera noise on the film and some of the levels are wrong. Anyway, he wants the world to know it was the Muldowney version that won the *Evening Standard*'s Best Film award.

'A lot of dealing with Virgin reminds me of school,' Perry says. 'Branson is a bit like a school prefect. There's a great deal of yah-boo-sucks style of negotiation. A lot of what happens is based on getting one back. Vendettas go on a lot of the time. It's very strange, really. 'Typical Simon,' they shout, when I point out that I've still got the rights to do something. 'Oh, you would say that.' It's that kind of stuff. Which on a good night can seem quite entertaining. We heard a lot of jokes about the Virgin inner party and outer party. Well, there is an inner party and they're all related in some way. A cousin. A brother-in-law. You know, like that. Our theory is that Virgin is still finally and absolutely a record company. And I think that they characterize us as the artist and his manager. Mike being the rock'n'roll performer who has to be comforted and kid-gloved, given everything he wants, flattered and told he's wonderful. And then they go out to the corridor and beat the shit out of the manager.'

The two things that all of the projects have in common are the basics of Branson's empire. One, he buys ready-mades. He sits in his houseboat and sifts through project ideas that come to him. Two, he changes those ready-mades to cater almost exclusively to the 'Virgin market', 15–35-year-olds who know music, consider themselves 'in' and have enough money in their pockets to convince everyone else that they are 'in'.

'You know when you're over the hump. And from there it's just a question of consolidating your position. Some people choose to take risks which will not consolidate them. We take calculated risks. All our risks are within a consolidated position. Such as the airline. But, no, I don't think I'm becoming more conservative as I get older. Not yet. I mean, I'm not a businessman like Gerald Ronson. He's older and he's had his time for learning. I'm still learning.'

But he's obviously learning well.

Eighteen months after he bailed out of the stock market, he decided he had to expand the international operations of his Virgin Music Group. They were already the world's sixth-largest recording company. But the five in front of him were huge: Time-Warner, Sony-CBS, Philips-PolyGram, Bertelsmann-RCA and Thorn-EMI. And even with sales of $400 million, Branson understood that he was much too small to face such stiff competition. So he looked around and tried to see where he could best patch someone into his network. Virgin Atlantic had just gotten a route to Japan, Virgin Music not only sells Western music in Japan but also records some Japanese artists, while a smaller Virgin business distributes Japanese home video games in the UK.

Best of all, Japan is the world's second-largest music market.

He sold 25.1% of Virgin Music to Fujisankei Communications for £96 million. They're Japan's largest communications group, owning television and radio stations. Now, with a partner in the Orient to sell – and play – his music there, Branson added a little cream to the deal by picking up the right to market Fujisankei's music CDs and other products in Europe.

That deal worked so well, he then started thinking about the possibility of cutting the Japanese into his airline.

Selling say 20% of Virgin Atlantic for £50 million would not just raise more cash for expansion, it would also improve Virgin's commercial alliance with Japan.

And there are a lot of profitable routes an airline could fly to from Tokyo.

Randolph Fields was born in Santa Monica, California, and moved to London in 1962 when he was nine. Educated in the UK, with one year at an American high school, Fields is a barrister who practised law for a couple of years in the States, and who came back to Britain in the early '80s with the idea of starting an airline.

He called it British Atlantic.

Fields wanted to make the Gatwick – JFK run with an all-business-class service. But he quickly saw the writing on the wall and opted out of Gatwick–Newark. The route had been assigned to British Air Tours and was, Fields says, 'the most closely guarded secret in the world. Before People's Express came along, British Air Tours, which is a charter company of British Airways, wanted to show that it would be a disaster of a route. Which it was, for them. It ran with atrocious load factors and they pulled off at the end of January 1983. That route then became open for the British to designate a replacement carrier. But the climate at that moment in time was that if the world's most popular airline couldn't be successful there, nobody else could'.

Then People's Express arrived. It wasn't a new mousetrap. It was merely a cheaper one. Yet the world still beat a path to their door.

Now Fields took another look at Newark–Gatwick.

'I'm a great believer in market segmentation, particularly on London–New York. It's such a large market that the best recipe for success is to appeal to a specific market and be overwhelmingly successful with that little bit of the market because it will fill your plane every day. There seemed to me to be two gaps in the market. One was that People's Express wasn't doing too well with the British visiting-friends-and-relatives traffic. Secondly, they weren't doing too well with youth traffic. Since Laker came off the route, youth traffic declined by two-thirds.'

He thinks Laker's appeal as a cult figure probably had a lot to do with it.

'With air transportation, apart from the must-go travellers, we're selling a commodity that people actually do not need. Like Virgin selling pop records. People don't need records. They buy records because they have disposable income so they're able to buy the records, and because their interest is aroused. It's the same with air travel. We're selling a non-essential product.'

Fields knew that to sell his non-essential product, everything relied on his marketing approach.

'The reason I came up with Richard Branson was because I conceived of an airline that would appeal to the British visiting-friends-and-relatives market plus the youth market through the use of entertainment. It was possible due mainly to the devlopment of new video projection systems. The classic problem with airplanes is that you've got all these people stuck in a metal tube getting bored out of their minds. There is no actual pleasure in the travel aspect of air transportation. After looking out of the window for five minutes – if you're lucky enough to have a window – you've had enough. So what you have to do is kill the boredom factor. With the newest video projection systems that have been developed, it struck me that you could show continuous entertainment throughout the flight, but you wouldn't have to darken the cabin. That's why the airlines only used to show one film. A lot of passengers don't want to watch films. So I conceived of this product where you would have entertainment and state of the art headphone technology. I had a lot of investor interest but I thought if you're going to have an investor you might as well get something from that investor. It occurred to me that if I got Virgin involved, not only would they serve as an investor, but also they would have the marketing expertise to reach the youth market.'

It took several attempts, but Fields eventually got Branson on the phone.

'I told him, I've got an airline project that's about to take off and I think you might be interested. I talked to him for a couple of minutes about it and he said, have you got a business plan. I said yes. He said, well, send it round to me and send a copy to my financial director. And I did that. The next day he called me up and said, look, we'd like to talk about it. We met the following day and thrashed it around. Over the course of the next week or so we talked about it. And burnt the midnight oil for a couple of nights. And came up with a deal. And then announced it.'

British Atlantic changed its trading name to Virgin Atlantic in February 1984.

Three months later they were in the air.

Within six months, Fields was no longer involved with the running of Virgin Atlantic.

'Well, yes and no. No, I don't think it was a boardroom fist-fight. It had to do with the underlying circumstances. In Virgin I went to bed with a very highly motivated individual. And that individuality permeates throughout all the companies. It suited both of our needs and purposes the way things developed. I committed myself to spending six months with it, getting it in the air, getting things running, and getting a chief executive. When we had a chief executive in place and we were able to agree that the guy we had should be made permanent, my job was pretty much done. Although Richard had asked me to stay on as chairman, I felt it was more appropriate that he should be chairman.'

In other words, Branson turned out to be a tougher guy to do business with than Fields ever imagined – than most people ever imagine.

'He can be very easy, but Richard is a very shrewd businessman. He's an incredibly tough negotiator. He knows how to negotiate a deal.'

When Fields presented him with all the facts, Branson took his usual approach to decision-making.

'If you sit down with accountants and look at profit and loss projections, they'll manage to come up with all sorts of reasons why something won't work. Well, I think if you've got a gut feeling about something, then trial and error can produce the best results. I think the only way to learn is to give it a try.'

Like almost every project that comes aboard the houseboat and interests him, it's only a matter of minutes before it becomes Richard Branson's project. Randolph Fields was quickly and smartly escorted to a back seat. And the headlines echoed that effect. Branson takes on British Airways. Branson picks up where Laker left off. Branson introduces Virgin Atlantic Airways.

Almost on cue, the moment Branson got involved, opposition was raised by British Caledonian. They felt that Branson was too young and inexperienced. Anyway, BCal. argued, the success of an airline should not have to depend on how many pop groups made it to the Top 10. Branson's argument was a simple one. He compared Virgin's profits with BCal.'s, and beat them two to one.

At the same time, Virgin Atlantic bought a 747 at a cost of just under $28 million. Included in the deal with Boeing for the three-year-old plane were all sorts of escape clauses in case the passengers didn't flock in the way Branson hoped. Actually all those escape clauses made it look more like a leasing deal. Branson could sell the plane back to Boeing at any time within three years, or sell it on the open market if he chose. The cost to him comes down to £2 million a year. And he covered that with his company's cash flow and currency options against distortion of the dollar/pound ratio. The way he structured the business, the worst he could lose was two months' profits on the Virgin Group. As it happened, the market for used 747s hardened and, at least on paper, one year after Virgin Atlantic went into business the Virgin Group showed a £2-million profit on the aircraft alone. Branson then used that increased value to buy a second Jumbo and start a London to Miami service.

Credit Branson now with the virtue of patience.

Instead of rushing into battle against the major airlines, he solidified his position first, establishing himself as a reliable player on the London Gatwick–New York run, landing at nearby Newark, New Jersey. Next step was London–Miami. After all, in those days he only had one plane. Again, with a constant eye on his prime market – that music-loving group of 18–35-year-olds – he bid for a third destination, Los Angeles. In the meantime, he opened the run to Japan, via Moscow. He also got permission to fly London–New York, now using JFK, which becomes an even more direct challenge to BA.

Not only was he offering his economy-class passengers with all the in-flight entertainment anyone could ever want, he also catered to the older segment of his market – the ones who had real money to spend – by giving them a first-class compartment at business-class fares. Consistently voted at the top of the 'best airline business class' league, Virgin's 'Upper Class' even became the envy of British Airways. In 1989, BA sent their spies on a few Virgin flights to see what all the fuss was about. In a confidential report, BA's evaluation was, 'The Virgin product is more akin to other airlines' first class.'

If that didn't worry BA – which it clearly must have – Branson came up with a few other ideas. He wants to fly to Singapore and several cities in Australia. Although he claims he'll stop expanding the Virgin route when he reaches 10 destination points around the world – using a dozen jumbos to service them – he also has his eye on the pride of BA's fleet, Concorde.

Branson announced recently that he'd begun talks with Air France to lease one of their supersonic planes, saying that if the deal came off, he'd redesign the interior, installing fewer seats and providing a better level of service on the North Atlantic run.

Over at BA, chairman Lord King and CEO Sir Colin Marshall have always said they welcome competition and are vanguards in Europe in the fight to decrease fares. Maybe. But they can't possibly be thrilled that real competition has suddenly been thrust on their front doorstep; especially real competition in the form of Freddie Laker reincarnate.

The Laker 'final solution' won't work this time.

BA might actually have to compete.

And in spite of their protestations about offering a better service, about always competing head-on, about being the world's favourite airline, it's odd that when the passengers vote on who's better, BA isn't the winner the chairman and CEO think it is.

With Virgin's pre-tax profits now in excess of £10 million and ever expanding, its 13.3% net margin means that it is the third-most profitable international airline in the business, behind Singapore Airlines and Cathay Pacific.

What's more, Branson has publicly stated that anyone who isn't happy with his 'Upper Class' service need only make a formal complaint and will get both a personal call from Branson asking why plus his money back on the fare.

One wonders how much time Mssrs King and Marshall would have to spend on the phone if they matched the offer.

5

Jacob Rothschild

Mayer Amschel Rothschild, patriarch of a legendary family fortune, is described by his biographers as having been 'an odd mixture of the philosopher and the entrepreneur'.

Six generations later, that same odd mixture is alive and well in the form of his great-great-great-great grandson.

In fact, the two probably would have gotten along very well.

'I drifted into business,' explains Nathaniel Charles Jacob Rothschild. 'I went to Oxford and nearly became an academic. There was a wish, I wouldn't say pressure, that I should go into N. M. Rothschild, which was our family business. So I went there.'

With a degree in history, it was decided that he needed some practical business experience. He spent six months at an accounting firm, counting steel bars to help the auditors tidy up some industrial company – 'It was the equivalent of starting in the mail room in the world of finance' – and was then shipped off to the States, to work at the investment banking house, Morgan Stanley. That was followed by a year's tour of duty back in London with a West End firm of financiers. In all, he was about two and a half years outside Rothschild's.

'Then I went back there. It was a fairly difficult place to learn as I was a member of the family. I was treated with too much respect and decorum. It's often easier to learn the hard way.'

Nevertheless, he might well have stayed in the family business for ever – it was either that or pursue his academic interests – except that in 1980 Jacob and his cousin, Evelyn de Rothschild, disagreed about how N. M. Rothschild & Sons should be run. The fight was a very bitter one and at one point

Evelyn actually tried to prevent Jacob from using the Rothschild name in any banking activities. He failed, and rifts in the family have still not totally healed.

Eventually the cousins agreed it would be best if Jacob went on his own. So he stepped out from beneath the family umbrella, a man determined to prove himself.

Under the terms of the separation, he was allowed to take with him a small subsidiary called RIT – Rothschild Investment Trust. Within a year he'd convinced David Montagu to join RIT, adding a definite heavyweight to his team. Montagu had built his reputation as Chairman and Chief Executive at his own family's business, Samuel Montagu & Co., Chairman and Chief Executive at the Orion Bank and Chairman of Merrill Lynch's international bank. Six months after joining forces, Rothschild and Montagu pulled off the first of several flashy deals – a £97-million absorption of the Great Northern Investment Trust. Before the end of 1982 they'd added a 29.9% stake in the London-based stockbroker Kitcat & Aitken.

Now called RIT & Northern, in August 1983 Rothschild bought the New York investment bank, L. F. Rothschild, Unterberg, Towbin. While the bank's founder, Louis Rothschild, was not related to any of the European Rothschilds – the name was strictly a coincidence – the purchase of a 50% share for £42 million was significant in a most personal way. Evelyn de Rothschild had also been eyeing the bank, hoping to pick up a controlling 51%. Because Jacob was willing to settle for half, he landed the prize.

It was not only a sound acquisition for RIT & Northern, it was a substantial moral victory for one cousin over another.

By November of that year, Rothschild had coupled RIT & Northern with the Charterhouse Group, a £400-million alliance that brought into the stable a merchant bank plus a varied assortment of industrial investments. Exactly six months after that, the newly named Charterhouse J. Rothschild (CJR) really made headlines by announcing a 25% stake in Mark Weinberg's Hambro Life Assurance group and plans for yet another merger. The new company, with over £1 billion in capital, was to be called Allied Rothschild Charterhouse.

Rothschild's idea in those days was to create a financial services empire, the likes of which the City had never before seen.

'At the time we acquired our original stake, we thought first of all that 25% would be a good investment. Secondly, we hoped and believed we would end up merging with Hambro Life. It didn't work out, which was a disappointment and a setback, for all sorts of reasons. One of them was that to have imposed a merger on an unwilling stock market would probably have resulted in a lower share price, and scepticism by the market for a number of years. That wasn't in our shareholders' interests. So both of us (Rothschild and Weinberg) decided to step back. Having stepped back, we had to demonstrate that the decision to acquire 25% of the capital was in fact a good investment.'

The Hambro stake represented a quarter of CJR's assets, a hefty chunk to cram into one basket. Yet Rothschild claims it was a measured risk and his faith in the deal soon proved worthwhile as the British American Tobacco Company (BAT) came along with an offer to buy. He notes it was easy for him to agree to the sale, but concedes it was a particularly difficult decision for Weinberg. After all, Weinberg had built Hambro. Nevertheless, in making the decision to recommend the BAT offer, Rothschild feels, Weinberg and his partners showed their true grit. They suppressed their own egos for the sake of the shareholders.

'If you can make those types of difficult decisions, then hopefully that demonstrates a quality of independence and objectivity which I think is very important. In a sense you have to change horses, don't you, because most companies are created by driven-ego types. But very often their ultimate destiny should be the very suppression of the egos that helped to build them up. In the case of Hambro Life they weren't stepping away from it, but instead putting their shareholders' interests in front of their own.'

Both sentimentally and ideologically there's no doubt that he would have preferred to merge CJR with Hambro.

'But realistically it wouldn't have made sense for either their shareholders or our shareholders because you're living in a period when financial conglomerates, or financial holding companies, whatever you'd like to call them, will sell at relatively low prices and relatively low multiples. To have disposed of our interests to BAT on a basis which was very acceptable to Hambro Life's management and also resulted in our shareholders being endowed with a significant capital profit in the course of a few months, seemed to us to be the right way to behave from the shareholder interest point of view. I can talk about the ideology of financial services but can't ask people to invest in it if the two don't happen to coincide. I discipline myself to that approach.'

So he sold CJR's stake in mid-December 1984 and the bottom line showed a £40 million profit. Ironically, Rothschild and BAT would meet again a few years later, but under considerably less friendly terms.

Worth noting is the fact that had the Hambro Life merger come off, Rothschild would have stepped down as Chairman, leaving Weinberg to run the company. In other words, like Weinberg walking away from Hambro, Rothschild would have walked away from the business he'd created. Even though it was at a time when he'd really begun to prove himself, he says he could have done it easily, and without any ego problems at all.

'I have plenty of other interests. No problem. The attraction of Hambro was that Mark is a superb businessman whom I happen to like very much, so whatever was created would have ended up in very good hands. It would have been a perfectly satisfactory way for the company I helped to create to have become independent of me, just as we've made other businesses independent of us. I find it rather satisfactory that one can be as objective as that about it.'

Within a month of unloading his Hambro shares, Rothschild stunned the City by divesting himself of Charterhouse Japhet plus his UK, French and Canadian development capital interests. The Royal Bank Group paid him £155 million. A few weeks later CJR was renamed J. Rothschild Holdings (JRH).

The financial press labelled it 'a retreat'.

In many ways, it was.

Timing may not be everything in life but it could be most things.

The sale of Charterhouse was not initiated by Jacob Rothschild. The Royal Bank approached him. However, agreeing to sell it probably had as much to do with when as it did with how much.

By the middle of the decade the City of London was becoming Wall Street East. Talk on both sides of the Atlantic was about 'Big Bang' and how American financial houses would squeeze their way into the City. The Americans came in droves. But so did the Japanese and so did the Germans. Everybody was out to make the big killing. Life in the City no longer had anything to do with Oxbridge gentlemen bankers in bowler hats. Change was what these times were all about.

For Jacob Rothschild, not all of the changes were to his liking.

'Suddenly there were too many sharks in the water,' Rothschild now says. 'I didn't want to be part of that. It's not the kind of company I keep. So we sold stuff and accumulated a big pile of cash. We then took that cash and reinvested it in very conservative ways.'

For the most part, what he did was to split his company in two. In 1988 he redesigned JRH specifically to concentrate on short-term dealing. He then modelled RIT Capital Partners on an investment trust to look after long-term stakes.

'I guess you could say we became a sort of investment company. What we do now is manage other people's money the same way they manage their own money.'

At first, one important part of Charterhouse that JRH kept was CHUSA, an American-based operation which concentrated on smallish buy-outs. Although he sold 75% of his stake within a year, he still managed to get involved in deals like the $340-million buy-out of the agricultural company, Central Soya.

'That was an area of risk, of transaction orientation rather than relationship orientation that we wanted to develop and foster. Except that I've always had an aversion to doing things on a hostile basis. And that's quite a disadvantage at times. Lots of people have made money out of hostile take-overs. But sentimentally or temperamentally, I'm just rather squeamish about hostile bids.'

Clearly agreeing with the critics who say that many of the hostile bids done during the '80s were anything but industrially constructive, he does think however that there are times when the deconglomeration of a company can result in far greater values for the shareholders than the stock market would otherwise put upon that company.

'Putting together a collection of diverse industrial interests under the umbrella of a holding company works extremely well under strong management and direction. But it's a kind of curious architecture, isn't it, because you have no theme in it. You have a neoclassical room, a Renaissance room, a rococo room, whatever you like. You're living in that mixture, that mélange. It's a curious phenomenon that this type of conglomerate is being embraced in the UK whereas in the United States deconglomeration is in fashion in what one might call the post-Geneen (ITT) era.'

Still, when the right opportunities come along, squeamish or not, he's more than willing to dive in. It's just that he prefers to do it with a partner more adept . . . or at least less squeamish . . . at swimming with sharks.

Enter Mr Goldsmith.

Sir James is to the world of contemporary finance what Hemingway is to mid-twentieth-century American literature, one of those larger-than-life characters with well tuned skills and a hearty following of fans who tell stories – some true, most not – that are the stuff of romantic, swashbuckling legend.

Undoubtedly, Rothschild and Goldsmith each saw qualities

in the other he admired – intelligence, culture, a bit of the pirate. A fast friendship was formed and several deals followed.

When Goldsmith went after the US paper-producer Crown Zellerbach, Rothschild was there with him, if not in person, at least in the spirit that his money represented. It was a very hostile take-over bid, not at all to Rothschild's liking, but as long as Goldsmith was willing to stand in front of the cameras and field most of the flak, Rothschild was happy to share in some of the profits.

He was also with Goldsmith in 1984 when the US-based paper, energy and insurance group, St Regis, caught Goldsmith's eye. Joining forces with Australian financier Kerry Packer and Italian automobile magnate Gianni Agnelli, they put $100 million into a pool as part of an 'investment' in the company. Goldsmith held 60%, Rothschild's stake was 30%, the other two divided the remaining 10%. The mere presence of Goldsmith had the desired effect. A panicky St Regis board simply paid everyone to go away. The group's $100 million had magically turned into $150 million.

Goldsmith had reinvented alchemy.

And Rothschild couldn't help but be impressed.

'I think there are once-in-a-lifetime risks that occur and then you've got to have the courage to take those risks. Those that are spread don't normally do very well. It puts a lid on their up-side if they're spread too much. So you have to have the courage from time to time to take important risks. But there's a difference between gambling and risk-taking. They're totally different. Gambling means that you can really lose everything you've staked in a short period of time. And the chances of losing everything you've staked are quite significant.'

In July 1989 Rothschild, Goldsmith and Packer teamed up again in a staggering £13.4 billion bid for BAT. Although it only ranked second in the world league tables to the 1988 take-over of RJR Nabisco which came in at £15.5 billion, it was a gigantic £10 billion ahead of Britain's highest-ever bid, Hanson's £3.5 billion takeover of Consolidated Gold Fields. As the *Sunday Times* pointed out, it made humble megabids look ordinary.

After all, the three were offering 'as much as the annual government grant to Scotland and Wales to acquire a company with a cash-flow as large as the GDP of Uganda'.

The troika came to do battle in a vehicle called Hoylake, a Bermuda-based company said to have been designed by Rothschild, supported by Packer and driven by Goldsmith. Obviously built to keep down-side risks to a minimum while maximizing their possible gains, the partners shared a 25% stake in Hoylake. The remaining 75% was controlled by the Anglo Group, made up of Rothschild and Goldsmith (11.3%) and BAT shareholders (88.7%).

Right from the beginning, Goldsmith, as spokesman, said they intended to unbundle BAT. No beating around the bush here. He claimed the company had mistakenly diversified out of tobacco, and into areas where it did not belong such as paper and packaging, perfume, retailing and financial services. He claimed that over the past 10 years BAT had invested nearly £7 billion in buying other companies and was, after all that, still worth just £7 billion. Goldsmith promised they'd sell off everything but the tobacco interests. Their offer of £8.50 a share already represented a premium over the £7 market price. However, certain analysts felt he'd underestimated the value and should be thinking of £15–19 billion, or £11–13 a share.

'Companies are stifled by the bureaucracy of large conglomerates,' Goldsmith continues to preach. 'They must be liberated in order for management to feel free to operate. It is', he insists, 'a form of privatization in the public sector.'

The one chink in their armour was the fact that instead of actually paying money for the BAT shares, they were offering secured debt, high-yield junk bonds and shares in Anglo Group. Some of the big institutions hesitated and the bid stalled. If it was difficult enough to convince anyone to take junk bonds before the fall of Drexel Burnham, it looked nearly impossible once that firm crashed. Yet Goldsmith, Rothschild and Packer continued to receive some support in the markets and much support in the financial press. Where BAT Chairman Patrick

Sheehy called them 'an *ad hoc* troupe of fianciers', the *Independent* announced, 'The arrival on the British scene of the "*ad hoc* troupe" is therefore welcomed. They will shake up managers who deserve to be shaken.'

It was always destined to be an uphill battle. Because BAT had insurance interests in the US, the marauders needed to get past various regulatory authorities in several states. They also had to get by the SEC in the States and the DTI, the Mergers and Monopolies Commission and the Office of Fair Trading in the UK.

Then there was also the BAT board to deal with.

Naturally, they actively denounced the bid. Sheehy labelled it 'opportunistic and avaricious. It represents a classic attempt to asset strip. The opportunism is self-evident. As for avarice, the trio who instigated the bid stand to gain billions of pounds, absolute billions, out of this operation at the expense of BAT's shareholders. Whatever Goldsmith says, this is a naked asset stripping proposal'.

It was an odd comment for anyone to make because: a) everything he accused the three of was obvious, and except for the label asset stripper – Goldsmith preferred the image of an unbundler – they'd quite openly admitted it long before Sheehy said it; and b) if they could unbundle the company and make 'absolute billions' for themselves, didn't Sheehy then have an obligation to his shareholders to do exactly the same thing?

As a matter of fact, doing just that became the vanguard of BAT's defence. The BAT board came up with the idea of 'unbundling' certain subsidiaries, among them their UK-based Argos catalogue shopping chain and their US-based Farmers Insurance operation.

And all this time there was Jacob Rothschild, his hands clasped together, slightly hidden by Goldsmith and the towering Packer, a 'squeamish' man in the middle of one of the most hostile bids of the century.

'As long as Jimmy Goldsmith is willing to stand in front, that's fine with me. And as for me being squeamish about hostile bids,' he shrugs, 'frankly, I still am.'

*

Call the game that Rothschild likes to play 'calculated risk-taking'. It's one where the bets are placed only on quality and only after all the homework has been done to minimize the risks.

'They should be macro-risks where you go wrong. I mean, if suddenly the American economy collapses or there's no steel business, or interest rates go through the roof, or there's a war, whatever, those are things that could occur. When you take any kind of investment risk you should think about that. But in the normal course of business you should be able to analyse out most of the risks. Especially if you risk a significant amount of the capital of the company you're running, which is earned after all by people who don't expect you to lose it. Due diligence, the soundness of the assets, the quality of the management, those are all things that are integral in the course of assessing risks. It's quite distinct from gambling.'

Here, of course, he's referring to the responsibilities of running a publicly quoted company. It is not necessarily the same game for people who run privately owned companies.

'They have a divine right or royal right to behave as they please. But once you're out of that domain and into the arena of being owned by widows, orphans, institutions and pensioners, then you've got a quite different set of responsibilities. And those responsibilities are paramount.'

Nicely enough, Rothschild is fast to admit that he's not the world's best businessman. But he's extremely proud of the fact that, internationally, he enjoys a reputation for being a straight and honourable businessman. Then too, he is a Rothschild, and since the death of his father in March 1990, he is the fourth Baron Rothschild, which means he has a long-standing tradition to live up to.

It goes without saying that he has been, all his life, financially independent, that personal gain is hardly his primary motivation. In other words, he can afford to be an honourable man.

'I think it's certainly partially that. Obviously, it's easier to be objective if one is independent. I'm fortunate enough to have been born independent in a materialistic sense. I think it makes

it much easier for me to, if you like, adopt the attitudes which I've spoken about. I think as a family, hopefully, we have a tradition of putting objectivity, particularly with other people's money and assets, as an extremely high priority. Perhaps the highest priority. So certainly there's a family tradition and history. And as I said before, that independence is also very helpful.'

When the Hambro Life deal was still on the cards, *Businessweek* featured Rothschild in a major cover story, calling him 'London's New Financial Whiz'. The article's subheading was 'Jacob Rothschild rebounds from a family feud to thrive on risk'. But rather oddly they described his style as 'aggressive and arrogant'.

It's a surprising comment because he is neither arrogant – 'Let's hope that you're right and they're wrong' – nor does he seem particularly aggressive.

'I think we're prepared to work extremely hard. But I don't think that makes one aggressive. I enjoy working hard and seem to have done without many holidays. I'm not sure it is always fun, but if you're looking for an answer as to why I do it, there can't be a very rational reason other than I enjoy it. We all need an element of therapy in our lives, but it would be exaggerated if I were doing it purely for therapeutic reasons.'

Anyway, he adds, he is a man of varied interests.

Appointed a Trustee of the National Gallery in 1984, he took over as Chairman of the Trustees a year later, succeeding Lord Annan. It was, he said at the time, a public service commitment that he intended to take very seriously. Which is exactly what he did.

Under Rothschild's stewardship, the National Gallery's finances have been put in order and the Trustees now manage the building, having taken those responsibilities away from the government. He's overseen a huge restoration programme of the main building, plus most of the £25-million Sainsbury Wing project. He also negotiated and helped set up the John Paul Getty Jr. Endowment, a £50-million fund for acquisition.

His term over in 1991, Rothschild says it was fun but has no qualms about leaving. 'I think seven years is enough for anyone.'

Anyway, he has plenty of other things to keep him busy, including his work at Waddesdon Manor, the last of the Rothschild family homes, now part of the National Trust.

Located on splendid grounds near Aylesbury, Waddesdon Manor is a 150-room, nineteenth-century, French Renaissance-style château, left to the National Trust by Dorothy de Rothschild when she died in December 1988. It's filled with period furniture, Oriental carpets and porcelain plus Dutch, Flemish, Italian and English master paintings, including portraits by Gainsborough, Reynolds and Romley.

'It's really a little National Gallery and I'm anxious to devote more of my time to it. After all, it's the last Rothschild home. At the same time, it requires a lot of attention. For instance, we're in the midst of a complete cataloguing of everything in the house. So no, I won't miss the National Gallery. It's time for the National Gallery to have someone else and time for me to do other things as well.'

His interest in the arts is well known.

But seldom have they ever been surrounded by the kind of controversy that he ran into when he decided to try to save *The Three Graces.*

In 1812 the sculptor Antonio Canova was asked by Napoleon's Empress Josephine to create a marble version of *The Three Graces.* He did and today that piece is at the Hermitage Museum in Leningrad. When the sixth Duke of Bedford saw it, he wanted one of his own and in 1815 he negotiated a commission with Canova. It was delivered to Bedford's home at Woburn Abbey in 1819. For the next 167 years it remained at one end of the great sculpture gallery in the temple that had been specially designed to house it. The sculpture has always been considered, without any doubt, one of the greatest works of art left in Britain, and was one of the major works sent to Washington in 1986 for the Treasure Houses of Britain exhibition.

That's where the trouble started.

Following its return to England, the Tavistock family, Bedford's heirs, announced that they'd sold the Canova to something called Fine Art Investment and Display Ltd of the Cayman Islands. In 1989 that company then sold the piece to the Getty Museum in California for £7.6 million. As Cayman Island companies are totally anonymous, no one except the Tavistocks knows for sure who's behind the sale. It's also possible they don't even know, as the company spokesman eventually turns out to be a lawyer in Switzerland. Speculation in the press has been that the Tavistocks themselves are somehow tied into the Cayman company. The Marquess of Tavistock has vehemently denied it. Whether they are or not seems a moot point if the sculpture leaves the UK.

Unlike other governments, such as France and Italy, which can classify a work of art a national treasure and thereby prevent its export, the law in Britain is such that export of a work of art can only be prevented if the price paid by someone wishing to export the work can be matched by someone willing to keep it in the country. Until Jacob Rothschild came along to try and save the work, the best the government could manage was righteous indignation. The Victoria and Albert Museum launched a fund and collected an embarrassingly small amount. There was indeed a public outcry at the thought of *The Three Graces* being sold to the Getty but public outcries alone don't pay for art. Money does that. But Rothschild knew where the money could come from.

According to the law, art and other national treasures can be given to the state in lieu of death duties, apparently at the joint discretion of the Minister for the Arts, the DTI and the Treasury. As he'd just been named one of the beneficiaries of a £92.8-million will by his late aunt Dorothy, Rothschild saw an opportunity to take advantage of the British tax laws to keep the statue in Britain.

Rothschild proposed that £7.6 million of the monies to be paid in taxes on his aunt's estate should instead go to buying *The Three Graces.* The sculpture could then be given to the government in lieu of taxes. His mistake was to say that once it was given to the government, it could then be put on permanent view, for instance at Waddesdon Manor.

Immediately the more cynical members of the public cried foul. They were convinced that Rothschild had somehow contrived a plan to both save some of the monies he'd otherwise have to pay in taxes, and also get the sculpture to keep. But it wasn't that at all and Rothschild is dismayed that anyone would take it so wrong.

'I wanted to save *The Three Graces* because I felt it was important to keep it in this country, to keep our national treasures here and not let them, one by one, go overseas. The money either had to go to taxes or be spent on the sculpture. There was no way we were saving a penny by offering to buy the piece and give it as a gift to the nation. And I only suggested Waddesdon Manor as one place where it might be housed. That has never been a requirement of the gift. There were never any strings attached at all. Whether it was to end up at Woburn Abbey or the National Gallery or Waddesdon or anywhere else is not the point and never has been. The important thing has always been to save *The Three Graces* for Britain. I take exception to anyone who presupposes that either I or anyone in my family has an ulterior motive for making the gift.'

In addition to his interests in the arts – and he can be expected to take his seat in the House of Lords whenever there is any debate on the arts – Rothschild is active in several other personal causes, notably the Hanaviv Foundation in Israel. That's the Rothschild family charity which built the Knesset. He also dabbles in businesses that can only be called slightly off-beat. He owns Clifton Nurseries, which he says he hopes is the best nursery garden in London.

'I'm not a gardener now, but I hope to be, when I'm older.'

A few years ago he teamed up with Terence Conran to help develop Butler's Wharf, a project he believed would one day become the Covent Garden of Docklands. More recently, he purchased the lease on Spencer House, right across the street from his office in St James's. Once the eighteenth-century home for the Princess of Wales's ancestors, it had been owned by the *Economist* magazine which is chaired by Evelyn de Rothschild. Jacob bought it to renovate as an investment property. Something his cousin might even have wished he'd thought of.

'I have those kinds of interests. They're personal interests. I don't see life as disintegrated between work and other things. I find these dividing lines that perhaps the English system tends to put on people are not necessarily valid in my case. There isn't something which is work between nine and five and then something which is something else after five. Although I have a family and children which is abolutely different from one's work. So I think life is something that goes on all the time.'

Rothschild continues to confuse the City.

They just don't know what to make of him.

Five years ago, Michael von Clemm, the former Chairman of Credit Suisse First Boston, Ltd said he saw Rothschild as 'a combination of long-range thinker on the one hand and an opportunist on the other'.

And Rothschild found that amusing. 'It's nice of him to say it. But let's put it another way. I think one of the most important characteristics of someone who is in the field of business is to correct his mistakes. So it may well be that you make a decision and it doesn't come off for one reason or another. We've spoken about Hambro Life in that context. Then you have a very big responsibility to correct it. If you take Michael von Clemm's kind phrase, maybe you make some decisions and it looks to outsiders like long-term strategy but to correct the mistake you have to be an opportunist.'

At the *International Herald Tribune* they saw him as a gunslinger who was good at pulling off 'flashy deals'.

But here too he disagreed.

'I don't think of myself as a gunslinger. Obviously not.'

Nor did he care to think of himself as merely the sheriff who heads up a posse of gunslingers.

'No, not that either. If you take a point I made earlier, we have an aversion to being involved as principals in hostile bids. The gunslinger somehow gives you a picture of someone who is endlessly making take-over bids of a hostile kind, and we're not that at all. It is perfectly true to say that we have bought and sold companies which we have developed. But I think that's a constructive thing to do. I think the building up of a conglomerate empire can be very successful over a period of many years. Ultimately there seems to be a tendency for such companies to end up being deconglomeratized by somebody else. You see that over and over again with the process of deconglomeratization in America. In our case, what we aim to do is stick to what we know quite well. We don't really have it in our mind any more to create some huge edifice.'

Five years later, in many ways, Jacob Rothschild is still something of an enigma.

Having come to the City with financial independence, at least in the beginning, he was seen perhaps as a dilettante. He proved them wrong and has, without any doubt, outshone his cousin by bringing a certain flamboyance to the modern Rothschild family image.

Yet, meeting him and speaking with him, the first thing you notice is that here is a man not at all out of the high-flyer mould. His office in St James's is a tribute to a man with refined taste. The furniture is splendid, the art on the walls is first-rate – a wonderful Lucien Freud portrait of Jacob Rothschild is surrounded by Giacometti drawings – while his desk is covered with small antiquities. Not at all out of context, there are also assorted auction catalogues and dozens of those little yellow stick-on notes reminding him of calls yet to make.

His ego, if there is one, seems insulated with old money, much like seven layers of fibre-glass wrapped around the water tank to keep the heat in. There is nothing of the self-publicist in Jacob Rothschild. He'd rather talk about almost anything than himself. When he was first told about this book and promised that his personal life would not be a part of it, that no skeletons in any cupboard were of any interest, he muttered with slight astonishment, as if everyone should know, 'I have nothing to hide. There are no skeletons.'

Not everybody in this book can honestly say that.

Still, when he refers to certain people with whom he's done deals, notably Jimmy Goldsmith, there is almost a glint of envy that flashes in his eyes.

It's not hero worship. It's something else. He and Goldsmith and Packer had to take their losses with BAT. But deep down, squeamish or not, there's little doubt that Jacob Rothschild feels this game is the most fun anyone can have vertically without laughing.

6

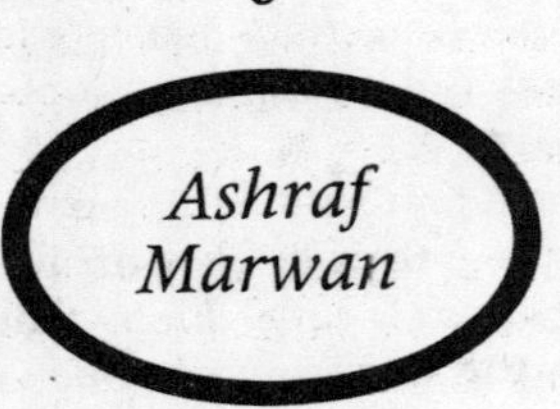

Ashraf Marwan

Five years ago the 'mysterious' Dr Marwan didn't think of himself as being all that mysterious.

'Why mysterious? I'm not mysterious. Everything is open. When you buy shares you buy them through stockbrokers and banks and everything is registered. So what's mysterious?'

Five years later he says, 'Nothing's changed.'

Well, maybe the thing is, you're mysterious if other people think you are. And lots of people still think he's mysterious.

Sic semper Egyptian risk-takers.

You step out of the lift at his office in Central London and find yourself facing a glass door looking into the reception.

A not-necessarily mysterious middle-aged Arab gentleman vets you before unlocking the door. He takes your coat while a not-necessarily mysterious young Arab woman explains that Dr Marwan will be right with you. Coffee or tea is offered. Everybody seems busy. People are constantly moving about. The waiting area turns out to be someone's office. We're crowded for space, the secretary apologizes.

When you're finally ushered into the corner office – a large room with Islamic art on the walls – the supposedly mysterious Mohammed Ashraf Marwan turns out to be a tall, starkly serious, but otherwise very cordial man. His receding hairline makes him look older than his 46 years. And at first it would be easy to mistake his character for a chilly dose of xenophobia.

'I have my PhD. in Chemistry.' His voice is low, laced with the sort of thick accent that gets used in films about the Middle East – the accent used by actors who are trying to sound mysterious. 'My BA and my Masters are also in Chemistry. It helps a lot in business because in chemistry you cut things short. One plus one equals two. Hydrogen plus oxygen gives you water. You see, I don't go for theoretical or hypothetical things.'

He is quite obviously a man who prefers to deal with facts. And one fact of life – as far as he's concerned – is that the British tend to think foreigners are mysterious.

'If you are a foreigner in this country – make no mistake about this – and if you try to become too successful, you will be absorbed by the financial establishment. You will be killed by them. You cannot fight them as long as you are a foreigner. You are single-handed. You know, we have a saying, if you cannot fight them, join them. Well, I have applied that system here but with a slight modification. If I cannot join them, I avoid them.'

In 1965, the then 21-year-old Marwan was a lieutenant in the Egyptian Army. Four years later he was named to a minor information and intelligence post in the Nasser government. Immediately following Nasser's death, Anwar Sadat brought him to real power as head of an office that in the West might be called the President's Advisory Board for National Security. He also served Sadat as Secretary for Foreign Contacts, a job that gave him instant access to all of the political and financial leaders in the Arab world.

Around Cairo they referred to him as 'the miracle child'.

By having shrewdly built up friendships with the most influential men in the Arab world, Marwan was appointed Chairman of the Arab Organization for Military Industry in 1976. It was a £1-billion joint venture between several Arab nations that Sadat hoped would establish an arms industry in Egypt. But it fell apart in 1979 when Saudi Arabia and some of the Gulf States decided that the Camp David Agreements had turned Egypt into an Israeli ally. Sensing the changes that were about to happen in Egypt, Marwan came to live in the West. He said at the time that he wanted his children educated in England. In those days his official residence was Monte Carlo.

These days he divides his time between London, the States and Spain.

Although you wouldn't know it by the way his name is bandied about in the City – suggesting he's had a history of influence on certain share transactions – he's only been doing business here since 1980. But then he didn't come to England penniless. The 'wonder child' was already a millionaire.

'I started in the 1970s by selling a piece of land in Abu Dhabi. That's where I first made my money. But I have to say that I was lucky. You know, business is all about knowledge and luck. Both must be combined. It's like two different people having two different oil concessions 500 metres apart. One drills and finds oil. The other drills a dry well. I was lucky because I had the land at the right time and there was a buyer. Sometimes you have some merchandise and there is a buyer. Sometimes there is no buyer. When there is no buyer you keep it. If you have good-quality material, there is always someone who will buy it. Like having a flat in Eaton Square. You can put any price tag on it. You can sell it in one day. You can sell it in two years. But eventually you will sell it.'

Unlike many wealthy men who love to tell you how smart they are, Marwan is alarmingly frank about the role luck has played in his own life. 'I'm not necessarily a bright man. It was a big piece of luck that President Sadat picked me for a job as his adviser.'

Well, not quite.

It happens that his father was a well-known Egyptian general, so the family had a sort of pedigree. It was most certainly a name respected enough that the dashing young Lt. Marwan could meet, fall in love with and wind up marrying President Nasser's daughter. Treated kindly by his father-in-law, his associations at the highest levels led him to the friendship with Sadat.

Because he knows what it's like to be on the inside, he doesn't hide the fact that he feels the cold in England, where he is decidedly on the outside.

'In the UK, everything is a club. If you want to go to a gym, you must belong to a club. If you want to get a good meal, you must belong to a club. If you want to meet the right people, you must belong to a club. It is a kind of discrimination, especially between the foreigners and the locals. In this country, if you do some small business, okay, they will leave you alone. But if you are a foreigner and you start touching the cream, the business establishment will close in on you.'

A 'concert party' has nothing to do with the Royal Philharmonic and crumpets.

It is, instead, an 'arrangement' between at least two parties to circumvent certain procedures laid down by law in regard to share holdings. The Companies Act says that notification must be given to a company if it is the object of 'a meeting of minds' between two or more parties for buying, using, retaining or disposing of shares. As an example, say someone has 29.9% of a company's shares and for whatever reason is not permitted to acquire more than that. Then say that person meets another person and offers to buy shares of a company through that second person or buy the shares already held by that second person, some time in the future when he is legally allowed to do so. Or, say that first person agrees to purchase those shares when the second person agrees to vote with the first in a certain matter before the annual general meeting.

In other words, a concert party is a type of conspiracy.

But then, everyone knows that and you'd have to be pretty stupid to get caught at it. There's no need to say, 'Let's conspire.'

Case in point: one very well-known businessman was, some time ago, engaged in a take-over battle. It was hostile, and a block of shares that would be potentially important for that person's victory was pledged against him. In fact, the owner of those shares let it be known that he would sell them to anyone in the world except the person leading the fight for the take-over. So another person – and it must be pointed out that neither one of them is Dr Marwan – heard about it and rang the first person. Despite the fact that there had never been any love lost between these two, the second was willing to buy those shares in his own name, with the intention of voting for the take-over, then passing them along to the first person once the take-over had been completed. He was willing to do it simply because it would be profitable for him to do it. A verbatim account of the entire conversation, as reported by that second person, went like this:

Second: 'Hi X, this is Y.'
First: (Laughter)
Second: (Laughter)
First: 'Thank you for calling. But I think I can manage it.'
Second: 'All right. Goodbye.'
First: 'Goodbye.'

So much for concert parties.

Where Ashraf Marwan first ran up against the establishment was when someone decided there must have been a concert party between Marwan and Tiny Rowland over several million House of Fraser shares held by Marwan and needed by Rowland to split Harrods away from the House of Fraser. After all, it was bad enough having foreign-born Tiny Rowland trying to run British-born Professor Roland Smith, then Chairman of the House of Fraser, out of town. But having an Arab do it as well was simply too much. Foreigners should know their place. Come on, we're not talking about some Pakistani buying a corner newsagent's or a Greek going into a High Street souvenir shop. This is Harrods. HM The Queen shops there. So does her daughter-in-law. So does Jackie Onassis. What did it matter if Harrods made money and the rest of the House of Fraser didn't. By God and Union Jack, we can't have these immigrants telling us what to do with Harrods. Anyway, the Professor obviously wasn't ready to accept as compensation just any old job at some medium-sized nationalized industry. Why shouldn't it be Sir Professor of Knightsbridge, or Lord Smith of the Food Halls? So someone rang the Department of Trade and Industry to profess that Marwan and Rowland had acted in concert.

The DTI appointed John Griffiths, CMG, QC, to investigate.

While he proceeded, Lonrho discovered the somewhat awkward fact that Griffiths had accepted a brief for and had appeared in court on behalf of the National Coal Board Pension Fund. Among the gentlemen connected at the time in one way or another with the National Coal Board Pension Fund were: Mr Hugh Jenkins, manager, Sir Ronald McIntosh, adviser, and Mr E. H. Sharp, member of the Investment Advisory Panel. Mr Sharp was also a director of the House of Frazer. Sir Ronald was also a director of S. G. Warburg, a merchant bank advising the House of Fraser and a supporter of Professor Smith. While Mr Jenkins – controlling at the time some four million shares – was also one of the more vocal House of Fraser investors in favour of the Professor's position against Lonrho.

Naturally Lonrho objected.

However, Norman Tebbit, in all his infinite wisdom as Secretary of State for Trade and Industry, ruled that this did not constitute any sort of conflict of interest.

It was the beginning of a long list of things that Mr Tebbit would do in all his wisdom.

According to Griffiths' report, Dr Marwan built up a holding of two million Fraser shares over four days in May 1983. Subsequently, he bought 1.2 million more. Another investor with an interest in House of Fraser shares at the same time was Mrs Adriana Funaro. It turns out that she is a member in good standing of the Fayed family who in early November 1984 bought £138.3 million worth of Fraser shares – the 29.9% stake owned by Lonrho. It also turns out that Marwan bought his 1.2 million shares from her.

Marwan had, Griffiths revealed, previous links with Lonrho. Tiny Rowland held a directorship in a Swiss company called El Sara and the office Marwan used on Piccadilly had been bought by Marwan's Mestimo Investments from El Sara. But that was pretty minor compared with the discovery of a Marwan/Rowland joint venture.

Ah hah, Griffiths must have thought, the plot thickens.

It seems that in 1980 Marwan purchased a 40% stake in

Tradewinds Air Holdings, Ltd. Lonrho had the other 60%. But three years later, Marwan chose to opt out. He wrote to Rowland saying that he was going to sell his shares to a certain Libyan who would be a thoroughly objectionable partner from Lonrho's point of view. Rowland quickly suggested lunch. The matter was resolved on 10 May, with Rowland eating vanilla ice-cream, drinking Perrier and coffee, and Marwan selling his stake to Lonrho at a loss for £500,000. Mr Griffiths never said what Dr Marwan had for lunch. Nor did he explain who paid the bill.

Griffiths did however look into Marwan's wealth. He discovered that since 1978 Marwan had invested in real estate, banking and other ventures in a number of countries and that, at least according to Marwan, by summer of 1983 he was worth about $20 million.

What worried Griffiths, among other things, was the motivation behind Marwan's interest in HoF. Marwan stated his decision to invest some £4 million in the company was based entirely on an article that appeared in the *Sunday Telegraph* on 15 May 1983. Titled 'Slater's Tip', one-time high-flyer Jim Slater wrote that anyone buying a million Fraser shares, worth £1.86 million, could tip the balance in favour of Lonrho at the annual general meeting in June. Slater figured that, if Lonrho were successful in splitting Harrods away from the Group, those shares would then be worth £2.5 million. He even promised, 'It cannot go wrong.'

Marwan said he read the article, liked the idea and bought the shares.

Griffiths didn't believe him.

He asked Marwan if he knew Mr Slater, or had ever heard his name. Marwan said, no. Then he asked, 'If you did not know who Mr Slater was, merely four short paragraphs to invest £4 million – it seems unusual.'

Marwan answered, 'Why? Last week I invested over £1 million, against the advice of everyone, even against the advice of my broker . . .'

But Griffiths firmly believed that there was more to Marwan's interest than the 'Slater Tip'. It was that 10 May luncheon. The Harrods demerger battle had been in all the papers. Griffiths was convinced that the two must have discussed it.

Question by Griffiths to Marwan: 'Did he (Rowland) say anything about House of Fraser?'

Answer by Marwan: 'No, but I was reading what is written in the newspaper for the past four or five years.'

Another question by Griffiths: 'There he was in the middle of a very sensational incident reported widely in the newspapers, midway between two meetings of House of Fraser and you did not speak at all?'

Answer by Marwan: 'I did not speak. Why speak? As I said, I had a very bad experience with Lonrho which cost me dear.'

Then it was Rowland's turn.

Griffiths: 'I would find it surprising if, in the middle of this foray, in the newspapers it seems to have been, you meet him, having done your business, and you do not move on to discuss this foray.'

Response by Rowland: '. . . It is possible that he asked me about the House of Fraser, but I do not know whether he raised it, I raised it, or whether it was raised at all. But it was not an issue. If you are trying to suggest that I said to him, "Look, I will pay you £500,000. It would be a good idea if you were to buy House of Fraser shares," you can dismiss that from your mind. That was not said by me and it was certainly not said by him.'

After further prodding by Griffiths, Rowland made this remark: 'I would not want to do business with Ashraf Marwan. We did the Tradewinds business and that was a disaster . . . because I would never know from day to day whether he was still my partner or whether he had sold his shares to a third party. Mr Griffiths, I have told you, I meet a lot of people – a lot of rich people. It may surprise you. It would have been easy for me to persuade a lot of people to buy shares in House of Fraser. I would not be such a fool – after all, we had given undertakings to the Minister – as to say to Dr Ashraf Marwan, who is totally unreliable when it comes to business . . . "Buy shares in House of Fraser and support us". I could have done it with reliable people. In terms of business Dr Ashraf Marwan is totally unreliable . . .'

Later still he added: 'I would not dream of asking a man like Dr Marwan to buy shares in the House of Fraser . . . I could have asked Robert Anderson to buy 10 million shares. I could have asked D. K. Ludwig to buy 10 million shares. I could have asked half a dozen or a dozen or dozens of people to buy 100,000 shares in the House of Fraser. Why pick on Marwan?'

When Griffiths questioned Marwan as to why he'd used his votes to support Rowland's plea for the demerger of Harrods from the House of Fraser, he got this response: 'Because if there are, say, 130 shops and one shop is producing 50% of the profit, there must be something wrong with the management of the other 129 shops.'

Griffiths' conclusion was that certain areas of Marwan's testimony did not carry 'the ring of truth'. For instance, he could not accept that the sole reason behind Marwan's decision to buy those two million shares was the article by Jim Slater or that demerger was not discussed at lunch.

When Marwan received his copy of the report, he tossed it in the dustbin. 'I don't care a damn what they think about me. That investigation was a waste of time and money. It led to nothing because there was nothing. You see, you can go to Hyde Park now and make a speech, allegations about anyone, right? Okay. That's what Professor Smith is doing. He makes defensive allegations to gain time. The Griffiths' report was just Speakers Corner.'

Even Rowland was incensed enough to write to Griffiths, 'If Dr Ashraf Marwan's position in England were equivalent to his place in Egyptian society, you would unhesitatingly accept his word, which is also supported by his financial and natural independence.'

Just for the record, it seems that Mr John Griffiths, CMG, QC is the same Mr John Griffiths, then merely QC, who in 1980, as Attorney-General in Hong Kong was involved with an official inquiry into the death of a police inspector. Two years later, an editorial in the *Hong Kong Law Journal*, reviewing his wisdom in that case, noted 'errors of judgement' and a public statement that was 'grossly misleading in a material respect'.

Oh well, you can't win 'em all!

On the other hand, you can win some of them.

In March 1990, after nearly two years of innuendo, denials, rumours, stalling, ministerial incompetence, muzzling the press, a flagrant lack of concern for the public's right to know and a general mishandling of the entire affair, the government released the Department of Trade and Industry's investigation into House of Fraser Holdings PLC.

If the report was a film, Marwan would be nominated as Best Supporting Actor.

The affair had been going on for just about 15 years. Mohammed Fayed met Lonrho's Tiny Rowland through Roushdi Sobhi, the Egyptian Chairman of the Allied Arab Bank in London. The two got along well enough in those days and breakfasted weekly to discuss the world's problems. They did a few deals together and in 1975, apparently at Fayed's request, Rowland invited him on to the Lonrho board. By the beginning of 1976, however, when the relationship did not prove particularly fruitful, Fayed left his Lonrho directorship. There does not appear to have been any further contact between Rowland and Fayed until 1983.

In the meantime, Lonrho bought a 29% stake in a company called Scottish and Universal Investments (SUITS) which happened to own 10% of the House of Fraser, and then a 19% stake directly in HoF. In March 1979 their successful bid for SUITS meant they now controlled 30% of HoF's shares. With that in their camp, Rowland launched an all-out £226-million bid for HoF. But the Monopolies and Mergers Commission blocked it. They also required that Lonrho not increase its stake in HoF. Rowland fought as best he could. But Trade Secretary

Norman Tebbit stood his ground. Unable to sway the government, Rowland tried to load the HoF board with a dozen of his own people. But Professor Smith fended off that move. Thwarted on every front Rowland sold his HoF shares to the Fayed brothers in November '84, although he immediately bought back a 6% stake. Five months later the Fayeds bid for HoF and that bid was not referred to the MMC.

Under the weight of Rowland's incessant accusations of bungling by both Tebbit and his successor Leon Brittan, the next Trade Secretary, Paul Channon, appointed a pair of inspectors – attorney Henry Brooke and accountant Hugh Graham Cazalet Aldous – to make a full report on the takeover. They began in April 1987 and sent their findings to the printers in July 1988. But the DTI refused to release the report as the Serious Fraud Squad now claimed an interest in the matter. Lord Young, who succeeded Channon, told the country on several occasions that he sincerely wanted to publish it but that the police investigation took precedence. In January 1989 Lonrho sued the government to force publication, and lost. Two months later an extraordinary midweek edition of the *Observer* – owned by Lonrho – hit the streets with the more defamatory sections of the report liberally sprinkled throughout. The DTI immediately won an injunction to stop the *Observer*. Copies of that edition are now collectors' items. It wasn't until Nicholas Ridley took over at the DTI that the government, forced by public opinion, published the report.

Then, despite the highly explosive information it contained, Mr Ridley – in keeping with the attitude of his predecessors – refused to take any action against the Fayeds.

It was as if the government had, for all those years, been spitting in Tiny's eye.

During this time, Marwan had been buying shares in HoF and siding with Rowland. He often describes their relationship as 'father and son'. When Rowland tried to cast aspersions on the Fayeds – their background, their character and the source of their funding – Tebbit, Brittan, the DTI and the OFT all turned a deaf ear. Even the press – with the obvious exception of the *Observer* – backed away. They didn't come out and say as much, but at least around Fleet Street, Rowland was thought of as a man unhealthily obsessed with Harrods and the Fayeds, and seriously stained with sour grapes.

It was Marwan who effectively championed Rowland's cause.

He'd gone to see Sir Gordon Borrie at the Office of Fair Trading and had written to Alex Fletcher, the Parliamentary Under-Secretary of State for Corporate and Consumer Affairs at the DTI, to stress three important points:

1. That the Fayeds were not, as they and their bankers Kleinwort Benson had claimed, part of a wealthy, old Egyptian family with cotton and shipping interests, but rather from very humble origins;
2. That the Fayed's total net worth was probably no more than £100 million and nowhere near the billions that some people at Kleinwort's had suggested. What's more, Marwan insisted, there was no way the Fayeds could have raised £600 million to buy HoF without outside financing;
3. That Mohammed Fayed was known to hold a power of attorney from the Sultan of Brunei in connection with the use of the Sultan's funds. Marwan's insinuation there was that the Fayeds had used the Sultan's money to buy Harrods.

Even though that point has been emphatically denied by both the Fayeds and the Sultan, and even though John Griffiths had said in his report that he could not rely on Marwan's evidence as 'the whole truth', Mssrs Brook and Aldous concluded, 'Dr Marwan's role in the dispute became of considerable importance between November 1984 and March 1985 because he had many contacts in Egypt and in other parts of the Arab world and they were all telling him that the Fayeds could not possibly be the beneficial owners of the money they claimed was theirs. Marwan also became satisfied that the Fayeds were telling lies about their Egyptian past'.

Marwan's evidence became the backbone for many of their more damning conclusions.

*

Ever since he first came into prominence as a player in the House of Fraser affair, Marwan has gotten his fair share of ink.

In June 1985, the financial press reported that he'd disclosed a 5.05% holding in Extel, the specialist news agency and advertising group. Over the previous 18 months, he'd bought and sold important stakes in Fleet Holdings and House of Fraser, which both had shortly thereafter become bid targets. For the next six months, he continued buying Extel and by January 1986, the papers said, he'd lifted his stake to 10.87%. A few days later, Demerger Corp. launched a £173-million bid. Twelve days after Demerger's bid hit the news, Marwan sold his shares to Robert Maxwell for around £3.95, a good 60p premium over the shares when he first started buying them.

He was back in the news a few months later, announcing a stake in the wire and engineering group, Bridon.

Next he was known to be buying Benlox, civil engineering and investment company, having acquired a 10.5% stake. That quickly rose to 19.4% and an offer to sit on the executive board as deputy chairman. He purchased another 5% just before Benlox – then valued at around £45 million – launched a £2-billion all-share bid for Terence Conran's empire, Storehouse.

Conran called the bid 'opportunistic financial engineering . . . ridiculous behaviour'. Marwan continued buying shares, raising his interest to nearly 9.4 million, at prices ranging from 48–54p. They soon jumped to 59p. Then word came that Marwan had been acting 'in concert' with Benlox. The Take-over panel rapped Benlox's knuckles over the affair, but never took any disciplinary action against either Benlox or Marwan. The bulk of their criticism seems to have been the fact that neither Marwan nor Benlox ever announced that Marwan would, in fact, not assume the Deputy Chairman's chair.

Within a month, the bid simply faded away. Benlox failed to get any sort of serious holding in Storehouse. Two months later, Marwan sold his 22% stake in Benlox with the share price at about 36p. However, three months after that he was back in the fray again, this time buying 2.5 million shares for a

5.78% stake. Over the next several weeks he increased his stake to just about 10%.

At the same time the papers noted he was building a stake in the British-based Kelt Energy. He has since become Kelt's second-largest single shareholder. Before 1988 was over, Marwan announced that he'd acquired almost 10% of Kelt. By that time Kelt's bid for Carless was announced. And when that hit the papers, so did the story that Marwan had been buying and selling Carless shares as well.

In January 1989 Marwan sold his 5.75 million Benlox shares. His name also popped up in connection with Bear Brand, a tiny company in which he had a 10% stake. The Bear Brand management had been trying to get a rights issue past their shareholders when Marwan objected. He held his ground long enough until he found a buyer for his shares, at the right price, then went away.

It would be difficult to know for certain, but in the space of these last 530 words, Marwan seems to have managed to profit somewhere in the neighbourhood of £2.25 million.

That's £4250 a word!

'It's very true that the first million is the hardest,' he says. 'If you don't have anything and you see chances, what can you do? That is the whole issue about business. You can buy any assets if you have the money. When people know that you have money, a lot of propositions are coming to you. But when people know you don't have money, who comes to you then? That's the way life is.'

So when you're wealthy, people come to you looking for deals. Marwan is wealthy. Therefore people come to him looking for deals.

Yes and no.

'A lot of deals come in over the phone but the good ones don't. You have to do your own homework. Balance sheets are fine. But what isn't on the balance sheet is also important. If someone offers you a palace, that's one thing. If it's in Shepherds Bush, that's another. It may still be a palace, but who's going to buy it?'

Most of the time, he says, he gets his ideas out of the papers.

'I do my research about a company's assets and look for real value. My hobby is reading so I read as much as I can. About 50 papers and reports a day. That's four to five hours. If you read, you know. No national in a country where I am would ever give me a tip. He'll never trust me because I'm a foreigner. Other foreigners usually only have a second-hand tip and by the time it reaches me it's passed through too many nationals. That's the way it is. It's a private club. Social. Financial. Either they accept you or they don't. Here in the City they don't like individuals. It's a fact. Individuals don't abide by the unwritten rules.'

In other words, it all gets back to being a member of the club. You play by the established rules. Especially in the City of London. He says that's one reason why he much prefers doing business in the United States.

'America is completely different. There are no unwritten rules in America. You just have to assemble a group of people to take over whatever you want. You can do what you want if you have the financial pull with the banks. England is 50 years behind America. There are very solid banks in the City but the rules are completely different. Here they loan you one to one. In America you can go three to one or four to one, depending on the project itself. With the same amount of money you pick up more growth in America. At the moment there are very good deals to be pinched in the United States. The savings and loan crash has created lots of sellers. There's property you can pick up at 15 cents on the dollar if you've got the money. I'm planning on holding my assets there for 15–20 years.'

In Britain he confines himself to share speculation and general arbitrage. The only bid he ever tried was Storehouse and he lost money. And while he's not too shy to put money on a company if he suspects a bid is on the way, what he prefers to do is invest in companies with strong assets, good turnover, a healthy earnings per share and very sound management.

'I always look at management. A gold mine without someone

to get the assets out of the ground isn't worth anything. Management is essential when I make a final decision about what I want to invest in. The most important thing to remember, however, is never to be greedy. When I buy, I say to myself, once I have so much of a profit, say 40%, I'll get out, even if the shares are still going up, that's all right. I decide what I want and stick to it. When it goes the other way, I cut my losses early. I only go into a deal after I study it. What's my high? What's my real risk? What's my down? You have to look at it all ways.'

He also feels the need to explain that he is not a wheeler-dealer.

'No. Wheel and deal I don't do. I never do trading. Because if you trade, you have to go to the door of someone to sell your goods. You have to understand the way most Arab investors think. They follow each other. Even if they are competitors, they do the same thing. If one of them goes into real estate, they all go into real estate. If one of them buys horses, they all buy horses. But they don't buy computers. Would you like to know why the Arabs have never invested in computers? Because computers don't look like anything. They can show off their horses and they can show off their real estate, but you can't show off a computer. I like creation. So we build things. After we build it, sometimes we sell it. Like an office building. Or we lease it. But we build things.'

He says he tends to divide his portfolio into risk factors, although unlike many conservative investors who never put more than say 10% of their holdings into high-risk areas, Marwan says he commits 50% of his funds to high-risk/high-return investments.

'I really am a risk taker. But the other 50% is safe investments which assure me of maintaining my life-style. Now, when I say high risk, I don't mean that I actually risk losing it all if an investment goes wrong. I can get in and out quickly. I was damaged in '87, like everyone else in the market, but I could afford to hold on and eventually, like anyone who did hold on, I got my money back. It's just that I personally believe my overall return on any investment, which includes dividends and appreciation, has to be more than I could get at the bank, otherwise it's pointless to invest. Just leave the money in the bank. It's much less headache.'

Next comes the question of long term and short term.

He answers, 'It depends. I make judgements ranging from about two to five years. It's not like IBM and Boeing. You can buy that and stick with it for 10 years because Boeing is Boeing and they supply the whole world. That's a fact of life. Their sales book is full for the next 10 years so whatever happens to the American economy, they're still going to be selling planes. You cannot go wrong there. But in the UK there'll be an election probably in 1991. You have to take that into consideration. So I'm thinking short term in my UK investments.'

Abroad, he's spent the past five years getting even more heavily into real estate. In America he's particularly bullish on land and residential units. In Monaco he's involved with building apartments. And in Mallorca he still owns the five-star hotel, Son Vida Castle.

'I bought Son Vida after a dinner. I had an operation on my back, so I went to Spain for a vacation with my wife, and I met some people, some friends there, who invited us for a dinner. There was a Spanish guy talking about a transaction he was doing for a Spanish group. I asked him how much he wanted for the hotel. He told me. Suddenly in the morning I called him and asked, is that figure true? He said, yes. I said, okay, you have a deal. Just like that. It was cheap. For a piece of real estate you can make a quick evaluation. For a company you have to dig. Look at any publication of any company. Are you going to believe it all? The hidden reserves and the real evaluation of the assets and the book value? You know how things are done. Creative accounting. But when you buy a building, it's a building. You can appraise it.'

Recently he's also begun investing in the Middle East.

He bought some land in Sharm el Sheikh, in the southern Sinai, and is building a four-star vacation complex there geared towards European tourists who want 365 days of sunshine a year and diving in some of the world's most beautiful reefs.

'It is a good time to invest in the Middle East because there is peace. And the peace is a lasting one. I can say that because everyone is tired. The two super-powers have made peace together and lost interest in confronting each other in the Middle East. None of the small countries, like Egypt or Israel, can fight without the support of the super-powers and the super-powers no longer give a damn about war in the Middle East. I remember Sadat saying, before Camp David, I want peace but it's difficult for the people who fought three or four times to make peace. Still, he did it. It will even happen in the Lebanon. We now have a trend towards peace worldwide and no one can stop it. It's contagious. Anyone who can't accept peace, is out of date. It's as simple as that.'

With peace seemingly breaking out all over the world, he is now also looking towards Eastern Europe for investment possibilities.

'I am looking to Hungary, Czechoslovakia and Romania. I'm not going to East Germany because that's going to be swallowed up by the West Germans. You can't compete with them. The same with Poland. That will be the German domain. In the other countries I want to make deals in property, hotels and technology. I'm going to Romania for one very simple reason and that's because most people are still afraid to go there. Their revolution hasn't yet finished. But it happens to be the only country in the East with no foreign debt. Once they start looking for credit, they should have less trouble than the other countries with $50 billion debt. There are some people who say Romania isn't stable. Okay, even if it isn't stable yet, it will be in a matter of time.'

So the mysterious Dr Marwan is off to Eastern Europe.

'Why mysterious?' He truly is bothered by the handle. 'You know, I travel about 1000 flying hours a year. But I fly commercial because I like to sit with people, to talk with people. Does that sound mysterious? And all that talk about conspiracy. Why conspire? All the tips you need to know are in the newspapers. They're all there. All you have to do is read the newspapers and you can find out everything. But you must make your own decisions. I never listen to forecasters. I'll tell you why. I was in Chicago and there was a programme on television where they took ten forecasters and a monkey. They all picked shares. Six months later they showed the results. The monkey won.'

7

Tiny Rowland

On Monday evening, 12 March 1990, five days after the Department of Trade and Industry released its report on the sale of the House of Fraser, the Attorney-General, Sir Patrick Mayhew faced an angry House of Commons.

The DTI had accused the Fayeds of lying. Yet the government was not going to prosecute.

Mayhew told the Commons, as the evidence was largely hearsay and therefore unsustainable, and as the likelihood was that the Fayeds could never be convicted on such evidence, the affair was closed.

At about the same time, Mohammed Fayed was throwing a party on the fourth floor of Harrods to celebrate the fifth anniversary of his ownership.

Testimonials were given to his friendship. Toasts were drunk to his health. He even took the microphone to say, 'The report has proven, once and for all, that the earth is flat.'

It was a swell party, with lots of champagne and lots of prunes wrapped in bacon and a huge birthday cake too.

Notably absent was Tiny Rowland.

Not that he would have come had he been invited. But talk around the party was that some people at Harrods actually thought it would be a hoot to send him an invitation.

Roland Walter Rowland, whose real name is Roland Walter Furhop but who's called Tiny by everyone – he even signs 'Tiny' on all things official, including letters to heads of state and on the bottom of the annual Chief Executive's report for his company, Lonrho – is a man with a definite presence.

His clothes are perfectly tailored. His bright blue eyes stare directly at you when he speaks. His handshake is strong. He collects art modestly, mostly African and German Expressionist, and has a number of cars, mostly Rolls-Royces and Mercedes. He's a man who doesn't sell his possessions. Cars and even clothes accumulate with the years. He has a mischievous sense of humour, but is, at the same time, very puritanical. He doesn't care for stories of drunkenness, debauchery or sexual revelling. At the age of 49 he married a woman he'd known in Rhodesia since she was three. They live quietly together with their four children.

He is a man who claims to have arrived at total independence.

'I am independent financially and socially.'

Financially independent means, 'I have more than enough money to do whatever I want to'. His salary has multiplied more than four times in the past five years, going from £265,000 to over £1.3 million, while his total annual income, thanks to shareholdings and other investments, is said to be ten times that.

Socially independent means, 'I have no friends. Every time I meet someone, an accountant, say, who makes £100,000 a year, I know he'll try to borrow some money from me.'

That independence is at the same time both his choice and his privilege.

'I'm a totally paid-up member of the Inland Revenue of the United Kingdom. I don't use tax havens. I don't go to dinner parties or cocktail parties. I have a happy family life. I've never been divorced and I don't plan on it happening. I don't belong to any clubs, so it's not likely I could ever be asked to resign from any. I enjoy meeting people but I don't keep a diary of appointments. I do whatever seems most important to do first. Some people talk to me about five-year plans, but with me five days is more like it. As long as I feel I want to work for Lonrho, I'll come to work. The day it bores me, I'll stop. I think in some ways I'm like a weed. You could plant me anywhere and after a few inches of rain I'd seed and prosper.'

Born in India in 1917, his mother was English, his father was German, a successful trader. Because Rowland sidesteps questions about his past, myths invariably fill the gaps. Some have him working as a railway porter. Others have him making £5000 a day by 1946.

In 1981, investigative journalist Charles Raw, writing in the *Sunday Times*, revealed that between the wars the Furhops returned to Germany. However, Rowland's father was an outspoken anti-Nazi, which forced part of the family to seek safety in England. Rowland attended Churchers College in Hampshire but left after a year. By 1937 he was working in his uncle's London-based shipping agency. In 1939, Rowland was arrested in Berlin for associating with anti-Nazis and spent two weeks in jail there. That same year he changed his name from Furhop, taking the W from Walter and putting it into his first name. Back in the UK he was conscripted into the British Army. His German roots restricted him from combat, so he served with the Royal Army Medical Corps in Norway and Scotland.

During the internment panic of 1940, Rowland's father was put into a camp. When Rowland was refused leave to visit his father, he went AWOL and was subsequently arrested. After 27 days in a military jail, he was permitted to join his parents in the camp. His mother died before the end of the war, and his father remained interned. When the war finished, his father stayed in England, having patented a carpet-making machine. He died in the early 1970s at the age of 93.

Rowland now went into business, buying and selling factories and was supposedly a millionaire by 1947. But after a hassle with the Inland Revenue over back taxes, he left for Rhodesia where he bought a pair of farms and settled into the life of a gentleman planter. Over the next 14 years his Shepton Estates expanded into gold and copper mining, a car dealership and made several acquisitions on behalf of Rio Tinto Zinc.

Enter here the London and Rhodesian Mining and Land Co., a lacklustre outfit that had been around for decades. In 1961, they acquired some of Shepton's assets and with them came Rowland as a joint managing director. In those days they employed 350 people, boasted assets of £2.15 million, turned over £4 million and had a pre-tax profit of £160,000.

Two years later the company name was changed to Lonrho.

By 1965, the year the Rhodesian government declared independence, Lonrho's assets were £13.2 million, its turnover £32 million, and its pre-tax profits £1.8 million.

Rowland had expanded quickly by taking Lonrho into new businesses – breweries, ranches and newspapers – and into new spheres of influence like the newly independent nations of Uganda, Kenya and Tanzania. These days there are few doubts that Rowland and Lonrho are one and the same.

'It's not at all like that. There are lots of chaps who work here. This is a comfortable, loose organization. Did you notice there are no closed doors in the hallway? That's the way we work. If anybody wants to see me, they simply have to come see me. I'm really just an amateur surrounded by professionals. I've farmed, mined, retailed, manufactured and wholesaled. Maybe you could say what I do is buying and selling and that I have a feel for what I believe to be a good deal.'

Rowland can say as often as he cares to that Lonrho isn't his show alone, but most people in the City know it is and the people who work with him act like it is. Yet when you ask him what Lonrho would be like without Tiny Rowland, you get a laugh and some modesty.

'Share prices would probably go up 50% once they (the City) realized that such an unacceptable character was no longer here. But I have no intention of leaving.'

His use of the word 'unacceptable' is well chosen because that was the handle Prime Minister Heath tagged on Lonrho.

'Edward Heath once called this company the unacceptable face of capitalism. It's the only notable thing he ever said. It's a boring phrase which is forever being repeated. But we've outgrown it. Although I don't think it was ever true. Of course, being called the acceptable face of capitalism would be equally insulting.'

*

Through business interests around the world, but especially in Africa and the Middle East, Rowland has built up long-standing and trusted relationships with several national leaders.

Lonrho's resilience to nationalizations is proof of that. Company assets in Africa have twice been nationalized – once in Tanzania and once in Zaire. And both times those assets have been returned.

'It's an occupational risk. But through those nationalizations we have never lost our friendships with those governments. We have never lost the sympathies of the people there. Developing countries need Western technology, skills that we have. You must be philosophical about such things. You must take the long view on a worldwide basis. Lonrho has a history and a tradition as a builder. The net result is, after both those nationalizations, we were asked back. We resumed those old friendships and they were perhaps even stronger as a result. That's very satisfying. It's a tribute to the company. Sure it costs us money in the meantime but, well, we must live with the world as it is.'

Rowland loves to play his part in the game of diplomacy whenever he's given the opportunity. It's a fairly well-known fact that he had a small hand in helping to arrange the Camp David Agreement between Israel and Egypt. Rowland had contacts with the Sadat government, one of them being Ashraf Marwan. At the same time, Lord Marcus Sieff of Marks and Spencer had access to Shimon Perez and Moshe Dayan in Israel. Because it could be kept outside regular channels, 'interested parties' felt these relationships could be used in the cause of peace. Rowland and Sieff were asked to test the waters, to make informal overtures that would pave the way for official contacts.

'Sadat had to be conditioned first,' Rowland explains. 'No one in America had access to Sadat the way I did.'

In the autumn of 1971, an even more revealing episode took place. And this one is not generally known.

There'd been a dispute between the Gaddafi regime in Libya and the British government over suspended contracts and the nationalization of certain businesses, including two British banks in Tripoli. At the request of the Foreign Office, Rowland was asked to help arrange some sort of settlement. The three interested parties were: Major Abdel Salam Jalud, Deputy Chairman of Libya's Revolutionary Command Council; Ashraf Marwan, representing President Sadat; and Anthony Parsons, then Under-Secretary at the FO. Within two months Rowland had forged an agreement that provided for a deposit of £25 million by the British government in a London bank which the Libyans would then spend on a £27-million Marconi air defence radar system.

Parsons told Rowland the cabinet would consider the agreement on 16 November. It didn't happen. Nor did it happen on the 23rd. Nor did it happen on the 30th. To keep the confidence of both Marwan and Jalud, Rowland flew to Cairo on 1 December with Parsons' assurance that the agreement would be discussed by the cabinet on 7 December.

At the same time, and seemingly unrelated, British treaties were due to expire with Bahrain, Qatar and the seven Trucial States. One day too early, British forces abandoned the Tunb Islands in the Gulf. A few hours later Iranian troops landed and claimed them. That England had allowed Iran to occupy their protectorate was regarded as a breach of trust by Colonel Gaddafi. He warned that if the British refused to take them back, he'd make reprisals against British interests in Libya. That clearly meant BP.

In Cairo, Rowland heard the news from Marwan. When Jalud arrived later that same day, Rowland took the initiative to ask for a cooling-off period. Jalud agreed that nothing would be done pending approval of the negotiated agreement by the British cabinet on 7 December. Rowland was then entrusted with a personal message from Sadat to the Prime Minister restating the Arab position. He returned to London and rang Parsons at 9.30 a.m. on 3 December. Parsons agreed by phone that everything would be done to obtain a quick decision, although it would have to wait until 7 December. Rowland related this to Cairo.

That Tuesday morning, Parsons rang Rowland to say that the cabinet would not in fact discuss the matter. He implied the government would not be pressured by deadlines and anyway that there were more important topics on the agenda. With no options left but to pass this news on to Cairo, Rowland sent a message at noon. A few hours later Gaddafi nationalized BP.

Three days after that, back in Cairo to discuss Lonrho business, Rowland saw the opportunity to confront Gaddafi personally. A letter was drafted with Sadat's approval, the text of which the Egyptian government hoped Gaddafi would issue to Rowland. The letter asked Rowland to intercede with the British government in gaining some form of censure of the Iranian government in exchange for promises from the Libyans to suspend the BP take-over. On 12 December, Rowland, Marwan and two Egyptian officials flew to Tripoli. They met with Gaddafi, who after three hours, signed the letter. Gaddafi then verbally confirmed that, as long as the UK would in some way censure the Iranians, the BP nationalization could be reversed.

Back in London, Rowland found the FO simply not prepared to make the slightest conciliatory gesture towards the Libyans. In January, when Rowland learned that the Libyans were about to negotiate a deal with the Russians for crude oil, he sought an appointment with the Prime Minister, hoping to convince him that a mission sent to Libya with the blessings of Downing Street might reopen the possibility of a settlement with BP. But the FO doubted the Libyans' sincerity, even though Sadat was willing to intervene with Gaddafi on Britain's behalf. Nothing came of it. Next, Lonrho's chairman, Lord Duncan-Sandys, went to Libya with the blessings of the Foreign Secretary, Sir Alec Douglas-Home, and met with Gaddafi, hoping that the Libyans might agree to arbitration of the BP problem. Gaddafi said no. Duncan-Sandys now told Sir Alec that Britain's best hope lay in disentangling the BP claim from the original commercial agreement as organized by Rowland. To buy time for the British, Marwan got Jalud to defer his visit to Russia to negotiate the oil deal. But on 20 February, when no word had come from London, Jalud and Marwan flew to Moscow.

Rowland refused to give up. He proposed that the government should purchase BP's oil and sell it onward to BP at the same price. In return, Libya should agree to sign contracts in the UK for some £400 million-worth of equipment. Based on certain assurances from the FO that the plan had merit, Rowland appealed to Marwan who spoke with Gaddafi. Marwan reported back confidently that a deal could be arranged. That's when Jalud summoned the British Ambassador. It seemed a simple thing. Jalud wished to confirm with the Ambassador that the British government was indeed aware of the possibility of a deal which would, in effect, solve the BP problem. Rowland claims the Ambassador had been kept informed from London. Jalud claims the Ambassador denied all knowledge of the deal, and in fact refuted it. BP was forced to write off the entire book value of their Libyan operations – £38 million.

He tells people that Lonrho is run strictly along the lines of Harvard Business School's theory of decentralized management. He says it has to be that way because Lonrho is a conglomerate of some 1000 companies spread through 100 countries. The group's annual turnover is these days in excess of £5 billion.

The main area of Lonrho's interest is still Africa, where among other things it is the largest single food producer. There are tea plantations in Malawi, Toyota distributorships and livestock in Kenya, gold mines in Ghana, sugar plantations in Swaziland, tomato estates in Mozambique, cosmetics manufacturing in Nigeria, civil engineering activities in Zambia, airplane retailing in South Africa and farm equipment distribution in Uganda. Adding in the rest of the world, there are hotels, oil and gas interests, printing plants, casinos, freight forwarding, postage stamp printing, finance, plumbing, stainless steel sink manufacturing, bed linen retailing, property management, insurance broking and newspapers, including the *Observer*.

'Some companies prefer to limit their areas of interest to specific fields where they already have expertise. I take a different approach. I can always buy someone with the necessary experience to run a business. When you've got the right man you've got the experience. On the other hand, there are certain areas I generally try to avoid. I stay away from manufacturing in the UK or in Europe. As far as I'm concerned, in Europe and even in parts of the US, we're living in yesterday's world. I see today's world and tomorrow's world in the Pacific Ocean. All developing nations are tomorrow's world.'

His dedication to Africa is deeply rooted and for many years Rowland was considered to have more influence on that continent that almost anyone in the world, businessman or politician.

'Africa is our life's blood. I don't see it as a risk area. It's more of a risk to manufacture in England. Do you think a tightrope walker in the circus is taking a risk? It may look that way, but he knows exactly what he's doing. There is no risk for tightrope walkers. I feel totally at ease in Africa. We have always had a fair deal in Africa. Our problems there have only been temporary. We cannot, however, say the same for the City of London.'

Lonrho is the most investigated company in the history of British business.

'We've had years of investigations. Believe me, it's sheer prejudice. It wouldn't happen if I were a member of the club, the establishment. But for me it would be a waste of time, going to all those boring dinner parties. All those investigations. They've been looking for the spot. Too bad because I could help them. I know the spot.'

In 1961, a man named Angus Ogilvy was sent to Rhodesia on behalf of his boss Harley Drayton. Among Drayton's holdings was a heavy share of London and Rhodesian Mining and Land. Drayton wanted Ogilvy to see if something could be done to revive the company's fortunes. A deal was struck with Rowland, who turned some of his Shepton Estates assets over to London and Rhodesian in exchange for 1.5 million L & R shares and an option to acquire a further two million. Rowland met with his first taste of criticism when questions were raised as to the actual value of those Shepton Estates assets.

In 1971, the South African government opened an investigation into a small mining company owned by Lonrho, claiming fraud. Lonrho's bankers, S. G. Warburg, resigned. A year later the South Africans dropped the charges, publicly apologized and even paid off some Lonrho officials. But the damage had been done. Lonrho's share prices tumbled.

That brought on the next crisis.

Lonrho appointed an auditing firm to investigate its financial position. In February 1972 they advised a reconstitution of the Lonrho board, including the appointment of a new chairman and new directors. When the annual report was submitted to the board, certain members openly questioned their confidence in Rowland. Leading the rebels was Sir Basil Smallpiece, the former Chairman of Cunard who'd been put on the board at the insistence of the Bank of England. Rowland forced a referendum. The shareholders voted overwhelmingly in his favour. Smallpiece and the others went into a hasty exile.

The Department of Trade then ordered a report which took three years to complete.

Rowland was emotionally hurt by the Smallpiece revolt, and that may account for those open doors on the sixth floor of his Cheapside Offices. It's a strange thought, but somewhere in the back of his mind he might want those doors open to reassure himself that none of his own are again plotting against him.

The 'boardroom coup' report was finally published in July 1976. In many ways it was critical of Rowland. Among other things, it detailed off-shore payments, heavy expenses, conflicts of interest over a copper mine in Rhodesia and suggestions that Lonrho had violated the 1965 sanctions ordered against Rhodesia. Given advance notice of the findings, Rowland bombarded the inspectors, his former bankers and those rebel directors with the most vitriolic responses. He also prepared dossiers on British companies he knew to have broken the sanctions. It created enough of a smoke-screen that he could

face some problems of his own making, notably that a group of Kuwaiti investors he'd just invited on to his board wanted a more important say in the running of Lonrho. In the end the Kuwaitis left the board, although they retained their holding.

The Department of Public Prosecutions recommended that no action be taken. But the sanction-breaking story reappeared, as if to haunt him, in May 1978 when Scotland Yard showed up asking for certain papers relative to the issue. Rowland fought back again, this time taking on David Owen who was Foreign Secretary.

'The problem with Tiny Rowland over sanction breaking', Owen recalls, 'was that he claimed to have documentation which he believed showed the British government had been involved and explicitly accepted that sanction breaking would continue back in 1967–8. I had established an independent inquiry, and I wanted to put the papers to them. But he was not prepared to let them free. He seemed to believe that you could negotiate with the British government. He would give the documentation in return for us letting him off the prosecution. But there was absolutely no way I could have dreamt of doing it even if I wanted to. There then grew a misunderstanding where I think, through talking to officials in my department, he got the impression that a deal had been made. In fact, no such deal had ever been made. But looking back at it, I understand why he got rather uptight about it. In his sort of world, deals are made which are not always expressed openly.'

Having seen Rowland close up, Owen feels one of the most interesting aspects of the man is the respect he commands in Africa.

'He hasn't got a trace of racial prejudice about him. That's one of his great virtues. He does deals and fixes things and organizes things exactly the same in Africa as if he were operating in London. And that's rather flattering. It's one of the reasons he's a success. He is also a loyal friend to people who help him when he's been in difficulties. That's the root of his friendship with Kenneth Kaunda who helped him when he was nearly ousted from Lonrho. I don't know the exact story, but I think you'll find that Kenneth Kaunda said, if you kick out Tiny Rowland then you don't do much more business in Zambia. Ever since, he had a great affection and understanding for Kenneth Kaunda. So when Kenneth Kaunda was on his uppers, when the Rhodesian sanctions were biting pretty hard, Rowland did everything in his power to sustain him and support him. In terms of his diplomacy, in some ways, Rowland was a nuisance. On the other hand, you couldn't help but admire the character.'

Owen sees Rowland as a great buccaneer. 'And like many buccaneers, they take short cuts. He's impatient with bureaucracy. I don't think a lot of his critics in England have ever understood the genuine affection that quite a lot of African countries have for him. He's certainly not an establishment figure, which is why the establishment dislike him of course. He's much too rough a diamond for them. But I say, if you had to quickly find out what was happening in Africa at this particular moment, you would get more information out of half an hour with Tiny Rowland than you would with the Foreign Secretary.'

That storm quietened down only to find the biggest one of all brewing on the horizon.

In February 1977 Rowland began building his stake in House of Fraser, first through a 25% holding in Scottish and Universal Investments, then directly through HoF shares. He got enough to put both himself and Duncan-Sandys on the HoF board. He then led Lonrho into a bid for SUITS, which put him on a collision course with the Monopolies and Mergers Commission. When they finally nodded okay, Lonrho acquired SUITS and topped up its HoF holding to 29.9%.

In January 1982 Lonrho saw Sir Hugh Fraser removed as Chairman, then bid for the company. But Professor Roland Smith, as Deputy Chairman, replaced Fraser and the MMC stepped in yet again. This time they ruled the bid would go against the public interest.

Having pledged not to increase his holding beyond 29.9%,

Rowland tacked into the wind with a plan to demerge Harrods from the House of Fraser. He reasoned, out of 130 stores, Harrods makes over 50% of the profits, so go with the profitable one and get rid of the rest. Smith answered that Harrods' profits were necessary to upgrade the rest of the group so that all the stores would one day be profitable.

Board meetings now got very nasty. Lonrho wanted rid of Smith, and Smith wanted rid of Rowland. An extraordinary general meeting was held on 6 May. A resolution against demerger and a vote of confidence for Smith was passed with a narrow majority of 1.8 million votes. Rowland managed to force another vote on 30 June. This time the demerger plan was effectively approved by a 53% majority of the shareholders. Except the cards were stacked. The motion required a 75% majority to win.

Cries of foul were heard all the way to the DTI. Someone thought it was pretty suspicious that four new shareholders, all buying abroad, had suddenly appeared on the scene to swing the vote to Lonrho. The DTI announced they'd investigate. That's when the Kuwaitis unloaded two million shares. A spokesman said they just felt the time was right to sell. Rowland noted they hadn't sold a single one of their 39 million shares for over three years. He suspected a leak from the opposite camp and asked for the sale to be subject to a Stock Exchange inquiry.

John Griffiths, CMG, QC was appointed by the DTI to carry out this investigation into Lonrho. He called over 175 witnesses, filled more than 400 pages with facts and theories, and couldn't prove that anyone had acted in concert for the demerger of Harrods.

So the battle for Harrods resumed.

Mohammed Fayed – who has for years called himself Al Fayed – was then 54. He claimed to be patriach of an old Egyptian family with interests on four continents. Together with his younger brothers Ali and Salah, their real estate holdings were said to include the Ritz Hotel in Paris, an apartment building on the Champs-Elysées, property in Egypt,

England and New York. Their shipping empire was said to consist of more than 40 ships, operating mainly out of Egypt and Italy. Their construction business was said to include projects in the Middle East such as the Port of Dubai and the Dubai Trade Centre, plus some oil exploration. Their banking interests were said to include the National Bancshares Corporation in Texas.

Born and educated in Alexandria, Mohammed Fayed always insisted his family was long established in cotton, that he'd taken his degree in Economics and at the age of 21 went into shipping. In 1961 his company, Middle East Navigation, was among other family businesses nationalized by the Nasser regime. That took the Fayeds to the Gulf States where they started again.

The truth is that he was born into a very poor family, that his father had been a schoolteacher and that his first job was as a sewing machine salesman. It is, frankly, a much more interesting story because he was obviously bright enough and ambitious enough to rise from there to become a man of wealth and stature.

Anyway, over the years, Rowland and Fayed had crossed paths several times. For instance, Rowland once purchased shares from Fayed in the civil engineering group Richard Costain. Mohammed Fayed even sat on the Lonrho board for a time in the '70s.

In late September 1984, at HoF's annual general meeting, Lonrho failed to get two more of its directors on to the board, although Rowland was re-elected. Exactly one month later, the Fayeds made a formal approach for Lonrho's stake. A deal was struck at £3 per share for 46.1 million shares. On 2 November, the Fayeds delivered a cheque to Lonrho for £138.3 million.

Although Lonrho could boast a £70-million profit, it appeared as though Rowland was finally giving up. At least it looked like that for three days until he came back on to the market and picked up a stake that made it the House of Fraser's second-largest single shareholder.

With a verdict due from the MMC on Lonrho's take-over

plans, the Fayeds announced in March 1985 that they would buy the entire group. Share prices shot up from near £3 to over £4. That's when Lonrho made the startling move of selling 9.7 million shares to the Fayeds. The deal netted Lonrho a £10-million profit, but also pushed the Fayeds past the 51.1% mark. Rowland, having kept 500,000 shares for Lonrho, said he expected the Fayed bid to be referred. That would drive the share prices down again, at which time Lonrho would be a buyer.

Rowland lobbied Trade and Industry Secretary Norman Tebbit. Questions were raised as to the source of funding that the Fayeds were using to buy Harrods. Was it their money or did some of it come from the Sultan of Brunei? Did some of it come from Dubai? Did some of it come from Kuwait? Rowland felt that the government clearly had a responsibility to assure equal treatment for all parties involved.

The DTI delayed one day before giving Lonrho permission to go beyond its previously restricted 29.9% limit, but added that the Fayed bid would not be referred to a take-over panel.

Utterly stunned, Tiny still refused to quit. He lobbied the Office of Fair Trading, claiming to the Director-General, Sir Gordon Borrie, that the Sultan of Brunei had given Mohammed Fayed a power of attorney for £1.5 billion, and it was that money which was used to buy the House of Fraser. If it was true and if Rowland could prove it, that would cast serious doubts on the Fayeds' story that they'd financed the entire acquisition themselves. Borrie asked for proof and Rowland refused to produce it at that time.

Speaking on behalf of the Fayeds, their bankers Kleinwort Benson admitted that the family had ties with the Sultan of Brunei and that Mohammed Fayed had acted on the Sultan's behalf in the purchase of the Dorchester Hotel. But, added the Fayeds, whatever powers of attorney existed were terminated before the HoF purchase.

Rowland demanded that the OFT look into the matter. Borrie stood his ground, saying he had no real evidence and that unless Lonrho was prepared to hand over the papers it purported to have, he couldn't act, or simply wouldn't act.

Furious, Rowland wrote to the Prime Minister: 'I believe that the decision to allow Mohammed Fayed to become the owner of the House of Fraser will prove to be a scandalous blot upon your Government's stewardship of the Department of Trade.'

How right that proved to be.

Now the Fayeds took the offensive. They protested that Rowland was using the *Observer* to launch unsupported allegations on their £615-million cash purchase of HoF. They pointed out that other papers, such as the *Sunday Times* and the *Financial Times*, had looked into Rowland's claims, and found nothing. They noted that the Sultan of Brunei himself had stepped forward to deny the claims. And that Kleinwort Benson's directors were totally satisfied that the monies used for the HoF acquisition were entirely Fayed family funds.

That's when Leon Brittan, the former Home Secretary, stepped in wearing his new hat as boss at the DTI. Brittan wrote to Lonrho that he could see no reason to reopen the case. He said that as long as no one had come forward with new evidence, hinting that Rowland's refusal to present what new evidence he claimed to have might mean that none existed, the matter would stand as is.

Brittan was replaced by Paul Channon who, with an election in sight, finally gave in and ordered an official investigation which resulted in the now famous report. But Channon was succeeded by Lord Young who read the report and refused to publish it. His excuse was that the Serious Fraud Squad needed time to investigate certain aspects of it. Young spent nearly two years saying that he wanted to publish the report but couldn't do it just yet.

Then came Nicholas Ridley.

Due almost entirely to Lonrho's insistence – at one point they even took Lord Young to court – it seemed as though by March 1990 the government had run out of excuses. Ridley had to publish it.

The report raised serious questions about the Fayeds, alleging that they'd supplied birth certificates which they knew to be false; that they'd not come from an old Egyptian family with interests in shipping, cotton and industry; that they'd altered their names from Fayed to Al Fayed; and that they'd knowingly misled the regulatory authorities at the time of the HoF bid. In short, the report stated that the Fayeds had dishonestly misrepresented their background, their wealth and their business interests.

Throughout the affair, both sides used the press. Rowland brought out several interesting volumes, in the spirit of old-fashioned pamphleteer, among them *A Hero From Zero*, the story of Kleinwort Benson and Mohammed Fayed. But his mainstay was the *Observer*, where stories hammered away at the Fayeds and the government, long after all the other papers had given up. The *Observer* even came out with a mid-week extra, containing large sections of the then still-banned DTI report. The government sued for an injunction and within hours had all copies removed from the street.

The Fayeds took a different, equally pragmatic approach. They sent whatever stories ran to their attorneys and answered many of them with libel writs, which served to keep most journalists far enough away.

It wasn't until the report was out that one could see how the press had been manipulated. But the press wasn't alone. William Rees-Mogg, writing in the *Independent* on 12 March 1990, hit the nail on the head. In his article, 'Shame on all their houses', he accused the press, the City and the government of gullibility and cowardice throughout the affair.

'The integrity of the City and of our system of company regulation is the issue at stake. That counts for more than Harrods or Brunei. It is a concern the City, the press and the government have, in this case, done singularly little to protect.'

Ask questions in the corridors at Lonrho and 'background sources' tell you the reason the report was so late in being published was to protect the Sultan of Brunei.

They claim the Sultan rules on an emergency decree that

must be renewed every three months and through that decree has his hands on virtually all the Shell oil production in Brunei. That, they claim, is worth $25 billion a year which is how he can afford to buy and refurbish the Dorchester and buy the Beverly Hills Hotel and build a palace for his second wife with 22-carat-gold ceilings.

They claim that in order to keep himself in power, much like the Shah, he's come to an understanding with the British foreign office who provide protection for him through MI-6.

They claim, the government couldn't publish the report without embarrassing the Sultan and Mr Tebbit, Lord Young and the then Chancellor Nigel Lawson.

The way they tell that story, the pound was scraping all-time lows when the Sultan met with Margaret Thatcher at Downing Street on 29 January 1985. Mohammed Fayed attended the meeting. The Prime Minister expressed her worries about the weakness of sterling and the Sultan offered to help. Over the next several weeks, with the Bank of England too depleted of reserves to have any further effect, the Sultan personally purchased £5 billion-worth of sterling. Working discreetly with one particular merchant bank, they claim that he and he alone brought sterling off the floor. Implicating him now in the Harrods affair, they claim, would simply not be the way to pay back a friend.

The only problem with that is it doesn't seem to match with what really happened.

On the evening of 29 January 1985 sterling closed at $1.1177. Although it rose to $1.1297 over the next two days, by 1 February the pound was falling again and by 28 February, a full four weeks after the Sultan is said to have agreed to intervene, the pound was down to $1.0820. It eventually bottomed out at around $1.03. Now, it's very possible that he took his time doing it and didn't really become a player until much later that spring. But the likelihood that the Sultan single-handedly saved the pound is remote.

On the other side of the fence, former BBC correspondent Michael Cole speaks for the Fayeds. He claims there never was a take-over battle between Rowland the Fayeds for the House of Fraser because Rowland willingly sold 36% of the company to the Fayeds.

He suggests, 'Perhaps Lonrho could not afford House of Fraser in 1985 and perhaps Mr Rowland has been trying ever since to recapture the chance which he threw away at that time. Perhaps the whole matter has simply become the obsession of an ageing man. Whatever the circumstances, Lonrho's shareholders are at least £20 million poorer and Mr Rowland can no longer capture the dream which has become everyone else's nightmare.'

Back at Lonrho the 'background source' explains, 'We were unable to mount a bid, being trapped by the government's insistence on an MMC investigation. We sold our 29% with a view to making a full-scale bid. But the government meanwhile made damn sure Fayed got 51% before Lonrho could launch their bid. Fayed's bid should have been referred but they ducked that in order not to have the can of worms opened. We sold 29% because we felt we would never get this thing off our backs, that we were never going to get permission to own Harrods unless there was a change of attitude. We sold our shares believing, mistakenly I suppose, that no one would approve of Fayed buying House of Fraser. We knew his background and assumed that, just as we'd been referred, he would be. But the government wouldn't have it.'

When the DTI report was published, quite clearly vindicating Rowland's claims about the Fayeds, the first question everyone asked him was, will you now go after Harrods?

Rowland's answer was, 'I wouldn't want it.'

When asked, why not, he responded, 'Getting Harrods is not what this fight has been all about.'

It's easy to see what he means. The fight had long since gone beyond having anything to do with Harrods. He was angry, he wanted to get even and he didn't care what it cost him. He says he never spent anything like £20 million, but he doesn't quantify the figure.

The Fayeds simply claim that Tiny shot himself in the foot

when he sold those remaining shares and only God can take Harrods away from them now.

Tiny vows to continue the fight.

But Tiny is 72 and he can't fight for ever.

It's not surprising then that there should be some concern about the future of the company. He can't run Lonrho for ever either. Except in the corridors at Lonrho they tell you there is no talk about the future of Lonrho without Tiny.

They tell you, 'We don't talk about succession around here. Tiny is fit and well and young and to sit around and ghoulishly deliberate is a very unhealthy atmosphere. Those things have a way of sorting themselves out.'

It's fairly well known in City circles that Tiny has not groomed a successor. Nor is he likely to at this point. While one or two of the directors have some flair, none of them is another Tiny Rowland. In the end, it may all come down to what Mrs Rowland wants. She's reportedly promised Tiny not to sell any shares for ten years after he's gone. That will give her a powerful voice in the company's future and in the man or men who will lead it. The most likely possibility is, at first, that a small group of insiders will form a committee, two or three or four of them, much like what happened at Shell after Sir Henry Deterding. The company will go on.

But without Tiny, it simply can't be the same.

8

Paul Raymond

The ashtray is still there.

The lipstick-stained cigarette butts are long gone.

Five years ago, in the middle of the ashtray in the middle of the lobby of Paul Raymond's office, above the theatre that used to be The Windmill and then La Vie en Rose, there were six cigarette butts – all of them ringed with bright red lipstick.

Oh how that lipstick filled one's brain with visions of some nubile lass, down from the provinces, just off the train at Victoria with no place to come but here . . . Okay, I'll do it but, I mean, do I actually have to take off all my clothes? . . . She waits in the lobby, chain-smoking, until HE appears, sporting a wide-brimmed hat and large lapels, literally dripping in gold chains and smoking a huge cigar . . . Come into my office my dear and slip out of that sweet little dress because, after all, we have to see what it is you've got to offer . . . and yes, certainly I can make you a star . . . now if you'd care for a little champagne while we discuss your career . . .

Reality is made of less romantic stuff.

No wide-brimmed hat. No large lapels. No gold chain collection. He smokes cigarettes. And there is no casting couch. In fact, at a distance of three feet, the bad boy of British business is considerably less sinister-looking than your average High Street bank manager.

He left school at the age of 15 – that would have been in 1940 – worked in markets and a shirt factory, and somewhere along the way learned to play the drums. Then he flogged nail varnish and hairnets at funfairs – slightly reminiscent of those snake oil salesman of yesteryear. But he gave that up to do a mind-reading act that he bought for £25 from a couple of palm readers at Clacton Pier. His father was a haulage contractor in Liverpool, although the old man disappeared when the family moved to Glossop. One grandfather was a cop in Liverpool. His mother always wanted him to have a proper job, you know, like an insurance salesman. But show business had bitten him. So for a while, after the snake oil, he was a part-time drummer and a full-time mind-reader. He might have preferred it the other way around, but he had to earn a living. It was only after doing his mind-reading act for the millionth time that he began to understand how real money might be made by booking acts, instead of being one.

The huckster turned mind-reader became an impresario.

The day he managed to talk two ladies in his show out of their clothes, Vaudeville Express became Festival of Nudes and the impresario became Paul Raymond.

'That is my real name,' he says, 'although I wasn't born with that name.'

Just to keep the record straight, he was born with the name Geoffrey Anthony Quinn.

'I suppose I changed it originally before I did the mind-reading act. I was a drummer in a band. And in those days, much like today, people in show business often changed their names. I was Gene Raymond, after Gene Krupa, one of the greatest drummers in the world. I wasn't as good as him, but you know, when you're young you go through all of that. Then there was Geoff Carlson, an appalling name. Then Geoff Raymond. And then came Paul Raymond. I've been Paul Raymond since my variety act days. Everyone knew me as that and it came to confusion when I started going abroad with a passport in the name of Geoffrey Anthony Quinn. There would be a phone call for Paul Raymond and I would be registered as Geoffrey Quinn. Or they'd know me as Paul Raymond and someone would ask for Mr Quinn and they'd say they'd never heard of him. In the end it was either go back to my original name or officially change it. It was easier to stay Paul Raymond.'

Not that it bothers him, no longer being Geoffrey Anthony Quinn. He doesn't miss it any more than he misses being a mind reader.

'Not at all. I don't miss not being on a stage. And I never do my mind-reading act, not even at parties. In fact, I'm very pleased. Had I been all that good I might still be doing my mind-reading act for a living.'

He earns his living these days as Chairman, Chief Executive Officer and owner of the Paul Raymond Organization Ltd – a series of companies he built from the ground up on the theory that men will pay money to look at ladies who aren't wearing clothes.

Raised a Catholic – 'No, I do not see any contradiction between being a Catholic, which I still am, and also being in the business I am' – he has, like Hugh Hefner of *Playboy* and Bob Guccione of *Penthouse*, long since managed to diversify, although his power base remains the naked lady industry. And while he didn't care to discuss his personal wealth five years ago – which was then estimated at £30–£50 million – he wasn't quite so shy this time. He said his property interests alone are worth £50–55 million and that his group profits in 1989 were in the neighbourhood of £7.5 million.

Not bad for an empire that was only conceived in the '50s, when he was booking shows for the variety hall circuit.

'How it all started really, was in the touring days, after my act, when I was producing shows in the UK. Towards the end, I had about 10 shows which each toured for about 40 weeks a year. This is the time when the music hall was dying yet all my shows did very very well.'

Some of his bigger successes from those days are now nothing more than memories and hand bills in simple frames scattered around his offices. *Follies Parisiennes*, twice nightly, featuring the only moving nudes. And, *Nude Neat and Naughty*. And, *Paris after Dark*. And *Piccadilly Peepshow*. For their day, they were pretty provocative. At times they were also filled with some rather elaborate stunts. For instance, *Les Nues de Paris* featured ladies undressed, standing in the middle of a cage where a lion tamer and a live lion did their thing.

'It wasn't pure burlesque because in burlesque there were strippers and the burlesque comics. You could say mine was an English version of American burlesque, for the want of a better word. They were revues, variety acts, and production numbers with the girls.'

There were no stars in any of these shows, although Shirley Bassey had seventh billing in one and in another he employed Larry Grayson.

'In 1955 Larry Grayson played in one of my shows at £25 a week. He wanted a rise to £27.50 the next year and I said no. He left.'

Raymond learned the business from the bottom up – how to stage shows, how to promote shows, the ins and outs of being an impresario. But some of those lessons came expensive.

'One of the best lessons I ever had was in the mid-'50s when I took a show to a nightclub in Vienna. It was a disaster. Yet I think I probably learned more from that time than anything else I have ever done. You see, one of the most difficult things to do is to get laughs. But if you're doing an international trade, it's very difficult to talk. The French don't understand, the Germans don't, and in the States it's a different sense of humour than it is here. So you do it visually. That's the best way to get laughs. But I wasn't too sure about that then and for the show in Vienna we booked two guys to speak a few words. They were Jewish comics. Two guys I had known for a long time. One did a clown act with a bit of Yiddish thrown in. The other could only speak a bit of Yiddish. It was close to German and I really thought everyone would understand so we could get laughs. I didn't know it but in 1954 they were anti-Jewish there. Believe me, the show was a disaster. I'm not saying only because of that, but it helped. However, what I did manage to do was learn a lot about the nightclub scene where before all I knew was the variety hall scene. I think I learned from that experience how to run the Raymond Revuebar.'

It was probably the Raymond Revuebar that took him from small-time impresario into the big time.

'The actual turning point? Well, I guess it all depends on what you call big time. There was no one deal. But certainly one would have to say the touring shows were important because they gave me the money to start the Raymond Revuebar. Or you could say that it was the Raymond Revuebar which then made that money into a lot more. And that money allowed me to expand.'

He opened a private club in 1958 with somewhere between £10,000 and £15,000 – he says he honestly can't remember the exact figure. He raised the money himself, although he nearly had a partner. There was a fellow he knew named Harry Kaufman who was a theatrical agent and also a very successful shoe manufacturer. The deal was to be Raymond 60%, and Kaufman 40%. But, on the day the contracts were to be signed, Kaufman suggested Raymond had got the figures the wrong way round. Raymond ripped up the contract and took on the world all by himself.

The Raymond Revuebar had to be a membership club because in the old days you couldn't do that type of show unless it was a club. Ten years later a change in the Theatres Act meant the Lord Chamberlain no longer had a say in what was done on the English stage. And that meant Raymond could run his Revuebar like a theatre. It was a major step. Foreign visitors didn't have to wait three days for their membership. He could sell tickets at the box office. That increased his revenue. His audience widened. Also, as a club he used to change his show every few months, trying to get the same people coming back. But as a theatre he could change the show less often, say every six months, then every year. That helped cut down on expenses. Profits became important.

These days he changes parts of the Revuebar show whenever he feels like it. He insists that it's a much more expensive show today than it ever was. Cast and crew wages have gone up, and so has his production budget. Sets are more elaborate. Lighting is more complex. But the show is still a money-maker. The

Revuebar averages around 500 tickets per night at £15. That's £45,000 a week. Drinks are extra, but the prices are way below the Soho norm.

£45,000 a week converts to £2.34 million per year.

The interesting thing is, he's hardly changed the original formula. It remains what it has always been – erotica mixed with humour.

'The show is acceptable but I wouldn't necessarily call it respectable. If it was respectable, people wouldn't come. The audience has changed from the early days. Then we had the older men who would look around, up and down the street, and dart in. Now they walk straight in. We get a much younger crowd than we did, and a lot more women. The show is much sexier, but I am an entertainer, not a pornographer. I have nothing coarse like those Sunday pub scenes with everyone shouting "Get 'em off" at the stripper.'

It goes without saying that, like much of London theatre, the Revuebar is a tourist attraction – for the Japanese and the Germans, and also for the lads down from Manchester on the razzle. There's nothing wrong with that and he never pretends that it's anything else. He knows exactly what audience he's catering for. And he's made his fortune by understanding that, for many tourists, London is The Tower, Big Ben and the Revuebar. It's a fair bet that if Flo Ziegfeld had been born in Liverpool, he would have been Paul Raymond.

Not that the Revuebar was a success from the start. Within a few days of the opening, the cops raided the joint. They took down the names and addresses of the 165 people in the audience. But within two years police harassment had pretty much subsided, and Kenneth Allsop, writing in the *Spectator*, observed that among the Revuebar's 70,000 members were 'enough businessmen and captains of industry to drain dry the Stock Exchange and the Savoy Grill'.

Raymond has had other run-ins with the police over his shows. Most of the time the charges proved fruitless, especially in the case where one police sergeant found it necessary to see a nude show no less than five times before he tried to close it.

'If I thought I was doing something wrong, I would not do it. People who talk about corruption always say it is not they who have been corrupted but someone else.'

He's won most of his battles, although one notable loss was the time he was fined a total of £10,000 for running a disorderly house.

'That was way back in the beginning. Running a disorderly house is a charge that isn't used much these days, but it certainly was then. It's from a law dating back to 1820-odd, and can be used on anybody who either has a stage show or a club that the police are rather against. It has nothing to do with prostitution or anything. It's something the cops can use when people get drunk and disorderly or shout obscene things. But it doesn't mean to say it's that as well. Because that wasn't the case regarding the Raymond Revuebar. In the early days, when we were backing up against the law the whole time, they went for us all the time because we were new and what we were doing had never been seen before. Running a disorderly house was the law they dug up.'

With money coming in from the Revuebar, he quickly began to expand. He bought the Windmill Theatre and the Whitehall Theatre and flooded the West End with shows – either as Paul Raymond Productions or shows merely booked into his theatres. In 1969, at the Whitehall, he opened a show called *Pyjama Tops* which featured lots of ladies without pyjama bottoms. That show was in profit within nine weeks, ran for a total of six years and grossed over £2 million. There was *Come into My Bed, Let's Get Laid* and, of course, *Oh! Calcutta*. They all made big money. His assessment of what the public wanted to see was proving right. Occasionally though, he missed, like he did with *Royalty Follies,* which cost £350,000 to stage and lost him a cool half-million.

As a theatre owner and theatrical producer, Raymond found himself in something of a minor crunch a few years ago when the West End looked as if it might be dying. *Anyone for Denis* closed at the Whitehall. It wasn't his production, he was just renting them the stage. And there didn't seem to be much around to take its place. So he invented the Theatre of War.

'I was sitting at home one Sunday afternoon, thinking what I should do at the Whitehall and came up with this idea. I spent nine months buying Second World War stuff. I made contacts with people who were experts, and they had contacts who knew about planes and tanks and that sort of thing. It cost me a lot of actual money today because some of this stuff in 1946 you could get for free.'

He hyped it as 'the greatest presentation of Second World War items in the UK. I think it had a great educational and historic value. At that time it was difficult to get a stage show in'.

A veteran of the RAF – 'I played the drums in the band for a time, then was put on a telephone switchboard. I liked that job because I was on shift work and you could always give someone a couple of bob to do your shift. You could only be there three days a week' – he says he spent around £1.7 million transforming the Whitehall and buying the equipment for the Theatre of War. But his name never appeared on the marquee. And that was very much on purpose.

'I didn't put my name to the Theatre of War because people would think there were naked ladies sitting on the side of the aircraft. That's what has happened to my name now. But I don't complain. As a matter of fact I am more than pleased because all I have to do now, if it has anything to do with sex, is to put my name to it and they will know exactly what it is all about. I don't complain about that at all because for 30-odd years I've been trying to build up a name.'

Within two years he ran up against Westminster City Council who claimed he'd changed the usage of the Whitehall Theatre by turning it into a museum.

'I argued that a theatre of war is the same thing as an actual theatre. They argued that it wasn't. They won, I appealed and they won again. Quite frankly, they were right. Oh, well, it was a good try.'

Westminster Council said he had to close the museum, so he

sold everything in it at auction for around £300,000. He took his losses, then sold the Whitehall as well, glad, he says, to be rid of it.

In 1964 he took his first dive into the world of magazines.

'I started a magazine called *King*. We started the same week and the same month as *Penthouse*. The first month we sold 75,000, which was very big for those days. *Penthouse* sold 40,000. The second month we sold 65,000 and they sold 55,000. Third month we sold 40,000 and they sold 65,000. *King* was originally to be the magazine of the Raymond Revuebar. But my editors and I didn't see eye to eye, so I gave it to them. I came out of the publishing side and swore I'd never go into it again.'

He swallowed about £30,000 worth of losses, but didn't keep his promise. Ten years later he tried again.

'A guy came to interview me for a magazine called *Men Only*. We got along very very well. He was then the editor, and he told me it was going downhill. Eventually he asked me if I was interested.'

That magazine was selling 35,000 copies when he paid £10,000 for the title. Within a month, by calling it *Paul Raymond's Men Only*, the circulation was up to 85,000. Now he's got a stable of magazines *Men Only, Club, Escort, Razzle*, and the *Model Directory* are monthly. There's a quarterly called *The Best of —*. Then there's a *Club* and a magazine called *Club International* which are edited in Britain but aimed specifically at the States – they're considerably stronger magazines than their namesakes in the UK. They also do a French edition out of London. Some years ago he franchised his magazines in places like Brazil but that ran into trouble when the Brazilians stopped paying in advance.

'We had been producing a magazine for them for two years that was a mixture of the English magazine and the American version. The States was too strong for Brazil and the British version too weak. Well, when we franchise we want so much money up front before we ship the goods. And in Brazil I don't have to tell you that with inflation and the difficulties in getting money out, anyone dealing with countries like that must be very very careful. Like all things, even supplying shirts, if you don't get paid you no longer supply the shirts.'

While he says he doesn't control every word of editorial or every cartoon that goes into his magazines – he's more concerned with the business side of them – he definitely doesn't neglect the editorial side.

'One, in my view, must let the editor run his magazine otherwise he can't work, providing he works to guidelines of what the magazine is all about. So the editor should have most of the control. At one time I okayed the centrefold and read all the copy. I don't have the time to do it now. I look through at proof stage and if there's anything I think really should come out, then I suggest that it come out. It's better to suggest than to insist.' Here he shrugs. 'Which is the same thing.'

Well, not always.

A few years ago he installed a new editorial director for his magazines and she's got a little more pull with the boss than most of the other editors. Raymond's daughter Debbie has taken over a lot of the day-to-day running of the magazines, and is – like Hugh Hefner and his daughter Christie – the obvious heir apparent.

'Heiress to the empire?' He grins with fatherly pride. 'I suppose, yes.'

But the empire she'll one day rule over is under seige. In recent years there have been some serious moves afoot to ban such magazines from general sale. It's something that concerns him greatly, not only from a commercial point of view but also because he feels that censorship of any kind is very dangerous.

'There have always been moves to stop men's magazines from publishing and every few years a bunch of MPs get together and sign a petition. You know, stop page-three girls and stop men's magazines, that sort of thing. It goes in cycles. I've been hearing the same things for 30-odd years. But it concerns me more lately than it ever has. Especially when newspapers and magazines take an editorial viewpoint in favour of any kind of censorship. I mean, how can the *News of the World* be taken seriously when they campaign against men's magazines? The argument isn't really whether or not topless girls are right or wrong, it's whether or not censorship is right or wrong. And if we lose that argument, free speech could be next.'

From magazines and theatres, he branched out into real estate – probably a natural extension of his interest in owning theatres. And these days Paul Raymond happens to be a major landowner in Soho and a bullish buyer.

'I am certainly a very large real-estate owner in Soho. I think in the past five years my real-estate interests have quadrupled. It's mostly commercial, you know, offices and shops, with some residential mixed in because it's part of the block. The wealth of the freeholds is tremendous. The beauty is that we're not heavily geared so we don't have to rely on paying back the bank. I've invested in real estate here because in my view Soho is going to become very big in not many years' time. I think it's going to be like Covent Garden. It has to happen here. It can't go any place else. The West End can only come into Soho. It can't go to Whitehall. It has to come this way. Values here in the last five years have gone up, out of all proportion.'

They continue to climb, in spite of the fact that since 1982 landlords could no longer get the astronomically high rents they used to demand from the sex shops and cinemas. That commerce, a part of Soho life that most residents would like to see controlled and continued – as opposed to abolished – is indeed being controlled now. A total clean-up of Soho would have changed it into something other than Soho and no one seems to want that. Least of all Raymond.

So when the Westminster City Council enacted licensing laws and a quota system on sex shops and sex cinemas, he was one of the very first to say, 'Quite rightly. Sex shops should be controlled. It couldn't go on the way it was before with doors filled with people, scruffy people at the door, the places were filthy. I don't think anyone in his right mind ought to complain about a sex shop. If you want to go buy sex toys, so go buy sex toys. But let's have them run in a nice way. They were opening up all over the place until the new law came in. Now they want to know who the owner is and who's behind it. Which is quite right. Although I don't think anyone here wants the Council to take over the place. They don't object to sex here, as long as we don't have indecent photographs in the streets, offending people, but I also think it's important for Soho to keep a bit of sleaze. We've got to have the right mix of food and shops and sex. It's a very special neighbourhood'.

He would say that. After all, he's got a major investment to protect, which in some ways explains why this has become a very favourite subject.

'Take displays in windows. I don't think it's right that, if a man and a woman are walking down the street with their little boy or girl, they should have to see all these displays. If you want to do it inside, okay. Of course, worse than that are the clip joints, the so-called topless bars where live sex . . . I mean, if they were doing live sex, okay. At least you're not being clipped. If that's what you want to see, at least you're paying for it. But people, more so from abroad than from out of town, won't see any show at all. They get clipped for £100 for near-beer or a so-called glass of champagne, which is not champagne. And some girl sits there with her top off and says, have one more drink, and it's £30 for her to sit down. I think that's a disgrace and is very bad for Soho. Clipping is one of the worst things here. It gives the police a lot of trouble too. What happens is that people go and complain, but if they come from abroad they're not going to come back to go to court. So there's nothing much anyone can do.'

It's happening less and less now that the powers-that-be have taken it upon themselves to carefully gentrify Soho. To keep the sexual overtones, but add better shopping and better restaurants and better housing. To block off certain streets as pedestrian streets. That's what he likes to see.

'I think the Trocadero site, which is not doing all that well, helps the place. I am not involved with that site, but I like the idea. I'd like to see more retail shops in Soho. I'm not saying that Gucci and Armani should come to Soho, but there should be good shopping. And more restaurants. And then the licensing laws do terrible damage. This has been going on for years. I'd love to stay open till 3 a.m. but the people who live around here say, oh no, too much noise, we don't want places open after 12 o'clock. Even the Soho Society, which has done a bit of good to be fair, is also against places being open late at night. Now, if you're going to close Soho at 11, there will be no Soho. That's the end of it as an entertainment centre.'

For many years another factor about Soho and investment there – too important perhaps to overlook or even to take lightly – was the mob element. Anyone bringing a business into Soho in competition with the local mob, especially the Maltese, could be inviting trouble. Raymond's operation is obviously far too big to have to worry. Although, according to him, 'I've been here 33 years and when I first started people said to me, you've got no chance, they won't let you live there, they'll control you. But it never happened. I pay my rates and if there is any trouble I'll call the police. You don't have to be tough with your fists. You've got to be tough with your head'.

Of course for years there have been rumours that the reason Raymond has never had any serious problems with the mob is because he's part of the mob, or controlled by the mob. It's something that he thinks is pretty funny.

'A lot of people think we have Mafia connections, which we haven't. But a lot of people seem to think I have. I suppose they think it's because I'm in the business that I am, and in Soho, and I've never been involved in any fights or anyone wrecking the place. Once upon a time someone who knew me years ago was told, leave Paul Raymond alone because he has Mafia finance behind him. They've been watching too many films. They see the Al Capone image and it's a natural thing if you're in the nightclub business – except I'm not running a nightclub – but they expect you to have a big Al Capone hat on, and big broad shoulders and a couple of blondes and, that's what they expect. I think they're rather amazed when they find out it isn't so.'

While he admits to having a certain knack in certain fields, not everything he touches turns to gold. At one point there was a foray into computer leasing.

'I thought it was something that would be a good investment for the company and make money. We leased computers to companies and councils throughout the UK. It was a pretty substantial operation. But we closed that down in 1989. I'd set it up because there were certain tax advantages which have now been stopped and I decided there was no point in continuing.'

When video hit the scene, he bought a wholesaler called Carnaby Video. It seemed like a good idea at the time. But he got his fingers burnt there too and closed it within six months.

'It was a disaster. I shouldn't have bought it in the first place. But it was the time when video was fairly new and lots of people were going into it and this was one of the main video wholesale firms. At that time, films came out from MGM and other studios and many of them started doing their own distribution of their own films. There was a lot of video shops, but there was a lot of the wrong type of person at that time going into the video game, like with all things that are new. No, my view on video today is, sure, if you're making a film it's got to come out in that way. But once the novelty's worn off, especially with cable coming out, unless it's a very good film you want to see, you're not going to sit at home and watch some old film. So I closed that out. I took a loss of about £250,000. I guess you could say I haven't got much faith in video. Even less now than I might have had a few years ago.'

He has however made some money in films, having partially financed two and fully financed two others – films like *Erotica*, *Let's Get Laid*, and *Hardcore*, which wasn't really hardcore.

'Film financing? Yes, we made some money, not enough to retire. But each film I was involved with was a success.'

He's also recently opened a new nightclub. Not quite what you might expect from Paul Raymond, the place is called

Madam Jo-Jo's. He says it's not exactly a transvestite room, but the boys who serve the drinks are dressed as girls and Madame Jo-Jo is a man. The show is all men in drag, although there is one girl.

'It's a fun place. There are straights and gays and people who don't know which way, in-people and yuppies, rock stars, everybody. It's an idea I had for many years. I started it in 1987 and it's a very in place, filled with people you'd never expect to see in a room like that.'

Most surprising of all, he's closed down the Windmill Theatre, once the home of his big revue, *La Vie En Rose*.

'I think the days of big revue shows are over. At least for the time being. You always hear people saying that someone should try to bring them back, but they lose money. *Ziegfield* was a flop at the Palladium and the producers lost hundreds of thousands of pounds.'

He took his own beating with *La Vie En Rose*, moved a disco in there called Paramount City and eventually, rather cleverly, turned the place into the only television theatre in central London.

'There are some small TV facilities in Soho, but they're really only for talking heads kinds of shows. You couldn't put an audience in there. I realized that with the television explosion in the next few years there was a need for a TV theatre, and the Windmill was ideal. There is nothing at all like it in central London and it has, since the beginning of 1990, been the home of the Derek Jameson Show for Sky television. The BBC is now planning on using it at least twice a week.'

Not counting the cast and crew at the Raymond Revuebar, he employs something like 65 people.

'We don't over-employ staff. I don't believe you should have staff unless they've got work to do. I'd like to think I delegate well. I'd like to think I'm a good manager. I don't think my staff will agree with me. But I think I am. I am not, however, a workaholic. What I like to do is come in at half-past two and leave at half-past six or seven. I like to, but I haven't always been able to. I have however slowed down a little. All the main decisions are still mine, but the day-to-day running of the business is left to the staff. I just oversee the whole thing because, after all, it's my money. It's important to have your finger on the pulse. When things are going good the company runs itself. When things are not going good, that's when you need a strong boss.'

He lives alone these days but can't imagine anyone seeing him as being a particularly eligible bachelor. 'I wouldn't have thought so. I go out less these days, but then I've never been one for going to Stringfellows to pick up young birds. One has had one's fair share, of course. Anyway, I don't think I could possibly live with any person all the time any more.'

He says he doesn't golf or fish, and he sold the houseboat he used to keep in the South of France many years ago. He used to travel a lot, when he was looking for new acts to book, but he stopped doing that a long time ago too. Antigua is a place he likes very much and for the past few years has been going there at least twice a year.

'I love being a real beach bum.'

Not having to worry about where your next conch is coming from is one way to measure success.

On the other hand, if he'd become Britain's greatest snake oil salesman, or another Gene Krupa, or if he'd truly mastered his mind-reading act to the point of Command Performances, there are some very obvious ways that success would be recognized. But as the man who's given the world the Raymond Revuebar, one wonders if he ever dreams about OBEs and knighthood. A royal warrant? Sir Paul?

'Absolutely impossible.' He roars with laughter. 'No, I can say that categorically, never! I could donate £10 million to charity and there isn't a chance of that. But then again, it's always a good thing to know what your limitations are.'

9

The house that James and Gordon built used to be called Hanson Trust but in 1986 they got themselves a listing on the New York Stock Exchange and, in New Yorkese, 'Trust' (as in 'Trust Company') is an old-fashioned type of bank while 'trust' (as in 'trust me') is what the fellow wants you to do when he offers to sell you the Brooklyn Bridge.

So they changed names to Hanson PLC.

But everything else stayed the same. They're still James and Gordon – Lord and Sir respectively. Hanson is still Chairman of the PLC. White is still Chairman of Hanson Industries, the wholly-owned Stateside subsidiary.

According to some of those who claim to know, White is the thinker and Hanson is the administrator.

'I guess I'm the more entrepreneurial of the two,' White says. 'Most of my time is simply spent thinking. No one thinks any more. Everyone is too busy spewing out paper. But decisions can't be made by committee. Someone has to make them.'

According to a few others who claim to know, White is the buyer and Hanson is the seller.

'I am very good at selling,' Hanson concedes, 'although so is Gordon. But he has this worry about doing anything. Once he's decided to do something and does it, he then worries about whether or not he's done the right thing. That may be all right when you're buying but with the selling side, that's difficult because you often have to make an adjustment at the last moment. I'm a relatively good horse-trader.'

Frankly, it hardly matters who's who because the two are, at least in business, interchangeable to the point that Hanson could run the US operation and White could run the UK operation, and no one would ever know the difference. They are cut from the same super-opportunistic mould. If someone offers to sell them a pound for 50p, they feel an obligation to buy. If someone offers to buy their 50p for a pound, they feel an obligation to sell.

Such is their reputation that – so the story goes – the Hanson helicopter landed on the roof of the wrong company one morning and that company's shares went up by 20% because the neighbours figured there was a bid in the offing.

In the meantime, Hanson and White are probably the most admired entrepreneurs in Britain today.

James Hanson was once a part-time entrepreneur and a full-time playboy. His most famous engagement was to a then-unknown Audrey Hepburn. Gordon White shared his interest in small-time business and big-time ladies, although he refuses to name-drop. Growing up in Yorkshire, he'd been best friends with James's brother Billy. When Billy died young, White says, he inherited James.

'We just sort of drifted into a friendship. We think alike. Sometimes it's weird how alike we can be. We'll come into a meeting and find that we're both wearing the same shirt and tie.'

Hanson's family had been in the transport business for more than a hundred years. Horse-drawn carts across the Pennines. He was running the Wiles Group, a Yorkshire fertilizer manufacturer and hirer of sacks, with interests in the trucking business. White tells people he was in publishing, although it was really more like the official programmes at sporting events.

Before long they thought about going into business together. They'd both seen humorous greetings cards in the States, decided that the same idea would work in Britain and started the Hanson and White Greeting Card Company. It's still in business, but they don't own it any more. They gave it up, only to find a few years later that they could no longer use the

Hanson and White name. James suggested they buy back their names, but Gordon said it wasn't worth the trouble. So in 1964 they called their business Hanson Trust.

Hanson, now 68, is based in London, and spends part of the year in Palm Springs. White, two years younger – but at 6'5" is three inches taller – is based in New York and spends part of the year in London. Hanson is on White's board but White is not on Hanson's board. That's by his own choice, which is probably indicative of just how secure the two are in their partnership.

Explains Hanson, 'Gordon and I are both very familiar with what's going on in the minds of the people who run this business and in the minds of the shareholders on both sides of the Atlantic. Inevitably, he does much more over there and I do things over here, but we talk a great deal and the lines are growing narrower. Anyway, Gordon and I are really just the front men. There's a very solid partnership in the company with four or five other people and when we sit down, if one of us has particularly strong views, the others will certainly try to dampen that enthusiasm.'

As defined by Hanson, the company is in the business of industrial management, of buying businesses or developing businesses to make them more successful. Hanson PLC is Imperial Tobacco, Ever Ready batteries, Consolidated Gold Fields, Butterley Brick, London Brick and ARC Limited. It's Hanson Amalgamated Industries (bathroom products), Lindustries (heating control systems and Seven Seas health products) and Hanson Engineering (stainless steel brewing equipment). Hanson Industries is Smith Corona, Kidde, Newmont Mining, SCM Chemicals, Hanson Housewares (small kitchen appliances), Hanson Recreation (Tommy Armour golf equipment), a lighting company, a building products company, an office products company, a firm that makes aerial access equipment and another that manufactures aircraft seating and galleys.

With over 150 companies on both sides of the Atlantic, the basic Hanson philosophy is strictly hands-off management.

'I know everyone preaches that and no one ever practises it,' says White, 'but we really do. I've never visited a plant or a headquarters. I've never gone to look at what I'm buying. I don't know why I'd even want to. I don't believe in royal visits. The guy who makes the money for the company is the guy who runs it. When we take over an operation, we're not interested in firing corporate people, we just send them back to the division where the money is made. Corporate headquarters, that's us, well we're there to lend them money and constantly review budgets. And to incentivize divisional management. The lower the budget, the quicker the incentives kick in. So what we do is to make certain that the divisional managers work with budgets that are fair.'

In reality they have an enormous hand in management because they hold the purse strings. Once a budget is approved, no one can spend more than £750 without the Chairman's personal okay. But except for budgets, there's no meddling in the businesses. Hanson and White control finances, devise methods to motivate managers and look to the future. For either of them to phone a shop steward would merely undermine the authority of the man running the business. They offer managers every opportunity to be successful. The only thing they won't do is provide him with any opportunity to blame them for a failure.

Judging success by return on capital employed, they acquire fairly mature, basic-industry companies that have been poorly managed. While they cringe at the thought of being called asset strippers, they do tend to shed excess baggage from any of their purchases. In many cases it helps pay for the purchase.

'Wait a minute,' Hanson cautions. 'I don't think we've ever bought anything with the object in mind of selling it or part of it. We do say nowadays, cautiously, perhaps there's some gravy in a deal, but we look upon every purchase as one which will become part of our organization. Sure, the financial men will say we've got to recover some of the output, especially if we've paid all cash for something. But if that's the reason, we won't do the deal because we don't want to commit ourselves to having to sell something.'

During the last decade, Hanson PLC bought a dozen different companies. Out of that, they sold just over 90 subsidiaries and properties. Still, Hanson is adamant about the point that they don't buy to sell.

'We try to acquire companies because we want what that company does. Therefore, it's always important to buy at the right price. That has priority over everything else. If we can't get something at the right price, we won't do the deal. But I honestly don't think there's been a single deal where we've been able, accurately, to say what we'd sell off. Yes, we have a reputation for being willing to sell. At the same time I hope we also have a reputation for giving fair value when we do sell. If you screw everybody right down to the last penny, you won't get any more deals. But again, we don't buy businesses because we have the ability to sell them. However, a hidden bonus is the fact that because of our ability to focus on each individual company's core business, we can make it a better business and at that point say to ourselves, do we really want to be number two or three in this particular business and if we decide we don't, we will offer it to someone who is more committed to it than we are.'

Once they take control of a company, corporate headquarters tend to disappear and so do most of the top-level managers. They favour giving younger managers a chance to be creative. Growth becomes a head office activity. Increased cash-flow settles their debt and provides them with enough money to buy something else.

To motivate managers, they rely heavily on incentives.

'Money is the ultimate motivator,' Hanson insists.

They pay a competitive salary, then throw in schemes which enable managers to receive bonuses up to the equivalent of their annual pay. In other words, they'll pay managers twice as much if they're able to materially improve both the return on capital employed and the profit over their budget. And here Hanson points out that budgeting comes from the bottom up rather than from the top down.

At many companies, financial experts predetermine a division's profit and impose budgets to fit their guess. Hanson expects the fellow running a division to come up with the figures. He will then stretch it with incentive schemes designed to encourage managers to be ambitious in their goals. The incentive schemes are redevised every year, based on the performance of the preceding year. That way, he says, it's always a moving feast. That way, budgets and incentives are always adapting to circumstances.

What you discover when you dig a little deeper is that every manager also understands that Hanson holds the sword of Damocles.

Divisions that don't bring in at least 25% return on capital are gotten rid of, unless someone can clearly see a way to get returns above 25% in the very foreseeable future. When Hanson invests in a new plant, he wants his money back in four years maximum. And four years is very much the outside figure. That manager had better do it in fewer than four years or Hanson will want to know why.

Two things are especially intriguing about Hanson and White.

The first is their overall, undisputed success. They have increased profits and increased dividends every year that they've been in business. Today Hanson PLC is one of those rare species whose profits are over the £1-billion mark.

The second is, they make it look so damned easy.

The UDS Group was a business developed over a long period by the Lyons family. It was Richard Shops and John Collier and stores like Allders. In 1982, if you'd been interested enough, you could have bought UDS shares for 60–75p. Stockbrokers were saying, 'The value of the assets employed has exceeded the rate at which profit growth has accrued.' Translated into English it meant they didn't have a lot of faith in the future of the business.

But a few people saw things differently. Gerald Ronson was one of them. Still smarting from his unsucessful bid to take over Associated Communications Corporation, by the autumn of 1982 he was thinking he could meld the UDS Group into his Heron interests. He valued the group at £191 million, or £1 a share, put a group of investors together – they called themselves the Bassishaw Consortium – and in January 1983 launched a cash bid.

Ronson went for the knock-out punch in the first round. But UDS had Sir Robert Clark in their corner. Chairman of Hill Samuel, a Director of the Bank of England, and a most articulate man, he is by anyone's standards a mean opponent. No glass jaw here. To ward off Ronson, Clark and UDS opened negotiations with Ralph Halpern of the Burton Stores Group, hoping to sell him the Richard Shops and John Collier. By the beginning of February a deal was done for £78 million. Ronson now tried to stop it with votes from shares committed to Bassishaw after the take-over bid had been declared. Clark countered by announcing a profit estimate that valued UDS at 140p, not counting Richard Shops and John Collier. Based on that, the UDS share price rose over the £1 mark and, in effect, nullified Ronson's bid. It forced Ronson to come back with 114p. Another good punch which appeared as if Clark would have to negotiate with Ronson.

At Hanson, they'd been watching this with the greatest interest. They believed Ronson was now ready to pounce, so Hanson rang Clark to see if UDS would welcome a White Knight. He told Clark, '125p.' In exchange for the UDS board's recommendation, Hanson offered five of his own shares for every eight UDS shares.

His timing was perfect.

It took Ronson nearly a month to come back with a cash offer of 130p. And when he did, he added, 'It's my final offer.'

Hanson went to 145p and won.

The price tag was £260 million in cash and shares. But then Hanson sold Richard Shops and John Collier for £106 million, plus a few other smaller business for somewhere around £70 million. He wound up with Allders Department Stores and the duty-free shops, a credit-selling business and some properties which represented a total outlay of £90 million.

In 1989 he sold those assets for £210 million.

Profit to Hanson, £126 million.

Then they went after London Brick.

A lacklustre operation with a 45% market share in the British brick business, it was the sole major producer of fletton bricks, a particular type of clay brick that comes on to the market cheaper than non-fletton bricks. A couple of years ago, London Brick attempted to take over the last independent non-fletton brick maker in the UK, Ibstock Johnson. Because any sort of acquisition involving more than 25% of an industry sector is subject to a review by the Monopolies and Mergers Commission, there was a hearing. The ruling that came down determined that the fletton brick business and the non-fletton brick business were non-competing. London Brick's stronghold on fletton did not prevent it from going into the non-fletton side of the business. As it was, London Brick backed away from the take-over because the price got too high. Yet the Monopolies and Mergers Commission ruling opened the door to London Brick for another assault on the non-fletton side of the business. And that had ramifications for Hanson.

He owned a company called Butterley Brick, a non-fletton producer that would merge quite neatly with London Brick. A possible take-over was in the back of his mind until December 1963 when London Brick announced their take-over attempt of two smaller brick businesses. It was obvious to Hanson that, if London Brick could pull off those take-overs, Butterley might be threatened. So Hanson rallied his troops and launched an assault on London Brick.

He offered £170 million.

Two years before, Hanson could have bought London Brick for 30p a share. Now he had to pay 89p for a block of seven million shares. His interest alone drove the price up to 104p. The London Brick board dug in and Hanson had a fight on his hands. It didn't matter at all to them that he was the reigning champ, having successfully manœuvred five major take-over fights in the previous five years. Nor did it matter that Jeremy Rowe at London Brick was something of a novice at all this, although he had the merchant banker Marcus Agius of Lazard Frères in his corner. Rowe and Agius decided that if Hanson wanted the company he'd have to pay plenty for it. Nothing personal. But let's face it, if you're going to get swallowed by a whale, Jonah, the least you can do is tumble down its throat hoping it'll wind up with one helluva stomach ache.

Rowe and Agius mounted their defences by telling the world that London Brick's estimated 1983 profits were up 70%. They forecast 1984 profits up 38% with a doubled dividend. They tried to make Hanson play an away game where the scoreboard read London Brick net assets were worth at least 215p per share. It forced Hanson to raise his bid not once, but twice.

No one had ever done that to Hanson.

He increased his offer from 120p to 150p, received a mediocre response, came back with 165p and even added a convertible loan stock alternative of 175p.

It netted him 29.9% of the company.

That Hanson could inadvertently underpin the London Brick share price at 175p was the risk he had to take to rally the institutional investors. But Hanson knew from experience that it was always much easier to get the additional 21% worth of acceptances out of the remaining 70% of the uncommitted shares than to get 40% if there were 90% of the shares left uncommitted.

Rowe and Agius refused to give up. The take-over deadline was set for Tuesday, 28 February 1984 at 3.30 p.m. And, with 20 minutes left to go, Hanson was still 1.5 million shares short of 50.1%.

'It generated a lot of emotion,' remembers Marcus Agius. 'The fact that Hanson had to increase his offer twice caused a certain amount of fluttering as everyone was concerned that Hanson may have got his sums wrong and, horror of horrors, he might actually lose. But he was very courageous. He just squeaked over the 50% mark. It was very close. Most exciting.'

The place where it happened was the noticeboard at the Stock Exchange. Hanson had to nail his declaration to the board, announcing that he owned more than 50% of the company, by 3.30. Had it gone up at 3.31 he would have missed the boat. As it turned out, a large block of institutionally held shares swung the game to Hanson. He wound up with 58.6% for which he paid £247 million, more than double his original bid. The notice went up with under 15 minutes left.

What impressed Agius most of all was that Hanson himself controlled the battle.

'It was quite clear that the whole thing was being orchestrated by Hanson personally. Very very tight control. Rothschild's (Hanson's bankers for this battle) was used pretty much as a post office. It was significant that press enquiries were directed only to Hanson's man. Rothschilds weren't allowed to talk to the press. That's most unusual. Hanson spent much of that time in America. Their press announcements went out at seven o'clock in the evening because it was obvious that the discussion of the content of the press announcement was never started until one o'clock London time, which is 8 a.m. in New York. Even earlier in California. Feeling it from this end, it was quite clear that the whole thing was being done directly by him.'

It was by all accounts a bitterly fought take-over. But Hanson always expects that.

'By the very nature of a bid,' he says, 'the predator is saying, we can do better than the present management.'

His thinking is that if you approach a company to make an offer, the board of that company must wonder, how do we know that's the right price? Because that board's first loyalty is supposed to be to their shareholders – and board members are often major shareholders – the best thing they can do is say, we don't welcome this offer, we want to see how far the company trying to take us over is willing to go. As everyone knows the first approach is never the last, or very rarely the last, bid situations in the UK – unless it's a white knight escapade where the besieged company invites somebody else in with whom they can do a friendly deal – are something to be fought.

On the other hand, Hanson is often quoted as saying, 'If

anyone wants to bid for my company, I'll send a car round to fetch him.'

In the States there are different rules because it's a different game.

'A hostile take-over in the United States is not always a good idea,' notes White. 'The cost of slugging it out legally, to me, doesn't usually make sense. It inhibits you from doing anything else. Although I admit that getting involved in a hostile take-over and what they now call greenmail is probably the only sure bet in the world.'

Although, if you look at White's record in the US – and Hanson Industries now accounts for more than 50% of the group's worldwide turnover – you might think another sure bet is the leveraged buy-out.

It was 1973.

Gordon White was closing in on the half-century mark, a time when most successful businessmen think of reinforcing their roots. But White felt it was time to do just the opposite.

'The Labour government had come to power and they threatened to squeeze the rich so hard that the pips would squeak. I just wanted to get out of the country, so James and I figured it was the right time to expand into the States. In those days there were exchange control regulations so we had to start up with what little money we could get. That was $3000.'

Today, Hanson Industries is listed among the 60 biggest companies in the States, and something like the eighth-largest foreign investor. That strikes both James Hanson and Gordon White as pretty funny, because the company has never actually invested a sou of foreign money in the States. They owe everything there to leveraged buy-outs.

'I sometimes think I invented the leveraged buy-out,' White claims. 'When I got to the States, the first thing I wanted to buy was a fishing company called Seacoast. But I had no money. So I said fine, I'd pay them $32 million over a period of time. I simply used the assets of Seacoast to secure the notes I gave to the family who owned it.'

It was the same thing when he bought 25% of Gable Industries. As long as it kept working, White kept buying, paying his way with what James Hanson liked to call 'Gordon White Promissory Notes'.

He picked up no less than nine textile companies, $75 million-worth of assets, with a leveraged buy of $35 million. He followed that with the purchase of Interstate United, although that was a public company and he had to tender for it. Once he got it, he stripped off some of the assets that were losing money – he sold a Michigan convention centre to the Shriners and divested himself of the Brass Rail Restaurants, among others – and what was left was a series of companies, including one in the food service business that sold hot dogs at baseball games.

In 1984 White managed to buy US Industries, a group with $1.2 billion-worth of sales from building materials, furniture, clothing and a range of industrial products. Originally for sale as a management buy-out, White offered $23 a share, or $531 million. The management team proposed a leveraged buy-out at $24 a share, but couldn't get enough support. Hanson and White moved in and mopped up.

It was especially attractive, says White, because USI was a series of companies where the risk was well spread.

'I'd rather have 700 companies making $1 million each than three companies making $250 million. The trick is to try to make sure that you're insulated in case a major division has a bad year. When I go to buy, I'm not interested in what I can make with the company as much as I am in knowing what I can lose if it all goes wrong. The up-side will take care of itself.'

Instead of going into USI, he says, he could have bought Norton Simon for $700 million, including Avis, the cosmetics side, and three or four other major holdings.

'I turned it down because the divisions were out of proportion. Any one of them going wrong would have tilted the balance. I'm not interested in a major one-product business, such as Boeing. It's too many eggs in one basket. Look at Warner when Atari got into trouble. That will not happen to us. We avoid making those kinds of mistakes, although I'm sure there have been other mistakes that I've made in not buying a company. When I turn down a purchase it's because I feel that if they went wrong they'd bust us.'

What he wants to see when he goes shopping is usually no further away than the company reports.

'The first thing I do is look back to see what a company has spent and also at its depreciation. If they've spent in excess of their depreciation, I might be interested. That's because I figure I'll be getting value for money. I never look at figures like the P/E. They're bullshit. It's not possible to judge a company that way. P/Es are nothing more than the number of years it would take to get your money back if the company paid all of its earnings out as dividends with tax put to one side. Except it never happens that way.'

The Hanson–White success story in the US is not one that many British firms have ever equalled. And credit for it really has to go to White's understanding of the American scene.

'Being successful in the States is not easy for a foreign company. Just look at the enormous number of failures. But we took our lessons from King George III. You can't run your American interests from London. He made that mistake in 1776. It simply doesn't work.'

There are, he says, lots of reasons why.

'Business moves much faster in the States. The mentality is very different. The US is a much tougher business environment than the UK. You can't even compare the two. In the UK you can featherbed inefficiency and high prices for ever. The thing about America is its freshness. If you want to see someone in America, they'll see you. If you've got something to sell, they'll listen. That's what's wrong with Europe. England is well known for having invented many new products, but it takes the US or Japan to make them commercially viable.'

He stops to think for a moment, then makes another point.

'You can't forget that the US is much more a lawyer-built society than Europe. Lawyers run everything. To survive in the States you have to know the ins and outs of the law. If you don't, the Americans will soon have you in knickers and necklace.'

America is a litigious country.

It's a nation of lawyers, with laws made by lawyers for the benefit of lawyers. At Hanson PLC there are five attorneys on the payroll. At Hanson Industries, there are 20.

Anybody who's ever done business in the States knows that when you have a disagreement in America, the first step is file a writ. Shoot first, ask questions later. There'll be time to talk about it when you get to court. Those are the rules of the game in the Colonies, and Gordon White had to learn those lessons early on.

'You see, the way it goes on, schools here are throwing out about 6000 lawyers a year. They hang up their shingles, and they follow ambulances, looking for anybody who might have been hit by a car. The system works on the basis that you don't pay your own legal fees. A lawyer here can work on a contingency and if you lose, that's it.'

Early in 1985 Hanson made a commitment to expand in the United States. Into its sights fell SCM, makers of the Smith Corona office machines, chemicals, foods and paints. SCM's year-end profits were fairly dull considering $2.2 billion in sales. Hanson and White saw money to be made – pounds being sold for 50p. Or, in this case, dollar bills going for a couple of quarters.

In mid-August, with SCM's shares languishing around $38–55, they offered $60. SCM said no. Brokers Merrill Lynch smelled money too, got in touch with SCM and within ten days announced a management leveraged buy-out at $70 a share. The board would continue to manage the company while Merrill Lynch and the Prudential Insurance Company would raise the needed $750 million to get a slice of the pie. So White increased his offer to $72. Merrill Lynch climbed to $74, but SCM voted a 'poison pill' clause that said, should anyone acquire more than one-third of their shares, Merrill Lynch would have the right to buy their most attractive divisions –

the paint and food businesses – at bargain prices. The result would be an asset lock-out, making a hollow victory for whoever took over SCM.

The next day, White withdrew his offer and went into the market. In under two hours, he bought $200 million-worth of SCM shares, giving Hanson Industries 25% of the company. SCM filed for a court order to stop Hanson from acquiring any more. And that order was granted. White appealed and won. Merrill Lynch then put SCM's paint and food divisions in escrow, to keep them out of Hanson's reach. Two days after that, White offered $75 a share, bringing his stake to 32.1% and effectively blocking the SCM/Merrill Lynch $74 gambit.

White's next move was straight into the US District Court in New York. He filed conspiracy charges against SCM, Merrill Lynch and Prudential. He claimed they'd broken the law by misappropriating at least $200 million of SCM assets. He said those assets had been taken from shareholders solely for the purpose of preventing those very same shareholders from getting the highest price for them, entrenching the SCM management and giving Merrill Lynch a windfall.

SCM countered by charging Hanson with illegally acquiring 3.4 million shares – the $200 million-worth bought in the open market. That, in turn, brought the SEC into the drama. They wanted to know more about that Hanson purchase.

Suddenly Hanson and White had a very major fight on their hands. This wasn't Gerry Ronson and UDS. This wasn't a few hundred million pounds. This was a heavyweight battle in the world's toughest financial arena, bare-knuckle and to the finish. At stake was a billion-dollar company, everybody's reputation, plus, perhaps, the very rules that would govern future hostile take-overs and poison-pill defences.

The court decided in favour of SCM, saying that the directors had in fact done their best to achieve a fair value for the shareholders.

Hanson and White had lost the first round.

By their own calculations, if they'd stopped right there they could have walked away with a $2–3-million profit. Small change maybe, but probably just enough to cover their legal bills. But quitting is not their style. They appealed, arguing that Merrill Lynch's option clearly denied the SCM shareholders of an offer that was in their best interests.

The appellate judge agreed.

And SCM fell into the Hanson stable.

Within three years they'd disposed of everything but SCM Chemicals and the Smith Corona typewriter divisions. They sold what they didn't want at a premium of 60% over the price they'd paid for the entire group. Which means, when you add in the £300-million annual profit from SCM Chemicals and Smith Corona, they'd more than doubled their money.

While Gordon White and the SCM bid were still in the New York courts, James Hanson, commuting back and forth from London, decided to go after the £1.9-billion Imperial Group.

The management at Imps had just agreed to a merger with the United Biscuit company which would have given the new group over 40% of the British snack business. But Hanson's desire for Imps got in the way of that. UB raised their offer. Then Hanson raised his. By combining cash with shares, the figures soon soared into the then dizzying heights of £2.5 billion. UB countered with a series of newspaper ads aimed solely at discrediting Hanson. Life got so rough that Hanson even filed charges, claiming the ads contained false and misleading statements about his US profits.

It was, to say the least, the most malicious street-fight Hanson and White had ever known. But then, when it comes to street-fighting, Messrs Hanson and White were not born yesterday. As the newspaper ads got nastier, Hanson increased his stake in Imps, tightening the garrotte, while the lawyers had a field day threatening everyone with suits.

Convinced that they would win, and with £2.8 billion at stake, UB boasted of its future plans for Imps and editorial comment swung in favour of those plans.

Equally convinced that he'd win, Hanson published a daily scoreboard to show how much better his offer was than UB's.

It was so effective that it not only got used in a subsequent take-over battle, UB copied it as well.

By 11 April 1986, the deadline set for the UB/Imps merger, UB's advertising bill stood at £2 million, Hanson's was at £1.5 million, and there was still no clear winner in sight. When the market closed that afternoon at 3.30, the shares were counted. UB fell just short of the 50% mark. That opened the door for Hanson and White, who came strutting in like they owned the place which, in fact, they did.

They have since sold off all but Imperial's tobacco business and Seven Seas Vitamins, netting back nearly £2.4 billion.

It was the same scenario, although slightly less spectacular, the following year with Kidde. A highly diversified American manufacturing and services company, he paid $1.6 billion, sold about $400 million-worth and has been sitting on the rest, developing the business and, almost certainly, waiting for the right buyers to come along.

Then came Consolidated Gold Fields.

A natural resources operation with mining interests so important as to make them the second-largest producer of gold in the free world, Hanson paid £3.5 billion. Within a week he sold 30% of Cons Gold South Africa to the Rembrandt Group for £368 million.

Unbundling was fast becoming the word for the '90s.

The single-most asked question of James Hanson and Gordon White is, what's the line of succession?

Hanson answers, 'You're talking to somebody who feels that he's the current succession. The company is in good hands, right now. Everyone in the company has the opportunity to take a pension at 60 and I strongly discourage that. But if I decide at a certain point that I don't want to go on, the timing on that is very very important. First of all, the moment you decide you're going to hand over or appoint a successor, you must get out. You can't hang around. You can guide him along, but just like prime ministers, timing is the most vital thing of all. It depends entirely on when. If some day I do retire it will be because I want to do something else.'

Like what?

'I'm very busy all the time. I've got plenty of things to do. Like at the moment I'm trying to hire a gardener. Over the years there have been offers, I don't think I can go into details, but there have been plenty of American companies who've approached Gordon and me. Especially Gordon, because he is an absolutely unique person in terms of being able to do what he does on acquisitions. There's no one like him anywhere in the world. And frankly when someone makes you a $10-million offer and says come and join us, we'll give you this much cash and this part of the action, of course we've looked at it. Gordon and I have also many times thought about starting again, either for Hanson or ourselves. But we decided we didn't want to do that because it's hard work. A lot of factors come into it. We're part of a team here. There's a lot of satisfaction in being part of that team and in achieving all that we've achieved. And I still have to hire a gardener.'

Anyway, he adds, he's still enjoying himself.

'I spend a lot of time now in Palm Springs. I get up each morning at five to go to the office and effectively finish their day's work by about nine. I have my breakfast, then take some exercise, you know, ride a bike or something like that. After that I come back to the office and work until about 11, which is seven in the evening in England. I can then take the rest of the day off until about four when I start to deal with what's happening in America.'

So, he stresses the point, even if he has picked a date in his mind to quit – and he's not saying he has – it gets pushed back further every year.

But what about ten years from now?

He concedes, 'What happens is that you have to think about your family and your health. If your health is fine, then it's okay to keep living this crazy life. But if that starts to be affected in some way or other . . . Well, Gordon is the fittest man in the world. I'm fit but not such a fanatic as he is. So I think if something went wrong with one's health, to slow any of us down, that would be the time to say quickly, okay, let's reorganize. Anyway, for succession, we've got all the people we need right inside this organization.'

Hanson and White bowing out gracefully as the next generation takes over is only one option.

'Everybody knows one day we'll leave. That's held our share price back for about ten years. If you listen to the analysts, every single one mentions this point. When is it going to have any meaning? I don't think it will. The important thing to remember about succession is that the company will only keep on doing what we have been doing. Gordon has a particular nose for deals of a certain type and if he were not available we might go in a slightly different direction. But don't forget that we're running a company that's much bigger than ICI in market capitalization terms, and we could go on doing that for years.'

There is however another possibility.

Timing and a sense of drama never escape these two, so when the hour comes to exit – if they can stage-manage it – look for something typically spectacular. It could be this:

Having aglomerated, they might just do the reverse.

What a final scene. Hanson and White simply unbundle themselves. And who more talented than they to do just that? The last act would bring in far greater value for shareholders than anything that could possibly follow.

They'd go right back down to nothing again and make enormous sums of money doing it.

It might even be remembered as the greatest exit of all time.

10

Gerald Ronson

These have not been good days for Gerald Maurice Ronson.

Five years ago, I wrote that he was what the Godfather would have been if Don Corleone was British, of Eastern European extraction and honest.

This was before anyone ever imagined that Gerald Ronson would find himself embroiled in the Guinness scandal.

Voted Businessman of the Year for 1984, Ronson is a tall, muscular guy who batters the King's English with an East London accent that is totally inappropriate because he doesn't come from the East End.

He's a man with a proven knack for making money. It's obviously a talent, like being able to stand on your head, walk on stilts, make a perfect soufflé or speak Russian. Some people just know how to do such things.

Five years ago when you asked him how life was, he'd say he was a contented, respectful, upstanding, happily married fellow who was totally in control.

These days the Guinness affair has taken over his life, monopolized his conversation and become a nightmare that will almost certainly haunt him for ever.

For Gerald Ronson, the most important thing in the world is his family. After that, he says, it's business. Then comes his charity work. Then come his boats.

'I have a reputation of being tough. I wouldn't say I have a reputation of being hard. If tough means no nonsense, if tough means I won't tolerate a lot of stupidity or a lot of bullshit going on around me, then absolutely. But hard, I wouldn't like to think of myself as being a hard man. I think you have to differentiate between being tough and being hard. Two different things.'

He quit Clark's College in Cricklewood before he was 15 to work in his father's furniture-manufacturing business. Today he is the fifteenth wealthiest man in Britain.

'I would not be what I am today if it was not for the training I got from my father. I started by sweeping the sawdust off the floor in the mill. That's a fact. I went through every single department in the furniture factory, which employed about 300 people. What I learned from him was the work ethic, your name is your reputation, a sense of responsibility, discipline and how to deal with people. He was very much out of the old school. He was a man who believed in working six-and-a-half days a week, getting into the factory before everyone else and going home after everyone else. It was that development of my character which gave me a good grounding for when I came out of the furniture business in 1957.'

He was 18 in 1957 when he decided to go out on his own. With £150–200,000 of the family's money, Ronson plunged into the house-building business. That led him into commercial property development. And that brought him, in a roundabout way, into the oil business.

As a property developer he started buying up petrol stations. Hardly the route most young take when they want to find their way into English upper-crust society. Even his pals said, 'Petrol stations? Look what Gerry is doing with his father's money.' But he didn't care what his friends said because he was in real estate, and he believed that petrol stations were prime sites that could bring in some income until he could afford to develop them.

In the meantime, he originated the self-service petrol station. Then came the oil crisis years. In 1973 prices went from $3 a barrel to over $12 in the space of three months. By the end of the decade they'd peaked at $40. The net effect was to create a hefty cash-flow which allowed Ronson to expand further into property, insurance, motor distribution and consumer products.

'If you look at how we built our business, it's been built brick by brick and with the reputation the company has. A lot of people think they can do it in five or ten years. But you've got to be a long-distance runner if you want to build up a serious business. You've got to have the right people, the right infrastructure, the right credibility, the right reputation. It's the persistence, and being able to put all these things together that make the business overall. It takes a lifetime.'

Making his own fortune didn't take him that long, however. He says he could have retired when he was 24.

'I remember saying to myself when I was 15, when I become a millionaire I'm going to retire. Then I said to myself, by the time I'm 30 if I make £10 million I'm going to retire. Which, looking back, I realize how ridiculous it was to say in the first place. Some people refer to me as a workaholic. I'm not a workaholic. I enjoy what I'm doing. If I didn't enjoy it I wouldn't do it. That doesn't mean I'm stupid and enjoy everything I'm doing, because there are days I don't enjoy it and there are days I find it frustrating and there are days I find it aggravating. But everything in life is a challenge and I enjoy my business. Just like some people enjoy golf or swimming or tennis or whatever their hobbies are. My hobby is my business and my business I enjoy as much, if not more than, doing those other things. If that wasn't the case, I wouldn't be at my business six-and-a-half days a week, I would be doing those other things.'

When he does take time off, he has a boat. He likes very big boats, the kind that always gets referred to yachts. He builds them himself. No, he doesn't put on the overalls and get out his hammer and saw. He fools around with the designs so that the boat will be to his personal specifications. Then he orders it built. He names it after his wife Gail, staffs it with crew and keeps it in the South of France. He plays with the boat until he gets tired with it, starts planning the next one and puts this one on the market. He sells it – to date he's done it eight or nine times – and each time he sells a boat, he makes a profit.

It keeps him in boatswain's whistles.

The company is called Heron.

The name comes from Henry Ronson, Gerald's late father.

It's a private company, apparently the second-largest private company in Britain. Ronson's salary is just over £830,000, up from £460,000 five years ago, but that's all he gets because Heron pays no dividends. The shares are owned by Ronson, several family trusts and three charitable foundations, all controlled by Ronson.

'I don't discuss my charities in terms of telling the outside world. It's not anybody's business. But I'm a great believer that if the Lord blesses you in terms of being able to make a lot of money, you've got a responsibility to do something with it. And more importantly, you've got a responsibility to show your children that those seeds have to be replanted.'

Structurally, under the umbrella of the charitable foundations, there's a two-tier board. The board at Heron International – a Netherlands Antilles-registered holding company – is four people. Ronson is Chairman and CEO. His three closest lieutenants are there as directors for finance, for property and for legal and commercial matters. Beneath that is the Heron Corporation Board, with those four plus the managing directors of the various trading companies. It fluctuates but there are about 14 in all. Heron Corp. is about 120 companies, although only around 30 are main active trading divisions falling under four basic headings – property investment, insurance, house building and general trading, which is consumer products.

In the UK, Ronson is the largest independent petrol retailer; office buildings and developments, auto retailing and distributorships including H. R. Owen Rolls-Royce, Massey Ferguson products plus concessions for Suzuki motor products and Lancia cars; audio, TV and video equipment; Baileys of Westbury, Ltd for haulage, parcel delivery and warehousing; Herondrive for fleet sales and leasing; and Heron Homes for house building.

In the United States, he used to be the Pima Savings and Loan Association of Tucson, Arizona but that went the way of so many S&Ls; Western American Financial Corporation and Western American Insurance Agency (both of Phoenix, Arizona); Media Home Entertainment for video distribution and film financing; plus Heron Properties and a 50% stake in the California developer Hall Properties.

On the Continent, especially in Spain, Ronson has picked up much of the property left by the crash of the Rumasa empire once controlled by Juan Maria Ruiz Mateos, then Spain's richest man.

'I have built up a team of what I would regard as 50 key senior managers. Although we employ something like 5000 people worldwide, I would say there are basically 50 people who are the key players. I think I delegate well, but I am also a very good detail person. I like to know what's going on in my businesses. Just look at our board meetings. I mean, we could sit here at Marylebone Road' – the office is almost directly across the street from Madame Tussaud's wax museum in London – 'and have all our board meetings here. But we alternate the board meetings to the major businesses. There's nothing like walking through a warehouse, a plant, a major site, a business or whatever, walking around insurance company offices, you get a feel for the business. Our approach is very much a hands-on approach. We believe that leadership should be in the front, there should be direct lines of communication.'

He usually travels 200,000 miles a year 'to visit the troops'. The Heron plane takes him around Europe. For the States, he generally Concordes to New York, and meets the Heron plane there.

'It's the same old persistence and dedication. It all sounds very boring. But that's what it's all about. You visit the troops. The people have got to feel that the business not only has a figurehead, but that person is visible, that person is there. Because if I don't make the effort, if they don't see that I care, I can't expect them to care.'

There is, he assures anyone who asks, a chain of command. But when you own the game and can make up the rules as you go along, that sort of thing probably doesn't matter as much as he says it does.

'I don't have a problem with the people around me. If I want to go direct to anybody, they won't object to it. They would object to it if I delegate somebody else to do it. Then they would take umbrage. But because they know my style of business, which is open – I'm not a politician in terms of how I operate within my corporation and you can interpret that whichever way you wish – but I believe things should go in straight lines.'

In other words – just in case there's ever been any doubt – Gerald Ronson is the boss. He is Heron. Although here too he tries to play that down. After all, he does have to live with the people he employs.

'As far as the business is concerned, it's all run by first-class managing directors and a very capable management team. A lot of these people have been with me 10–15–20 years. You never hear about people leaving Heron, because they don't leave. But every ship has to have a captain on the bridge. Every team, there has to be a team leader. I'm the leader of my team. Yes, I'm the architect of the business.'

He stresses though that strategy and planning is these days much more of a team decision than it was than it was 15–20 years ago.

'We work on four-year rolling corporate plans, which is current financial year plus three. I don't believe you can look out much further than that. Some major corporations look 10–15 years. But in my opinion there is no way in the world we live in today you can look 10–15 years up the road. You're very clever if you can guess it right three years up the road; in some businesses, three months up the road. But we've worked for the last 15 years on a four-year plan. You get more sophisticated as time goes on. More experienced with the input and the way the plans are structured. Our plans are very complex in terms of assets, cash flow and development of specific businesses. We update our four-year plan in the last quarter of our calendar year. All my managing directors of every division participate in the input, because obviously this is the way to involve the whole team. You've got to have people around you who are thinking forward all of the time, because if they're not thinking forward they're thinking backwards.'

Because he wants to maintain extremely tight controls on the corporate finances – his annual turnover is now well over $1 billion with pre-tax profits closing in on the £60 million mark – he gets a full weekly management package, and full monthly figures on every single company in the group.

'Our financial directors are watching daily the movement of cash and treasury. It is very important to keep tight controls. Especially when you're in eight different currencies. You've got to be watching this.'

To protect his foreign exchange exposure he matches and swaps but never opens positions in currency.

'We don't gamble. We make sure we know where our exposure is and our exposure is a controlled exposure. I'm not a gambler. I'm not in the business of gambling. Gambling is for the needy and greedy. There are risks in my business but there are risks in everything. You analyse the risks. You take a view based on experience and judgement. As a business gets bigger your approach is much more conservative, much more careful. Now, if you'd have spoken to me 15 years ago I might have said I'm going bonko on something. But that's not how we run this business now. We haven't run this business like that for maybe the last seven years.'

It was the middle-1970s when the penny dropped.

'The banks had over-extended themselves by loaning to people who were not responsible or professional property developers. Half the secondary banking system went bust. Even the major banking system needed the encouragement and support of the Bank of England. You just couldn't sell a property for its real value. When you see institutions today buying on a 4–5% yield, you couldn't have given away those properties on an 8–9% yield. There was no confidence in property.'

A lot of people he knew were suddenly broke. And he thinks that Heron was lucky to have come through it basically unscathed.

'We realized that it could have happened to us. You know, there but for the grace of God go I. Thank God we had a very successful petrol business, among others, which generated the cash flow to take us through that hump. It was worth 25 years of business experience. Now I'm probably one of the most conservative businessmen you'll meet.'

Still, he doesn't discount the luck element in everything he does.

'Luck is very important. You've seen some of the cleverest people in the world screw up situations. Why? Over-confident. Wrong time. Wrong place. Luck plays a very important part in what you do. I've seen the most stupid people make fortunes. Especially on the other side of the ocean, where I've seen people with vast wealth that don't particularly have any great ability. But they were in the right place at the right time. They struck a hole in the ground and found oil, or found gold. Or they were sitting on a piece of land their grandfather left them which was umpteen thousand acres.'

While he never sat down to work it out, he figures if you're lucky half the time you'll come out a winner.

'I wouldn't say today that we're putting 50% luck into the equation for our decision-making. But that luck factor plays a very important part. You've got to get the deal right, you've got to get a lot of the pieces together, but that luck is the difference between success and failure.'

Being successful usually means you can minimize the luck element by controlling the game. And, at least until the Guinness scandal came along, Ronson always considered himself a man in total control. Where business deals are concerned, he would never figure he's half right and hope his luck would carry him through. He insists he wouldn't and doesn't rely on his luck in anything. He relies on the judgement of the deal.

The luck element comes into play when the deal works out better than he ever imagined.

Sometimes.

Heron was once the only foreign company in the United States to own a savings and loan association, the American equivalent of a building society.

Ronson went to Tucson, Arizona, to buy that savings bank, at a time when most people in the UK had never heard of Tucson. The Howard Hughes estate came up for sale – 12,500 acres of the most valuable land in Tucson – with a price tag of $75 million. But it had to be cash. And anybody in the world could have bought that piece of land if they had the cash. Ronson would never have heard about it or looked at it had he not already been in Tucson with his savings bank. Realizing immediately that this was the finest land in southern Arizona – it's the 20 square miles between the airport and the city centre – Ronson jumped on it. He could see that if the city was ever going to expand, it had to go towards and on to his land. It simply couldn't go the other way because there's a mountain. So, in spite of interest rates then running at 17%, it was an opportunity he didn't want to miss. He put together a few partners, and bought the land, having pre-sold $40 million worth at the closing. He then sold another $80 million. Not wanting to flood the market, he and his partners only released so much of the land every year. They could afford to sit on it because they were also looking at the appreciation. In the end, a conservative guess is that the deal netted him $200 million.

Is that luck? Or is that just Gerald Ronson doing his thing? He says where the land deal is concerned, it's luck.

'I call it good luck that I first came to Tucson, Arizona. If you had said to me ten years ago, Tucson, Arizona, I would have looked at you and said I never heard of Tucson. It's cowboy country. But how did this Englishman from Marylebone Road find himself in Tucson, Arizona? Elements of luck. Now you may give me a strong argument that there's no luck there because I did my homework and I looked at the metrics and this and that. Yes. If you were talking to somebody with a

Harvard MBA, he could give you that argument. But I bet he wouldn't have had the nose. He wouldn't have got on his bike to go to Tucson. He would have gone to California or Houston or Dallas. Elements of luck put you in a position.'

But then there's the story of the Puma Savings and Loan Association.

It looks like good luck doesn't always stick around too long.

The bank was hit by a severe downturn in the property market. Losses had been piling up since 1987. Ronson spent 18 months trying to sell the bank to anyone who'd have it. But no one wanted it. And in March 1990, US Federal regulators finally took control.

In the end Ronson might have lost as much there as he made on the land. Oh well, at least he got to spend some time in Arizona.

Gerald Ronson may be a pretty good street-fighter but he's not undefeated. He's gotten his nose bloodied a few times.

And the Guinness scandal took him down to the canvas.

In 1982 he got into a skirmish with Robert Holmes à Court for the Associated Communications Corp., Lew Grade's former empire. Holmes à Court had opened the poker game for the £120 million company with a bid close to £35 million. Ronson raised him 30% with a £46.6 million bid. Holmes à Court matched it, and Ronson raised to £49 million. Then Holmes à Court came back with £60 million and Ronson folded. He lost the bid. But ACC was burdened with lawsuits, and riddled with a £38 million overdraft and another £67 million worth of debt. Once the smoke cleared it looked as though Ronson may not have lost as badly as some people thought he did.

He even told *Forbes* magazine, 'Sometimes when someone is too greedy he gets left holding the bag.'

A year later he bid for UDS – the United Drapery Stores group of manufacturers and retail outlets like Richard Shops, John Collier, Allders Department Stores and the duty-free shops at Heathrow and Gatwick airports. This time James Hanson beat him.

'Hanson bid for the company and was the successful acquirer, and it's been a very good deal for Hanson. I'm very pleased that it has been a good deal for the Hanson Company because we were major shareholders in Hanson Trust. But having said that, I know they didn't do their homework anything like we did. Again, the reputation of Heron. If we're bidding X for that, other people figure that must be right because Heron does its homework. They didn't have any qualms about going in and overbidding us. Of course they're in a position to, I won't say overbid or pay more, but they use paper. And if you have paper that yields 3% that's a lot different than using pound notes that cost 10% to borrow.'

There is another consideration he always makes when he puts a price on a company. And that's all about goodwill.

'I'm not in the business of paying for goodwill. There is a price for goodwill, but when you're buying a business for cash and when you're spending your own money, it helps focus your mind very clearly. The more hard assets that you're buying for your dollar or your pound is where it's all at. Goodwill at a stroke you write off your balance sheet. But if you've got hard assets, if a business doesn't always turn out the way you expect the business to turn out, then you have something tangible. If you have a lot of hot air, then there's nothing tangible unless you're in the balloon-racing business. Remember that when you look at our balance sheet you're looking at hard net worth. There's nothing in the balance sheet for goodwill.'

To bid for UDS, Ronson put together the consortium called Bassishaw. It was half-owned by Heron, half-owned by institutional investors.

'I'm sure that we knew more about UDS when we were ready to bid for it than the management running the company. In fact, I know we did.'

Using only one broker – plans stay quieter that way – Bassishaw built up a whole load of shares.

'I think we had 4.9% or 5.1'%. We had an agreement with certain partners of ours that they would tender their shares with us. So I think at one stage we had 10% of the company. I'm pleased to say half of those shares we bought at very low figures when the company's results were very bad, which was maybe 12–18 months prior to when we bid for the company. But it's much harder to bid for a major company all cash, believe it or not, than it is to just do a straightforward paper exchange where I'm swapping my shares for your shares. That's a great game to play, until the wheels stop spinning and the last fellow in line holding the stick looks up and says, what happened? That's not the business I'm in. I'm in the business where I have to make real money with real cash, a positive return with proper cash-flow and just keep it very simple and very old-fashioned.'

He started at £1 per share. He says he had a pretty good idea what he was prepared to pay for the company. But he was almost certainly not expecting as tough a fight as he got and was quickly forced up to £1.14 by a feisty UDS board.

'There was a time when we went to a certain figure. There was also a time by the way when we actually agreed a deal with the board which they reneged on. People are very good at hiding behind boards of directors. It's not a game I've ever played. I can give you a big long list of people who have agreed deals with me over the years and have reneged on them. They say, "Well, I've taken it to my board and although I've recommended it, the board won't go along with it." Well, when a chairman and CEO recommends the bid, the only reason the board doesn't go along with it is because in between somebody else came along and offered more money.'

Ronson was eventually forced to raise his bid to £1.30, which is where he announced, 'This is my final offer.'

When Hanson walked away with UDS, the pundits turned around and said Ronson's mistake was the 'final offer' remark. You aren't supposed to do such things in a take-over battle because it means you've reached the end of the line. Once you say this is the end, that's the end. It's like throwing in the towel. It opens the field to the next guy. It's admitting defeat, unless of course you're simply not prepared to pay a penny more for the company because you don't think it's worth a penny more.

Asking him point blank if his 'my final offer' was a mistake, the answer you get from him is, 'You've got to interpret these things as you want to.'

Gerald Ronson says his handshake is his bond.

'When you shake hands with Gerald Ronson, the deal is done.'

He nods, pauses, then comes up with the story of the deal he once negotiated with the British head of an American oil company.

Ronson was selling some sites, and the two came to an agreed price. The next day, Ronson received a call from another company willing to pay more for the sites. Ronson refused to sell at that higher price and stuck with his original deal.

'They thought I was stark raving mad.'

But that's the way he says he likes to do business – on both sides of the Atlantic – which, he adds, is not always the case with everyone else.

'In certain places in America, especially the South-West, because of the structure of the community your word is still important. Everybody knows everybody else. All the players know who the other players are in the market-place. If you give your word, or if you do a deal, your reputation is very important. You get into a different ball game in California, or even in New York. I'm generalizing because there are certain businesses where people know who the players are, such as in the diamond business. If the people know one another, a word counts for something. But generally you need to read the fine print very carefully on every contract you look at in America. There are always armies of lawyers on both sides and it's a whole different ball game than the European attitude where reputation and integrity, I think, have different values and meanings. It really depends on where you're coming from.'

Heron is a cash-rich company, which means Ronson can buy almost anything he wants to.

'Cash gives me the ability to purchase when the right opportunity comes along. So does leverage, yes. But with leverage you take a bigger risk. Leverage and cash are two different things. Having the cash enables me to go out there and do it. Leverage, well, you're leveraging your assets and then you have to go out and get the cash. You're in a much stronger position to do deals if you have money when you don't need it.'

Why not, he's asked, simply go public?

'Because I like Heron being a private company. It's a luxury we can afford.'

Deals come along on a regular basis because everybody knows there's plenty of cash around if Ronson wants to buy. They also know that as a private company he can often move a lot faster than a public company where boards have to consider the eventual reaction of their shareholders. Still, he picks and chooses his deals with great care. As he says, he's spending his own money.

'You don't have to jump on every bus coming along up the street. A proportion of our acquisitions have not come out of a great scientific development plan, they've come out of opportunistic deals. And any entrepreneur who says he's never done any opportunistic deals is either kidding himself or not telling you the truth.'

Yet Ronson labels himself a runner of businesses and not the kind of entrepreneur who buys businesses, strips and sells them.

'That's not our style. We build up business and we build up the management. That is how I have all these businesses. Therefore, when people know you're out there as a major player, and that you're in a position to sign a cheque for a big number, then who do they pick the phone up to call? They don't pick the phone up to the faceless crowd. And in the UK there are only half a dozen people who are in a position to write out a cheque and can make a decision like we can make a decision. In fact, I'm not even sure there are half a dozen out there.'

Who are they? He shakes his head, refusing to list them.

'You know who they are.'

Obviously he's one of them. Over the years, Ronson has become a favourite of the crystal ball gazers. When a company looks ripe for a bid, somebody invariably whispers with a knowing nod, 'Gerald Ronson'. It's as good a guess as any.

Five years ago his name was linked to a possible take-over bid of Burmah Oil so often that he alone might have been the only businessman in England who doubted Gerald Ronson's intentions towards Burmah.

He said at the time, 'I think that can be a figment of people's imagination because we own a reasonable stake in that company. But having said that, I would not assume that Burmah is the one. I can think of other companies that we've got stakes in that nobody talks about. But then I read about a lot of companies I'm supposed to have stakes in that I don't have stakes in. Every Sunday I open the newspaper and I laugh because I see last week I bid for Burmah with a Saudi consortium, and the week before I was bidding for some other company. I mean, what's the guessing game this weekend? I'm surprised how irresponsible some Sunday papers can be that they don't do their homework properly.'

On the other hand, he does his homework.

'Yes, we do our homework. We are very conservative people because we are spending our own money. Our reputation is on the line. If we borrow money from banks, we give them information, we give them facts and figures, and they've got to be right.'

The way he comes into the market to buy or sell has to be right too. He may quite happily make money on a lost take-over bid but he won't get involved with games like 'greenmail'. Actually Ronson cringes at the thought of being put in that category.

'I'm not in the greenmail business. If I wanted to take advantage of Heron's charisma in terms of Heron buying shares in companies, then we could make a lot of money playing those sorts of tricks. But that is not where our reputation is.

We are serious business people running a serious business, not playing out there in the market to make opportunity killings in the stock market on either side of the ocean. In America, it's a different ball game. In America, very respectable people play that game and it's not looked down upon or frowned upon the same way it is in the City of London. But in the City of London, if you want the right reputation – and I believe I know the reputation we want and we have – then that's not the game you play. That's not the game Heron will play.'

Nor does Heron go in for the 'back door' approach to takeovers.

Ronson says they don't use shell companies in strange places to do their bidding for them, hoping to keep their intentions quiet as long as they can. Life can get expensive for guys like Ronson when lots of people find out what he's up to. But that's one of the things he just has to live with because, for Ronson, playing the game is not enough. Somewhere deep in his psyche there is the compelling need to play by the rules.

'It's very difficult to stay quiet about anything. You may be fortunate to pick up a block of shares over a period of time. But we don't hide behind back doors. Within the rules of what you can do, we do. We don't get involved in all those funny shareholdings, etc. That's not our style.'

Even though he once said he could have built his empire six times faster had he been working in the United States, Ronson remains strongly committed to Britain.

'This is where I live, which to me is very important. I am a man of roots. I'm a family man. This is where I've been brought up. This is where my commitments are to my community. This is where my commitments are to the people who have been with me for many years. That to me is very important. I don't want to live anywhere else other than where I'm living now.'

Ronson is now 51. In nine years he'll be 60 and he's always said that by the time he reaches that age he hopes he will have found someone to take the reins.

'At 60 years of age I wouldn't want to be running around quite as much as I'm running around today, that's for sure.

Looking five years out, I would like to be in a position, instead of being Chairman and Chief Executive, of just being Chairman and having a Chief Executive who is following in the footsteps. Not a yes man. But someone following in the footsteps of the development of the corporation. I would like to step back more, to look at where we're going internationally, in terms of corporate planning, and bring on my team. In actual terms of where the business will be ten years down the road, well, if we're going on at the same momentum that we've been going at for the last 30-odd years, and we know what's there for the next five years, we will keep on growing. We could short-cut that by floating off parts of our group and going on the paper chase, building up much faster and accelerating the group, but there are no plans for a public flotation or any plans to go that route.'

Although now he adds, 'Things could change. The important thing in business is to be flexible.'

And lucky.

The Guinness Inquiry was the largest case the Fraud Squad had ever undertaken.

It was the most complex and involved the most money – an enormously complicated maze of wheeling and dealing through the £2.7-billion Distillers take-over, of accusations that included share manipulation and fabulous fees paid to various people for their help in the take-over.

The Department of Public Prosecutions sent the case to the police at the end of April 1987. Detective Superintendent Richard Boatwright and Detective Inspector John Wootton were put in charge. Together they hand-picked a team of officers – they averaged 15 years' CID experience each and at least three years on the Fraud Squad – broke the group into smaller units with specific briefs, and began collecting the necessary back-up professional experts – accountants, financial advisors, stockbrokers, bankers and attorneys. They claimed at the time it was the largest *ad hoc* grouping of professional advisors the police had ever assembled to help them with an inquiry.

They officially went into business on 1 May.

Five days later they arrested the former Guinness chairman, Ernest Saunders.

Within a matter of weeks the police also arrested financier Sir Jack Lyons, stockbroker Anthony Parnes, mergers and acquisitions wizard Roger Seelig, merchant banker Patrick (Lord) Spens, stockbroker David Mayhew and Gerald Ronson. The eighth man of great interest to the police eventually turned state's witness, former Guinness finance director Olivier Roux.

Before the year was out the case had been taken away from the Metropolitan Police and turned over to the newly formed Serious Fraud Office. Charges were lodged, the defendants were split into two groups and nearly three years after those initial arrests, the first four – Saunders, Lyons, Parnes and Ronson – found themselves in the dock.

The prosecution contended that Saunders, in his desire to be head of a large multinational, had used his position as Chairman of Guinness to organize a take-over bid for Distillers, which had also been the target of a rival bid from the Argyll Group. It was alleged that in order to make the bid attractive he needed to keep the Guinness share price artificially high. To do that, he called on the other three. Parnes and Lyons then went on the lookout for people prepared to buy the Guinness shares in return for an indemnity against any losses and a success fee if the bid went through. Ronson, who has always claimed that he believed the agreement to be legal, was supposedly paid £5 million in success fees and £800,000 for expenses. It also must be said that as soon as questions arose about the legality of his actions, Ronson immediately returned all the money.

Still, he was charged with conspiracy to contravene the Prevention of Fraud (Investments) Act, aiding and abetting Saunders to authorize or permit Guinness to contravene the Companies Act, false accounting and theft.

Like the others, he pleaded not guilty.

But unlike the others, he was a loser long before the trial ever started.

He never hid the fact that so much of his life had been aimed at one goal. But all his ambition, all the charity work, all the cash in the world can no longer buy what Guinness has cost him.

The dream of one day becoming Lord Ronson of Heron is over.

11

O ye of little faith.

Had you put £800 into a penny share called Polly Peck on the first of January 1980, ten years later, on the first of January 1990, your shares would have been worth £1,012,720.

That works out to a return of precisely 126,590%.

There isn't another stock listed in London now – or has there ever been a stock listed in London – to rival the decade's performance chalked up by Asil Nadir.

And yet there are still some folk in the City who think he's a flash in the pan.

The north side of Cyprus is the Turkish side. That's where he was born 48 years ago.

'My father was a very innovative businessman in Cyprus. He was the first man to do public transport there. He brought double-decker buses from the UK. He also started rental libraries, although it wasn't a very good business because my father believed in education and used to rent out the books at cost. He was a very wise man, my father, and used to say to me, don't ignore successful people because you can learn from them. I've never forgotten that.'

When he finished his studies in 1965 – he got a degree in economics from the University of Istanbul – Asil Nadir moved to England.

'My family had to leave Cyprus because all our businesses were taken away during the crisis. We thought we could get a better start here. For the next two years I divided my time between the UK and Turkey, trying to find myself, trying to decide what to do. Then in 1967 I started a company called Wearwell. The rag trade is, I think, one of the few industries you can enter without too much capital.'

However, it wasn't until 1978 that he hit the big time, that he saw how real money could be made in the part of the world he knew best.

'We had a request from the Turkish-Cypriot government. Citrus was their main export but they were having massive problems. They weren't able to compete internationally because they had no marketing expertise and lacked the right kind of packing facilities. They called me and said, can you help?'

There's always been speculation around the City about that call. After all, his critics shrug, why would someone in Cyprus concerned with the fruit business ring a garment manufacturer in the East End of London? It might not make much sense to British logic, but when you put it into the context of Nadir's world, it comes into focus. The fact is, he was connected. He grew up there, comes from one of the right families, and was known in Cyprus as having made a success of himself in the UK. Even the sometimes cynical *Financial Times* calls him 'the best-known Turkish-Cypriot businessman in Britain'. So when his pals in the government looked for one of their own to talk to, the field was pretty narrow. They weren't phoning a garment manufacturer, they were calling Asil.

'In all these countries you find that they actually think the centre of the world is the centre of some tiny village. They come to decisions or organize themselves only within their own sphere. They thought because I knew the outside world I would be the right man to give them some expertise. But if they hadn't phoned me, I would have visited them myself. It was an idea whose time had come.'

Once he got that call he did what any bright, educated young businessman would have done – he set up a feasibility study. It didn't cost much to look into the problem and anyway, he was helping the people he'd known since he was a kid. But what that feasibility study showed him was startling. He discovered that even though there were plenty of fruit exporters on the island, they were all making the same basic mistake. The fruit was good when it was picked and good when it was packed but wasn't arriving at its destination with the same quality or in the same quantity.

The packing was wrong.

It was really that fundamental.

So he thought to himself, why don't I build a fruit-packing plant in Cyprus?

Now, here's where the story gets a little complicated.

Wearwell was designing clothes in the UK, but most of their manufacturing – the higher labour-intensive work – was done in Cyprus. They were then exporting 70% of their goods to the Middle East. Nadir took the company public in 1972 and secured his own future. He was making a lot of money in that business and could have gone on making even more by simply sticking to Wearwell.

But Nadir has always been ambitious and driven by success.

A two-time winner of the Queen's Award for Export Achievement, by 1980 Wearwell was capitalized at £12–13 million. So his first idea was to build the packing plant on the back of a Wearwell rights issue for £1.5 million. It seemed like the simplest way. However, his financial advisers argued that foreign investment should not be done in Wearwell because shareholders had invested in a UK garment manufacturer and they might not take kindly to such a risk.

He tried to explain there really was no risk but when they wouldn't accept that he started looking around for a shell vehicle. The one that caught his eye was Polly Peck, a textile firm that made some money in the '60s but had run into trouble during the '70s. He bought a 56% stake, with 34% of that going through Restro, a Jersey company he'd set up to handle his personal investments.

The cost of the Polly Peck shares at the time was minimal, about five pence. He made it clear to Wearwell shareholders that the purchase of Polly Peck was conditional on their approval of a rights issue to invest in the packaging plant, which would be called Uni-pac I. And when they agreed, he went into the fruit-packing business.

'When I spoke to my friends in Cyprus about packaging, I had to explain that I didn't just mean packing something in a carton. I tried to make them understand it's got to be to the standards of the Western world. It must get the items to the consumer in perfect shape. You know, if you examine all these countries, they're not using the right technology, they're not using the right expertise to produce their cartons. They're using recycled paper. They penny-pinch. If a carton should cost 40p, they only want to pay 30p. They save 10p per carton, ignoring that within the carton the value of the produce is, say, £5. It becomes an educational process. You actually have to teach them.'

He taught them, while learning himself along the way. And before too long he wondered, if the problem exists in Cyprus, then maybe it exists in other countries too. He went to Turkey and found that, in fact, it did.

'Turkey has massive resources. Millions of tons of citrus fruit, millions of tons of grapes, millions of tons of tomatoes. We found they were excellent up to the growing stage. But from there, they didn't know what to do. Spain was exporting something like 66% of its crop. Turkey was exporting 20%. Like most of the developing countries, their economy is inward-looking. They don't always think beyond their own borders. Yet, with the deficits and inflation, they have to find so many more dollars just to survive. Unless they start looking outward they are not going to survive. They need technology. Their capital markets are in such a mess. They haven't got a chance to survive unless you take them inexpensive capital and technology. In return, you mobilize those massive resources.'

That's precisely what he did.

It was as if he had the key to a vault.

Almost from the day he opened Uni-pac he started making phenomenal money. Profits quickly headed up towards £10 million. It was clear to him that Cyprus couldn't have been more ripe for something exactly like this, so he built Uni-pac II. Next, he put his own Sunzest label on oranges and lemons. New markets were opened. Polly Peck shares, which had been on a one or two times earnings basis, suddenly had a new look to them. There was speculative buying. That drove the share prices even higher. The profits kept coming in. And the share prices took off. Having gone from five pence to nine pence, they stayed at 35p for a while. Then, with dizzying speed, they hit £8.

From there they went to £10, then £12, stopped for a pause at £20 and raced up to £35.

Everyone was talking about Nadir and Polly Peck.

Analysts who wouldn't have given him the time of day a couple of years earlier were now saying things like, the agricultural industry is severely under-developed you know, and Cyprus had previously been importing packaging, so this Nadir chap comes along, you understand that he's got an in with all the politicians there, hum, yes, and so he comes along with this start-up business . . .

He became the wonderboy of the City.

'The speculators did that. Not me. You have to understand that share speculation does a lot of harm at times. Others speculate and we get the blame. The shares should have never gone up to £35 at that time. If you look at the P/E ratio it didn't make sense.'

Fast up, fast down, and they did come slipping down. They fell to around £22 before being split 10 for 1. Word around the City was that he had no staying power, that it was all a fluke, that his organization didn't have the infrastructure of a business pretending to be so important, that he was probably some sort of Turkish-Cypriot spy here to steal the secrets of capitalism.

'In this country there are people who believe that it's a sin to be successful. I don't know if it's jealousy, but the attitudes are not constructive. I go to a country where the produce is not worth anything because it's wasted. I pay them a proper price. Because I'm efficient and integrated, I earn a higher margin than someone sitting here just distributing food. Tell me why I should be criticized for that. I ought to be complimented because I've gone to a developing country, created employment, and put up plants. Instead for this I get criticized!'

These days, little has changed, except the size of the game. His philosophy is exactly the same. Solve the problem in one country, find another country with the same problem, and implant the same solution.

But to some people it looks as if those big profits only come at the expense of big risks. Not everyone wants to put their money into areas sometimes described as politically shaky even if the dangling carrot is 40–50% returns.

He shrugs off those criticisms.

'There are political risks only if you don't know the country. What happens with many multinationals is that they get a bad surprise from some division. That wouldn't happen with us. We believe in communication with the grass roots. Whether it's financial or general information, we have people based in those countries who mix with the people. We're always trying to get a better feel as to how the country is doing. Of course political stability is important. But any fluctuation or any movement towards instability starts as a rumble among the people. That's where you have to listen. The rulers are the last to know. When they find out, it's too late.'

Perhaps. But there are still some people in Cyprus who worry that one day the Greeks will get fed up with the Turks and start fighting again and then what would happen to his investments there?

'You're asking the question because you don't know the country. Everything in life is a balance of power. Not only in Cyprus but all over the world. You have the Western bloc, you have the Eastern bloc. I must say, by the way, that we're not a political entity. Please understand that. My business has nothing to do with politics. But doing business in a place like Cyprus only looks like a political risk if you don't know the country and don't understand this concept of the balance of power. You have the smaller Turkish community in northern Cyprus and you have a bigger Greek community in the south.

You have Greece, with eight or nine million population. And then you have Turkey. So although the balance is to the advantage of the Greeks in Cyprus, you then have to add in the size of Greece, economically and militarily, and the same for Turkey. When you balance the whole thing, although you think it's politically insecure, the risk element is one we can accept. Today I feel there would never be any trouble in Cyprus unless the Turks want it. And we know that the Turks don't want it. The whole problem in Cyprus was that a minority wanted the same rights as the majority, to live without the fear of being annihilated. Today I reckon there is less of a risk in Cyprus than the radical left-wing unions taking over in England.'

Enter here Greeks bearing rumours.

In early 1983, the Greek-Cypriot government began to realize that, apart from the Turkish-Cypriot government, Nadir and Polly Peck were the major industrial investors on the northern side of the island. As the Greek-Cypriots have a stake in ensuring that the Turkish-Cypriots never become economically viable, so they put out the word.

A Greek banker in London became the mouthpiece.

Big-risk area, he said. Big-risk taker this Nadir. Could be a big loser very fast. He talked about Nadir and his huge margins. Nadir and his profits tied to nothing more than currency fluctuations. Nadir and his political connections. Say, what do you think would happen if the Restro Investments books were made public? Restro holds a heavy block of Polly Peck shares. But, according to the *Observer*, Restro is just a subsidiary of a Manx company called Hillgate. And, while Hillgate is owned by Nadir, Restro has several other shareholders besides Nadir. Among them are shares registered to nominees at various banks, including one in the Cayman Islands. The *Observer* said shares are held by Ashraf Marwan, another Egyptian businessman named Hani Abd el Salam, a Panamanian company called Shadow Valley Inc., a Liberian-registered company called Mosel Investment Corporation, and something known as Kipeco Finance SA.

'Restro doesn't concern anyone,' Nadir has always argued. 'It's a private company. The press can insinuate anything they want as far as I'm concerned because it really doesn't matter. I can assure you, nothing moves me. We know the goal. What we have to do. We know what we're doing is right. They're the wrong ones and we don't have to be proved right. No, it doesn't matter at all.'

What he does point out is that he has, all along, continued to buy Polly Peck shares. He says he's never lost faith in the company and puts his own money into it because he knows how good the company is. There is an adage that goes, if the man running the company doesn't spend his own money on it, chances are something must be wrong. If that's true, then the opposite might be true as well. When the man running the company does spend his own money on it, chances are something must be right.

The *coup de grâce* in the rumour market was the story that Polly Peck's seven-year tax holiday in Famagusta was non-existent. That it was just a Nadir pipe-dream. That all his fancy profits were pre-tax and destined to disappear into the Turkish-Cypriot treasury.

As it turned out, the story was totally false.

The tax holiday was very much a reality. Nadir had cut a deal with the Treasury there and was so much the better for it. But people got nervous. Share prices had gone too far, too fast. They were overcooked.

Just as Polly Peck was about to absorb Wearwell, the share prices fell.

The Greek banker's timing was immaculate.

Nadir's own bankers decided it was wiser to wait until the prices stabilized before Polly Peck went ahead with its plans to digest Wearwell. The planted stories effectively caused a 13-month delay.

What little good news there might have been easily turned sour. In one case, perhaps even negligently so, a British journalist went out to Turkey to have a look at a mineral water bottling plant Polly Peck was building in Niksar. He did't find it as complete as he thought he would, and he told the world. Nadir tried to argue that the journalist got it wrong, that he wasn't looking in the right place. The journalist stood his ground. Nadir filed a whopping libel suit. But it was too late.

Buoyed up and keyed up by tremendous hopes – by balance sheets that showed over 40% return on turnover – Humpty Dumpty had a great fall.

And, at least for a couple of mornings, Greek bankers everywhere dined out on scrambled eggs.

For some reason he is forever being labelled 'mercurial' and 'slightly controversial'.

It may have something to do with the fact that from fruit-packing he branched out to mineral water production, electronics, tourism and not so long ago even opened the first Pizza Hut in Turkey. It may also have to do with Nadir running his company from the front and over the years having had problems with keeping top-class executive managers.

When a senior manager walked out a few years ago, Nadir regretted his departure but explained, 'There was some confusion over who was the Chief Executive.'

Or it might be tied up with the fact that the City institutional investors have never forgotten how, in 1985, all sorts of fancy profits were promised but when the annual reports were published the estimates were off by several miles.

What baffles people is that mercurial or not, controversal or not, Nadir has – with the exception of that 1985 hiccup – constantly delivered staggering results. By 1988 he'd become one of the most profitable fruit distributors in the world. He'd also built up a global electronics business, using a cheap manufacturing base in Turkey.

'Why shouldn't they, in Turkey today, have the same quality of video or television as other consumers in the West? When we looked at the market, we saw the Japanese were selling only a few thousand sets per annum there. Ask them and they'll tell you that their studies show there is a very big market but they just can't seem to sell there. To have the right product and to have a huge market and not sell, there must be something wrong. In their case it was a lack of understanding of the area.'

And none of that, he insists, has anything to do with taking risks. Instead, it's all about minimizing risks.

'I keep hearing stories about political risks, but throughout the 1980s I worked hard to broaden our base, to expand our manufacturing and sales bases into other areas. We went into electronics in Turkey. They only got colour television there in 1984 and we were there to feed that market. When it peaked, we looked to sell our products in Western Europe. Televisions made in Turkey are now sold in the UK. When I bought Capetronics, I opened our electronics market in Japan. We bought Russell Hobbs and Tower domestic appliances which we sell throughout Europe. We built up our fruit operations in Spain and Uruguay and have a special sourcing arrangement in Chile. That fruit is as profitable if not more profitable than the fruit we sell from Turkey. And yet everyone keeps talking about all the risks we're taking in Cyprus and Turkey and areas like that. It simply doesn't make any sense.'

'He's a gunslinger,' one City broker says. And it's exactly that reputation which gives Polly Peck the look of a personalized business. Polly Peck is Asil Nadir and Asil Nadir is Polly Peck, and often the twain shall meet.

'It's not a personalized business.' Nadir doesn't like that reference at all. 'It's a team effort. I'm merely the face of the company because dealing with the City or the press is so time-consuming and I want to keep my management busy with the job we have to do. But the real problem is not that. It's that the British don't understand or know much about Turkey or Cyprus. They don't know much about the potential of those countries. Many people in the UK don't know that Turkey is self-sufficient in food, for example. They have a fairly negative view and are a bit nervous about those areas as an investment. They've not understood what we're trying to do.'

That sort of misunderstanding seems to haunt him.

Even as late as 1989, after Nadir managed to pull off a pair of spectacular deals which helped turn the company into a global business, the *FT* couldn't help but use sobering tones.

Acknowledging that Polly Peck was successfully transforming itself from 'an opportunistic and erratic trading group into a truly international electronics and agricultural business', the *FT* couldn't help but insist that Polly Peck still had a way to go before it won the public relations battle. 'The company has not entirely put its reputation for nasty surprises behind it.'

Nadir simply can't understand it.

'I am a workaholic. Work is my hobby. But this is not a one-man show. Why do I have to keep saying that? How could one man run all this?'

Yet as he explains it, and even when he shows you videos to prove that he's doing what he says he's doing – to prove that the profits are there, that the infrastructure is there, that the business is indeed as important as the City once said it was – there is still some lingering doubt. The press has helped create an image and the Greek merchant bankers probably can't afford to let it die.

Deep down he knows that, probably better than anyone.

'When you look at the inaccuracies in the press it's unbelievable. In the end, we don't really need public relations. We feel that by doing what we're doing perfectly, given time, it will be understood. But one hopes that, given time, the quality of journalism will be better.' He shrugs. 'One hopes.'

Spotting opportunities is basically what his business is all about. And, he claims, it is not difficult once you know what to look for.

'It's like being a doctor. Once you've seen a hundred cases of the measles, you recognize it right away. Believe me, opportunities stare you in the face. I suppose one has to have a certain degree of intelligence and knowledge of business, but the opportunities are massive.'

The secret of making money once you spot those opportunities is integration. Call it, if you will, the 'full trading circle method'. By starting with a natural resource product, like fruit,

Nadir finances his other investments. The fruit is exported, which turns Turkish lira into hard currencies. Those hard currencies are then brought back into the country to create further investments, such as cars or video recorders. In turn, they're sold for Turkish lira which are then pumped back into products for export, and more hard currencies. The circle cushions the foreign exchange risk while also allowing Nadir to take his profits whenever he wants.

'There is a tremendous mistrust with the West. They look at these countries and think they're risk areas, that it's unsafe to trade there. And so the attitude out there is that the Western world always wants to take advantage. We've seen a lot of bad examples. In the pharmaceutical industry, for instance, left-over products are pushed into those countries. Business ethics – without specifically pinpointing any Western companies – are non-existent. They start by taking the developing countries for granted. The quality of goods shipped out there is usually sub-standard. I think they try to sell there because they can't find a market for certain products in the West.'

One of the ways he's tried to capitalize on that and, at the same time, expand is to reshape Polly Peck – he now calls the group Polly Peck International, or PPI – with redefined priorities. He's totally divested out of textiles in order to concentrate on three specific areas of interest: food, electronics and leisure.

In food, mainly fruit, he's taken a completely integrated position. His companies pick fruit – and in some countries like Turkey they actually own the trees – package it, ship it and market it.

Electronics is mainly audio and video equipment.

The leisure area includes hotels in Turkey.

In order to successfully expand his fresh fruit business, he knew he had to look towards the United States. So in 1987 he bought Prevor Marketing International in New York. They had a strong export business, from Latin America, shipping fruit and vegetables to the States and Europe. He also purchased a similar operation in California and formed Sunzest marketing subsidiaries in Japan and Hong Kong.

Then he went after the biggest catch of all.

In September 1989, he paid $875 million to RJR Nabisco for the Del Monte-brand fresh fruit business – the world's largest supplier of fresh pineapples and the third-largest supplier of bananas.

It not only gave Nadir one of the most famous brand names in the world, it consolidated a series of small, locally based businesses to turn PPI into a global force, as the third-largest fruit company in the world.

'This was an absolutely extraordinary opportunity, one of those once-in-a-lifetime deals. Not only is it the most famous brand of fresh fruit in the world, but the business we had and the business we bought matched perfectly. They were truly complementary. PPI is strong in citrus fruits and in Europe. Del Monte is strong in bananas and pineapples and has it's principle markets in North America and the Far East. We will now put the Del Monte name on all of our fresh produce.'

He's prepared the ground for 1992.

There's little doubt that Brussels is looking for Europe to become more self-sufficient in its food supply. The importation of products that aren't grown in Europe, like bananas or pineapples, could be restricted to European companies or growers in, say, former French and British colonies. It opens the door for PPI to supply British bananas and British pineapples, even if they come from Honduras or Hawaii.

But buying into Del Monte was one thing.

After all, other British-based businesses have bought into US companies recently.

Yet when Nadir went to Japan in October 1989 and wound up as the main story on the national TV news, and on all the front pages, even his sceptics in the City had to sit up and take notice.

His purchase of a 51% stake in the Japanese audio group, Sansui, for £69 million, made PPI only the third foreign company to win control of a quoted Japanese firm. (The BOC Group purchased Osaka Sano, a gases company in 1982, and the US drugs group Merck took control of Banyu Pharmaceuticals in 1983.)

'Today is almost an historic landmark in the relationship between Japan and other trading nations,' he announced to the Japanese press. 'The myths that Japan is not open to companies from foreign countries have been demolished at a stroke.'

Wait a minute, the sceptics cried. The only reason the Japanese sold out was to unload the thing. You don't think they'd have sold anything that was making money, do you?

As a matter of fact, it's true that the Sansui board had been looking around for help from several sources and that they only accepted Nadir's offer after it became clear that no Japanese companies were interested.

Nadir had to shake his head and laugh.

'It's incredible isn't it. If this company couldn't make money I wouldn't have bought it and if they didn't think I could make money for them they wouldn't have sold it to me. What's more, there is no denying that I have opened a door that has remained shut for many other Western companies. Here is a nation that is constantly criticized in the rest of the world for putting up cultural barriers. They come to the West to buy but when a Western company goes there and bangs on the door, they get nowhere. But my approach was different. I didn't pound on the door. I knocked on it softly and waited for them to open it. Too many Western companies forget that in Japan dealing with us is also a cultural problem for them.'

What Nadir plans to do with Sansui is use it exactly the same way he will use Del Monte.

His Capetronic operation in Europe needed a well-known brand name in addition to a base in the Orient. Now that he's got that, he'll bring Sansui into Europe, switching production from South Korea and Taiwan to Turkey, while expanding it's sales throughout Europe and the Mediterranean.

It also capitalized PPI at over £1 billion.

'An extraordinary performance,' the financial press wrote.

'It is a turning point,' he agreed. 'And I hope now it will

vindicate my claim for all the achievements we have made. We have done as much work in 10 years as other people do in 20.'

Asil Nadir's office, in a period building off Berkeley Square, has got to be the most stunning office in London.

He is a man of enormous good taste – Western good taste – with the money to back it up.

The building is filled with antique furniture, fine oriental rugs, old master paintings and tapestries. In the reception area on the main floor, there's a fabulous eighteenth-century writing desk. In his own office one flight up, plants and small trees surround period furniture. It looks more like an extremely comfortable gentlemen's library, with huge French windows, some terrific Persian carpets, more paintings and tapestries, a roaring fireplace and a spectacular old mirror above it.

'Not everyone is invited in here,' he makes a point of saying.

It's understandable.

This is not only an office, it's a home-made museum, something very personal and in a way very private.

'Yes, I have tried to make my office like a home. I spend so much time here I want to feel comfortable.'

He is easy to be with, a nice-looking man with a good smile and a strong handshake, a man with Middle Eastern/Mediterranean charm and a British savvy of how to deal one-on-one with writers.

Of course coffee is served.

So are all the usual pleasantries about friends and family.

In addition to running PPI – which he points out is a full-time job – Nadir has personally become a major investor in Turkey. His private interests span banking, a small charter airline and publishing.

Late in 1988, he made his first move into Turkish media when he bought a series of publications that included *Gunaydin*, a daily broadsheet in Istanbul. In January 1989 he added to his interests there with the Gelisim chain of publications, which include *Ekonomik Panorama*, an economic weekly, and *Nokta*, a popular weekly, described as 'radical chic', with an appeal to younger readers. A few days later he announced the purchase of *Gunes*, another daily in Istanbul.

'But you must understand something about my newspaper interests. I have set sound editorial standards but do not exercise any editorial control. I have stressed to the editors that they must be fair and objective. But I have not expressed my political views to them, nor would I.'

There has been some comment in the press that since he took over the newspapers they've taken a more softly-softly approach with certain politicans. But Nadir refutes that.

'They've taken a more cautious, more professional, more objective approach.'

He has a huge mansion in Turkey now, on the Bosporus, where he spends some time every month.

But Britain is home. His family is here, he's raised his sons here and he carries a British passport.

And that's why, he says, he's decided it's time to start giving something back to Britain. In association with the National Society for the Prevention of Cruelty to Children and the Spastics Society, he's made an initial donation of £5 million of his own money towards the creation of a remedial centre for behaviourly disturbed adolescents.

'We're building it near Milton Keynes. My idea is that there are homes for disturbed children but not much for young adults. And when they grow up they are no longer taken care of the way they should be. So I've formed an association that will be the pilot programme in helping to care for these people. At the same time it will be a training centre for staff.'

And like everything else he does, he promises that if it works in Milton Keynes, he'll find way of exporting it to other places where such help is needed.

'It's about time that charities were directed by people who understand sound business principles. It's the best way I can think of to give something back.'

12

Ian Posgate

Ian Richard Posgate will for ever be remembered along Lime Street as 'Goldfinger'.

But the nickname wasn't born out of affection.

He was the most unanimously disliked man who ever stalked the insurance market that is Lloyds of London. He was frequently rude, often contemptuous, and even at the best of times difficult. At the time, the highest-paid man in the UK, he was also undoubtedly the most flamboyant underwriter Lloyds has ever seen – or, for that matter, is ever likely to see.

Then came the scandals. They rocked the very foundations of the insurance business. Yet a hundred years from now, if Lloyds of London still exists, 'Tales of Goldfinger' will still be told – the way folks in Dodge City still talk about Wyatt and Doc and the OK Corral.

Lloyds of London is a market-place where brokers bring risks and where underwriters openly compete against each other to insure those risks.

Today it's housed in a modern glass and steel structure filled with hanging plants and escalators, and people asking each other how to find the well hidden washrooms.

But in Posgate's day Lloyds operated out of an over-crowded, out of date, much more romantic building, the heart of which was 'The Room' where underwriters sat crammed into 400 uncomfortable wooden stalls – a sort of accountants' *souk*.

The game they play, however, has not changed.

A broker begins the process with a form called a 'slip', which gives the details of the insurance cover he's seeking. Slip in hand, he literally walks around the room shopping for someone to underwrite the deal. As the insurance business is based on the concept of spreading risk, underwriters generally only take a small percentage. For example, one may sign on for 2%. Another may go for just 0.5%. The broker has done his job when he's filled 100%. If there's a claim, the underwriter pays his agreed percentage. If there's no claim, he receives his agreed percentage of the premiums.

Except, in practice, it isn't that simple.

For many people, Lloyds is also an investment. Each underwriter represents a syndicate in which people have pooled their wealth to cover risks. These 'names' – and there are currently about 28,000 of them – have committed the full extent of their personal fortune to cover claims. Going bust means losing everything – cash, homes, cars, silverware, paintings – at least, everything that hasn't been safely transferred to a husband or wife. To become a name you must be worth £100,000–500,000, depending on where you are and where your fortune is. The further away, the higher the ante. A certain portion of this must be liquid. But, nicely enough, none of your liquid assets need ever leave your savings account, unless there is a claim. So your £100,000 can pick up 10–15% at the building society, while on the syndicate's books at Lloyds it might earn another 15% in premium income. If the syndicate has a good year, there might also be a share in the profits – perhaps another 15%. It's not unheard of for names to find themselves 40–50% ahead at the end of the year, and some of it is tax-free. On the other hand, if the syndicate has a tough year, you get a bill from them. That's recently been known to be the plight of several once-profitable syndicates; although it must be said that the long-term gain is the rule and total loss is extremely rare. And even if the more conservative folks at Lloyds hate to admit it in public, being a name is sometimes said to be almost as good as having a licence to print money.

Making money was what Ian Posgate wanted to do when he left Gonville and Caius at Cambridge without a degree after one year in 1953.

He came to Lloyds to learn the underwriting trade. But he never wore one of the correct school ties, never had one of the correct regimental ties, and at Lloyds those things matter. Still, by the time the '70s came along, his undisputed genius for the insurance game and his stunning ability to make both money and enemies brought him superstar status. In 1965 he'd been underwriting for fewer than 30 names. By 1980 he was underwriting for 5–6000. One estimate says that almost 10% of all the business conducted at Lloyds was coming through him. And in 1980 Lloyds did nearly £4 billion-worth of business.

With nearly 25% of Lloyds' names on the books of the four syndicates he controlled, Posgate had a reputation for taking big chances – war risks, satellites, kidnappings, hijackings – and coming out ahead. Not surprisingly, jealousy ran high. And that merely helped to breed more contempt. His lack of friends and his maverick reputation meant there were plenty of people stalking the bushes, waiting for their shot at him. Yet as long as he made fortunes for people – including himself – the names on his syndicate figured they could learn to put up with his temper.

'I don't know if I was the best who ever was,' says Posgate. 'I think Roy Merritt was very good. I think I was the best there was in the '70s. But it's very difficult to say. It's like comparing one baseball player of one generation with one baseball player of some other generation. Roy Merritt was doing the same thing except I suppose the field was smaller and in those days you wore longer trousers.'

The Committee of Lloyds, acting like a board of directors, took their first shot at Goldfinger in 1970, officially censuring him for 'writing on the back of the Central Fund'. It was, and still is, a favourite trick of the high-flyers. It was, and still is, against the rules.

One of the main safeguards built into Lloyds is a multi-layered series of reserve funds maintained to ensure that a policy can always be paid, even if all the names in the syndicate go broke. Billions of pounds are set aside to insure the insurers.

Since each syndicate is limited by the wealth of the names, overwriting means that policies are written for more than that amount and the underwriter is risking not only the total wealth of his names, but also the funds held by Lloyds in reserve. If the underwriter has guessed wrong, the names go bust and the reserve funds must cough up the difference. But if the underwriter wins, the names of his syndicate make more money than they otherwise could have hoped for and the bookkeepers who look after the Central Fund are none the wiser.

'I was not popular in '70,' Posgate says. 'And the unpopularity remained. I would have suggested it was jealousy.' And no, he still insists, he was not writing on the back of the fund. Anyway, he adds, 'I've always believed that Lloyds should be net underwriters, risk-taking underwriters. And I don't think there's any question, with the spread of my account, of writing on the back of the fund. As was proved, the idiots who wrote huge lines on computer leasing (a £222 million fiasco for Lloyds), who were safe syndicates, were far more likely to wind up on the central guarantee fund than in fact I was.'

Chairman of the Committee in those days was Paul Dixey, an elegant man whose father had also been a Committee chairman, and who was the third of four Dixey generations at Lloyds. He makes no bones about saying that he thinks Ian Posgate is 'a ruthless bully who has consistently and deliberately broken the rules. He is a most unpopular man'. But then Dixey gives Posgate his due by admitting he was very successful, especially when times for other underwriters were bad. And, yes, 'that can breed envy and jealousy. He may be a man of courage, single-minded and completely self-reliant. He has a wonderful memory and a terrific head for figures. But I would say that he has a complete lack of moral scruples.'

Yet Dixey and the Committee stopped short of total banishment and agreed to let Posgate underwrite for a managing agent. They wanted him to have a babysitter.

Enter now the Alexander Howden Group.

It was a flashy, entrepreneurial UK brokerage house, the brainchild of Ken Grob. He was just the man to see the possibilities of joining forces with Ian Posgate. All Grob had to do was be a minder. All Posgate had to do was make money. It worked so well that at times during the '70s Posgate was able to post 40% annual profits. 'To some extent,' Posgate says, 'Ken Grob was quite a good minder because he was adaptable. I made a lot of money for a lot of people including Mr Grob.'

The way Grob sees it, Posgate was not as great an underwriter as he was a risk taker. 'He was a risk taker, that's for sure. But of course he had huge reinsurance facilities behind him. He was essentially a dealer. He'd say to a broker, look, I want your war risk account. And the chap would say, well you can have 5% and Pos would say, no, don't be silly, I want 100%. They'd finally compromise with Pos probably writing 50%. Or the broker would find that Pos would undercut his rates to his competitor. He was that sort of dealer. It was marginal stuff. But he had got a flair for the short-term risk. He loved war and kidnap and ransom, that type of thing. He wasn't the kind of underwriter to whom you'd take a really serious complicated risk, because he couldn't be bothered to read it. He always had 30 people waiting to see him. I don't want to denigrate him because I have the highest opinion of his ability in the market to stir things up and get the market business. As great underwriters go, no, he simply wasn't one. As a great risk taker, yes, he was.'

For a while, the Howden Group and Goldfinger had the world at their feet. There were big cars with fridges in the boot to keep the champagne cold during Royal Ascot. There were country estates in the UK and holiday mansions on the Riviera. They had cash in their pockets and art on their walls.

Even Horatio Alger couldn't have invented Ian Posgate.

Jack Bogardus watched it all from the other side of the Atlantic.

In his mid-50s, tall with light hair, his father had been a big deal in the US insurance industry, and he was determined to be just as big. With great determination Bogardus jun. worked his way up the ladder at Alexander and Alexander Services, the second-largest insurance broker in the United States, manœuvred a boardroom shuffle and took control. Then he did what most men do to prove that they're in control – he made decisions. Under the previous chairman there had been flirtations with Alexander Howden. But A&A always walked away.

Now in 1979 Bogardus was shopping for a way into Lloyds. He gave Howden another look. And suddenly he liked what he saw. Posgate was part of the deal. A fortune was in the offing, so there were meetings in London, afternoons at Grob's villa in the South of France, and expensive lunches in New York. But Bogardus hesitated and eventually confessed to one member of his board, 'These guys are too rich for our blood.'

Unsure of himself, he turned instead to the much less glossy Sedgwick Group, Britain's largest independent insurance broker. They courted for two years. They held hands. There might even have been some goodnight kisses. But one day the romance ended. Interestingly enough, near the end, Bogardus reportedly mentioned to someone that if the deal fell through he'd go back to Howden. The advice he got was, 'I wouldn't touch them with a bargepole.' Bogardus denies it. The source of the advice dined out on the story for a year. But then Bogardus also denies that at least one member of his own board also cautioned him against Howden. True or not, it instantly became a moot point because two days after the Sedgwick deal fell through, Bogardus rang Grob to ask, 'Are you still for sale?' Six weeks later the deal was made.

Bogardus handed Grob $300 million (then £170 million) for Howden, their very complex network of more than 200 companies worldwide, and the wheeling-dealing skills of Posgate. On 1 January 1982, Alexander Howden became the 'Third Alexander' at A&A.

But it quickly turned out that $300 million merely got Bogardus into the game. Unknowingly, and/or clumsily, he stumbled into the biggest scandal the City had yet seen.

While this was going on, in December 1981, Posgate ran for a seat on the 16-man Committee of Lloyds. He lost. In January another seat came vacant. Posgate ran again. And this time, to the Establishment's horror, he won by 27 votes. 'My election to the Committee infuriated Peter Green who was then Chairman. In retrospect it was probably a very bad thing. I wonder whether certain things would have happened if I was not on the Committee.'

Then came the Qantas scandal.

Insurance for Australia's airline was up for renewal on 1 April. In March, to everyone's surprise, the account was taken away from a company called Bain Dawes, which had placed it for 30 years, and wound up at Howden's. When the slip went around the room, the top line was a whopping 15% signed by marine specialist Ian Posgate. It caused a stir for three reasons: aviation insurance is usually written by aviation specialists; the largest piece of the action most underwriters take is well below 15%; and the $5 million Posgate quoted for the business was way below the going rate. Aviation underwriters screamed 'foul' and in the end Posgate couldn't find enough associates to pick up the remaining 85%. The Qantas affair put Howden in an embarrassing light. To set the situation straight, they soon announced that Posgate had been replaced on the Qantas account by another underwriter who would take it for $5.5 million, with Howden paying the $500,000 difference. To some people the episode pointed up the flaws in a system where one firm could represent both the insured and the insurer.

In the midst of this, on 16 March 1982 Posgate resigned from Howden's board. 'I was unhappy about being left out of the merger talks between Howden and Alexander and Alexander. Because it was quite wrong. And it was very dangerous.'

Before long, a steady trickle of Howden names were defecting to Posgate's own syndicates.

Unbeknownst to Bogardus or Grob, Posgate had been thinking about his swansong with Howden for some time. A bill had been introduced in Parliament that would separate the powers of brokers and underwriters. If it were passed, Posgate would be free of his minder and, in a sense, have *carte blanche* to take with him the names he was otherwise dividing between his own syndicates and Howden. Grob and every other broker in the market petitioned to defeat the Lloyds Bill. And they might have swung it had Posgate himself not gone down to Westminster to testify before the House. His argument was so damaging to the case against the bill that he alone might have been the reason it passed.

'If you like, I made two mistakes that I would do over and over again. I stood for the Committee and got on. And I fought the Committee and (the then Chairman) Peter Green on divestment (i.e. splitting the jobs of brokers and underwriters). Green and all the major broking houses hated me for that. But I think that in a hundred years' time the most important thing of this century, for Lloyds, is the recognition of conflicts of interest and the consequent divestment. There is no question that, without me, divestment would not have taken place. I single-handedly got divestment through and I paid for it. I was the only person who gave evidence for divestment. But divestment moved Lloyds into the new century and towards facing up to conflicts of interest, which in fact have been faced in America for some years but have not been faced in the City of London.'

On 3 July, the House of Lords approved the legislation. On 4 July, Posgate shook the market by announcing that he would cease underwriting for the two Howden syndicates. 'I wanted out.' More names defected from Howden to Posgate. But the best was yet to come. Bogardus had at last asked for an audit of Howden. And the accounting firm of Deloitte Haskins & Sells reported 'discrepancies'.

The operative word became *reinsurance*.

Once an underwriter signs a slip, he's committed his syndicate to that percentage of the action. However he can, if he wants, hedge his bet by reinsuring the percentage elsewhere. And reinsurance was something Posgate understood very well.

As Grob explains, 'He was a natural-born man to sit there in his box, with no one telling him what to do. I mean, no one had any control over him at all. I forget the numbers now. But where he had, for example, a £90 million capacity after reinsurance in 1982, I think his final net figure was £120 million. He'd gone over his limits by a third. That didn't put him on the Central Fund, all it meant was that if individual names as a result of his overwriting had exceeded their individual limits, they'd have to put up pound for pound. If he had a really major loss, he had two things: huge reinsurance protection running something like £100 million on which he could call first of all; then he'd call on these 4000 or 5000 names. I used to say to the Committee, don't worry because there's no such thing as a risk which Posgate couldn't pay if the market was still there. I mean, one could envision a risk, obviously, which Posgate couldn't pay, but then nor would anyone else pay it. It would be a national catastrophe and the nation would have to fund it. Or the Americans would have to fund it, like California falling into the sea.'

What Deloitte believed to be happening was that Posgate's syndicates were reinsuring through the Howden-owned Sphere Drake company, and then, somehow, monies were being filtered through various companies and trusts until they disappeared. One of those companies was registered in Panama as Southern International Re (SIR) – the 'Re' being the generally accepted abbreviation for reinsurance. And all of this might have been fine except this time the 'Re' stood for real estate. Making matters worse, SIR was secretly owned by the 'Gang of Four' – Ken Grob, Howden directors Ron Comery and Jack Carpenter, and Howden finance chief Allan Page. That disclosure, while required, had not been made. Putting SIR under the microscope, Deloitte then found some money going through SIR being used by the Gang of Four, and possibly Posgate, to purchase a bank in Geneva called the Banque du Rhone et de la Tamise. The Deloitte conclusion was that a lot of pennies were missing – like $55 million-worth.

Now Jack Bogardus had to make a tough decision. If fraud was involved, he had to call the cops. On the other hand, if this was simply a matter of accounting procedures, maybe he could get the money back without upsetting his shareholders in New York. He must have figured it worth a try because on Friday night 13 August he and the Gang of Four sat down to do some big-league haggling.

Posgate was not invited.

Bogardus showed up at the meeting well armed. He even had the code names the four were using to keep money supposedly hidden in Liechtenstein trusts: Grob was Bloomers, Comery was Blissful, Page was Karoli and Carpenter was Skyair. In the end Posgate turned out to be Hereford.

The result of that meeting was a secret agreement whereby Alexander and Alexander promised not to take civil action against the Gang of Four in exchange for more than $29 million in cash and assets. In the final draft the word 'civil' was used, although in the initial draft the words 'civil or criminal' appeared. The word 'criminal' was struck out at the insistence of Rod Hills, who was linked to the meeting from his home in California by an open telephone line. His advice carried a lot of weight with Bogardus, not merely because Hills was Chairman of A&A's audit committee, but also because Hills was a former chairman of the American Securities and Exchange Commission (SEC).

The agreement was signed in the early hours of Saturday 14 August. A contingent from A&A arrived at Posgate's home near Henley-upon-Thames later that day for lunch. 'I was on very good terms with them,' he remembers. 'I thought at the time I could work with Bogardus. With hindsight, I do not know.'

Nine days later, Bogardus mysteriously announced that A&A was severing all ties with the Gang of Four and that Posgate would be Chairman of Alexander Howden Underwritings. Four days after that, Bogardus admitted there was a $25 million shortfall in Howden's assets. Then came the first public claim that the Gang of Four had secretly controlled a company that did extensive reinsurance business with Howden. That announcement was totally unexpected by the Gang of Four because in Clause Four of the secret agreement all the signatories, including Bogardus, pledged to honour the confidentiality of the agreement. And in case of disputes, they'd all agreed that arbitration would be the proper step. Bogardus had gone back on his word.

Sir Peter Green and the Committee of Lloyds sat nervously on the sidelines.

Firstly, no one on the Rota was particularly thrilled to see Posgate there. Certain Committee members apparently felt entitled to be on the Committee at Lloyds because their fathers had been there before them. And in their eyes, Posgate was a 'parvenu'. But then Posgate always said that one of the main problems with Lloyds was that it suffers from 'the second generation' syndrome.

'It definitely has. It still does. The problem, and this applies to Miller (Peter, former Chairman and great nephew of Thomas), Chester (Henry, nephew of Guy), Merritt (Stephen, son of Roy) and Green (Sir Peter, son of Toby), is that the people who inherit, who have not in themselves created, spend most of their time protecting what their family created. They're inward-looking and that's led to the problems Lloyds has.'

Secondly, it was hardly their fault that Posgate had been elected to the Committee. However, given time, they would find a way to even that score by throwing him off and banning him from Lloyds.

Thirdly, and very importantly, some people at Lloyds, including Committee members, felt that the less the public and the authorities knew about the actual workings of Lloyds, the better. Many of them were well aware of the all-too-many entangling alliances that could come to light if the scandal spread.

Case in point: the potentially embarrassing explanations that would have to be made by Committee Chairman, Sir Peter Green. 'Gang of Four' member Allan Page had worked for Toby Green, Peter Green and Peter Cameron-Webb. As a senior partner in an auditing firm, Page acted as their adviser. That firm was also auditing Howden's books. One day Grob offered Page a job. Only later, when full disclosures of hidden assets became the rule at Lloyds, did one notice that some of Peter Green's offshore reinsurance interests had a familiar ring to them. They were very similar to the ones in question at Howden. And similar again to the ones which were run by Peter Cameron-Webb and which would eventually drive him out of Lloyds. Nothing illegal of course. That would hardly befit a second-generation Chairman of Lloyds. Just familiar.

All this time Bogardus was still saying that there was room for Posgate in his organization. 'I get along fine with Mr Posgate. It often happens that the best people in any company are the most entrepreneurial and of course those are the most difficult to control.' He also said he didn't expect Posgate to steal away into the night with Howden's names. 'If Mr Posgate decides to leave, that is something that we will have to worry about when it happens.' Even though he too had heard the rumours that Posgate was thinking about cutting out, as late as 30 August Bogardus was still telling the world, 'If we lived on rumours we would all be committing suicide hourly, especially in London.'

Yet by 8 September, Lime Street was in turmoil.

The Lloyds Committee had no choice but to ask their own auditors to look into the matter. And a lot of people at Lloyds were making phone calls to places like Panama, trying to divest themselves of certain interests before it became too late. Then, on 20 September, A&A filed what is known as a 'Current Report/8-K' with the SEC in Washington. There is some reason to believe that, during the meeting on 13–14 August with the Gang of Four, Bogardus had been urged to sign the secret agreement on the advice of Hills who assured him that he, as a former SEC chairman, knew what kinds of agreements the SEC would accept. But when Hills failed to get SEC approval for that agreement, or when the SEC, on their own, looked askance at it, he warned A&A to immediately cut bait. They had no choice but to file the 8-K. And that's when everything hit the fan.

Bogardus fired Posgate and Lloyds suspended him. The Department of Trade stepped in, and with them came the City of London Fraud Squad. A&A filed civil actions against the Gang of Four and Posgate. And then they filed for and were granted an Anton Pillar against Posgate. That's a draconian order allowing lawyers and accountants enormous powers of search and seizure without giving the victim any protection by the police. Posgate's home and offices were searched. So was the home of his assistant, Laura Davies. They literally turned everything upside-down, paying particular attention, Ms Davies said later, to her underwear. The lawyers and accountants took with them everything they personally deemed relevant. That was followed by a Mareva injunction, a writ forbidding Posgate from disposing of any assets pending trial. His assets were frozen, although he was allowed a weekly pittance on which to live.

Posgate also claimed he was being followed by private detectives. 'It was very insulting. The Anton Pillar. You know, looking through underwear and this sort of thing. Looking through female underwear and getting a delight. I think they were rather kinky, personally.'

It was until 13 October that Posgate was able to rally his forces. He started proceedings against A&A, Alexander Howden and the Committee of Lloyds. The next day the Gang of Four announced through their lawyers – where an entire office devoted solely to their case was dubbed 'The War Room' – that they had answers to all of the questions being asked.

In 1983 the courts ruled in favour of the Gang of Four in their motion to force Bogardus back to arbitration. Both parties knew that a loss in arbitration could involve gigantic sums. So, at the initiative of A&A, with total legal fees on both sides quickly approaching the £1 million mark, they sat down to settle out of court. An agreement was reached in April 1984. In that settlement, A&A received some £300,000 worth of marketable securities, a Renoir painting, and a house in London. In exchange, among other things, Ken Grob got back the villa in the South of France. Carpenter and Page resigned from Lloyds.

The Courts ruled in favour of Posgate and against the Committee's suspension, saying that they could not deprive him of his livelihood. They unsuspended him as they were ordered to do, then simply re-suspended him, renewable every six months. At the end of 1984 he was suspended. When a guy is down, it's wise to keep him down or some day he may get up and remember. Earlier, a boardroom coup at his own agency, Posgate and Denby, deposed him, sending him into exile to a small office across the street.

When his underwriting suspension expired in January 1986, a heavier, older, but much wiser, Ian Posgate tried to return to The Room. The Rota said no. They said he was not a 'fit and proper' person. Posgate vowed to fight on, but didn't get very far.

Anyway, by this time the A&A/Alexander Howden scandal was being pushed off the front pages by others. The papers were filled with scandals – Minet . . . Sasse . . . Peter Cameron-Webb . . . Peter Dixon . . . Unimar.

Lloyds was so rife with fraud and larceny that the Committee was forced to hire a full-time Chief Executive, an accountant named Ian Hay Davison. Under his guidance, and obviously under some pressure from the Bank of England, the Rota passed a series of regulations that require everyone at Lloyds to thoroughly disclose their interests. At the same time, Sir Peter Green announced he would not stand again as Chairman.

According to Davison at the time, 'It's an internal matter in Lloyds and concerns the relationship of names and agents. I think the steps Lloyds has taken to correct those situations has been different from what people expected. They assumed that matters would be swept under the carpet and there would be the good old nudge-and-fudge compromise. You know, at the end of the day we'll meet the bill, sort of thing. Instead there's been much more of a root-and-branch reforming approach. Lloyds is clearly anxious to be seen to get its act cleaned up and get the crooks brought to book. In addition, the rulebook is being changed and in particular accounting is being brought into line. The motto is, you know, sunshine dries away the mist. I would remind you that in July or August 1984 the accounts of all the syndicates were placed on public record. Two years before, it would have been inconceivable.'

But then that was at a time when he was paid to say that kind of stuff. He has since resigned. The reason was reportedly due to 'great differences in opinion' with the ruling Committee on precisely what regulations should be put into force. Privately, it's said that Davidson was an honest man who simply became too great a threat to certain less honourable forces.

There's probably more truth in the latter. It's just odd that, in those days, when you tried to pin him down to know if Lloyds was squeaky clean, you always got a less than direct answer.

Question: Weren't these scandals just the tip of the iceberg?

Answer: 'There are no other cases, to my knowledge, of plunder other than those that have been reported in the papers.' (Within six months, other 'irregularities' came to light.)

Question: So Lloyds is now clean?

Answer: 'Well, no, I didn't say that. I didn't say that. There are no other cases of plunder, that's to say large-scale depredations of the PCW type (the Peter Cameron-Webb affair). The papers have found and reported on all the cases of plunder.' Although eventually he admitted, 'There are, I believe, still widespread misunderstandings about the proper handling of conflicts of interest, the proper accounting for secret profits as between mains and agents. But these have not led to major depredations and they still fail to be corrected in the sense of disclosed, and in some cases the arrangements discontinued.'

Seven years after the Howden affair first hit the headlines, the case went before a jury. But only Posgate and Grob ever faced justice. Ron Comery was killed in a car crash that some people believe was, in fact, suicide. It's been alleged that at least one note, if not two, was found on his body instructing his next of kin and/or his solicitor what to do about his death. At the same time, the courts ruled that Allan Page was too ill to stand trial and then that Jack Carpenter, who became ill during the hearings, was not well enough to see those hearings completed.

Posgate was accused of taking part in one conspiracy to

defraud and another conspiracy to steal. Grob was charged with 16 counts of theft, four of false accounting and three of publishing false statements. During the trial the prosecution dropped several charges. Fifteen weeks later, the jury deliberated for nearly 21 hours before returning not guilty verdicts on all remaining counts to both men.

At Lloyds, and around the offices of the Serious Fraud Squad, the general attitude was of 'despair and nausea'. Said one Lloyds employee, 'We were sick as wet hens at having lost. The verdict seems to show that juries are simply not capable of understanding the complexities of such cases.' Added someone from the prosecution's team, 'In this country you have to satisfy the jury beyond reasonable doubt. When you get a complicated fraud case, if it were possible to ask any member of the jury just what it is that the defendants stand accused of, the number who could do it would be nil. It supposedly takes ten years to train a good reinsurance broker. How could anyone just off the street figure out what had been going on in only 15 weeks?'

Grob and Posgate however did not share those opinions.

Once the not guilty decision was handed down, they both did the usual 'I feel vindicated' speech. But Grob made a point of adding, 'The best thing has always been a British jury and this sort of case proves it is right.'

Originally it had been planned that Grob would stand trial a second time on further charges. But before long the courts ruled Grob was not well enough and, anyway, that material witnesses had either died or were too ill to give evidence.

His eight-year ordeal finally over, Grob is retired.

Posgate, however, is not.

'I've got an office and I'm playing around on a few things. I don't know much about anything except insurance so I'm advising various people. My days as an active underwriter are finished. Anyway, there's more money to be made by organizing other people and by being fractionally lazy.'

He still has his farm with 400 head of cattle plus certain financial interests in insurance companies and is still, ironically, a name at Lloyds. 'The only thing that keeps me from resigning is that it would please the buggers if I do. But there's really no basis for being a member of Lloyds at the moment. There are losses around, the premium is falling, they're losing names. But what is much worse is they're losing business. It's unlimited liability and the risks are too great on what they're writing. It's much better to be a shareholder in a limited liability insurance company than in Lloyds at this moment in time.'

At Lloyds they suggest that Posgate's opinions are nothing more than sour grapes. 'It's true that quite a few of the so-called low-capacity names have in fact resigned. People whose life-styles would be affected by say, £20–30,000 losses. But against that, quite a few of the wealthier names have increased their commitment. The result is that the capacity of the Lloyds market is as high now, if not higher, as it was two years ago.'

Posgate totally disagrees.

'Lloyds is really rather a mess. They're getting into tremendous problems. The business they've got is now this enormous spiral of reinsurance upon reinsurance. Half of the business is reinsurance between one syndicate and another. And that must end in disaster. There's no question that Lloyds would fight like mad if I tried to go back. But I really wouldn't want to go back either. I admit one comes before the other, but it is a very sad place. Anyway, the Americans are getting surer of themselves. Most of the major brokers are now owned by the Americans. They'll eventually hijack the whole thing. In fact I think the whole thing will slowly cease. It's an anachronism. All middlemen are lazy and now there are other markets. There's the Institute of London Underwriters who, rather grandly, write insurance directly. And there's about to be a reinsurance exchange, which is being spearheaded, I regret to say, by some American companies. That means there will be three market-places instead of one and Lloyds hasn't adjusted. On top of that, Lloyds started life as a coffee house and well, the ILU also serves a better cup of coffee. It all gets down to the coffee.'

13

Sir Clive Sinclair

Clive Marles Sinclair is undoubtedly the most recognizable inventor in the world. After all, how many inventors can you name who regularly get stopped on the street by fans wanting an autograph?

'Sure I like being recognized. It also sometimes helps getting a table in a restaurant.'

Having roller-coasted between success and disaster several times, he earned a knighthood for high-flying in the hi-tech world of mass-market technology and, at least once, came back from near bankruptcy to find himself among the wealthiest men in the kingdom.

In October 1984, when the *Sunday Times* published their list of the nation's 100 wealthiest businessmen, Sinclair was said to be worth an even £100 million. He was ranked sixth, behind Gerald Ronson (No. 2: £300m) and Robert Maxwell (No. 4: £151m), but ahead of Terence Conran (No. 8: £74m), Tiny Rowland (No. 10: £63m), Asil Nadir (No. 11: £59m) and James Hanson (No. 64: £9m).

Unfortunately for him, it didn't last long.

Five years later, when that same newspaper published a list of the 200 wealthiest people in the kingdom, Ronson was number 12 (£500m), Maxwell was 11 (£675m), Conran was 109 (£56m), Rowland was 36 (£196m), Nadir was 37 (£192m), Hanson was 75 (£95m) and Clive Sinclair was nowhere to be seen.

Five years from now, that may not be the case.

*

A smallish man with a receding hairline and a bright-red beard, he was born in London in 1940, the son of a mechanical engineer. An inventive kid who showed an early interest in calculating machines and electronic gadgets . . . 'I can only concentrate if I can do what I want . . .' his mother was most anxious that he become an academic. 'I knew that if I went to university I couldn't just study electronics, which interested me. I'd also have to do electronic engineering, which didn't interest me. Of course, now I've got honorary degrees. But those things get flung around all over the place. They don't do you much good.'

Leaving school at the age of 17, he made his way into the world as a journalist, producing small books for the electronics hobbyist, most of which he wrote himself.

'Being a technical journalist seemed a good idea, as it was an attractive and lucrative way of being employed. It got me about and gave me considerable freedom. It also gave me the opportunity of learning at someone else's expense. I learned far more about my subjects than anyone who ever read what I wrote.'

But becoming an inventor was what he really wanted to do and that in turn meant becoming a businessman.

'You can't really separate the inventor and the businessman. The idea of the lone inventor sitting in an attic somewhere is pretty impractical. By its very nature, invention itself is improbable. If you rush around with all your ideas in a brown paper bag, knocking on doors of big companies, those big companies are going to say, no. The way society arranges things makes it very difficult for all inventors. So the way you get around that problem, the way you turn your invention into something, is by being a sort of businessman. You go out there and you start a company and you get your own invention off the ground.'

Accordingly, in 1962 he founded a company called Sinclair Radionics to sell radio and amplifier kits by mail for under £3. Five years later he added hi-fi's to his list. In 1973, with his annual turnover well over £100,000, he invented the pocket calculator.

'I really believed it would be a fabulous thing.'

As it happened, he changed the world.

Those original pocket calculators – there is one in the permanent collection of New York's Museum of Modern Art – cost £79. Today you can buy them, complete with solar energy cells, for under £4.

'I'm so pleased that these things exist because they make my life that much easier. Same with the digital watches.'

They were next.

From there he went on to the pocket television set.

And that's when he nearly went bust the first time.

'We ran short of cash in about 1976. But no, we weren't going broke. We were a bankable proposition. We got investment in from the National Enterprise Board. It seemed a good idea at the time but it didn't turn out well at all. Originally the chap running it backed us, quite rightly, on the strength of our flat-screen television programme. Unfortunately, he soon left the NEB and they brought in someone else and they took a totally different view. As it happens, a wrong one about which way the company should go. They also appointed a managing director who was really not satisfactory. I was Chairman. And, well, by a combination of things, the net result was really disastrous.'

The NEB wanted him to go into the instrument business. Sinclair wanted to stick with consumer electronics. In 1979 there was a formal parting of the ways and he formed Sinclair Research. The first product he put on to the market was the Sinclair ZX 80 personal computer. The price was so low – under £100 in the UK and under $100 in the more competitive United States – that just about any home could afford one, whether they needed it or not. He sold 130,000 of them. The following year he came out with the even cheaper ZX 81. The price of that one hovered around £50/$50. And in the first 18 months that they were on the market he sold, worldwide, 1.1 million of them.

Then there was the Spectrum, a 16k basic language home computer with a full range of add-ons, followed by a 48k model, and the Spectrum Plus. At one point Spectrum accounted for nearly 80% of his turnover.

Next came the QL – the Quantum Leap – Sinclair's first real stab at the world of business computers. But it proved to be a costlier venture than originally planned.

'As far as the man on the street was concerned, our computers didn't change the market, they created the market. Of course there were always hobbyists interested in home computers, but that wasn't true of the general public. The average guy doesn't think he needs one. What I think our computers have done, priced for the average guy, is to give him the chance to learn how a computer can work. Our initial sales were made to people who wanted to learn. Now, many of our sales are based heavily on the games market. Although we never intended the computer to be a toy.'

In those days he justified the relationship between computers and games by saying that lots of the games aimed at the home computer market actually required intelligence to master and could be very demanding to play.

These days he concedes it was a business he never really wanted to be in.

'At least it wasn't the business we'd originally intended to be in but that's the way it turned out. We wanted to go on to serious machines but our games' machines had been so successful that they completely dominated the business.'

In his mind, those early computers were simply the first step towards computer literacy.

'That's really what the ZX 80 and ZX 81 were all about. The game stage was next. But it was only a stage, to be followed by functional applications. The machines being developed today are coming with those changes. The actual application of computers as an integral part of the home are a little way off. Before it happens in the home it has to happen in the office.'

Oddly enough, there are no desk-top computers in the Sinclair offices. He still doesn't own a computer. 'I don't need one.' Although he says he'll probably have one some day. It's just that he doesn't feel that there are any machines available right now that can do anything more than, say, store data. What he says he wants is a truly useful machine. And that, when it comes, will be the final stage in the home computer evolution.

'I'm talking about machines that you might call intelligent. The money-dispensing computer at the local corner bank is a stupid computer. It can only do what it's told to do. I see computers coming along that will be able to reason. For instance, in the personal computer for the home, we haven't really begun to teach. Or take the place of the doctor in diagnosing illness. At the moment it's not easy to get all the information necessary for medical diagnosis into a computer. But I don't think a computer diagnosis could possibly be as dangerous as some doctors I've seen.'

The idea is that, one day, a computer working in a logical fashion will be sophisticated enough to draw inferences from information. Life will not be black and white. There will be many degrees of grey. George Orwell might have finally won.

'Computers are not yet teaching. What people are learning to do with them is program. I think the day will definitely come when computers themselves become the teacher in their own right. I think a computer can much better teach children than teachers as we know them can. The ratio can be brought down to one per child. A computer is infinitely more patient than a human teacher. The possibilities are at their earliest stage right now, but I see no reason why a computer shouldn't do anything that a teacher does now.'

When and if this ever happens, it will represent a leap forward so spectacular that comparisons are difficult to make. A computer that thinks, and might even surpass man's intelligence, would be similar to Christopher Columbus in the year 1492 somehow reaching the moon. It will, not surprisingly, reap untold wealth for the man who makes it happen.

'Computers are the roots to the latest frontier. They've been around for years, but the sudden explosion in technology has been changing computers at a drastic pace. Machines of immense power are now within our grasp. They will change society. No doubt about it. That kind of thing has been said before. This time we mean it.'

Sinclair does say that there's no need to worry yet about being owned by a computer because it's not something that is just around the corner. Although he thinks it could happen in the next decade or two. 'Machines will absolutely begin to exhibit intelligence. Might even happen around the turn of the century. And I don't necessarily see that as frightening a prospect as you might. The jobs that computers will be able to replace could create for us a golden age which in turn will give us more time to educate our children as original thinkers. I'm an optimist.'

So was Murphy!

He insists that his main interests lie in innovation and not in what might be termed a conventional market.

'Older companies of any sort find it very hard to innovate, not because of any intrinsic reluctance, but because once they have an established manufacturing base they find it hard to change direction. Layland can't just suddenly go out and make plastic cars, and throw away all its capital equipment. It might suddenly be the right thing to do, but it's wrong from the accountancy point of view.'

What he feels he does best is to identify what people want but still can't afford, then build one that's affordable. In the end, the Sinclair version might not suit the buyer's needs right down to a 'T', but it's so far been close enough and so far been affordable.

Some times he gets it very right. Witness the pocket calculator. At other times he has been known to get it very wrong. Witness the pocket TV.

'I thought there was going to be a huge market for that. Back in the early '60s, when pocket radios came out, they went from nothing to 30 million units a year. I thought pocket TVs would do the same and so I put a lot of effort into it. I developed a flat cathode ray tube, the first time that had ever been done in the world, plus a single chip that would do everything. It was a huge effort and took huge investment. But sales were pitiful. Then the Japanese leapt in and dozens of companies invested huge amounts, absolutely unbelievable, and they substantiated what we'd already discovered – that there was no market at all. The first one we did was black and white and we developed a colour one and so did the Japanese and the result was still pathetic. I guess people simply don't want pocket TVs.'

He also got it wrong with the QL.

There he tried to take on the big kids.

'What happened to the QL is actually very sad because that was a successful machine in it's own right. Still today there are a huge number of QL users and a magazine devoted to it that sells something like 20,000 copies a month. The mistake we made there was that we were not IBM-compatible. We didn't particularly want to be IBM-compatible because I always felt that their standards were sadly deficient. But IBM is IBM and you can't swim against that tide, not for long anyway.'

The thing is that each time he's wrong, he figures it's merely another step along the continuum. The important thing, he feels, is to keep trying.

'We depend for our early sales on people who have great tolerance to new ideas. With the computer, that was the sort of person who, if you put it down in front of them, would just want to play with it straight away. We get the product to them, other people see it, it becomes more familiar and they lose their fear of it.'

But at no time in his career did he ever make a bigger blunder than when he came up with the C-5.

Of course, the idea of an electric car is not a new one. There have been electric cars on the drawing boards and even on the market for decades. Every golfer who rides his 18 holes does it in a battery-operated cart. What Sinclair seriously hoped to do was take those carts off the golf course, make them a lot sexier and much more economical, and put them on the street.

'I'd been toying with the idea of doing an electric vehicle for years, and had done various little experimental vehicles to try out this idea or that. But it wasn't until a few years ago that there had been enough innovation in all kinds of fields to give us a package that clicked. For example, the steady progress in battery design hadn't seemed particularly impressive in any one year. But over the years it rolled up to a considerable advance. The science of lightweight materials advanced to the point where we could actually buy a body with the right strength/weight ratio. Other people's problem-solving made our project possible.'

Although he designed the C-5 completely from scratch, when you ask him why he went into such a different field – cars require specific areas of technology that computers don't – he tells you he never saw it as all that different. 'My business is consumer products that are basically electrical, and the electric car falls into the category. There's a massive difference, in a way, between hi-fi's and computers. I don't see any greater difference between computers and cars.'

The main obstacle he faced with the electric car was the classic one. Even today's most improved batteries won't provide very great range without recharging, and then they won't recharge very often without burning out. Yet Sinclair believed there was a big market for a modest-range town car.

'You must of course be able to find the market spot and meet it. If you're GM, you clearly hope it won't happen. It's not really the role of the large companies to explore new realms because it invariably threatens their capital base.'

Previous failed attempts in search of the same market didn't daunt him.

Perhaps they should have.

Sinclair sincerely believed there was a market for a souped-down version of a golf cart. The C-5 vehicle was a three-wheeler with bicycle pedals just in case the battery failed. The range was 20 miles, if that. The speed was just 15 mph. There was no roof – which makes one wonder how well suited it could ever be for the British climate. There was room for only one person – which ruled out Sunday afternoon family outings. And the boot was notably too small for golf clubs, a baby seat or even heavy grocery shopping.

Almost immediately Sinclair's critics cast a doubting eye. Sure, they said, the world laughed at Alexander Graham Bell and the Wright brothers. But General Motors tried electric cars and they couldn't make them work economically enough. The Sinclairmobile may cost next to nothing to run, but then so do electric golf carts. Furthermore, electric golf carts are big enough to be seen when you drive one next to a lorry, and comfortable enough to sit in for more than a few blocks.

Having sunk more than £7 million of his own money into the C-5, Sinclair was heavily betting on his judgement of the market. He was obviously hoping the C-5 could do for urban transport what that first ZX80 did for the home computer market. His projection was that within the first year he'd sell 100,000 C-5s.

He was very wrong!

Sales failed to take off. Some dealers thought it should have been marketed as an expensive toy. Sinclair insisted it was serious transport. Then the British Safety Council suggested that 'there was a potential safety hazard' when it came to the driver's visibility where other road users were concerned. Almost immediately plans for a proposed second assembly line were 'postponed'. Then the Advertising Standards Authority started publicizing complaints from users hinting that the C-5's advertised range was not as great as had been promised. Within three months of the C-5's launch, Sinclair supported the continuum theory by announcing that he was working on a C-10 model – a 30m.p.h. two-seater – and that by 1990 he would bring forth the C-15 – a four-seater with an 80m.p.h. range of several hundred miles.

Within seven months of the C-5's launch, some 110 creditors were lining up, claiming to be owed £700,000. The car's production ground to a halt. Only about 9000 of the cars were made and it was reported that less than half of them had been sold, despite the £399 price tag. Some dealers tried getting rid of their C-5s at a knock-down £99. And still the public said no.

The receivers were called in.

'It was basically aimed at the bicycle market. It was small, which I think was the fundamental mistake. Although it was safe, because it was very visible to other road users, people didn't necessarily feel safe when they were in it. That was another problem. It was a psychological thing. But then, people suppose the C-5 was a passion of mine but it wasn't at all. The passion there, which remains, was for a full-range electric car. I had no particular desire to do a single-seat electric car except that, the full-range electric car was going to be so expensive I though that if I could find a stepping stone that would make some money, I could do that. Obviously it wasn't. My biggest mistake, I suppose, was to do a product I wasn't all that passionate about.'

Ironically, there is still a market for them. Sinclair produced somewhere around 10,000 and sold them at £399. If you want one today, expect to pay around £1000 in the collectors' market.

And just as an aside, he has not abandoned his desire to invent a viable electric car. A French car manufacturer not long ago announced their intention to do the same thing, but Sinclair feels, 'They're just pissing in the wind. All they're doing is taking an ordinary car and putting some batteries in it. The thing will go 50–60 miles, if you're lucky, and then stop. That's no use to anyone. The fact is that anyone can make an electric car. The trick is to make one that has a proper range and some performance.'

Riding high in 1982, Sinclair had no trouble selling off 10% of his company to some institutional buyers in the City. He said at the time he planned to use the money to finance an array of projects, including his stated intention to take over the defunct De Lorean factory in Northern Ireland. He told the world he was interested in building a petrol engine automobile there. But the take-over never happened. Nor did the petrol engine automobile.

'I'm convinced there are enough new products waiting to be put on the market to last me the rest of my business life. I can see a whole range of ideas that I want to do. They're always swimming around in my mind. But it's hard to describe the sort of judgement you make whether a venture is going to be a success. It's in the subconscious, really. It's a question of building up a mental image, a feel for the market.'

Needless to say, the inventor's mentality is a special one.

Consider then, something that might be called 'the theory of the inventor's continuum.'

Simply stated, you can't get to invention number 10 until you've gone through inventions 1–9. In many cases, the inventor has no idea what will follow each particular invention. It's a path without a road map, littered with other inventors' carcasses and, like a maze, branching out to all sorts of dead-ends. The trick is to keep building on your ideas, and stay alive long enough, so that if you've made all the correct turns you might possibly find the pot of gold at the end of the rainbow, if indeed there is one.

It's a terribly complicated way to earn a living. In fact, most inventors either don't, or simply can't. But the ones who do, the ones who understand how to work this 'continuum theory' and who are also able to combine their inventing skills with a modicum of business skills, at least they've got a shot at making something work.

Build a better mousetrap, so the proverb goes, and the world will beat a path to your door.

Except it isn't that easy.

The C-5 was almost certainly a better mousetrap, except nobody wanted to get caught in one and they nearly bankrupted him.

Actually, they were only part of the problem. The C-5 ran into trouble at exactly the same time that his main business, Sinclair Research, was having problems too. Creditors were worried. Computer sales had slipped. The pocket television was late in proving itself a money-spinner. Nor was the £400 QL an overwhelming success. There were delays and changes, and the company's reputation was seriously marred.

On to the scene galloped Robert Maxwell.

Proclaiming Sinclair a national asset, Maxwell said he felt

obliged to do something. So on a warm Sunday evening in June 1985, Sinclair and Maxwell struck a deal. Sinclair himself would step down from the board of Sinclair Research, giving up the everyday management of the company in exchange for a consultancy. Maxwell would inject £12 million cash into the company through a rights issue which would put a £16 million value on the company – as against the £136 million value less than two years before.

With £34 million in unsold computers sitting in the stock-rooms, Maxwell merely had to do his arithmetic to realize that this might be a terrific deal. Long a man with heavyweight connections in computer-less Eastern Europe, even a half-price sale of the unsold QLs to the Eastern bloc could bring in £17 million. That would represent a clear £5-million cash profit. He'd also wind up owning Sinclair Research, as icing on the £12-million cake.

On paper it looked marvellous.

In practice it never happened.

Maxwell pulled out. For whatever reason, he said no. He might not have been able to secure Eastern bloc orders quickly enough. Or the Mirror Newspaper Group might have been attracting too much of his cash. Or he might have worried that Sinclair could start a rival company. Speculation in the press touched on any and all of the possibilities. At the same time, Sinclair didn't exactly give the impression that his new best friend had deserted a sinking ship. As the *Economist* noted, 'Sir Clive looked far from sad to see him go.'

With Maxwell out of the picture, Sinclair announced that the price of the QL would be cut in half. Some of the major creditors said they'd ride with him until the end of the year, until after Christmas when they could reduce the computer mountain and bring in some cash.

The ploy worked, but only for a while.

'We got into financial difficulties when the home computer business went into an uncontrollable nose-dive. For two successive Christmas seasons, the major High Street outlets had totally underestimated demand for home computers. They'd found themselves seriously understocked. Inevitably, the following Christmas, they overreacted. But the market had rapidly been approaching near-saturation, and by November 1985, once they realized that sales weren't going as they'd expected, they started cancelling the bulk of their orders.'

Although Sinclair Research had a lot of other projects going in a lot of other fields, all of its income, all of the money it was earning, was coming from the home computer side.

'We found ourselves caught in a very serious cash position which made it difficult to pay our various suppliers. At first we thought we only had one option, which was to accept an offer from a very large company to take a minority stake but they didn't want me to continue our other research activities. They didn't see that as the future of the business. It was a plausible route but it wouldn't have satisfied me. I saw research as the most important part of the business and home computers as a bit of a bloody nuisance. It made us a lot of money but it wasn't a business I'd intended to get into in the first place, nor was it a business I knew a heck of a lot about.'

The major electronics' retailers, like Dixons, were very concerned about the future of the home computer market. Some of them thought there might be something in an Amstrad/Sinclair merger and pointed this out to Alan Sugar. Their original idea was that Sugar would become Sinclair's major investor to help bolster the home computer side. But that would again mean sacrificing Sinclair's reasearch interests. So in April 1986 he and Sugar struck a deal where Amstrad would take over the home computer business and leave the rest of Sinclair Research to Sir Clive.

Sugar paid £5 million for a business which was once worth nearly 20 times as much.

'It was a pretty drastic measure for us because Sinclair Research didn't have any trade. But I felt that simply getting finance for the home computers and ditching the rest was like throwing out the baby and keeping the bath water. Anyway, I didn't think there was a lot of growth left in home computers. I didn't see it as a very exciting business.'

Alan Sugar has since run into trouble with his computer business which, Sinclair feels, was probably inevitable.

'I think it's exactly the same thing that happened with us in the home computer business. When you're in a rapidly growing field, the day will come when it stops growing. But you can't accurately anticipate when that day will be. It's not that it necessarily kills you, but you've suddenly got huge stocks and no cash.'

Sinclair himself licked his wounds and slowly began to regroup.

'I took a personal beating. But I can't say I was terribly embarrassed about it because money has never been very important to me except as a means to an end. Yes, I had an airplane, which I haven't got now, so that changed. Also, I sold my house in Chelsea and my big home in Cambridge but I think I would have sold them both anyway. But my life-style didn't really change. Although I'm clearly worth a lot more today than I was a few years ago. But that's all on paper, so it's academic. Frankly, to be rich is nothing. Making money for the sake of money is bloody easy. What I've always tried to do was use the money to make products.'

He lives alone in London, reads poetry and jogs. He was married in 1962, but he and his wife split up before the crash. They have three children, all grown up. And he's now a grandfather. 'My daughter has two children and I'm very much a doting grandfather. The older boy is three and that's very exciting.'

Looking around for projects he cared about, Sinclair quickly convinced shipping magnate Fred Olson – who also owns Timex – to back him in a company called Shaye. Together Shaye and Sinclair had overseen the pioneering of pocket telephones and now supply British Telecom with all its Tele-point phones.

'Our idea was to create a pocket phone which would work anywhere. It's not fully exploited yet because we've only got the Tele-point side of it, but very shortly we'll start producing a box you put in your office and that means wherever you go all you need is the telephone in your pocket. Shaye also has a joint project with Mercury and Motorola which is the call-point system, in competition with Tele-point.'

A second company he founded after the Amstrad deal was Cambridge Computers. Controlled personally by Sinclair, he's now back in the computer business, with a lap-top model.

'Ours will run 20 hours on pen light cells. It's a radical development. There will be two models. One with a 20mb hard disk, the other with an 8mb solid state equivalent. The computer business is one I like. I love the technology and we've got lots of long-term plans in that area.'

Cambridge Computers is also developing a satellite television receiver.

'I don't run these companies on a day-to-day basis. I generate business, that's what my job is. I hire managing directors to run them because they can do that better than I ever could. Ten years ago it was different. I couldn't attract young talent. But with the Thatcher revolution people have realized the potential of getting into a young, fast-growing company so now I can attract the right managers and that means I can get on with what I do best.'

Like personally taking it upon himself to reinvent the bicycle.

'Early in the '80s the thought crossed my mind that bicycles were very, very nice ways of getting around cities and towns except for one thing. They were fine while you were peddling them but a damned nuisance when you arrived somewhere. You've got to secure them in some way which is not always easy and anyway, you can't take them on public transport. You couldn't, for instance, bicycle to the railway station, put the bike on the train with you and then bicycle from the station to your office. I decided that if I could figure a way around that problem it would radically change the way people use bicycles.'

He had an image of a bicycle that would be much lighter than a conventional bike and instantly foldable.

But it was easier said than done.

Folding anything into however many parts turns out to be

nothing more than a complicated design problem. Getting a bicycle to weigh a lot less than they normally do is another matter. For the most part, bicycles today weigh about the same as bicycles did 100 years ago. Even with lighter materials in the frame, it works out that the frame of the bike is only about 20% of the weight. The wheels, the cranks and the peddles make up most of the weight.

'Originally I thought the use of light alloys, like aluminium, would be the answer. But it turned out to be a much bigger problem than I ever thought. We turned out a very nice bicycle but it was only 25% lighter than the lightest one that already existed. And even though it folded readily it still wasn't the sort of thing you could take on the train so it was therefore unsuitable.'

It is a project he unashamedly labels as very dear to his heart.

'There's a need for this. It's a chance to produce something that can make a difference. I personally worked on it for a couple of years. I found that in order to do what I wanted to do I had to be very radical not only in the form of the bicycle but also in the materials. I don't think there's a single piece on ours that is a standard bike part. The average bicycle weighs something like 22 pounds. Ours will be under 10 pounds. It will also fold instantly. I get these sorts of passions from time to time.'

However, his two greatest passions remain the electric car and artificial intelligence.

'The progress towards artificial intelligence has been steady if not spectacular over the past five years. For instance, wafer scale integration is a necessary technology for that.'

And in that regard, he has just scored a very handsome victory.

One of the first projects he turned his undivided attention to was this wafer scale integration. Without getting at all technical, it has to do with the horrendously complicated process of manufacturing pre-linked computer chips. It's a concept that had been around for a couple of decades. But each company that had so far pursued this Holy Grail of the semi-conductor business, including IBM, had sunk hundreds of millions of dollars into the search, only to come up empty.

Sinclair however knew something the others didn't. 'Back in the '60s, there was a man in this country named Ivor Catt, who'd come up with a different approach to wafer scale integration. Although he'd got some work done at universities, he never managed to get the large backing he needed. I believed his idea would work and bought the rights to it.'

He formed a company called Ananartic . . . a made up word which might have meant 'free from fault' had the Greeks ever thought of it . . . put a 20% chunk of it into Sinclair Research's holdings and brought in other major investors, including Barclays Bank and Tandem Computers.

They are already shipping product and Sinclair is confident that unless something very strange and totally unpredictable happens, this will be a billion-dollar business in the very near future.

Sinclair 1, Holy Grail 0.

14

Five years ago he worried about things like *pâté aux cèpes*.

He'd just bought a house in the South of France, not far from Arles, and in the city of Arles there's a hotel called the Jules César where they make the best *pâté aux cèpes* in all France.

Pondering that for a moment, he shook his head. 'Yes, we pass the hotel on every trip down there. But I didn't know about the *pâté aux cèpes*.'

For Sir Terence Conran, who once ran a chain of restaurants called The Soup Kitchen and whose current wife Caroline writes and translates cookbooks – ex-wife Shirley writes best-sellers like *Superwoman* and *Lace* – knowing where to find the best *pâté aux cèpes* in France was not something he was likely to forget.

Five years later he has other things to worry about, such as the future of the empire he built and named Storehouse.

A retail operation that spans the globe, it all began with a store concept called Habitat in 1963. He is probably best known as the first, if not the only, retailer in the UK who went out of his way to try to create excitement in what must be called the otherwise dull world of British retailing.

The way Conran has always seen it, the retail business in this country only started changing about eight or nine years ago. In fact, it's really only been in the past 15 years that the rest of the world has seen changes in retailing. But this country has been particularly slow to change.

'Like Sunday trading laws. We were one of the great promoters of Sunday trading in the UK. But the main changes in England have come about because retailers are starting to understand the importance of design. Until recently, it was only the manufacturer who worried about design. Now the retailer is becoming the catalyst, deciding for himself what he can offer to the public. That represents a major breakthrough.'

The idea is one that has been popular in supermarkets for years. It is known as 'private labelling'. Goods are packaged under, say, the Sainsbury or the Safeway label and inherent with the product comes the retailer's reputation for quality. Probably the best-known example in the UK is the St Michael label at Marks & Spencer. In fact, M&S take the private labelling concept to the extreme. Whereas Safeway will put a competitor's strawberry jam on a shelf right next to their own-label strawberry jam, M&S will not sell anything but goods bearing their own label.

It's always been a slightly different approach at Habitat. Conran likens his kind of private labelling to designer collections.

Instead of doing what M&S do, that is, provide some decent-quality but otherwise bland goods that try to cater to the widest-possible taste levels, Conran imposed very specific design ideas about the goods being sold in his market. Either he went to specific manufacturers and asked them to produce something of Habitat's own design. Or he took the manufacturer's designs and amended them to suit his markets. Unlike a Harrods or Selfridges, which by their nature must offer something for every taste level, Habitat really only caters to one taste level. There is a well-defined Habitat client – a young, married, upwardly mobile white-collar worker, probably living in their first home, without children. They can afford restaurants once or twice a week, sincerely want to become urbanized, and do some entertaining at home. They cannot afford Picassos but are perfectly at ease with dhurri throw rugs, red and white striped saucepans, and ersatz hi-tech metal units for records and stereos.

'The process of design is interrelated to business. I'm not only concerned with how our products are retailed, but also how they're made and how they're marketed. My greatest pleasure in life is not balance sheets but products. I make it my business to concern myself with how those products are designed. I concern myself with how they're advertisied. I get involved with the design of the shops. Everything comes through me. I try to go to all our merchandising meetings. I try to have some say in about 95% of all that's sold.'

But this, he insists, is not at all a question of ego.

'One of the most important things I have learned as a businessman is to delegate. To get people around you who you can work with. People you trust. People who become part of a team. In the early days it wasn't easy for me to realize I was also part of that team. That I too had to be a team member. That I had to take my position and let the others on the team take theirs. So, although I try to have a say in everything we do, my point of view is not the one that necessarily wins. There are times when the team tells me no and we do it their way.'

Still, the basic concept remains his. Terence Conran was, after all, knighted for having been the man who conceived and built the foundations for what is now one of the most copied formats in retailing.

Born in Surrey in October, 1931, Conran was hailed as one of the hot-shot designers of the 'swinging '60s'.

'Growing up in England before the war meant life was extremely austere. During the war we had rationing and there were no materials for building. So in design schools they taught that design actually had to have some social intent. And I think what we as students in those days saw at the time was that good design could make a big contribution to the quality of life.'

In the early 1950s Conran opted out for some time in Paris, and worked there at a restaurant. That's when he first discovered Les Halles – the Parisian markets – and years later he would return to Les Halles to buy kitchen utensils and equipment for his stores, hoping obviously to re-create that same feeling in the Habitat kitchenware departments. However, during that first stay, among other things, he learned to make soup. When he came back to London, he and a friend decided their future lay in soup, so they opened a restaurant called The Soup Kitchen, just off London's Strand. Conran decorated the place in a bright, clean way and, although he didn't realize it at the time, the embryo for the 'Conran style' was fertilized.

He'd been designing furniture during those years, selling mostly to the trade. But he wasn't yet the Terence Conran he would become. His partner in the Soup Kitchens eventually decided to take the restaurants off in a direction slightly different from the way Conran saw them going, so he sold out. He began to concentrate more on design, and little by little started to refine his vision of design coupled with retailing. If he first saw it around Les Halles, he certainly started to materialize it when he helped to create the market atmosphere by designing Mary Quant's Bazaar on the King's Road.

By 1963 it all came together in the first Habitat.

'I think the reason I went into the retailing business was because I believed that there was another way of selling furniture. The way I see it, the art of retailing is understanding that selling your product and creating an atmosphere to show off that product is exactly the same thing.'

That original Habitat store was generally categorized as a child of the swinging '60s. London then was the King's Road and Carnaby Street, the Beatles, *The Knack* and *A Hard Day's Night*. But then Conran isn't quite so sure that the '60s were swinging any place else.

'Frankly, looking back on it, I think the term "swinging '60s" was merely a media catch-phrase for what was happening in a very small area of London. And only there. What was going on in those days wasn't happening everywhere. It began with a few designers opening their own shops. We had just emerged from the extremely dreary '50s where nothing at all happened and some of us wanted to put our stuff in front of the public. Music came first. Then design. A few Italian restaurants came to London and suddenly there was a renewed interest in food. But this "happening", if that's what you want to call it, really only touched a few people until the media came along. They're always searching desperately for something to print, so they made it much bigger than it was. Take that first Habitat store as a good example. In reality, other retailers saw the first Habitat store and said, It's okay for Chelsea but it's not for Manchester.'

Not only did it turn out okay for Manchester, but he took his act on the road, throughout the UK. And on to the continent. And into North America. And into Japan. And also into a few off-beat places, like Martinique and Iceland.

He knew from the beginning that he had a winning formula, but he also realized that a winning formula in Britain might not be a winning formula in another country. He believed that, to retail successfully in other places around the world, he'd have to make various amendments. For instance, in some countries you can't sell bedlinen that isn't 100% pure cotton. The people there simply won't buy it. In other countries, they only want percale. So what he did is cater to the locals. The designs on the sheets in England and the designs on the sheets in France were exactly the same, but the material was different.

'We've been in France and Belgium since 1973. And I think the highest compliment we've ever been paid there came from a real-estate agent who told me that Habitat was a French company. I said no, it was English, but he insisted that I was wrong, that Habitat was French. I guess that means we're doing the right things in France.'

It was the same story in most places where he set up, although he faced an unusual problem when he went to Japan. There, vast cultural differences always play a role. In Conran's case, he minimized his risk, not by asking if he was ready to expand into Japan but making certain that Japan was ready for Habitat.

'Some serious cultural changes are happening there. They're acquiring Western taste. They are trying to become a Western country. They're rejecting their own traditional culture. People there are wanting to live like Americans and Europeans. They're even trying to cook exactly like Westerners, which is pretty funny because Westerners are trying to cook like Orientals.'

He had problems converting the Habitat formula to suit the Japanese, this time largely due to the physical differences between Orientals and Europeans.

'Because the size of rooms in Japan is much smaller than in the West, everything there is neat and precise. To fit in with the size of the rooms, we had to scale down our products. Especially seat-related products such as chairs. We actually scaled them down by about 7%. The Habitat style represents young European and US taste. Yet there is also a slight connection with the more formal Japanese traditional style. So maybe we're a transition.'

The most difficult area to conquer, however, was the United States. Business there is littered with the carcasses of British companies gone in search of the vast riches. Conquer America and you've conquered the world. Yet too many firms come a cropper there. And Conran feels, where retailers are concerned, that the enormous size of the country is one hazard. A second is the thoroughly unique American attitude towards retailing.

Both are mistakes he keenly tried to avoid.

'I spent a week doing a whistle-stop tour of the States. I got to see a lot of America, and I can tell you that the best retailer I saw was absolutely terrific. There are lessons to be learned. It was Macey's in San Francisco. What they've managed so wonderfully to create is a store filled with excitement. That's because they've got the right management. I especially liked the management style, and believe me, you could see just by walking through the store that it was a close-knit team. What you usually find in retailing is that the marketing people and the retailing people never talk to each other. But they do at Macey's, San Francisco. You can see it the moment you step inside.'

It's very much the feeling he'd hoped to create when he opened the first of his stores in New York in 1977. Called Conran's, because there's already a chain there called Habitat, establishing himself in the States turned out to be more difficult than he'd imagined.

'It was during the time when New York City real estate had

ebbed, and the only building going up was Citicorp's. Well, first we managed to swing a long lease with a low rental. Then we got a fantastic amount of publicity. We honestly thought our business would just go through the roof. But New Yorkers didn't understand what we were doing. Until we came along, there was never anything quite like a home-furnishing supermarket. You know, take-away furniture. Lots of people came to look, but it took about four years to get it off the ground.'

In fact, it was only in 1983 or so that the American side of his business started showing profit. It took that long because retailing in the States is not like retailing in England.

'No, there were some new things we had to learn. For instance, America is vastly over-shopped. It's more difficult to make money in the States than it is in the UK, for a variety of reasons. The country is so big that distribution can be difficult. There are also lots of climatic changes. Florida is different from Boston, so you have to have the right merchandise in the right place at the right time. Management is also more costly. Although one of the joys of retailing in the States is that it can go very fast. There are shopping malls everywhere in America. There are relatively very few in the UK. Then there's sales promotion. In the States, a higher percentage of turnover goes for promotion and advertising. Ads in the UK cover the entire country. In the States, again because of its size, there are no national newspapers so you have to take the time and expense to target your advertising.'

Just as importantly, the word 'sale' doesn't mean the same as it does in England.

'Sale in the UK means that you've bought something badly and want to get rid of it. Or you've got damaged goods to get rid of. Or you've actually bought in goods to be marketed on sale. In the States, the word sale means this is the regular price. I'm afraid that Americans are incredibly gullible. Before we managed to figure that out, our competition in the States came from retailers who used to scream, Sale. To get even, we simply joined the bandwagon. We started promoting ourselves very heavily. Although in the end we've actually found very little real competition for what we're doing in the US. The department stores, for instance, don't sell furnishings with the same sort of conviction we do.'

Conran clustered his first stores in the north-east corner of the country because he felt it would be a mistake to attack the huge American market by thinking that it's just one country.

'I don't look upon the States as one country or 52 states, but rather four very distinct regions. The North-East, the Midwest, the Sunbelt and the West Coast. I think that's the way you have to see America. I think you're looking for trouble if you say, I'll just go across the States with a chain and cover the entire country like that. You have to adapt your product range to suit these four different areas. You find lighter colours in Los Angeles than you do in New York. California is obviously less metropolitan and that is reflected by requiring slightly different shades and styles. You've got to cater to the local tastes. The secret to success in the States is that you must take advantage of regional management, marketing, product and store design. I honestly believe that, if you get it just right, there's a lot of money to be made. If you simply try to pick up what you're selling in the North-East and drop it on the West Coast, you won't be as successful as possible.'

'Terence Conran's handwriting spreads to everything he touches,' says Robin Guild, one of Europe's most successful interior designers.

Guild, who owns the London store Homeworks, also just happens to have been one of Conran's first retail accounts back in the days when Conran was designing and manufacturing furniture only for the trade.

'There is no doubt at all that his was the first business empire in this country built around style, taste and design. I'd say he's brought style to a certain level of the English public and drastically changed furniture retailing. He opened up a whole new world for that middle-income, professional management, white-collar type. He made stylish good taste affordable.'

Even five years ago, long before he ran into trouble, asking various analysts around the City what they thought of Conran got you the overall impression that he's never been a financial whiz-kid. But then, he's never pretended to be anything like that. He is a designer, first and foremost, whose greatest talent is in merchandising. He makes his shops look attractive and makes what's in them look attractive.

Yet in spite of his design skills, Conran's rise in the world of business was hardly meteoric. Nine years after he opened the first Habitat, his empire was a mere 15 stores. Then again, in those early years, Conran made a few less-than-satisfactory deals. One of them was buying into and nearly merging with Rymans, the stationery and office supply chain. It tied up a lot of his capital and a lot of his energy. It wasn't until 1972, by getting out of that deal, that he managed to raise enough capital to begin his expansion.

It was January 1982 when Terence Conran pulled off a terrific coup. Under the Svengali influence of Morgan Grenfell's Roger Seelig – he of Guinness scandal fame – Conran managed the reverse take-over of the Mothercare chain. Habitat sales were then about £78 million with profits at a mere £6.6 million coming from just 52 stores. Mothercare, however, was turning over £117 million and making a profit of £20.6 million with 429 stores in 11 countries. Based on the number of employees alone, Mothercare was three times the size of Habitat. It was also getting a better return on turnover than Habitat.

'As far as we were concerned, all you had to do was go into one of their stores to see why they needed us. Mothercare had lost its way. The shops had no direction. They didn't look good. The product line wasn't right. Our idea was to turn Mothercare into a pre- and post-natal version of Habitat. I bought the chain because, in spite of their problems, they still had 35% of the market. When I say in spite of everything, I mean that while they had good sites and good management, they had dull products and had lost the middle-class market.'

He financed the Mothercare acquisition by taking Habitat public. Except Mothercare wasn't being talked about publicly when Habitat went to the market. And that raised some eyebrows in the City. Some analysts thought the reverse take-over was too risky a move so soon after going public. Others went so far as to warn their clients to be careful because Conran and Habitat were 'trendy'.

That's a term he's heard often. That's precisely what the banks told him when he tried to raise capital for expansion in the States.

'We've suffered too many times at the hands of the all-too-usual near-sightedness of the British banking community. None of the British banks wanted to know. 'You're reasonably successful, they told us, but you are very trendy.' They saw us as some sort of Carnaby Street jeans merchant, here today and gone tomorrow. It was all very disappointing after struggling very hard for years.'

Being a retailer, he's usually been able to depend on financing growth out of cash flow. When Mothercare and Richard Shops came along, he started using convertible unsecured loan stock. That gave the group the look of a high-leverage operation.

Next Conran went after Heals.

A popular store in London's West End, it was the closest thing Conran had to a competitor. He bought it in 1984 and immediately made some changes. But his reason for buying it was not to wipe out the opposition. Instead he envisioned turning Heals into 'a mature man's Habitat'.

In between Mothercare and Heals, he picked up a 48% stake in Richards Shops, opened a chain called Now for the teenage market, built up a strong base business for Conran Associates – which is a design consulting firm that he closed in 1986, restructured and now calls the Conran Design Group – and joined forces with Paul Hamlyn for a joint venture in the book business.

Early in 1985, Conran also found himself involved in merger talks with the Debenhams Group. He obviously felt those shops could be made to meld nicely with Habitat–Mothercare. So he came up with an offer, Debenhams' Chairman, Robert

Thornton, rejected it, and after some shadow boxing, Conran went away.

In the meantime, he started hanging out with Ralph Halpern. A thin, nervous man with a receding hairline, Halpern became chairman of the Burton Stores Group of clothing stores in 1978. Before he took over, Burton's was very much the same kind of ailing operation that Mothercare was when Conran came along. In 1978 Burton's profits were running just under £7 million. Seven years later Burton's balance sheet showed profits had increased more than eight-fold.

Halpern too had ideas for the Debenhams group. He believed that, by combining his retailing skills with Conran's design skills, the world could be their oyster.

What the two of them envisioned was a 'galleria'. They believed that the old-fashioned department store was a dinosaur. That the future lay in a modern version of a much sexier shopping environment, like *La Galleria* in Milan. The idea was that the store would provide the walls, plenty of glass and lots of green plants, assure a general quality of merchandise and establish an overall shopping ambience. However, the merchandise offered for sale would come from trading partners. Call it a min-shopping centre, if you will – an accumulation of boutiques pretending to be hi-tech High Street.

Debenhams attracted them for several reasons. Beside having an already established specialist retailing operation, there was also shoe manufacturing, and Welbeck finance – a boomingly successful consumer credit operation. But the best part of the deal was to be the group's two major properties – a sensational Oxford Street location, and Harvey Nichols in Knightsbridge.

Unfortunately, the management of Debenhams had their own ideas. As Halpern was planning his attack, Thornton was planning his defences.

Now, it almost goes without saying that Terence Conran has never been mistaken for a Lord Hanson or a Gerald Ronson. His style is very different. He's much more laid back and isn't the kind of street-fighter they are. Nor could anyone doubt Ralph Halpern's track record as a retailer. But when it came to wheeling and dealing and nasty take-over fights, neither of them had much success in the ring – least of all Halpern who'd just lost a bitter battle for UDS. He went up against Gerald Ronson and James Hanson, and Ralph Halpern came out a definite third.

But that didn't stop them.

Halpern's Burton Group launched an attack on Debenhams. Thornton dug in. As the battle hotted up, Halpern announced for the first time that Conran was with him. Although he wasn't bidding himself, Conran would revamp the group's 67 stores, take up 20% of the group's trading space and hold an option to buy a 20% stake in the redesigned Debenhams group. Halpern's announcement was followed by national newspaper ads showing a smiling Halpern and a grinning Conran, and promising, 'Either of them could turn Debenhams around. You are being offered both of them'.

Thornton pooh-poohed the *Galleria* concept and outrightly rejected Halpern's bid. In the middle of the fight Professor Smith of House of Fraser got in on the act, with the Fayeds behind him, and picked up around 25% of the Debenhams shares. His move looked as if it was aimed at foiling Halpern. Then Gerald Ronson showed up and with Phil Harris, Chairman of Queensway. They grabbed 7% of the Debenhams shares.

Halpern and Conran might have been thinking about gallerias, but now the big kids were in the game and they were trying to get their hands on the real pearl in the oyster – the £40 million Harvey Nichols site. Halpern suddenly had to negotiate with Ronson and Harris – the same as Gerald Ronson did when he found Ralph Halpern getting in his way during the UDS bid. But business is business and none of them could afford to let personalities get in the way. In the end it was the Ronson/Harris 7% stake that eventually swung the group to Halpern. The press called it one of 'the bitterest and most colourful take-over battles the city has seen'.

Not to be outdone, less than four months later, Terence Conran managed what was then considered a very major

British retailing coup. In Novemeber 1985 he overshadowed both the Debenhams deal and the UDS deal by announcing a merger of Habitat–Mothercare with the basically sleepy and otherwise staid chain, British Home Stores. Although BHS shareholders would have 55% of the newly named Storehouse PLC, the merger announcement was quick to point out that Conran would be Chairman.

Suddenly Conran was operating along every economic spectrum of the High Street. A redesigned BHS to fight Marks and Spencer. Habitat, Mothercare and Now for the younger, hipper crowd. Heals for the more upmarket group. A galleria'd Debenhams for the boutique set.

In less than a quarter of a century he'd gone from Soup Kitchen to chairman of a billion-pound operation. The designer-turned-businessman had all the glory that the business world can offer.

And that's when everything started to turn sour.

Under the terms of Habitat's merger with BHS, Conran became Chairman of the new group which they named Storehouse. But those former BHS board members who joined Conran on the Storehouse board soon became disenamoured. Within two months of the merger, Storehouse's market value fell from £1.5 billion to £1.1 billion. And that worried the institutional investors. In June '87 Conran mentioned that Storehouse might be up for sale. Geoff Mulcahy, who turned Woolworth into Kingfisher, met at least three times with Conran. His idea, agreeable to Conran, was to take Mothercare and BHS and leave Habitat. Those former BHS board members were anything but pleased.

Over the next few months the boardroom rift deepened.

Mulcahy pulled out of his talks with Conran and Tony Clegg now stepped in. Chairman of the Mountleigh property group, he was allegedly prepared to offer £4.45 a share for Storehouse, when the market price was lingering between £3.50–4.00.

Conran came close to making the deal, then, mysteriously, said no. He had decided that he no longer wanted to sell the business.

Looking back, that was his fatal mistake.

The City lost confidence and support for his shares began to slip.

Other suitors followed, like Peter Earl who teemed up with Ashraf Marwan to make a run at Storehouse. The stock-market crash in October 1987 knocked a full pound off Storehouse's share prices.

Management changes brought fresh faces to the top, with a new Chief Executive taking over the day-to-day running of the business from Conran. But the overall downturn in the High Street store sector, brought on by high interest rates, hit the group very badly. The bottom fell out of the home-furnishing business and Habitat lost its way. So did Mothercare. So did BHS. As one analyst put it at the end of 1989, 'For all the talk of Storehouse's brand strength, the cruel truth is that if BHS, Mothercare and Habitat vanished overnight from the High Street, few consumers would miss it.'

Word around the City is that certain big institutional investors have agreed to support Conran until October 1991. In other words, when he hits 60, it's over. In the meantime, the sharks have been circling in the waters for some time. Asher Edelman, a New York raider has had a keen eye for Storehouse, so has British entrepreneur David Rowland. But then, the list gets longer every day. And anyway, it probably doesn't matter as much who, but when.

Too bad.

Conran deserves a better exit.

His soul is dedicated to good design and he's tried to promote it every way he could.

Some years ago, he went to the Victoria and Albert Museum and put together a tiny design museum in their basement, called the Boilerhouse Project. Then he joined forces with Jacob Rothschild, Lord McAlpine and Roger Seelig, among others, amassed £200 million and bought Butler's Wharf.

The 17-acre site lies on the south bank of the Thames, a few hundred yards below Tower Bridge. Conran's aim was to develop a complete village there, a sort of south bank Covent Garden, mixing residential space with offices, workshops, botels, restaurants and boutiques.

As he said at the time, 'We want to have a place that attracts people excited by the idea of being part of a new community, where they will live and work, not a collection of flats where people go home to Surbiton at the weekends.'

The main Butler's Wharf building is a late nineteenth-century warehouse. Conran preserved the façades while modernizing the interiors. Next door he built Spice Quay, a riverside office complex where Conran himself now holds court. But the spirit of the development is the Boilerhouse Project grown up, a full-sized design museum.

A white building with a flat roof, narrow windows and glass brick walls, it is privately funded by the Conran Foundation. The permanent collection includes some 400 items on display – things of superior design, from chairs to kettles, from silverware to automobilia – with a library of videos, books, and journals dedicated to good design. There are also temporary exhibitions of new products and prototypes.

As the first museum in the world devoted entirely to industrial design, it is very much a symbol of the '80s.

So too perhaps, Terence Conran.

Thanks to him, good design filtered down from the yuppies to the working classes. Design as an industry has boomed.

Whatever his legacy as a businessman – and that's still open for debate – his place as a major British designer and patron of good taste is absolutely assured.

15

Robert Maxwell

Scene from the Life and Times of Chairman Bob: No. 1.

The Chairman is a man of many talents.

Included in the long list of his achievements is *Dodo – the Kid from Outer Space.*

It seems that back in 1954, one of his ventures was called Harmony Films. The company didn't exactly evolve into Twentieth Century Fox, and he never exactly became Darryl Zanuck, but the Chairman – in those days known as the Producer – did give the world 52 cartoon episodes in the life of Dodo.

However, as one kid from outer space does not a movie mogul make, he also funded several filmed opera and ballet performances.

At one point during the filming of a Bolshoi production of *Giselle*, the prima ballerina was having a difficult moment, so the Producer himself jumped on to the stage to guide her through the finer points.

The mind boggles at the ballet career he might have had.

Robert Maxwell likes to think of himself as the British version of America's Armand Hammer.

At least, when someone makes that comparison, he doesn't argue the point.

Since the end of 1989, much-publicized former friendships with Romania's Ceaucescu and East Germany's Honecker have been down played. Win some, lose some. Readily more available these days are photos of Maxwell trying to help Mr Gorbachev realign the Soviet economy.

He does, by the way, travel with his personal photographer so that no unforgettable moment will be forgotten.

In large part because he understands how to play the media game and has become so adept at it, he is one of the most famous men in the country. He is, almost certainly, the nation's most recognizable entrepreneur. Ask almost anybody in Britain who Robert Maxwell is and they're bound to know at least two things people know about him. The first is that he owns the Mirrow Newspaper Group. The second is that he was once ruled unfit to run a public company.

But not necessarily in that order.

In 1984 he used his considerable take-over skills to negotiate and win the *Mirror*. Sir Alex Jarratt, Chairman of Reed International, had announed a public flotation of the group, originally hoping to raise £75 million. But a re-evaluation by his advisers brought that figure down to £60 million. That's when Maxwell came along to offer £100 million. It put Jarratt in a most uncomfortable position. He'd been hoping to spread the shares as widely as possible in a public sale but at the same time didn't want to turn down Maxwell's extra £40 million. If he floated the company, Maxwell might just bid everyone out of the sale. On the other hand, if he thought about it too long and Maxwell pulled out, he might wind up with even less than £60 million.

Sensing Jarratt's dilemma, Maxwell turned the heat up by raising his bid to £113 million. The message to Jarrett was clear, that to refuse would be financial suicide.

In reality, Jarratt had little choice. The deal was agreed on Friday 13 July at 2.30 in the morning. Four hours later, the Mirror Group Chairman of just six months, Clive Thornton, walked into his office and found Maxwell already sitting behind his desk.

A day or so after he took over, Maxwell addressed the *Mirror's* union members. They'd been openly hostile to him because they believed that wherever Maxwell went, redundancies followed. He asked them to work with him to make the paper Britain's largest-selling daily. He told them he didn't want to go into battle with them.

He said, 'I don't want to spend years in trench warfare.' Then he asked rhetorically, 'Do you think I'm on an ego trip?'

The audience shouted in unison, 'Yes.'

The Mirror acquisition was the culmination of a long march that started on the wrong foot 15 years before.

It was 1969.

He and the American wheeler-dealer Saul Steinberg decided it might be time to join forces. Steinberg's leased computers (Leasco) and Maxwell's magazines (Pergamon Press) were supposed to enjoy synergistic bliss. Steinberg had agreed to buy Pergamon shares at 173p.

Maxwell's version is, 'Somewhere in the middle of our dealing, Steinberg decided to pull out. I think he was probably short of cash.'

Steinberg's version is that Maxwell's profits were grossly exaggerated, that the share prices were inflated.

Maxwell says, 'He turned on me to make me seem to be the villain. It is classic American business practice. Steinberg had paid $6 a share for his interest in the partnership.'

No indication where that $6 figure came from because, even at the 1969 average £1 = $2.39, the £1.73 price only equals $4.13.

He goes on, 'I bought his shares for 25 cents.'

He actually paid 12p, which is what Steinberg eventually wrote them down to when he took a derisory loss on his own balance sheet five years later.

Adds Maxwell, 'I spent $5 million. They say that he's only had two failures. Chemical Bank (a costly and bitter take-over bid Steinberg lost) and me.'

Reached by phone in New York, the impression Steinberg gave was that he wanted nothing at all, absolutely nothing, really and truly nothing more to do, ever, with Robert Maxwell. But, he was asked, is it true that Robert Maxwell is the only man ever to have got the better of Saul Steinberg? Not an easy task considering Steinberg's reputation. His answer was, 'Bullshit!'

The Stock Exchange suspended dealings on Pergamon Press. The City Take-Over Panel was called in and they cited 'misgivings'. The Board of Trade ordered an investigation. Steinberg had used his shares to remove Maxwell from the Pergamon board. Leasco also filed a $22 million lawsuit against him in New York.

Throughout the inquiry, Maxwell argued that the methods used by the investigators denied him justice. He called it a Star Chamber – it was – and claimed he's not been given the opportunity to confront, cross-examine and/or otherwise refute unfavourable testimony.

Despite his objections, when the report was published it was critical of Maxwell.

The government concluded that he'd inflated his company's profits through dealings between Pergamon and a group of his private companies. Today the case is one of those cited in great detail by the Department of Trade and Industry in their Handbook of the Companies Inspection System. The points raised and debated have set precedents and in some way changed the system.

But they also marked Maxwell for the rest of his career, because the inspectors ruled that, as he'd been recklessly optimistic, he was therefore 'unfit to be a steward of a public-quoted company'.

Scene from the Life and Times of Chairman Bob: No. 2.

It had once been the custom at the *Mirror*, as it is around many newspapers, that editors stock their offices with suitable liquid refreshment at the company's expense. But the Chairman has a great aversion to needless expenses and can get quite stroppy about it. So, when he took over, he ordered that any expense-account booze had to be approved by him. Discretion being the better part of Scotch on the rocks, most of the editors did not push their luck and instead paid for their own. However, one editor figured, to hell with this, went to the

Chairman's penthouse suite, banged on the door and found him relaxing in front of the television. 'Here,' he said, pushing the expense voucher for a bottle into the Chairman's hands, 'sign this.' Much to the editor's surprise, without saying anything, the Chairman signed it. A week later the editor's phone rang. 'This is Robert Maxwell. Would you come upstairs to see me, please.' Suddenly worried for his job, the editor went to see the Chairman who greeted him at the door with, 'Come in, sit down, would you like a drink?'

It seems he was getting lonely and this editor was the only guy at the newspaper the Chairman knew who drank.

Maxwell is a fighter.

The Leasco scandal knocked him down, but it didn't knock him out. He got up and he clawed his way back. In 1974 he retook Pergamon Press, buying it off Steinberg for $6.25 million to settle the case.

His come-back to the chairmanship of Pergamon also created another reference that won't go away – from that day forward he's been known as the Bouncing Czech.

By 1979 he'd built Pergamon's pre-tax profits up to £1.5 million. But he was still, by international standards, small potatoes. He didn't begin to make the big time until 1981 when he went fishing, hooked and actually landed the British Printing Corp.

Losses at BPC were in the £10–12 million range. But assets weren't being used to their fullest – it was the nation's largest printing company – and he had loads for them to print. From the moment he took control, he made all the typical Maxwell moves. He tightened the management screws and slashed a large chunk out of the work-force. He renamed BPC the British Printing and Communications Corp. and, within a year, the company showed a tiny profit.

Fair-sized fish swallows small whale and both live happily ever after.

It's a talent that has made him a fabulously wealthy man and, in a not always flattering way, a legend in his own time.

But he didn't start out rich and famous. Once upon a time he was a poor refugee on the run from the Nazis in his native Czechoslovakia. His father was shot by them. His mother died in a concentration camp.

'I worked for a time with the underground in Budapest helping to smuggle people to Yugoslavia when I was captured and sentenced to death. I escaped to France and fought there for a while until an American consul in Marseilles offered me a chance to go to the United States. He offered me a scholarship and a visa. I turned it down because the war was on. This was 1940.'

His first sight of England came in September of that year. He arrived with, literally, not a penny in his pocket. He spent a brief period in a refugee camp, before enlisting in the Pioneers and North Staffs, thinking it was a fighting regiment. Four years later, he was in the British Army fighting in Normandy and earning himself a battlefield commission.

'It caused a lot of problems, not for me but for the War Office. Technically, I was a German or a Hungarian at the time. It took General Montgomery to personally intervene.'

Monty pinned the Military Cross on Maxwell's chest. Actually, he pinned it on Jan Lodvick Hoch's chest. That was the name he was born with but, when the War Office found out that a foreigner was wearing the Military Cross, he was given near-instant British citizenship and a new name. From Hoch it became Du Maurier. He'd seen it on a cigarette package and should probably count himself fortunate that today he isn't known as Bob Luckystrike. Then for a brief time it was Jones. Somehow it wound up Maxwell. To a 21-year-old Czech kid who had just fought a war, it had a terrific British ring to it.

Having shown a great ability for languages during those years – he claims to speak nine of them fluently – Maxwell spent a couple of years after the war in Berlin. Through a publisher there he discovered piles of technical studies done by German scientists. He decided a world-wide market for them might exist. So he bought the rights to as many of them as he could, and published them wherever he could. He says that by 1948 he was already a millionaire.

In 1951 he bought a small publishing company called Verlag Heidelberg from Butterworth & Springer for £13,000. He renamed it Pergamon Press. And that company became the backbone of everything he's done since.

By 1964 he was a Member of Parliament. 'I spent seven years as an MP for the Labour Party for Buckingham. But that ended in 1970 (a year after the Leasco scandal). I got kicked out by the people. I lost an election.'

He's always been a staunch supporter of the Labour Party and vowed that the *Mirror* would always be a Labour newspaper. It is and he is quite obviously very sincere about his socialist tendencies. However, with a personal fortune estimated to be worth £675 million, making him the eleventh wealthiest man in Britain, the Labour Party doesn't know quite what to make of him. Some of the powerful print union factions have at times tried to kick him out of the party. But that may be less for his wallet and more for the fact that he's never hesitated to make severe cuts in his work-force when he felt it necessary, has closed plants and made some very naked threats. For instance, the first day he met with the *Mirror*'s union members, he told them if there was ever an illegal strike he'd shut down the paper. Just like that, he said, he'd close the doors and walk away.

Whether or not they believed him is one thing. The fact is, some real-estate experts have claimed all along that the *Mirror* building at Holborn Circus is actually worth more as a property than Maxwell paid for the entire group. Shutting the *Mirror* would have perhaps been a blow to his ego. But it might not have been a suicidal blow to his wallet.

Holding closure above their heads – like the way he issued redundancy notices to everyone in the group in late 1985 so that he could force SOGAT into agreeing to manpower cuts – has quite clearly earned him points with bankers and financiers around the City. Many admire his relentless energy and single-minded determination. Many openly admit that Maxwell's methods have helped to bring a nineteenth-century industry into modern times.

Just as Maxwell can be so very charming when he wants to be, the red capes of certain union leaders turn this bull into a tactless rage. And that, most assuredly, has not won him a lot of friends in the union movement. Then again, he's stood up and played tough with the unions before so he probably didn't have too many friends in the union movement to begin with.

'I really have no time to worry or care. And that infuriates my enemies. I'm a socialist manager. But they have their job to do and I have mine. I still love them as brothers but business is business.'

Long before the *Mirror* came along, Maxwell was already claiming to be the world's largest publisher. Pergamon Journals publishes a list of almost 1000 technical magazines, annual subscriptions to which can cost hundreds and even thousands of pounds. *International Abstracts of Biological Sciences Monthly* is 11 separate magazines per month at the combined rate of over £1000 per year. Computer state of the art reports costs nearly twice as much. While a combination subscription to *Insect Biochemistry and the Journal of Insect Physiology* is a bargain at around £500.

'I'm the smartest publisher in the world because I do what none of the others do. I get writers to pay me.' Besides that, as all subscriptions must be paid in advance, he's got a positive cash flow of over £100 million.

Scene from the Life and Times of Chairman Bob: No. 3.

The Chairman was having lunch with some friends. He was going on about how the British establishment had never taken to him. He slammed his great big fist on the table and said, 'I defy anyone who's ever done a deal with Bob Maxwell to say that he didn't get a full 12 annas for his rupee.'

There are, however, 16 annas to a rupee.

Blind faith and loyalty are not the top two qualities Maxwell inspires amongst his troops.

It's no secret that he can be a bully, that he sometimes fires people in the most humiliating fashion and especially in front of their peers. Former employees have been known to describe him as an erratic and mercurial autocrat, saying you pay attention to him, not because you like him but because he's screaming at you. Yet, after describing a man with that sort of temper, many of them will then admit that they admire him as a hard-driving entrepreneur who's attained great success. They admire him for being a workaholic, shrewd, astute, clever, at times charming, often brilliant with details, and someone who claims to possess a near-photographic memory. People who've worked for him say that he's got a short attention span but when he is paying attention, he makes decisions on the spot. They say that if you got to him with a deal and he likes it, he'll say yes right away and find the money to back it. If you can get his attention, there's no red tape. On the other hand, if he doesn't want to do something, he tends to totally disregard it. He doesn't answer memos and isn't available for meetings. Many things he doesn't want to do simply fade away, without him ever having to say no.

Naturally he has his enemies – in the nastiest sense of the word. But even they credit him with being someone who displays great love and admiration for his family. He's been with his wife for 45 years and they've had nine children – although two have died. He says that his main regret in life is that business has all too often kept him away from his family.

Yet business is business and with Robert Maxwell it's almost as if there is an insatiable drive for the next deal. The game is the thing. He certainly doesn't need the money and says as much.

'I am not motivated by money.'

As far as he's concerned, the best thing about money is being able to have someone drive your car for you. He tells people he lives in a council house, but that council house turns out to be the biggest mansion on the block, on a hill overlooking all of Oxford. He claims he works as hard as he does because 'I wish to be of service'.

As there's no confusing Robert Maxwell with Mother Theresa, that can't be the only reason.

Some people say that his success if nothing more than an expensive ego trip. Not long ago in Belgium, corridors leading to a Maxwell press conference were lined with huge photomurals of him. While a recent Maxwell Communications corporate video features Maxwell as the star attraction, with the music swelling every time he appears. One person who saw it commented, audiences could be forgiven for not realizing that the company has 17,000 other employees.

Others say the motivation is nothing but power. He obviously enjoys rubbing shoulders with world leaders. Otherwise he wouldn't court them the way he does.

Still, even if the past 45 years have been nothing but an ego trip or a chance to play the game of power, it would be understandable – the poor Czech boy who survives to do it all. Maybe that's why he kept putting his picture on the front page of the *Mirror* when he first bought the paper. Or why he wrote all those editorials in the *Mirror*. Or why he constantly reminded people, 'I'm the publisher. I'm involved in everything.'

Whatever he does, there's no denying that he does it with total commitment and *élan*. He can street-fight with the big kids. How strange it was then in 1983–4 when he took on a little kid, and found the little kid just big enough to knee him in the groin.

Maxwell wanted to buy a company called John Waddington, a Leeds-based printing business that owns the UK rights to such games as Monopoly, Lexicon and Cluedo. In June 1983 he launched his first attack and came within a few percentage points of taking the company. A year later he took his second shot and fired off a £44 million bid. But this time David took aim at Goliath. Waddington's Chairman, Victor Watson, said that as long as BPCC wanted to own his company, and as long as BPCC was then 61%-owned by Maxwell's Pergamon Press Ltd, and as long as Pergamon Press Ltd was 100% owned by a Liechtenstein trust called Pergamon Holding Foundation, he felt he had the right to know exactly who owned the Liechtenstein trust. After all, he argued, whoever owns the holding foundation would, in reality, own Waddington. That immediately raised more important questions, such as who really owns the Mirror Group.

Maxwell instantly denied that he owned the *Mirror*. 'I am not a proprietor, I am a publisher.' To that he added, 'Look at the record for over 30 years. Every public statement I have ever made has made it clear that neither I, nor my wife, nor my family will inherit one penny of all the wealth that I have managed to create.'

The 1981 Companies Act gives public companies the right to demand that shareholders disclose beneficial ownership of their stakes. So Watson sent a letter to the resident director of Pergamon Holding Foundation in Liechtenstein, requesting such information. The official answer was, I'll speak to my lawyers and let you know. But Watson didn't have to wait. Maxwell conceded defeat and started selling his Waddington shares.

As for who really owns the Liechtenstein trust and in turn the Mirror Group, there have been several stories. At the time of the Waddington bid, the official word was that ownership was split between a series of charities and members of Mrs Maxwell's family. She's French – they met in Paris in 1944 – and her relatives are not resident in the UK. That was as much of an answer as Maxwell was then required to give. More recently he's explained that the trust is owned by the Maxwell Foundation, which was started in 1953 when his sister Brana, a survivor of the Buchenwald death camp, had deposited a few thousand pounds of her savings in Liechtenstein. The foundation, which holds a majority stake in the Maxwell Communication Corporation, the main Maxwell company, will reportedly one day give all its money to charities that support medicine, science, young entrepreneurs in the media industries and education in the cause of peace.

Maxwell insists that the foundation is not, nor has ever been a mystery and has nothing to do with tax avoidance. Yet he has always appeared almost obsessively secret about it.

It's still never been made totally clear who actually controls the foundation. Or, perhaps, he just figures it isn't anyone else's business.

Scene from the Life and Times of Chairman Bob: No. 4.

A young man nervously drank a coffee in the waiting area in front of the Chairman's office. From the gold ring on the fourth finger of his left hand you could tell he was married. From his rosy cheeks you could tell he was newly married. This probably wasn't his first job. But it could have been his second. And by the way he was whispering to himself, you could tell that he had a speech for the Chairman.

'Now here's the way I see the situation, sir.'

He'd practised it the night before while his bride lay on her satin pillows and watched him with wonderment. 'That's right, I'm going to get into the Chairman's office and say to him, the way I see the situation, sir, is that improved cash-flow will allow us to make further investments in related businesses.'

He looked like an accountant, wore accountant-type shoes and an accountant-type suit. God only knows, he probably also had an accountant-type wife.

'Oh yes, dear, yes, that's very good,' she nodded to reassure him.

'From my experience with such matters, sir, I can recommend a cost accounting method which would in turn assure that stock control . . .'

By God, he was going to give the Chairman a first impression of a young man on the way up. A team player. An organization man. A young man who was going to find his way on to the board before his thirtieth birthday . . .

The Chairman came out of his office and walked up to the young man. He extended his hand and said in a very strong voice, 'I'm Robert Maxwell.' He did not add, however, 'But my friends call me Bob.'

The young man jumped to his feet, nearly spilling his coffee, fumbling with the cup and saucer before putting it down to shake the Chairman's hand. 'Hello . . .'

'You're the new accountant for the printing works, I presume.'

The new accountant for the printing works tried to recall his speech.

But the Chairman had met new accountants for the printing works before. Hundreds of them. Thousand of them. He'd heard their practised speeches. He knew exactly what to expect. And he had long ago learned how to cut short that kind of thing. The Chairman is a very large man, tall and bulky, an expert at using his body weight, and at using his air space.

'Now here's what I want,' he said, moving in on the new accountant for the printing works, towering over him and poking his finger into his chest. 'I want a system which will allow you to report to me . . .' The Chairman's direct orders lasted two minutes. Then he asked the new accountant for the printing works, 'Is that understood?'

The new accountant for the printing works was barely able to utter a feeble 'Yes, sir'.

'Good,' the Chairman smiled victoriously. 'Thank you for coming to see me.' He shook the young man's hand, turned around and walked away.

In 1988 Maxwell predicted that his Maxwell Communications Corporation would be one of the world's largest communications groups within two years.

He didn't make it, but it wasn't for the lack of trying.

Hungry to buy, he purchased shares in the *Kenya Times* and the *Montreal Daily News*. When Rupert Murdoch announced that he'd leased four transponders on the Astra satellite to be launched that November, Maxwell announced that together with British Telecom and W. H. Smith, he planned to launch seven channels on satellite. That month he also purchased a company called Science Research Associates for $150 million, finally establishing a US publishing base for himself. A few weeks later he acquired 5% of France's Havas communications and media group, and immediately began negotiating for another 5%.

Maxwell went after the *Melbourne Age* newspaper but the Australian government pulled the rug out from under the deal in the wake of a public outcry against Maxwell. He then announced a huge venture with Société Générale de Belgique. But that fell through when SGB decided that they couldn't do business with him reportedly because 'Maxwell always wants 200% control'.

His next step was to take over the British-owned AGB Research PLC, one of those companies which measures media audiences, to team up with a group of private investors to buy into a Hungarian newspaper, and to bid for, but get beat with a $412.5 million offer, the US supermarket tabloid, the *National Enquirer*. He was successful however in purchasing Sphere Books from Penguin for just under £14 million. He followed that by doing a publishing joint venture with the Soviet Academy of Science. The idea is to publish non-classified Soviet scientific and medical reports.

Before long he announced his intention of launching the *European*, a *USA Today*-style newspaper to serve Europe. But making it work was not as easy as he thought it would be and he found himself continually backtracking, with the launch being delayed over and over again.

He set up a $1 billion investment fund to finance joint ventures in Central and Eastern Europe and got into the travel business by purchasing Thomas Cook Travel Inc. from Dun & Bradstreet, which included all of the Official Airline Guides.

Then he paid $39 million for a 27% stake in the Israeli high-tech firm Scitex, which produces computer-imaging systems that dominate the world publishing market, and $30.4 million for an 18% share in Teva Pharmaceuticals, Israel's largest drug company. He offered $250 million for a stake in Clal, Israel's second-biggest company, and also went after a stake in the *Jerusalem Post* newspaper.

Maxwell is today the largest individual investor in Israel.

He opened negotiations with Italian media baron Silvio Berlusconi for joint ventures, and joined forces with arch-rival Rupert Murdoch in a multimillion-dollar agreement to link satellite and cable television in England. He offered $49 million for De La Rue Company's Crosfield electronics unit, then bought a 14.5% stake in composer Andrew Lloyd Webber's musical-production company, Really Useful PLC.

Looking for major expansion in the States, he embarked on a hostile bid for publishers, Harcourt Brace Jovanovich. But they were so dead against having anything to do with him that they went into a dance which can only be described as 'a wildly leveraged recapitalization' simply to avoid being taken over by Maxwell.

It had been an especially frustrating time for Maxwell in the States. He'd eyed Bell & Howell but they ran for safety into the arms of Robert Bass. He'd considered buying Scientific American, the CBS magazine division and even Doubleday. He struck out three more times.

Now he set his sights on the Macmillan Publishing Company.

Over the course of three months in late 1988, he faced off against Kohlberg Kravis Roberts, the Wall Street trio who became world famous for their $25 billion mega-bid for RJR/Nabisco. With deadlines drawing near, Maxwell looked like the winner at $89 a share. But KKR suddenly came back with an eleventh-hour offer of $90.05. Furious that he'd been topped like that at the last minute, he upped their offer by 20 cents, for a cash total of $2.6 billion. He desperately wanted Macmillan and he was not going to be denied.

Just as he thought he'd won, the Macmillan board said that they'd rather stick with the KKR bid. Outraged, Maxwell raced into court to block the deal.

When the smoke cleared, Maxwell emerged owning the company. And within a month he installed his son Kevin to run it.

He wanted the company to take a more aggressive stance in international publishing with a world-wide distribution network for its scientific, educational and professional titles, bringing them back into a field abandoned eight years previously. He then linked Macmillan's educational division in a joint textbook venture with McGraw-Hill, worth $190 million to Macmillan, signing at the same time what is known as a 'stand-still agreement', which barred him from putting together a take-over bid for McGraw Hill.

USA Today now reported that Maxwell was eying Chicago's world famous skyscraper, Sears Tower, intending to move Macmillan into it and rename it Maxwell Tower.

His more immediate intentions however were to float 8.4 million shares of Macmillan's Berlitz International, a language training unit. He also announced plans to float shares in the Mirror Group.

His prediction to become one of the biggest communications groups in two years might simply have been over-ambitious.

He's still a buyer, although time is running out.

In his late 60s, he'd obviously like to do it soon, before he hands over, probably to one or two of his sons – Kevin and Ian are the prime candidates – who will then face the even more ambitious test of keeping dad's ship afloat.

Scene from the Life and Times of Chairman Bob: No. 5.

The Chairman turned 60 years old in 1983 and figured it was reason to celebrate. He threw a party for his 2000 closest friends. It was a do to out-do even the annual Ewing barbecue. Seen at the birthday party were the Soviet Ambassador and the Bulgarian Ambassador. They were heard at the party too, as they read official tributes from their governments to the Chairman. Then the Chairman's wife Elizabeth took the microphone and read from a book she'd prepared containing lots more tributes to the Chairman – these from a cross-section of the world's leaders who unfortunately were unable to attend. A photographer never stopped taking pictures. The Chairman liked one in particular so much that he used it for his Christmas card that year. It had been a party worth remembering so he wanted the several thousand people on his Christmas list to remember. In the picture on his Christmas card was a banner with the words, 'Happy Birthday, Bob'.

And you thought Christmas had something to do with Jesus.

People who know him well say that in the last 20 years he's had two dreams, a Fleet Street newspaper and peerage. But in getting as far as he's gone, he's really never played the Establishment's game. Peerage is very much about playing that game, about having friends in high places, and markers that can be called in. He says he doesn't care what people think about him. 'I'm the man everyone loves to hate,' he boasts.

Some people who've done deals with him say that when you get into bed with Robert Maxwell you always end up with the rumpled end.

Others more generously suggest that he is a gambler.

Yet perhaps the best description is the one that goes: he's neither a cunning nor an evil man. He's not at all a calculating man. Instead, he's a man who has an amazing sixth sense for a deal. He is, the theory goes, a man who has intimidated people into believing that his instinct is calculation. Which it is not. It is instinct.

He's made his own victories. He's suffered his own defeats. There have been good deals that have worked out splendidly, and bad deals that have hurt him badly. He's a survivor in a game where it's not merely the weak who don't survive. It's most people.

His only mistake in surviving, they say, is that he's become Robert Maxwell. And the problem with being a legend in your own time is that you might start believing everything you hear about yourself.

Three books on Maxwell were published in March 1988.

They were, *Maxwell – The Outsider* by Tom Bower (Aurum), *Maxwell – A Portrait of Power* by Peter Thompson and Anthony Delano (Transworld/Bantam) and *Maxwell* by Joe Haines (Macdonald).

While his vanity must have been massaged by the fact that some people thought his first 65 years on this planet were worth the forests felled for 1150 total pages, his litigious side got the best of him and he did not let the books go unnoticed.

In February, with the *Sunday Times* about to begin serialization of Bower's book, he issued a series of writs against Bower, Aurum Press, Andrew Lloyd Webber's Really Useful Company which owns Aurum, and the newspaper. He claimed he was seeking assurances, and if necessary an injunction, preventing the repetition of material written previously by Bower in two magazines. He was also objecting to material in the book obtained from a former Maxwell employee, whom Maxwell claimed, had been in breach of a duty of confidentiality. He added that the book contained eight specific libellous references.

Aurum answered that the book would be published on schedule.

At the same time he went after the Thompson and Delano book, citing 27 libellous references.

To put pressure on both publishers, Maxwell also threatened booksellers and newsagents. He even issued a writ for libel against Blackwell's, the Oxford-based bookseller where both books were on sale.

Blackwells said they saw the issue as a matter of principle and, while they would obey the law if the courts injuncted them, they would continue to sell the books so long as they could lawfully do so. The two books remained on sale.

The third book, written by Maxwell employees Joe Haines, published by Maxwell's Macdonald Press and serialized in Maxwell's *Sunday Mirror*, was the so-called 'authorized' version of his life.

No injunctions against it were even contemplated.

Which is too bad for Haines because it lagged in sales behind the other two, which, thanks to Maxwell, were getting an inordinate amount of publicity.

To keep their books on the front shelves, Aurum and Bantam offered indemnities against any damages Maxwell might be able to claim. It reassured some booksellers. But not W. H. Smith. They held the books in the warehouse while their lawyers studied the implications of the indemnity offer. Maxwell sought to exert pressure on W. H. Smith, and other booksellers who might try to sell the books. Certain booksellers became so furious at Maxwell's approach, they now threatened to pull all Macdonald titles off their shelves.

The tone of the matter changed in late March when Maxwell's case against Transworld/Bantam was heard. It was alleged and subsequently proven in court that the book contained serious libels and was therefore 'wholly destructive of Maxwell's character and reputation'. The courts awarded him undisclosed but substantial damages and a public apology. Bantam conceded they'd made a 'grave error', recalled what copies they could from booksellers and, along with stocks held in their warehouse, pulped them. They also gave an undertaking that any reprint of the book would not contain the libels.

Hoping to salvage something from the affair, they quickly reset and reissued the Thompson/Delano book in May. They'd taken out the offending comments. But they infuriated Maxwell, yet again, with one word in the blurb on the back jacket.

Maxwell flew straight back into court for another injunction.

Looking at the books objectively, the main problem with all three is not so much anything that they've said about him as the fact that Maxwell himself may be too big a subject to get right the first time around. However, the three books do provide the ground-work for what might some day follow, a frank, unemotional, extremely well researched book that can dig more deeply, that can uncover the truth about a man who has layered on, or had layered on to him, so much legend that it's easy to get fact and fiction confused for each other.

But that book might not be soon in coming.

In fact, it might not be until he's gone that his family, friends and enemies would feel comfortable enough to tell the whole truth, to give a real inside look, to come up with the best stories.

Scene from the Life and Times of Chairman Bob: No. 6.

The Chairman is an ardent non-cigarette smoker. He likes

big cigars, but there are certain areas in his offices where smoking is absolutely *verboten.* One day while walking through a non-smoking area, he spotted a man sitting on a chair puffing away. The Chairman bellowed that the culprit had been caught red-handed. He reminded the man that the penalty for such an offence was immediate expulsion from the firm. The Chairman demanded to know of the man how much he was earning. The man answered, £75 a week. The Chairman reached into his pocket and took out a month's pay – £300 – gave it to the man and said, 'You're fired.' The Chairman pointed to the door and the man sheepishly left.

But the man was only there making a delivery.

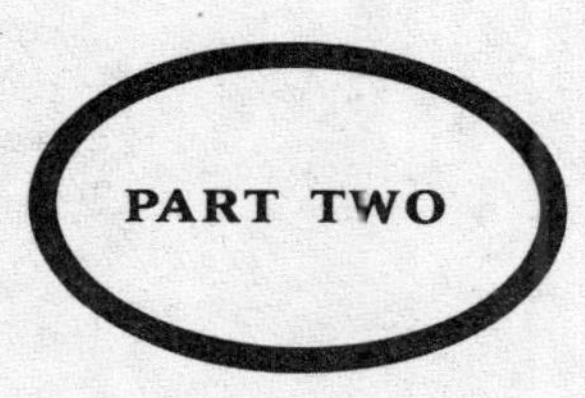

PART TWO

The New Risk Takers

Introduction

Do you know the story about the man with the elephant for sale?

A fellow, call him Harry, is walking down the block one day and bumps into a friend, call him George, who says, 'How would you like to buy an elephant?'

Harry says, 'How would I like to buy a what?'

George answers, 'I've got an elephant for sale. Wanna buy him?'

'An elephant.' Harry shakes his head. 'What the hell am I going to do with an elephant?'

'This is a terrific animal,' George says, now putting his arm around Harry's shoulders. 'You know how some elephants can stand up on one leg? This one can do that and also tip right back on its hind legs too, like it's sitting up.'

'That's not what I mean,' Harry says. 'I mean, what am I going to do with an elephant? I live in a one-bedroom flat on the third floor of a walk-up. Where am I going to keep an elephant?'

'Let me tell you something,' George goes on. 'For £450 you could have an elephant that not only does those two tricks, but also knows how to count. You say to him, how much is two and two and he raises his trunk four times. It's a great trick. A real party-stopper.'

'George, listen to me.' Harry needed to make his friend understand. 'An elephant has to be walked and bathed. An elephant has to eat. Where am I going to walk him? How am I going to bath him? I could never afford to feed an elephant.

George, you're talking about an animal that weighs four tons. Where would I keep him?'

George snaps his fingers as if he's just thought of something. 'Know what, Harry? This could be your lucky day. The elephant came out of a circus. Very bright animal. But in the circus he had a mate. A girl elephant. Now the two of them do this trick together where they walk backwards to music . . .' He stopped and pulled Harry even closer. 'Tell you what I'm gonna do. I could arrange to get the mate for you and give them both to you for £700.'

Harry swung around and looked at George. 'It's a deal.'

Does that tell you anything about the people in this book?

If one week is a long time in politics, five years is an eternity in business.

And five years ago one of the big players was Alan Bond.

He burst on to the international scene in 1983, off the coast of Newport, Rhode Island – heady days of top-secret winged keels – when he took the America's Cup race trophy away from the United States. But he'd been wheeling and dealing in Britain and Australia since he was a teenager. Legend has it that as a teenager in London he worked out a scheme with a local supermarket to sell them back empty jam jars. After emigrating to Fremantle, Australia in the '50s, he saw more profits in organizing newspapers boys to work for him than in selling the papers himself. A few years later, in Perth at the age of 19, he did a little land deal which made him enough fast money that he was hooked. Property and mining, especially gold mining, became the basis of his fortune. When property crashed in the mid-1970s, he nearly went bust. But he bounced back, using as much leverage as the banks would allow him, rebuilding his empire and putting enough aside to go after the America's Cup several times.

It was his third shot at the trophy that proved lucky.

And winning at Newport – sponsoring the first yacht ever to beat the US in a century of racing there – did for him what none of his other business deals could.

Bond became an international star.

He was a hero. Suddenly everybody wanted to do business with 'Bondy'. He parlayed his yachting success into breweries and television stations in Australia, property in England, and more breweries in the United States and a telephone company in Chile.

The best buy of all was Vincent Van Gogh's masterpiece, *Irises*.

In November 1987, when the picture came up for sale at Sotheby's, Bond bid the price up to $54 million (£30 million), making it the most expensive work of art in the world. The problem was, as Sotheby's eventually had to admit much to its embarrassment, Bond never paid for it. Sotheby's had agreed to lend him half the hammer price. Whether or not he had to leave the painting in New York as collateral is still unclear because that's where it was when the story of the Sotheby's loan leaked out, but the newspapers were filled with pictures of Bond and the painting at his offices in Perth. The rumours were that the Perth version was a copy.

Whatever, Bond didn't pay and couldn't pay and Sotheby's looked the fool for playing the game they did, too.

It has since gone to the Getty Museum in California who, supposedly, took it off Bond's hands – and Sotheby's – at a substantial discount on the hammer price.

Around the same time, he tried to rescue a bank in Perth and that cost him some money. He wanted to build a petrochemicals plant in Western Austrialia but fell out with the state government there and that cost him more money. He took a beating when the stock market crashed in October 1987. As highly leveraged as he'd been, increased interest rates weren't helping his cash flow. He'd over-extended himself and probably needed to cut back. Instead he tried to take over Lonrho.

Messing with Tiny Rowland was his fatal mistake.

Tiny can be one of the most charming men in the world when he wants to. He helped Jim Slater come back when Slater Walker crashed, despite the fact that he didn't really know Slater. He tried to help Freddie Laker get started again when Skytrain went down – again, someone he'd just met a few times casually. When Ernest Saunders was arrested at the opening of the Guinness scandal, Tiny helped Saunders – also someone he hardly knew – arrange bail.

Bond misjudged both his own business prowess and Tiny's patience.

The story is told that Bond had built a stake in Lonrho, showed up at Tiny's house in the country one weekend afternoon, knocked at the door and when Tiny answered, told him, 'I'm going to take over your company.'

It's not true.

It didn't happen at the house in the country.

Knowing that Bond was having troubles, Tiny believed that Bond might be looking to hide some of his debt in Lonrho's assets. He explained to Bond that it didn't work that way and that he – Tiny – wasn't thrilled with him – Bondy – having anything at all to do with Lonrho. The hint was, there will be no take-over, there will be no seat on my board, there will be no more buying of my shares! Bond allegedly agreed not to increase his Lonrho stake. The problem, as Tiny saw it, was that he went away and immediately started buying again. A message, that the people around Lonrho found to be 'insulting', then arrived from Bond, asking Tiny when he might be received.

Tiny's answer was to set about to destroy him.

The Australian press called it 'a broken-bottle attack'.

All he did was arrange to have his leverage pulled out from under him. Bond got caught in a cash crunch – like for $3.7 billion – as the banks trumpeted for the receivers and the walls came tumbling down.

Not all Australians have fared as badly. Several have done rather well. Some have even done so well they're no longer Australians.

Take for instance, R. Murdoch, American Citizen.

He and his family own a company called Cruden Investments. In turn, Cruden controls the Austrialian-based News

Corporation, which has two wholly-owned subsidiaries – News Limited, an Australian holding company, and Newscorp Investments, a British holding company. News Limited controls Ansett Transport Industries – which is Murdoch's only non-media investment – and owns and/or controls various Australian newspapers. That company also controls News America in the States which is the *New York Post*, the *Chicago Sun-Times* and the *Boston Herald*. Murdoch also owns Triangle Publications – whose lead title is *TV Guide* – and Harper and Row Publishers. The British company owns outright News International, which in turn owns and/or controls British subsidiaries like *The Times*, the *Sunday Times*, the *Sun*, *News of the World*, a holding in Reuters, Collins Publishing, Sky Channel and Sky Television. He also publishes the *South China Daily* and has interests in a Hungarian newspaper.

In 1983, he tried to buy Warner Communications – the former film studio turned entertainment conglomerate. Losses there had been running heavy and Murdoch spotted an opportunity. Before the year was out, he'd spent just over $100 million (then about £71.4 million) to acquire 7%. By the first week of January 1984, he'd had filed his intention in the US to purchase 25–49.9% of Warner's stock. His bid for the company was checked. However the fight to keep Murdoch out of Warner was hot enough to raise the value of the shares he was holding. He walked away with a $40 million profit for his trouble.

Two years later he paid $250 million for a 50% stake in TCF Holdings, parent company of the film and entertainment conglomerate Twentieth Century Fox. The shares had previously been owned by commodities speculator Marc Rich. Within six months Murdoch turned around and offered his new partner, Denver oilman Marvin Davis, $325 million for the other half. In between, he paid $1.55 billion for six Metromedia television stations. The American press suddenly proclaimed Murdoch a major US player.

So it really came as no surprise to anyone in 1989 when he intervened, unsuccessfully as it turned out, at the very last minute with a $1.8 billion bid for MGM/UA. What he lost out on was United Artist's 1000-film library.

Since buying Metromedia – ownership of American TV stations is restricted to Americans, hence his change in passport – Murdoch's been trying to set himself up as the fourth American network. But to do that, he needs product. Along came Sky and his appetite for more product, especially movies, became insatiable. His own studio has a 2000-film library and adds roughly 30 a year from current production. But it's not enough. Bidding against the rival networks, the BCC, ITV and BSB for films in the rest of the market has made buying an expensive exercise.

But then, Murdoch has always proven himself to be a long-term thinker and someone with a vision who, when he undertakes a project, sticks with it. Sky, for instance, costs him around £2.2 million a month. Yet he remains firm in his five-year commitment to the four channels because he believes the future of television is satellite and cable.

Another Australian who seems to make the papers is Kerry Packer.

Having taken Murdoch's title as the wealthiest man in Australia, Kerry Francis Bullmore Packer is often compared to the feudal landlords of old. As chairman of the family concern that he inherited from his father, Consolidated Press Holdings, he is a big man with a tough expression and large hands. And even if he is a teetotaller, he's still probably not the kind of guy you want to insult in a rowdy bar. Known for his heavy gambling and fierce temper, he's been highly successful in publishing, the media, chemicals, real estate, mining, livestock and financial services.

The story that usually gets told about him has to do with his penchant for always being on time and insisting that everybody else always be on time too. So one morning he waited at the front door of one of his newspapers to see who was coming to work on time and who wasn't. He announced he'd fire the last person in. As it happened, last to work that morning was his own son.

So he fired his son.

Packer is also well known for having changed Test cricket for ever. Over Christmas 1978 he hired some of the best players in the world and staged his own World Series Cricket Tests. He owned the Nine television network in Australia and needed programming for the holidays. The Australian Cricket Board wouldn't stage any matches, so he did.

He's also known in Australia as the man who sold the Nine network to Alan Bond for A$1 billion – at least twice what it was worth – and as soon as Bond's empire crashed, rushed in to buy it back at greatly deflated prices.

In the UK he's become known as the third man in the Hoylake take-over of British American Tobacco – alongside Jacob Rothschild and the incomparable Jimmy Goldsmith.

One of the most urbane, fascinating, ruthless, cunning and totally off-beat men in the world of international business, Goldsmith understands perhaps better than anyone else how to make money by always being in control.

For the past several years he's devoted himself to building his own 'Disneyland' in Mexico. He bought a huge property where he's building himself a gigantic home which is surrounded by several other houses – it's said there's one for every woman in his life – tropical rain forests, lagoons and even his own volcano.

Born in Paris in 1933, Goldsmith has divided his life between France, the UK, the States and, now, Mexico. He has a taste for the finer things in life, including beautiful women. There have been several wives and a few near-wives. He's got a whole slew of children and being a family man – albeit not exactly of the most conventional variety – he simply divides his time between all these various families.

He's been wheeling and dealing ever since dropping out of Eton at the age of 17. He joined the British Army as a private and got out two years later as a lieutenant. At the age of 20, with £100 in his pocket, he purchased the French rights to a British rheumatism cream. Three years later he sold his interests for £250,000 and started a dietary foods company, which served as the basis for his early international forays where he took over ailing companies and slowly built the third-largest food conglomerate in Europe.

Right from the beginning the Goldsmith touch has been recognizable: high risk, high gearing, a complex structure.

In 1984 he went after the forestry and insurance group St Regis. He bought shares, panicked the board and backed away with a $26 million profit. Unfortunately for the board at St Regis a number of Goldsmith's pals followed him and they all walked away with handsome profits. One of them later described that three-act greenmail opera simply as 'gang-rape'. Although for once it did disprove Goldsmith's so-called motto – 'If you see a bandwagon, it's too late'.

Two years before, he went after the forestry group Diamond International, paid $752 million for it, dismembered it and, at least on paper, became a billionaire. One source says that he's made more than $500 million on their land assets alone. In June 1984 he took a stab at the Continental Group, a packaging, insurance and forestry operation in Connecticut. He lost that take-over battle too, but ended up $35 million richer for his troubles.

He got himself into a real fight when he tried to take over the Goodyear Tire Company. The townsfolk lobbied their Congressmen and a Sub-Committee subpoenaed Goldsmith to explain what he was going to do with the company. He told them, nakedly, 'Make money.' It wasn't what anyone wanted to hear – which is odd because that's what Goodyear should have been doing all along. Anyway, they burned him in effigy and symbolically ran him out of town. In reality they bought him off. He took his money and the result is that he's the only fellow on his block with a volcano; although it must be said that Goldsmith himself doesn't feel that any sort of 'swashbuckler of the decade' award belongs to him.

As he put it, 'Rupert is the only man I know who makes me feel like Liberace.'

Not all risk takers are swashbucklers.

And in the past five years, with the Thatcher Revolution in full swing, all sorts of opportunities have opened up for all sorts of different types of people.

Richard Thompson is 26.

His father is David Thompson of Hillsdown fame. David had inherited his dad's meat business and built it up into a huge, international food industry. In the mid-80s David sold, took his money and with his son set up Thompson Investments. These days David spends his time taking care of his racing interests and a property development in Portugal. He's left the day-to-day running of the family business to his son.

'I finished school at 18 and couldn't wait to get into business. I worked for Hillsdown for three years, in all sorts of areas, and have been here now for five years. We're a private company dealing in property, commodities, and shares in public companies.'

They own Windsor Race Course – which is not a great money-maker – and the First Division football club, Queens Park Rangers – which does make money. And Richard is Chairman of both.

'Football needs a radical change over the next few years. We need to bring excitement back into the game. We need people in football who understand how the Americans and the Europeans bring excitement into sport. The problem with English football is that there are too many people trying to make the important decisions. Everybody's got their own interests to protect. All the owners have their own club to protect. It's difficult to find someone to take a decision while looking at the industry as a whole.'

Robert Lefever is a tall, thin, quiet-mannered family doctor who feels so strongly about what he's doing that he mortgaged everything he owns just so he could keep doing it.

Twenty years ago he'd established a thriving National Health practice in London. Ten years later, discontented with the system, he walked away from his public practice, went into hock and opened a private practice right next door.

Now, it's one thing trying to run a business that charges people for something they can get for nothing three feet away. It's another thing again to then open a subsidiary in which the public generally does not believe and from which the client will often try to escape.

In 1986, Lefever remortgaged his house and added his office to the bank's holdings so that he could set up a private alcohol and drug treatment centre. He receives no financial support from the State or local authorities and charitable donations amount to less than 2% of his running costs. As many private insurance policies specifically exclude alcoholism and drug addiction, he gets no support there either. Compounding the problem, the public and many doctors believe all the answers to addiction problems lie in will-power. Bankers can be even more sceptical. Crusaders, it turns out, are not on the top of their better-risk lists. But Lefever is unmoved in his beliefs and his personal indebtedness now tops £1.5 million.

He has of course broken the first rule of risk-taking, which is never play with your own money. But then, he's the only person in this book whose risk-taking is all about saving lives.

John Newman was a chartered accountant who spent seven years at Hanson Trust.

In 1987 he and Nick Shipp, a stockbroker, decided to go out on their own. They started with one small company, which they bought, acquired other small companies and eventually reversed them into a Sheffield-based engineering group called Tyzack Turner. Today, they call their holding company TT.

'We look for companies which have been well established in their market for a long time,' says Newman. 'We look for companies with a good solid product and with management that isn't performing as well as they should be, Yes, it is the

Hanson formula. It is a simple formula and it's good to keep it that simple.'

Like Hanson, TT is in fairly unsexy businesses. They are in packaging, industrial supplies and building supplies. And while Newman plans to see his company grow and prosper through sound acquisitions, he is convinced in the gospel according to Hanson and White.

'Yes, it's the down-side that's the important thing.'

Gregory Hutchings is another Hanson/White refugee.

He worked there from 1980–3 doing corporate development. He'd just gotten an MBA and, until Hanson, had always worked for himself. His three years were essentially involved with head-office buying and selling.

He bought a shell called Tomkins, and has used that as his holding company.

'There's no question but that Gordon and James are very downside-orientated. That's the reason why they're here 25 years later and the Slater Walkers aren't. Their main concern, while they built up the company especially during the late '60s, was to buy limited-downside companies. Down-side is the thing. And that's what Gordon taught all of us. Try and lower the risks, there are enough risks already built into making acquisitions, so try to lower them wherever you can.'

So he has stayed with low-technology, low-risk investments, and a few years ago bought the famous US gun maker Smith and Wesson.

'The gospel according to Hanson and White, as I see it, is more of the same but younger. There may be a few variations but essentially the philosophy is the same. Gordon is a brilliant trader. He buys and sells companies like no one else in the world. I don't think I have that ability so we don't count on that as part of our philosophy. We spend more time trying to develop companies because we're not as good as Gordon and James are at buying and selling. But then, no one is.'

*

What makes Christopher Miller, Philip Turner and David Roper unique is that their company Wassall has impressed Hanson and White enough to own 13% of it.

Miller had been Associate Director at Hanson, handling some of the day-to-day running of the group. Turner had been Acquisitions Manager, following Greg Hutchings into that office. Roper, a skiing friend of Miller's, had been in corporate finance at Dillon Read.

'To be honest, it's been bloody scary,' says Roper. 'But at the same time it's been a lot of fun. The three of us started with nothing more than the idea we could do it. We wanted to do something for ourselves and somewhere down the line, at the end of it, we wanted to be able to look back on it all and say, we did a good job, we did it properly, we built something up that is worthwhile and successful and never cut anybody's throat while doing it.'

The traditional way of starting a company is to buy a shell, run the share price up, then do a rights issue to bring the institutional investors in at the higher price. You then sell enough of your rights to get all your money back, or maybe even make a profit, and that puts you in the game for nothing. You start doing your deals with the institutional investors' money and if things go bad, they lose, you don't.

Says Miller, 'That's not the way we did it. We brought the institutions in at the same price as us. On Day One we all got in at the same price, which effectively means we were giving away some of our action to them. And some people thought we were crazy to do this. The reason we did it, and there can only be one reason, is because we took a long-term view. We decided, if we're going to be around for a long time and, as a public company, need institutional backing, maybe they'll remember that they came in at the same price as we did. The idea was to set the tone. Now, we've got a good bank of institutions behind us who, so far, think we've done it the right way.'

The company they bought was in the shoe business. They

then went out and bought a couple of office-furniture businesses and a luggage manufacturer and eventually sold off the shoe business. Then they got involved in their first hostile bid.

'We really liked the look of Metal Closures', Turner says, 'because it was the kind of business we wanted to be in. It's a basic production business with big market-shares in its core businesses. We also thought we could get it at an attractive price because it had been disappointing financially for a few years.'

They were lucky enough to pick up a 30% stake in the company right away, which gave them a base to launch a full-scale bid. Of course Metal Closures, which makes bottle tops, fought the bid, claiming that it was derisorily inadequate. But the fight didn't last long. Wassall's £50 million was enough to win the bid and immediately they went about merging this new business into theirs.

Miller continues, 'One of the lessons of Hanson has to be, only buy what you can manage, what you want to keep, what you think you can do something to. In other words, buy it to improve it. That's what we did. There's no doubt that we try to imitate that. We don't kid ourselves. We're not the world's greatest marketeers, nor have we great technological insights. What we think we've got is a hard-nosed, common-sense preparedness to make changes in a business that needs changing. Now, if that is a high-technology business or a people business we're going to make complete fools of ourselves because you have to know too many things to run those specific kinds of businesses. But bottle tops and batteries and bricks and office furniture and suitcases have a lot of things in common. They are simple, straightforward businesses that don't depend on a couple of whiz-kids who go home in their Porsches at night, or depend on some brand new machine that's going to be invented next week by the Japanese and cost £5 million. You avoid a whole lot of things, and must always avoid them, and look at what's left. You look for something you can improve on. Then it gets down to such considerations as what's available and how much is it going to cost.'

*

Nowhere in the Bible is it written, 'Thou shalt automatically become rich and famous and thy success is indeed part of God's divine plan for the universe.'

Making it is hard work.

Keeping it is even harder.

Michael Ashcroft fought his way to wealth by being brash, hyperactive, extremely ambitious, tough on the people around him, often temperamental and by constantly playing up to the *enfant terrible* image that has tagged him for so long that one would think he now does whatever he has to in order to perpetuate it.

Born in Chichester in 1946, he spent much of his early youth travelling abroad as his father was in the colonial service. He attended a grammar school in Norwich and when he couldn't get into university, he opted for an HND course, studying business. From there he got himself a trainee's appointment at Rothmans, where he spent two years bored silly. His next job was at a cleaning firm, as assistant to the financial director. At 26, he dropped out of that job, got himself a shelf company for a pound, somehow convinced a bank manager to lend him £15,000 and bought his way into another cleaning business.

That he may or may not know one end of a mop from another is irrelevant. He knew how to take a small, insignificant company and build it into a viable one and four years he later sold it to Reckitt and Coleman for £1.3 million.

He then took some of that money and bought a pair of clapped out companies – Hawley Leisure and Provincial Laundries. He also spent some of his windfall buying shares in quoted companies on the stock market. At one point in his career it was reported he had stakes in no less than 1000 companies. Repeating his resurrection act, he brought both of those companies back to life and used them as his base for a staggering number of deals in a very short period of time. He bought stakes in Miss World, bid for Black and Edgington, acquired Oxford Building Services, acquired Derwent Cleaning, bought a 40% share of Security Corp. and 72% of a Canadian shell company called Midespa and 12% of the fitted-bathroom manufacturer, I.D. & S. Rivlin. He also tendered for a 20% stake in Cope Allman, the fruit machine to engineering group. All of that in under four months.

He branched out to the United States to buy a security group. He also invested in a bedroom-furniture manufacturer and a coachbuilder that stretches Fords into armoured limos and hearses.

At one point he launched a dawn raid on the cleaning firm that had once employed him. He managed to thoroughly alienate the management there, lost the bid and reportedly walked away with £5 million profit for his trouble.

Teaming up with David Wickens of British Car Auctions, Ashcroft finally made a full-scale bid for Cope Allman. He managed to get 29.9% while Wickens came up with 14%. Amidst allegations of concert parties, Ashcroft managed to take over as Chairman.

Next he turned his attention to Henley's, a leading British Leyland distributor, using Midespa to launch his bid. He then bought from Wickens a 32.5% stake in Atwoods, the quarry and waste disposal group whose Deputy Chairman was Denis Thatcher.

The buying spree continued – 250 acquisitions in 15 years – coming to a head in 1986–7 with three major purchases. The first was Pritchards, the cleaning group that had first hired him and later beaten off one of his first take-over bids. The second was Wilkins British Car Auctions. The third, and most important, was the US-based security company, ADT.

He reversed the empire into ADT, using that as his main company, and began disposing of activities that he considered peripheral to his main businesses which he defined as security and auction services.

Recently he's taken positions in Christies auction house, which makes sense if he's got a take-over in mind. And the British Airports Authority – which doesn't make a lot of sense if he wants to own it one day because it's protected from a take-over by a government 'golden share' and rules which cap any single investor at 15%. He claims he'll challenge the 'golden shares'.

And everytime he comes up with a plan like that, he confounds the City.

But then he must enjoy doing that.

He has had his share of controversy. There was an investigation into some of his dealings at the time of the Blue Arrow affair. And as ADT is registered in Bermuda a lot of what he does can't necessarily be seen. Bermuda is a good base for attracting investors from the United States. Of course, so is New York. For that matter, so is London. Although there are certain tax advantages to Bermuda. There is also the advantage that any contributions to the Conservative Party – he is a firm supporter of Mrs Thatcher – don't have to be revealed.

If he doesn't care for the speculation about him that often appears in the press, it might get back to the fact that he doesn't do a hell of a lot to clear up any mysteries.

And then there are the slightly odd contradictions.

As Judi Bevan reported in the *Sunday Telegraph*, he drives a grey turbo Bentley with the number plate A2. When she told him she was going to use that in a story, he asked her not to. She wondered why. He said if she mentioned it he wouldn't any longer be able to drive around surreptitiously. And she had to point out to him that, for starters, anyone truly wanting to be surreptitious didn't drive a car like that.

Someone equally 'misunderstood', or at least so he'd have you believe, is George Walker, the East End boxer who runs the brewing to betting shop group, Brent Walker.

He is tough, no-nonsense character whose left hook has been replaced by teams of solicitors with libel writs when anyone takes his past out of context or suggests that there is anything nefarious in his present.

Growing up in Stepney, East London, his father was a drayman. He was a tough kid who left school at 14 to work as a porter at the Billingsgate fish markets. But he had a good pair of hands and found out he could box in the RAF. Demobbed at

21 – he was by then the RAF's light-heavyweight champ – he rose through the amateur ranks, winning the British title before turning pro. But Walker was a fighter with a difference. He had some good, inborn financial sense, and the first money he made in the ring was invested in a transport business he set up in Billingsgate. He fought 54 times, went as high in the world rankings as number eight, and was forced to quit the ring in 1953 after a terrible defeat for the British title that temporarily cost him his vision in one eye.

That's when he got into trouble. He wound up serving two years for theft. But he was young, it was a mistake that he has recognized for years to have been a mistake and he has paid for it.

By the time he got out and had begun to put his life back together again, his brother Billy had started to box and George became his manager. Besides taking care of his training, George did Billy the greatest favour anyone could ever do for a boxer – he made sure the winnings were well invested. Billy was better than George, fought 35 times as a heavyweight and reportedly earned as much as £250,000. That became their stake for G. & W. Walker. The company's first venture was a chain of baked potato restaurants.

They went from there to garages, ice-rinks, discos, taxi cabs, restaurants, boxing clubs, a chain of cinemas and a nightclub. By 1974 he was savvy enough in the world of business to know where the big money was. He merged with Hackney and Hendon Greyhound Stadium, called the new entity Brent Walker and in 1979 went public.

Billy took his share and retired to Jersey.

George went into property – creating the Brent Cross shopping centre on the old greyhound stadium grounds in North London, built hotels in Egypt and a leisure complex in Westcliff. He also got into films, backing Joans Collins's best known epics, *The Bitch* and *The Stud*. He was, at times, a bit reckless. Within three years of his stock-market listing, the company was in trouble. He borrowed the money he needed to buy back the shares and take the company private again. That gave him the breathing space he needed to regroup. Three years later he was back at the stock exchange, raising £11 million in a flotation that allowed him to develop the Brighton Marina. Next, he bought 385 pubs around London from Grand Metropolitan. He took over the troubled Goldcrest Films, bought Elstree Studios, branched out into whiskey, hotels and casinos, bought the William Hill and Mecca betting shops, and developed the Trocadero Centre in Soho.

And all of this happened because he lost the fight for the British title. Had he won it – and he's been known to say that's his only regret in life – he might still be working at the fish market.

Had Tony Ryan not stumbled onto a great gimmick, he might still be helping passengers board Aer Lingus flights.

Ryan – who likes to be called Dr Ryan, with an accent on the honorary PhD. – founded GPA, Guinness Peat Aviation, and runs the most important aircraft-leasing company in the world. When they go public in late 1991, which it seems they will, GPA will become Ireland's biggest company, capitalized at around I£4 billion. And Ryan will become Ireland's wealthiest man.

His is an unparalleled success story.

Here's a man with a minor education and even less charm, who had enough good luck to be in the right place at the right time and enough common sense to figure out how to turn that into a colossal fortune.

Born in Tipperary 53 years ago – and affectionately referred to as the 'Tipperary Farmer' – he is one strange dude.

To begin with, he had a lot of trouble understanding the main two-word title of this book.

'I am not sure I am the right man to carry the title of "Risk Taker", he complained. 'A successful business must, of course, constantly manage risk and GPA is no exception. But ours is a very orderly and conservatively managed enterprise and we have a significant group of international shareholders who rely on me to ensure that its specific risks are assessed and managed in a prudent fashion.'

I assured him that was exactly the point of this book. I confessed that the book probably should have been called 'Risk Minimizers' except that's a horrible title, and tried to allay his fears by explaining that it was a serious look at extremely interesting, but serious, businessmen.

He still couldn't understand, and now suggested that he'd be happy to tell me what I wanted to know about him if I changed the title.

'My reservation continues to be the name of the book,' he said 'as it has unfortunate implications.'

Maybe in Tipperary farm-speak it does, who knows?

He went on, 'I believe I could take a more positive attitude if the book had a different title, for instance, "The Risk Managers".

Yawn!

'My favourite quotation', he continued, 'is from Walter-Wriston who when admonished that businessmen adopt risk strategy – stated, "there cannot be accomplishment without risk. Businessmen are paid to take risks, if they don't, they should be kicked out of office." Since the art of business is essentially the management of risk, perhaps you could reconsider the title and I would therefore be more comfortable . . .'

Again I explained, gently out of deference, that the title had to stay, especially because it was the same title from five years ago.

I don't think he ever got the point.

I know he wasn't comfortable.

The son of a train driver, Ryan went to work for Aer Lingus back in the 50s, starting at Shannon Airport as part of the ground crew. Some of the people who worked with him in those days remember that he was very shy – he hasn't changed all that much – but was a hard worker. He spent time as a dispatcher, then Aer Lingus sent him to Chicago for a while, where he went to some night school and got a degree in business administration. Back in Ireland in the early 70s, he worked in the Aer Lingus leasing office. Because the carrier was heavily dependent on seasonal travel, someone in management realized they didn't need all their planes all year long. They found out that they could lease them to other airlines for part of the year, bringing them back to Ireland for the heavy-traffic summer months.

After leasing a jumbo jet to a Thai company which operated from Bangkok to Honolulu by way of Hong Kong and Seattle and Tokyo, Ryan started to see a host of benefits from leasing in terms of growth for aviation, particularly in South-East Asia. He reasoned, the world was full of countries that didn't have the necessary capital to buy airplanes. Many of those same countries welcomed the chance to get into international air travel because it brought them much-needed foreign currency revenue.

Out of that arose GPA.

In 1975 he put a proposal to Aer Lingus and they backed him. The merchant bank, Guinness Peat matched Aer Lingus's share and Ryan managed to squeeze out 10% for himself.

With one client already built into the system – Aer Lingus – he went in search of others.

An Aer Lingus associate recalls, 'Just after the American pull-out in Vietnam, Tony did a deal with the Vietnamese for a Pan Am 707. That's the kind of opportunist he is. He isn't the sort of guy who likes an open-door situation. He loves a challenge. He never seemed interested if it was too easy.'

While aircraft production has increased gradually over the past decade, demand for aircraft has increased rapidly. Not only are more people travelling but more countries are trying to get into the airline business.

Ryan and GPA have amassed the largest single fleet of airplanes in the world, nearly 200. He either owns a plane and leases it, or buys a plane, sells it, leases it back and then leases it out again. Normally, all leases are on a one-month, renewable basis, paid one month in advance. A few years ago when Air Florida's finances were shaky, leases were on a day-to-day basis. Someone from GPA stood around waiting for a certified cheque every morning before allowing the airline to use the plane.

The company is a mirror reflection of Ryan, which is to say, aggressive. A few years ago, believing that there were enormous profits to be made by taking a future share of all planes coming off the assembly lines, Ryan bet the ranch. He bought planes not yet built for leases not yet arranged.

Although Ryan himself plays up the team's contribution, he is surrounded by some fairly unpleasant people, none of whom hide either their admiration for or their fear of Ryan. He is said to pay them very high wages in exchange for their commercial souls. He has been known to fly off the handle and berate staff members who aren't living up to his expectations.

His offices, at GPA House in the tax-free zone at Shannon airport, contain a small collection of paintings and a huge collection of model aircraft, all decorated in the colours of his leasing clients. Upstairs there's a briefing room worthy of a spy film, with three computer-controlled projection screens, dark-blue walls, and microphones at each desk position. Ryan's private office is downstairs, on the ground floor, there on purpose, so they say, to enable him to see who's coming and going.

He lives on a 300-acre estate called Kilboy about 45 minutes drive from the office, although he can helicopter back and forth. The main house, a restored seventeenth-century country mansion, is magnificent. There is a huge entrance-way stocked with an eclectric bunch of antiques. There's even a piano shoved off to one side. His living-room is done with extreme good taste . . . money shows . . . as is his library, where dinner can be served for four. Further along there's a covered swimming-pool and downstairs there's another of those spy-film command posts where he can keep track of every plane he owns.

For the most part he lives alone. His marriage broke up some time ago – his wife lives in Dublin – and his three sons are grown-up. His friendship with Miranda Guinness, Lady Iveagh, is not a topic for discussion. He is fast to say that he lives in a small country and doesn't want everyone to know when he goes to church, or when he doesn't.

Even at home he is not totally relaxed.

Maybe it's the company.

He does not warm easily, is laconic, forces a laugh out of politeness and shows great discomfort with anything more than minimal polite small-talk.

You get the feeling there's a great sense of insecurity that surrounds him. Which may be why he surrounds himself with the board members that he hand-picks. Among the men he's invited on to the GPA board are former Chancellor of the Exchequer Nigel Lawson, former Irish Premier Garret Fitzgerald, and former Chairman of ICI, Sir John Harvey-Jones.

'He has a vision,' Harvey-Jones explains. 'His mind is open and he's alway thinking constructively. The extraordinary thing is that when you talk to him you discover he actually doesn't have a very disciplined mind. By which I mean that his mind jumps. I'm a sort of rather plodding sort of guy in my own mental processes. Tony doesn't do that. He jumps from A to M and then back to F and as far as he's concerned you fill in the bloody bits afterwards.'

To be perfectly fair, Harvey-Jones, who is Deputy Chairman of GPA, claims the Tony Ryan he knows is a lot more attractive a man than the one I met.

'He's been described as being uncharismatic by a number of writers but I don't see him that way. He can charm the birds off the bloody trees if he wants to. He's got a very nice sense of humour and one of the reasons we get along so well is because both of us have an irreverent sense of humour and spend a hell of a lot of time laughing.'

Harvey-Jones also credits Ryan with great skills, for having built GPA out of nothing.

'Tony always sees an opportunity. In fairness, none of us are infallible and some of his ventures outside the aircraft business have not been successful. He's tried to diversify into one or two other things. But he really does understand the aircraft business absolutely backwards. He knows everybody. He's indefatigable.

He really does work his butt off. He's alway in the bloody aeroplane. He has an immense range of acquaintances. He's got a very good information network and a very good sense of feel for what's happening in that business.'

It's odd that he should be so successful in GPA and not be able to match his great successes elsewhere. According to the *Irish Times*, he lost I£600,000 in a failed attempt to back the *Sunday Tribune* newspaper. He also lost money in a pub he owned called Matt the Thrasher. Two of his sons run Ryan Air and that's not been doing very well either. Although he immediately says that he has nothing to do with the airline, no one doubts that he set it up and has funded a large part of it.

Money is not a problem.

Based on dividends from his 8% holding of GPA and his salary as Chairman and Chief Executive, one fair estimate puts his annual income at around I£10 million; although in April 1990, GPA voted him a cash and shares bonus of I£60 million.

And don't forget there are special tax concessions allotted to GPA because of their duty-free location.

But then the company is making a lot of money by maintaining its huge share of the market. Ryan really only has two competitors, one in California and one in Australia and neither of them come even close to doing the size of business he does. On top of that, he's now in the middle of a raging bull market.

John Harvey-Jones again. 'It's quite difficult for him to fall off the end through the 90s. I suppose his outstanding example of risk-taking was at the time when the airframe makers were in a very bad way, he was prepared to take the risk of forward ordering and establishing positions with all the main makers which in fact airlines were not prepared to do. Now, the result of that is that he actually commands something like 10% of the aircraft coming off the lines. And of course the demand for aircraft has gone on and on and on and looks as though it will go on. So he has the products which he's bought very well in a market which, as far as one can see will go on increasing.'

The only fly in the ointment, it seems, is the public offering.

It's not Ryan's idea of a good time. It's the banks' and some of his shareholders'. These days GPA is roughly one-third Japanese-owned, one-third European-owned and one-third North American-owned. The list of Japanese shareholders includes Mitsubishi Bank and Mitsubishi Corporation, which together own 14%, followed by Long Term Credit Bank of Japan, Japan Leasing, Kawasaki Enterprises and Mitsui. In North America, Air Canada has an interest. In Europe, both Hanson PLC and Jacob Rothschild hold stakes.

But the investors want to track the shares. Three years ago they were somewhere around $240. By late spring 1990 they were $650.

'You will doubtless recall,' says Harvey-Jones, 'in the middle of all that there was the stock-market crash. Now you try and think of any other share that has gone straight through the stock-market crash without any sort of backward glance. It's difficult to find one. It's a very considerable achievement. And it's been achieved because we have not been subjected to the vagaries of the market. For anybody who wants to sell out of the company, we've always had a long list of people who want to buy in. We've been able to establish liquidity that way. The problem is that the shareholding is now getting diffused and, particularly when you get institutions into the thing, those institutions want to be able to play. They want to be able to run with the market when it goes up and down. That's the way that professional investors allegedly earn their keep. So that's where the pressures for going public are coming from. But there's little doubt that operating as a private company is very much in the interests of the shareholders and the employees, who are in fact shareholders.'

16

Call it the curse of the second generation.

You know, all those spoiled rich kids who've drunk too long on their fathers' wines and think they know what they're doing.

Not as motivated as the founding first – and there's really no reason why they should be – they make their way into their birthright business and either screw it up because they don't know what they're doing or spend their lives trying to come out from under dad's shadow.

Not so Gerald Ratner.

'All too often, when a son comes into a business, he's elevated too quickly. Or he comes in very late because he's had a good education and gets pushed up the ranks. Well, I don't have a good education and I didn't get pushed up the ranks. I worked in the shops, and in the factory, and on the buying side, and on the office side. A lot of people who come into their father's business won't make the tea or run down the block to fetch something. But all of that is crucial if you're going to be at the top. You must understand what makes the business tick. And you learn that by starting at the bottom.'

Leaving school at 16, he spent the next 18 years working his way up the ladder, slowly, rung by rung. He learned the business inside out, until he knew everything there was to know.

He learned how to sell jewellery.

And today, he is the world's largest jeweller.

'I don't know a lot about other businesses. But I know that this business is all about getting the basic approach right.

Because I started at the very bottom, I don't walk around today with my head in the clouds. This business is not about sophisticated marketing formulas. Calling in high-powered advisers is not the answer. To get the figures in at the end of the week you have to spend the week working very hard. You've got to sell at the right prices, keep the windows clean, keep the stock clean, keep the displays tidy, motivate your staff. There are no magic formulas. You have to work at all the nitty-gritty little things.'

Leslie Ratner opened his first jewellery shop in Richmond, Surrey in 1949.

It was one of those traditional jeweller's, a store front with bars on the windows and glass-topped counters filled with gold chains, bracelets, watches and rings.

But he had bigger ambitions and over the next 30 years he built his business into a nationwide chain of more than 100 shops.

Now, instead of traditional, the key word was bargain.

'When my father started out, the only jewellery chains were H. Samuel and James Walker. But their jewellery was expensive and their profit margins were high. What my father did was to keep his overheads to an absolute minimum which in turn helped keep prices down. It's true that Ratner's didn't have the quality image of the other two, but everyone knew that Ratner's was as good a place to find a bargain.'

Then came the '80s and Ratner Sr. made a crucial mistake.

'I don't know why it always happens that whenever someone has been successful down-market they get it into their head that they should go up-market. You see it all the time, as if that's the next logical step. And that's exactly what my father did. He went up-market. He called in the designers. Suddenly Ratner's was no longer thought of as a place to get a bargain. And it was a disaster.'

By 1984 the company, some 120 stores capitalized at £10 million, was suffering heavy losses.

Believing the business had lost direction, Gerald now got it into his head the time was right to take over. However his father had different ideas about that and what ensued was a family feud, although Ratner *fils* prefers to label it 'a little bit of a power struggle'. Gerald won and was named sole Managing Director. Two years later he succeeded his father as Chairman. Needless to say, it was a stressful time for the Ratner family.

'My father wasn't anxious to step down but I felt if I didn't take over soon, it was going to be too late. It might have been different if the business had been doing fantastically well, but it wasn't. Of course I know how difficult it was for him. But now, when he looks back on it, he says he made the right decision. And we're on fantastic terms.'

The first thing that Gerald did once he took control was to turn back the clock. He moved the company down-market again. He returned to the business of bargains. Then he revamped the inventory system so that computers in the warehouse could process point of sale information overnight and resupply the shops the next morning. He also created various incentive schemes which translated directly into enormous bonuses for the staff. He wanted them to be more aggressive, more determined. He put a more competitive edge to his selling approach.

Immediately two things happened.

Profits came back. And the rest of the nation's jewellers resented Gerald for declaring war.

'Of course they hated me. I forced them to compete. Until I came along jewellers never priced their goods so when you went into a shop and chose something you liked, the price was whatever they thought they could get for it. They'd make up a price. It's still like that at the top end of the market. It's a bit of a rip-off and you have to be very careful. What I did was clearly ticket everything and describe each item in great detail. It forced many of them to do the same. But where we were concerned, it was a very important step. If you're going to do volume business, you can't rely on your staff. In mass-market shops you just have to accept the fact that the sales staff doesn't know what they're selling. One reason is that it's very difficult to train thousands of people. Another reason is, at least in a lot of shops, the sales staff isn't properly motivated so they just don't care. I geared the system to make everything as simple as possible. I want the customer to understand exactly what he or she is buying so that the moment they walk into the shop, at least to a certain degree, the item is pre-sold. And I want the staff to know that they'll be rewarded for working that much harder.'

Simply put, Ratner's trading approach is nothing more than a modern variation on the original formula for retailing success . . . pile it high and sell it cheap.

And Gerald Ratner makes no apologies for being so basic.

'It's something we unashamedly do. It's a decided advantage to be in the lower end of the market, espcially when everybody else has gone the designer route. As it happens, we're in all areas of the market. But in Britain the lower end is where the money is. What I can't understand is why the press continually regard somebody who's selling something very competitive and low-priced as less desirable than somebody who's selling something expensive. Especially the financial press. They seem to think down-market is a bad word. I was reading a comment in the papers that Terence Conran had failed to get rid of the down-market image of British Home Stores. But in fact, he did get rid of it and that's been part of his downfall. BHS has always been down-market and if it had remained the basic warehouse where you knew you could get the cheapest, most basic product, it would still be doing huge business. Trying to turn BHS into something it isn't was a mistake.'

A mistake, he feels, that lots of companies have made in the past few years.

'Marks and Spencer is a good example of what can happen. They had a bad patch for about six months when they went too far up-market and did nothing more than alienate their customers. They tried to sell cashmere sweaters and things like that, but quickly realized it was a mistake and reverted back. I guess they read in the newspapers about the success of Next and guys like Ralph Halpern and felt that because the press love all this talk about changing life-styles, about more sophistication and about bringing expensive products to the High Street, this was the way to go. But it was a load of nonsense.'

At the same time that he was taking Ratner's down-market, he was also buying other business, aggressively going into the market to win control of other jewellery chains which would allow him to segment his empire into five very clear-cut areas. These days he's got Salisbury's, which is his costume jewellery outlet, then Ratner's at the cheapest end of the real jewellery market, H. Samuel's in the middle, and Zales stretching from the middle towards the top. He also owns Watches of Switzerland which covers the very pricey top.

'We're just jewellers. That's our only business. Today we represent 30% of the UK jewellery market and show profits of £130 million. That's not bad considering that five years ago we only had 2% of the market and were losing money. Our intention now is to get to 50% of the UK market. And I believe that there's nobody who can stop us from doing that. Not even the Office of Fair Trading. I think if they were going to say anything, they'd have done it when we acquired Zales a few years ago, which took us to 25%. The thing is we only have 1000 or so shops out of the 7000 jewellery shops in this country. The others are mainly mom and pop businesses, with secondary positions, very little stock, no systems and very expensive product. They can't hang around for ever and we're taking their business very quickly.'

To hit that 50% target in the next few years, he's not only outlined each segment of the market, he's deliberately customized the weighting in each segment. There are about 250 Ratner's shops, where the average ticket price is £15; 500 H. Samuels with an average price of £25; and 250 Zales, where the average price is £50.

'Those are our multiple businesses. Unless we diversify, we don't want any more stores in the UK. We can reach 50% of the market with what we already have so we don't want to dilute the market buying more stores.'

Then there's Watches of Switzerland, about 20 shops, with an average ticket price of £1000.

'You couldn't have 100 stores like that because there aren't enough towns in Great Britain where people spend that kind of money. We bought Watches of Switzerland specifically for areas like Bond Street and Knightsbridge. After all, when you go from the High Street to Bond Street there's a big jump in people's incomes. Watches of Switzerland is also mainly a tourist market. Quite frankly, even I sometimes think the prices are totally ridiculous. We recently sold a watch there for £375,000. That's complete madness.'

Needless to say, not everything Ratner sells is 'on sale'.

But most of it is.

Until he came along, 'Sale' in Britain meant January and July. He broke the mould by using the American method where everything always seems to be on sale. At Ratners and H. Samuels and even at Zales, every day is sale day.

'It works. We more or less have a sale going 12 months of the year because people are always looking for bargains. Especially in jewellery. I'm proud of the fact that we have a very good marketing strategy. Having said that, our prices are very low. Perhaps we sometimes give the impression that they're lower than they actually are. But that's all right too because that's the name of the game. There's a technique to sales. The wrong technique is to simply cut all your margins. That's the surest way to go bust. There's no point in cutting 25% off everything because your profits will go down by 75%. What you have to do in a sale is to reduce the stock that people will appreciate having reduced.'

Having changed retailing in the UK, at least jewellery-retailing, he isn't shy about what he sees remaining from the 'bad old days' when he himself goes shopping.

'You walk into a store in the States and everyone is pleasant, very helpful. Sometimes I think they're maybe even too helpful. That 'Have a good day' stuff gets on my nerves. But that's because I'm British and while the Americans are generally happy, we British are generally miserable. Okay, Americans may be a bit too friendly, but we British are unbelievably unpleasant. Just look at the way you get treated in shops in this country. If you can find someone to serve you, you're lucky. Most of the time you can't. When you do, it's usually someone totally apathetic who, instead of selling you something, would just as soon get you out of the shop so they don't have to do any work. Or, if you do buy something, you have to wait an hour while they fiddle with the credit-card machine because they're not properly trained. It all takes too long. It's too much of a hassle. You won't find that at Ratner's but I do find it at a lot of other shops I go into. There's nothing fun about shopping in Britain.'

Gerald Ratner's corporate headquarters in London's Mayfair used to be the home of a banana magnate.

A listed building with large period chimneys and high-ceilinged rooms where Mr Banana covered the walls in dark mahogany panelling, the building boasts a central staircase to rival the one at the Connaught.

Fittingly, the offices are decorated with antique furniture, Oriental rugs and minor-master paintings. There's also a good collection of antique silver scattered around various rooms. The only modern things you find in the building are the phones, the plumbing and the basement gym.

'Whenever I have problems to worry about, I go downstairs and run on the machine. It's fantastic. My problems just go away. Otherwise I walk a lot, swim and play a little tennis. I love being at my house in the country where I've got one of those 1930s boats on the Thames. I used to enjoy playing poker, but I stopped that when winning or losing a few hundred quid didn't mean anything. Then too, Michael Green and I used to play serious snooker. We played for a long, long time. But we dropped it because we weren't getting any better at it. In fact we quit because we were actually getting worse.'

His gymnasium notwithstanding, the place looks about as far as you can get from the High Street stores that have paid for all this.

'A lot of people who come here are very surprised because

my image is so down-market. But this is my personal taste level. My shops are totally commercial. They're where they are and look how they look simply to make money. You know, with many other retailers, you find they do up their shops the way they like them or the way their friends would like them. They want people to believe that the shop reflects their own taste. Conran's, for example, is a beautiful place. But I don't give a monkey's about that. Watches of Switzerland in Bond Street, which is beautiful, doesn't give me any more pleasure than an H. Samuel in Barnsley. In fact, the one in Barnsley gives me more pleasure because it makes more money. It's purely commercial.'

Another purely commercial aspect of his business is that he's sold off most of his freeholds because he believes that if you're going to be a successful retailer, you need all the money you can lay your hands on to get the right stock at the right prices and to motivate your staff. He feels it's a very rare luxury for any retail business to keep money tied up in property. Because he's expanded so fast, especially in America, he's taken the view that he can make more by selling jewellery than he can by also being in the property business.

But then jewellery is a fairly peculiar business in that most of it is based on Christmas. The month of December accounts for 30% of his sales and 70% of his profits.

'People in this country really only buy jewellery in a big way at Christmas time. Now, seasonal trading can be a problem for some sectors. Sometimes you hear the clothing people complain that there's not been a summer. But there's always Christmas. And even if things are bad, the way they were in 1989, people still come out at Christmas and spend. Our problem is dealing with all those customers in such a short space of time. Did you know that we make more money in December than any other company in the UK, including giants like ICI. We're talking about as much as £100 million in a 3-4 week period.'

Because he's never been able to figure out a way to open only for Christmas and devote the rest of the year to skiing or swimming . . . 'Wouldn't that be nice!' . . . he has to work at the business 12 months a year. Most of his time is spent in London. Some of it is spent in the States. But the rest of it is spent travelling around Britain, seeing the stores. He usually devotes a day or two every fortnight to being on the road. As Christmas approaches, he doubles that, making surprise visits to stores at least one day a week.

'They've got to be surprise visits because I won't learn anything if people know I'm coming. If they know I'm on my way, there won't be any problems by the time I get there. So nobody knows when I'll be there. I want to see if there's a broken counter. I want to know that because their computer is up the creek they're out of 50 good-selling bracelets. I'll even do things in the wrong order you know, drive 100 miles out of my way, just so that no one knows where I'll turn up next. But I've got to know what's going on. I've got to find out what's happening from the customer's point of view.'

He is, needless to say, a very hands-on chairman.

'Wait a minute. I'm very hands-on when it comes to marketing. I want to know how the shops look. I want to see what our promotions are like. I want to see our posters. I'm very hands-on when it comes to changing managers and opening new shops. But those are the parts of the business I know best. I'm less hands-on when it comes to something like buying because I don't have any great ability there.'

By his own admission, he is also fairly hands-off when it comes to the American side of his business.

'I've been in the jewellery trade in the UK for over 20 years, and I'm confident when I make a decision that I've got a better chance of getting it right than most other guys in this business in this country. I still sometimes get it wrong, because that's how difficult a business it is. But in America I've got no chance at all. It's a totally different world. All those British retailers who were arrogant enough to think they could transplant a British formula to America, even a very successful one like Marks & Spencer, have run into trouble.'

What Ratner knew he had to do if he was going to crack the

US market, was buy the best-performing jewellery business he could find there. Sterling Jewellers, based in Ohio, wasn't the country's largest chain but he liked their numbers and especially liked the people running the business. He coughed up $210 million for that business, a staggering ratio of 25 times profit. However, he points out, one of the major assets he acquired was a man named Nathan Light, Sterling's chairman. Some 15 years Ratner's senior, Light is now on Ratner's main board. And very much like Ratner, he too had spent his entire life in the jewellery business.

'We paid an unreal price for Sterling but that included 110 shops and their management. Today we've built that up to 500 shops. Yes, we've influenced them. We've told them about our electronic point-of-sales systems and we do a lot of joint buying together. But we're not running the business there. Nat Light does that. Sterling shops look like American shops, not anything like a British shop transplanted into the States. The people running that business are American jewellers, not British jewellers.'

But then Nat Light and Gerald Ratner share a common passion – that is, selling vast quantities of jewellery.

'My ambition is to repeat our UK success in America and I believe we can do that. To a certain degree we're quite lucky. The jewellery business is not as cut-throat as, say, the electronics business. It's a sleepy area, or at least it has been for many years. The competition is weak, they don't have inventory systems, they don't have the benefit of going to Bombay to buy parcels of diamonds at rock-bottom prices, they're just not as aggressive as we are. Something like 70% of the jewellery shops in the United States are independents, you know, mom and pop shops. And it's a fact of life that the multiple retailer will always have a huge advantage over the independents. If you look at any other field of retailing, you'll see how the multiples have taken market share. This never happened in the jewellery business before we came along. It was a totally new concept for the UK jewellery business. And we believe we can make it happen in the US too. After all, how can they possibly compete with us? The independents have huge overheads while we're distributing to 500 shops from one depot. We're already taking more money and making more profit than any other jewellery retailer in America. I'm certain we'll eventually have 1500–2000 stores there. That's what we want.'

Some people in the City of London think Gerald Ratner is a very brash young man.

Well, yes, he concedes, he may be very brash in the way he markets his products, screaming 'Bargains' from every shop window. But then, he argues, there's nothing wrong with being very competitive. On the other hand, he insists, a lot of people get their lines crossed when they confuse him with his business approach because he doesn't think he is personally brash.

Judge for yourself.

Start with Ratner on the telephone.

When someone rings him, he picks up the phone. You don't have to go through a series of secretaries and assistants. So when he rings someone, he expects the same treatment. And he can be very short-tempered if he doesn't get it.

'When I need to speak to someone, I make certain I have their direct line. I've built up a library of direct lines, which I find very valuable. I don't care who it is, from the Chairman of Barclays Bank or Morgan Stanley to any of our suppliers. I don't want to go through a switchboard or be passed along from secretary to assistant. In some cases I may not even say hello. I've actually been known to say nothing more than, are you going to lend me £50 million or not? Either they say yes or no. I just can't stand all the usual beating around the bush and time-wasting.'

Then there's Gerald Ratner when he deals with the press. He's accessible, answers questions directly and does not couch his feelings in clubby euphemisms.

'That's the way I do business. Not everyone takes it well. And yes, it sometimes gets me into trouble. I have at times been quoted in a lot of ways that, perhaps, I shouldn't have been quoted. I'm very frank about my opinions and not necessarily afraid to let someone know what I think. It isn't always done that way in this country. Being up-front is not always something that's appreciated here.'

Because his style has at times rubbed people the wrong way, his company has not always been particularly well accepted in the City. There are those who say it's too much of a one-man band.

Ratner says they're wrong.

'Our share prices have increased from 25p to £2.50 in five years, that's tenfold, so the City can't disregard me. I deliver. But our rating is very low. They don't like a company that issues paper on a regular basis, that's acquisitive the way we are. Sure, a lot of people have come up very quickly and disappeared even quicker and some people in the City worry that will happen to me. The difference is that our shops are suddenly not going to be run badly, we're only in one business, we're very careful to always get things right and we're much better than our competition.'

The problems he occasionally has with the City, he claims, compound themselves by the fact that he doesn't take himself as seriously as some folks in the City take themselves.

'I've never bothered trying to cultivate an image with the City, although I guess some day I might have to start. Maybe I've even gone too far in the past to upset people because I just can't stand the boors you find there. They drive me around the bend with their stuffy, non-committal approach. They don't ever do anything because they're too terrified. They're always saying, 'No comment.' Then I come along and make some outrageous statement to the press and maybe even throw in a joke. It doesn't amuse them. But I believe that if you're in the business of making money, you've got to be a bit street-wise and mix with people. You can't sit up on a pedestal and do nothing all day. That was Britain 50 years ago. Maybe even 20 years ago. But it's not like that in America and it's not going to be like that here in the '90s. Yes, of course money is deadly serious. Some fund managers are dealing every day with hundreds of millions of pounds. But they take themselves too seriously and I don't and that unnerves them a bit. Too bad.'

Everybody makes mistakes but few people are as haunted by theirs as Gerald Ratner is over 'the one that got away'.

'I believe in the paralysis of analysis. If you go too far down the road with research you find you've wound up nowhere. So I follow my gut feelings. I try not to ask too many people for advice or to over-analyse things because I can look at something and, in many cases, instinctively know what needs to be done. I get gut feelings about things and they've never yet let me down.'

At the beginning of 1989, when he heard that the American jewellery chain Gordons was for sale, he knew right away that it was a perfect fit with his US business. His gut feeling told him to go for it.

His mistake was letting himself get talked out of it.

Gordons was the H. Samuel of America. Even though they'd been losing money, they were still the second-largest jewellery chain in the States. Most of their 500-plus properties were either owned outright or on low-rent leases. Best of all, the company had no debt. He'd already purchased Sterling and a pair of smaller chains, giving him something like 350 shops in the US. Gordons would have more than doubled his size overnight. He estimated that by carefully melding Gordons into his US operation, he could make nearly $100 million out of the purchase the very first year.

At $300 million, Ratner saw it as an incredible buy, a once-in-a-lifetime opportunity.

The City wasn't so sure and the moment the 'For Sale' sign went up at Gordons, Ratners shares dropped 10p. Undaunted Gerald flew to the States and, without first securing the full backing of his board, offered $39 a share. Gordons told him that someone had offered $38 a share but that $39 was better and they could do a deal. When word of the offer hit the City, his own shares took a second plunge. Fund managers all over town found themselves feeling very queasy about Ratner's penchant for issuing paper to finance acquisitions. If he wanted to do it with real money, that was one thing. To gear at a ratio of more than 100% was not for them, this time.

When he returned to London to announce his *fait accompli*, two of his board members were not amused. In spite of the huge earnings potential of Gordons, those two saw their own net worth diminishing daily and voiced their objections. Ratner gave in.

But his gut feeling about the deal wouldn't go away.

Two days later he announced it was on again.

Unbeknownst to him, the $38 suitor was Zales US, from whom Ratner had bought Zales UK. They were putting pressure on Gordons to sell and warned that if they didn't make a deal right away, their $38 offer would drop $1 a day until they did.

Ratner came running back to Gordons to buy.

But by that time it was too late. Zales US had picked up Gordons for $36.75.

'I was sick. It was a beautiful deal and losing it really bugs me. It's the worst mistake I've ever made in business. It was an old established, very conservative company with very good sites. It was the perfect business for us to buy. You don't want to buy a business after someone like me has been in it because I've taken out all the goodies. This one still had them all. I wanted to buy it. And it was ours. We had the banks with us and the agreement worked out, it was all ready to go. We dithered about it too long and lost it. That's something I've never done before. That was the one time I was ever influenced to go against my gut feelings and if nothing else it's made my resolve even greater towards following my nose. Whenever I've wanted something, whenever I've spotted a target, I've done everything possible to get it. I've even overpaid in some cases, I don't care, just to make certain that I've got it.'

Some people might think that's a bit reckless. But he disagrees, saying that's the way deals have to be done.

'If you really know that this is the right business for you, and it's a fantastic deal, there's nothing reckless about it. When you produce the numbers that we do in the jewellery business, you've got to get the shops before someone else does. You've got to get them quick. If you over-pay it doesn't matter. The people who are too careful are going to lose out. When I want something, because I know it's the right thing, I want it at all costs. Listen, I know my own limitations. Where some other bloke will go in head first, my success has come from knowing my market back to front. Because we do so many deals, many people think we rush right in, that we're complete megalomaniacs, prepared to buy anything. But the reason we do so many deals is because we're so confident about the jewellery business.'

And that is basically where he intends to stay.

However, he doesn't rule out the possibility that he might one day diversify out of jewellery. At the beginning of 1990, he took an abortive stab at playing White Knight for Dixons, then under heavy pressure from a bid by the former Woolworth management under the Kingfisher banner.

In fact, Dixons might have been just the sort of business Ratner would like to be in.

'In time we probably will diversify out of jewellery, at least in this country. I don't know where but I'd like to pick up a business that is in the same sort of situation that jewellery was in before I came along five years ago. Some business that hasn't yet been brought into the twentieth century. Of course it's risky because the jewellery business is the business I know. Mind you, we wouldn't go into it like a bull in a china shop. We'd go about it very cautiously. We're always looking and in the past we've looked at a lot of areas. But frankly, there's nothing around that's as good as jewellery at the moment. Our profit margins are very very high. we've got no real competition and the jewellery market is growing faster than any other sector in the High Street.'

Diversification, he insists, is therefore neither a compulsion nor a necessity.

'We've got the States which has a huge potential in jewellery. So we're not in a tearing hurry to diversify. But again, if the right opportunity came along we'd be terribly interested. We're retailers. I believe that our marketing skills and our systems could work elsewhere. It will put 10p off my share price but I don't care.'

There are certain areas he rules out immediately, labelling them 'the three Fs'. That's fashion, furniture and food. That leaves the rest of the High Street, selling everything from electronics to shoes.

It also leaves department stores.

'That's a very sleepy industry and might be rekindled into an American-style operation. What I think would work over here is the K-Mart or Wallmart-type store, or the price clubs. I think that over the next ten years you'll see a lot more out-of-town shopping where people are less interested in the trimmings, like service, which you don't get anyway nowadays. People will simply want to buy something very cheaply even if they have to do it in some fairly unglamorous shop where the retailer is only working on a 5% profit. Look at Argos. They're brilliant. They're one of the country's most successful retailers. But that's a catalogue showroom. I'm talking about a different thing. In America you find people buying tyres in places like Sam's Club. You see them rolling tyres right out of the store, not minding about that because they've bought so cheaply. I can't see why that won't work here.'

The one place he doesn't see himself working is in Europe.

The coming of 1992 is, as far as he's concerned, irrelevant.

'It's certainly irrevelant in that if it's a good idea to go to Europe it's a good idea to go any year. The problem is that Europe is a lot of different places. I know the British business and Nat Light knows the American business. But nobody knows the European business. Each country is a different market. In Holland they use 14-carat gold. In Italy they use 18. In Germany it's eight. In France it's 22. On top of that, they all have different tastes. The Dutch, for example, like much heavier jewellery than the French, and then they take an hour to make up their minds before spending two guilder. Nor do the Dutch give Christmas presents, whereas the jewellery business is all to do with Christmas. For us to go into Europe

at times running presses, at other times selling. But this time Wray said no.

'I have no idea why. Maybe it was nothing more than a bit of rebellion.'

Rebellion might be a worthy cause, except if doesn't pay the rent. So he thought about what he wanted to do with his life . . . besides being capped for England . . . and decided merchant banking had a nice sound to it. He wrote letters to banks in the City and took his first job as a trainee at Singer and Friedlander because they offered him £35 a week, £10 pounds more than Charterhouse.

'The choice was obvious. As it happened, it wasn't a bad choice. It's a nice place with nice people and a weird name.'

Four years later, bored to tears with merchant banking, he quit. His salary had nearly doubled by then but he'd been playing the property market on the side and just happened to have made £100,000.

'Singer & Friedlander's greatest strength, and maybe even their greatest weakness, is that people never leave. The guys I worked with are still there. It gives the company tremendous stability but is not so good for guys who want to do unconvential things, which is what I wanted to do. Now, in many ways, you need to be very young to make lots of money because when you're very young you don't see the pitfalls, you just charge blindly ahead. It also helps a lot if you have a bull market. To be perfectly honest, I really didn't know what I was doing. I was just cashing in on the tail-end of a boom. I didn't have a clue at the time how precarious the whole thing was.'

Or how bad his timing could be.

The so-called Secondary Banking Crisis of 1973 soon turned into the total crash of Britain's property market. Wray, far too close to the end of the tail, went all the way back down to zero and only just got out of it. Everything he had went to pay off borrowings and to builders to get houses completed so he could at least try to sell them.

A huge whack to his confidence, 1974 was the year he discovered that he didn't have the Midas touch.

'I think it's sheer luck that anyone ever comes back from that. If you lose confidence, to an extent, you think you're useless. It was happening to all sorts of people at the time, but one's thoughts concentrate on oneself. I was extremely worried and embarrassed. I'm not exactly a loud-mouth but when I made that 100-grand I probably talked a little too much about being successful and then when you become thoroughly unsuccessful, no matter what other people think, embarrassment is the right word.'

Still, there were valuable lessons to be learned and he took those lessons to heart.

'It taught me just how vulnerable one is. The important thing is to do things, if you can, from a solid financial base. You need the good balance sheet. Otherwise, you're forced into making decisions when you don't want to, like selling when the prices are wrong.'

Finding himself unemployed and out of the property market, Wray meandered into the financial newsletter business, publishing a tip sheet called *Foresight*. He saw it as an interesting, untapped market and a great cash-flow business. After all, people paid for their subscriptions 12 months in advance. He'd always enjoyed looking at small companies and now he believed he could write about them in an interesting way. At one point, he thinks, he even had 200 subscribers.

In fact, he might still be in that business today had Lady Luck not played her hand.

His competition at the time was the *Fleet Street Letter*. The fellow who owned it yearned to live in France and through a mutual friend wondered if Wray wanted to buy it. For £6500, which Wray could just about afford, he got 800 subscribers, a £16,000 turnover and a balance sheet filled with red figures in the loss column. Originally it had been a foreign affairs newsletter with some investment tips but Wray quickly changed that because there's no money in foreign affairs. He spent what little money he earned visiting companies and writing about them, and at the end of the first year he had a whopping £98 in the bank.

He was also learning how the market worked.

Within a couple of years the *Fleet Street Letter* was making money and within four years Wray was savvy enough to know how to take the company public with an offering on the Unlisted Securities Market.

'I seem to remember we were one of the first companies to go public on the USM. I can't recall how many shares I sold but I received a cheque for a quarter of a million quid. To be perfectly honest, had someone offered me £150,000 for the whole thing a year earlier, I'd have taken it.'

With *Fleet Street Letter* faring better than he'd ever believed it could, Wray discovered that if he could sell one newsletter, he could sell two, three, four and five and that each one could feed off the others.

He learned about marketing and cross-marketing and how to sell financial services through the newsletter.

Profits were spectacular.

However, despite his successes, even as late as 1983, tip sheets never had a great image in the stock market and that's something he still finds odd.

'Generally speaking people look down their noses at tip sheets. Especially the brokers. And yet their entire lives are spent tipping shares. It always struck me as being very curious. But that's how it is. There was no point in me trying to change all the rules on my own. It wouldn't work.'

Enter Lady Luck yet again.

He met and got to know Michael Green who then owned a printing business. Well, printing didn't seem any more attractive to Wray at this point than it did a dozen years earlier. But within Green's company, there was another called Carlton, and inside that was a video business called Carlton Studios. Essentially they made pop promos for Adam and the Ants. Video struck Wray as being very exciting, so he and Green negotiated a merger of Carlton and Fleet Street Letter. Green wanted it to go 60–40 in his favour because Carlton was making more profit and had a better image. Wray got him all the way down to something resembling 59–41.

'I owned about 30% of the Fleet Street Letter Group, and the Fleet Street Letter Group owned 41% of Carlton's shares. So there I was in 1983 sitting on lots of paper, some debt and no money.'

He continued running his side of the business within Carlton until they sold the *Fleet Street Letter* for £12 million to a sort of mini-conglomerate named Barham. Wray became a director of Barham and stayed on the board until Barham was bought by IBC for £98 million, at a time when the Fleet Street Letter Group was accounting for about half of Barham's profits.

With even more paper in his pocket, some debt and not a lot of real money, Wray went looking for something else to do. In October 1986 he bought a property company called Gilbert House Investments, then capitalized at about £5 million.

'I bought 83% off the guy who owned 83%. He'd been making a 16p offer to his own shareholders to go private because he'd been fed up and didn't think he was getting anywhere. I said, I'll give you 18p. Obviously that made sense to him and his shareholders. I hadn't been into property for a long time but I'm comfortable with property because it's assets. I understand assets and gearing.'

Using Gilbert House as a shell, he purchased a company called Centrovincial, which had a portfolio of West End London properties plus some commercial and industrial properties in Worcester and Croydon. He paid just about £50 million for it and almost immediately saw the net asset value rise from 15p to nearer 50p. The earnings per shares went up as well. He degeared the company by selling a few things, then took a deal to his bankers – who just happened to have been his former employers – Singer and Friedlander.

'I knew the management there and also knew that they were unhappy lying inside the Britannia Arrow Group. So, because I believe that if you don't ask you don't get, I suggested that Gilbert House bid for Singer and Friedlander. I didn't even know at that stage how much money was involved. I thought it would be about £100 million, although I'd underestimated the strength of Singer's property assets and it turned out to be £145 million.'

Much to Wray's credit, that deal appears to be the only one struck in the City at the time of the 'Black Monday' stock-market crash that has succeeded.

'If you look at every single deal done in the run-up to October '87, Blue Arrow, Eagle Trust, Peek Holdings, you name them, Colorall, virtually the whole damn lot has come unstuck. The Gilbert House/Singer and Friedlander deal has not because profits have gone up and asset value is getting close to the 110p rights issue price. It's a good solid business. Our's didn't come unstuck because our's was a balance-sheet deal. The people were right, there was no question about that. They were good solid people. And the assets were there. It all made sense. None of those other deals had balance sheets.'

Suddenly Wray found himself right back where he started – at Singer Friedlander.

Except now he's Deputy Chairman.

He doesn't however, have any day-to-day responsibilities.

'I don't want to work at Singer's, I did that 20 years ago, and don't particularly believe they want me to work there either. They've got good-quality people. So my role there is really with the holding company, in terms of acquisitions. Actually, I haven't been to an office on a regular basis for some years.'

Well . . . not quite.

He has his own personal office, a house in Hampstead which he bought a few years ago. Yet, unless he explains that this is his office, one automatically assumes that this is home. 'I happen to like my office looking like a home.' Actually, he and his wife and their daughter live 15 minutes away in a Jacobean house with some oriental rugs and a few good paintings. 'Not megabuck paintings but I like them.'

Holding something in the neighbourhood of 3–4% of Singer's stock, Wray is their largest individual shareholder, although the institutions have bigger chunks. 'But I still don't have any cash.'

So to help keep himself in hot lunches, he then bought control of a company called Chartsearch, which was quoted on the USM. It's newsletters and a database, a business he says he understands. After that he bought a property company called Burford, which had a wonderful growth record and strong, entrepreneurial management. Next he took a stake in a nursing home group called Takare.

'That's a major growth business, although it's capital-intensive because you've got to put up nursing homes. I couldn't support it as an individual so I sold my shares to Singer's and they've built up their holding to about 22–3%, capitalized at about £60 million. It's property-backed because they're building nursing homes, and it's got the people. That's crucial. In business, you can't be totally clinical and unemotional. It's not only about balance sheets, it's also about people. At the end of the day, if you've got good people you want to cling on to them, if for no other reason than the fact that there aren't a lot of good people around.'

Frankly put, as a high-flying financier, Wray is something of an oddity.

He is a quiet, modest man who doesn't, in any way, shape or form, live up to the wheeler-dealer image.

There are no yachts or Lear jets. There is no fleet of chauffeur-driven Rollers. He may be worth £53 million, or slightly less than half that after taxes and gearing, but that's still more than enough for most people to live with considerable flamboyance. Yet hanging out with him, you'd never know he's got that kind of money. 'Tycoonery is an anathema to me,' he's fond of saying. And in this case that's not just reverse snobbery. He's neither impressed with the trappings of great wealth, nor does he appear to want them.

'I was brought up in a middle-class family and guess I have a very puritanical streak in me. I happen to have got where I happen to have got. And having got there, I'm incapable of going and sitting on a beach. I'm not intelligent or worldly enough to sit in libraries for the rest of my days. So a bit of me is stuck with being in business. I feel that if you're going to do anything you have to do it well, so obviously a part of me is ambitious to that extent. But I do so little entertaining, it's not true. If I go out a couple of times a year, that's a lot. I'm not out to impress anyone. I don't think I have an ego problem. I don't think you'll ever find my face on a mug being handed around to all the staff. I'm not desperately into any sort of advancement. I've never been to 10 Downing Street and can't possibly imagine that they'd even want me there. I do not want to be seen at the best dinner parties with Lord and Lady so and so. I can't overspend for things. The idea of paying £52 for a bottle of champagne in a nightclub is beyond me. I also dislike ostentation. To me, that sort of thing is a noisy, flamboyant gesture. It's something I don't like.'

The obvious question is, then, what drives him?

'Funny, but I often have this conversation with Michael Green. I think one is driven by a sense of insecurity, partly self-imposed, because obviously one borrows money to enable one to do more and the moment you borrow money you worry, how can I pay it back? I have an investing mentality. For me, the money you make with an investment is something you plough back into an investment.'

It's very much a part of the 'businessman as game player' syndrome.

'Yes, it's like a game of chess where you're pitting your wits against other people. I think of money as a yardstick which measures your ability to play that game. I mean, once you get to a certain level, which is probably a nice house, you can clothe yourself, put food on your table and maybe go on holiday, there aren't really that many people who really want to go to the Nice Hilton every weekend to give a party. From then onwards, people ask, why are you working. But in my case I'm not working because I'm greedy, I'm not working for money, I'm working because it's fun. I don't mean there's a sense of frivolity and that people don't count because people do count. But look, in cricketing terms, you don't say to a chap who's just made a hundred in a Test match, why are you still playing, why do you want to keep scoring, you've already made a hundred. You don't say to Jerry Rice or Joe Montana, you've already got one touchdown, why do you want to score another? By the same token, you don't say to a businessman, you've already got one million, why do you want more?'

Except perhaps in Britain. There are people who say just that. It's one of the distinct side-effects of Mrs Thatcher's free-market economy. She's inadvertently polarized strong feelings about the capitalistic instinct.

'It's odd the attitude towards business success in this country. If someone wins the football pools for a few million, that's okay. But if someone builds a business and then sells out for a few million, they've exploited people. There's still a strong element in this country that says success in business is not very acceptable. Yet it's all right for a pop singer or an athlete. Without any doubt, there's a tendency to regard companies as a piece of paper. And that's wrong. A company is much more than a bit of paper. It's people lives. If you want a good company, you've got to respect that because you want the people who make up the company to be pulling together as a team. But to write people off as exploiters is a bit silly. Quite clearly, they are creating something. They might not be terrifically altruistic and intending to create employment opportunities, among other things, but they inevitably do in their path.'

At the same time, he agrees that there are some valid criticisms to be made, especially with some of the more popular games of the last decade, such as greenmail.

'I've never been involved with greenmail or hostile take-overs. I disapprove of them. One of my sort of bugbears at the moment is seeing vast salaries being paid to people doing an indifferent job. People regarding companies as their own, reacting with outrage at the thought of a take-over as if they're being personally violated. Whereas I haven't yet bumped into a shareholder who woke up on a Monday morning when his share was being bid for, found it 40% higher and was hugely upset about the thing. That's where directors really run the business for themselves and not for their shareholders. Then there's this appalling thing at the moment whereby people really make a mess of the damn thing and have to get a million pounds to leave. That's disgusting.'

Another common practice he objects to is when the chairman of a company magnanimously gives something to a charity, is profusely thanked in front of the assembled masses and maybe even eventually gets a knighthood.

'It's all so bloody easy for him because he's giving away someone else's money. I do object to that. I don't mind a company being socially responsible. I think that's a very good thing. But the trouble is, I often suspect the motives of the guy doing it. Please don't get me wrong. I think it's important to give to charity. But if the chairman of the company who's making the donation feels that strongly about it, let him give his own money, not the company's.'

Nor does he think directors should have many of the perks that are common in business today. Not that there's anything wrong with the perks themselves. It's rather that the perks are bad for the success of the business.

'People start confusing their money with the company's money. Marble staircases appear and the Roller sits outside. It happens all the time. Just for the sake of argument, I don't think I've ever even had a lunch bill on Burford, to say nothing about the car and driver. But that's me. Now, I do think people who work hard should be well rewarded. But good management, the way I see it, is the type who runs a company lean and tight, who looks after people, pays them well, and doesn't abuse the situation where perks are concerned. It's not so much a question of someone having a Rolls Royce which costs a certain quantifiable amount, it's the attitude of mind that's gone behind that. Maybe the business can afford the car and the entertaining and the executive who puts his gardeners on the payroll. But the attitude is wrong and it grows like a cancer.'

The right management, the kind he respects most and looks for in whatever companies he deals with, are keen to generate the right attitudes and the right motives throughout the company. But even that isn't necessarily enough. He is convinced that good motives poorly executed, which probably means bureaucratically executed, merely create bureaucratic black holes. Just chucking money into something that has become bureaucratic is therefore always a disaster. The money can never get through to where it's needed. By definition, a bureaucrat will simply hire more bureaucrats. That's how bureaucrats become more important and eventually higher paid. The entrepreneur, he says, is almost a reverse bureaucrat. The entrepreneur doesn't surround himself with flunkies because that's not what's important. He's not even sure a real entrepreneur pays much attention to his own salary, either.

For the record, Wray notes the highest salary he's ever earned, and that was only for a short period of time, was £70,000. These days he draws about £40,000 a year.

'I must admit that when I see people being paid half a million quid for doing a cock-up job, I sometimes think maybe I should be paying myself more. But that doesn't really interest me. What does interest me, to express it crudely, is to create wealth. But I do that through building a business.

And although that is easier in Britain today than it was back in the '70s, it still isn't as easy as it is in some other countries. Britain, he believes, still had a long way to go.

'The differences between the way business is done in England and the way it's done in, say, Japan, are basically cultural. You often hear people in England saying, if the pound was lower we could export more. That's got to be rubbish. Who are the best exporting nations of the past ten years? Japan and Germany. And look how strong their currencies are. The fact is, if you give the Japanese an appreciating currency, they'll climb over the top of it. If you give us an appreciating currency, we'll look at it as a road block. It goes straight back to education and life-style, I'm sure. But then the supreme irony of England is that we're moving more and more towards a service economy and yet the average Englishmen hates giving services. You can't get service with a smile in this country any more. You get service with a snarl.'

It is just possible that a negative correlation exists betwen formal education and entrepreneurial success.

Wray has a degree, but he's very much in the minority among the people in this book. For instance, only three of the original 17 risk takers went on to university. Jacob Rothschild read history at Oxford, Ashraf Marwan has a PhD. in chemistry from Cairo while Asil Nadir took a degree in economics at the University of Istanbul.

'If one took the entrepreneurs of today, just the ones I can think of, say Michael Green, Michael Ashcroft, Elliott Bernard, none of them have had any higher education. I doubt if they've got an 'A' level between them. I remember Nigel Rudd of Williams Holding saying that he didn't have an 'A' level on his board. Maybe once you get into higher education, your mind is broadened, you're interested in a wider spectrum of things. Perhaps that also means you're less narrow in terms of your business, which is one of the things I think you need to succeed. A narrow vision is important in the respect that, if you've got a good idea, you need to flog it to death.'

But that's only one element.

As far as Wray can tell, the key to success as an entrepreneur can't be neatly packaged into a couple of concise sentences. It's far too complex a result for there to be a single formula behind it. If there was a formula, he says, then presumably there'd be schools doing nothing but turning out successful entrepreneurs.

True, there are some high-flyers with MBAs from Harvard. But not many. The School of Hard Knocks seems to produce a much more interesting crop.

'Remember when Hanson took over SCM in the States? There was a huge court case and Gordon White was on the stand and they asked him something like, what did you do before you bought the business and he said he'd commissioned Coopers and Lybrand to do a report. Then someone asked him if he'd ever read the report. And he said no. Now, if entrepreneurship was as simple as getting Coopers to write a report on a business and you bought it and it went well, hey presto, there'd be a formula and everybody would be doing it. But it's not like that. Okay, by all means have someone do a report. That's common sense. But at the end of the day it's got to be the entrepreneur who says, something about this feels right, it's the right thing to do.'

Obviously his own sense of that has been finely developed over the years. Although he's the first one to admit that he sometimes gets it wrong. Still, he feels, he's fortunate enough to have evolved to the point he is today.

'There are very few people, I suspect, who actually set off on the road and at the end of their lives are still on that same nice straight road. We all go along the road and there are turnings off it and we make choices. Turnings you couldn't have envisaged at the start of that road. I'm certain if you asked James Hanson or Gordon White whether they thought 20 years ago they'd be doing what they're doing now, I'd be staggered if they said anything but, of course not.'

One of the many times he got it spot on was in 1981 when he first heard about a small company called Polly Peck.

'I went to Cyprus with Asil Nadir to see what he was doing there and found the company amazingly exciting. My only mistake was in not holding my Polly Peck shares for ever and ever. It proves my philosophy that you really only make serious sums of money by staying with a company, not one year or two years, but ten years. Nobody is that damn clever that they can always buy at the low point and sell at the high. And even if you do buy low and sell high, odds are you'll never get back in because it will never look right again and you'll miss out on the great wave. A few you will get wrong but if you stick with the right ones over the long term, it doesn't matter that you've got some wrong because the multiples you make on the ones you get right are so enormous.'

Enormous is an understatement.

He bought Polly Peck at about 18p. The shares at one point

touched £35. 'The great thing about Asil Nadir and Polly Peck is that he proves it can be done.'

On the other hand, one of the few times Wray got it wrong was when he put a fair bit of money into a private venture capital company with one particular holding in a public company.

'They'd gone up three- or four-fold. So it was an incredibly profitable investment. And then it just disappeared. They ended up going bust. The reason was that the businesses the management was investing in fundamentally had no assets and no balance sheets. They were over-geared. So when things did go wrong, there was nothing left.'

That cost him about £300,000.

'Obviously I've lost a lot more than that on paper in the stock market in October 1987 in a single day. But that's paper. This £300,000 was real money.'

While it appears that he's constantly wheeling and dealing, he claims that appearances can be deceiving.

'I don't do a lot of buying and selling of shares just for the sake of wheeling and dealing. I'm much more interested in the largest holding I can possibly get in a growth company with people who are entrepreneurial and with an eye to ten years down the line. That's when I think it all happens. I'm good at assessing opportunities but I have serious problems looking beyond the end of the week. Maybe not actually that bad but I don't see myself as someone with a vision. Not like, say, Michael Green. I don't think his visions occur as he thought they would, but he's broadly on the right track. He sees things in a broad pan. I don't have that sense. But I do understand that the huge rewards come if you stick at it long-term.'

Unlike some of the other people in this book – Michael Green, Gerald Ratner, Martin Sorrell, Robert Maxwell, Gerald Ronson, James Hanson, Gordon White – all of whom who are known to be very tough negotiators, Wray sees himself as anything but.

'No. Not tough at all. I know what's sensible. Not all the time but most of the time. It's either a sensible deal and it's fair or it isn't. The thing is, it's no good waiting until you think the market is right to sell because, by then, everybody's made that decision. But I don't see any point in screwing people into the ground. If you're doing a deal and it actually matters to the last penny, then you probably shouldn't be doing the deal anyway. You must do deals with plenty of margin. After all, who's that clever that you can get it spot-on. You need margin as your cover for mistakes and for when things don't go exactly as you thought they would, which they hardly ever do.'

Plenty of margin, strong assets and a sound balance sheet.

He makes the point clearly. Especially about the balance sheet. He says he can't emphasize strongly enough, that at the end of the day the balance sheet has got to look right. It is, after all, the most accurate reflection of the personality of the people running the company, how it's organized and how it's structured.

'I like to know what's going on. Monthly figures must be on time. But other than that, I leave people alone. To a certain extent, people have to sink or swim. I think it's terrible that, generally speaking, people don't use their brains. The great majority of people spend much longer at work than they do with their family. And most people do not think. Even when they produce figures, most people don't think about what those figures mean. All too often, the fact that figures have been produced is the end in itself. Well, it isn't, it's really just the beginning. Once you've got the figures, you've got to look at them and decide what they're saying. It's not very complicated but most people don't do that very well.'

He not only looks at the figures and devotes a lot of time to thinking about them, he uses them to help him assess the risks involved and make a judgement about the down-side of every deal.

'At the end of the day we're all idiots. The winners are just less idiotic than the losers. There are obvious exceptions, but if you look at the people who've led the great banks of the world, I think the way they've spent money in certain countries and lost everything, you could make out a reasonable case that they are idiots. Those deals have all come unstuck because they were idiotic to begin with. Start-up ventures are a completely different science altogether. Your only chance there is to do ten of them and hope a few come right. I'm much happier dealing with businesses that have a track record you can get your teeth into. I think if I hadn't lived through 1973/4 I'd have made far more money in the 1980s. But I knew first hand how the stock market had fallen 150 points because I'd felt it. I knew how property values had collapsed, because I'd felt it.'

That's why, he claims, his gearing has always been sensible. And pre-October 1987, whenever he was asked why he'd gone for Centrovincial or Singer and Friedlander, he answered, because they had a balance sheet, because he knew that one day the music was going to stop and when it did, he wanted to know there was something behind the company to back it up.

'I was saying this as late as September 1987 because I'd foreseen the end of the bull market. A lot of people did because bull markets can't go on for ever. Unfortunately. Of course I had no idea it would be in October. Nor had I ever seen a two-day bear market. No one had. I looked at the television and saw Wall Street down 300 points and thought, silly buggers, must be a misprint. Then I turned to the other channel and it said Wall Street was down 400. I watched the news at 10 o'clock and they said Wall Street was down 500. It was the first time since 1974 that I'd experienced that sinking feeling in the pit of my stomach. It was quite frightening. You could see the possibilities for panic. Obviously, I've taken risks along the way. But being cautious is the only way to invest. Being cautious means you see a lot of value in your investment and also that you know your down-side. After all, none of us knows when the market is going to have another crash. I'm always keeping half an eye on the clock because you never know when midnight is coming.'

18

Michael Green sits behind a large glass table that is his desk, with his shoes casually cast aside, facing a Richard Avedon photo of a coal-miner.

'The important thing about that photo for me is, here's a guy who actually works for a living.'

His office, in the heart of Mayfair, is a white-walled, somewhat stark, uncluttered place with just his desk, a few chairs and several good contemporary paintings.

And that coal-miner staring back at him.

It is a daily reminder, perhaps, of how lucky he's been.

'I firmly believe that the world is unfair. That's important to understand. When I started in business with the little capital I had, and I must say it was small, if I'd lost it, the worst that would have happened is that I'd have gone back to a very comfortable home. Most other people who think about starting a business usually also have to worry about a house, a mortgage and kids. They think about going into business on their own, see how much down-side there is and decide they can't afford to take the risk. I understand that. In most cases there's so much down-side, they'd be crazy to take the risk. If you come from a good secure background where you've got nothing to lose, of course you can be bold. It doesn't mean you're brighter or more clever than anyone else. You simply have the security of knowing that if you fail it isn't real catastrophe.'

Green's mother is a psychologist and his father, now retired, was a successful businessman so his story is hardly a tale of rags to riches. He was raised in a relatively wealthy, middle-class family, by parents who wanted him to be a doctor. In fact his mother always hoped one day he'd become a psychiatrist. To help him on his way, he was sent to Haberdashers' Aske's, one of the country's better public schools. But he wasn't much of a student. Instead, he had what is politely called a very active social life.

'What I did, I suppose to rebel, was purposely not take much interest in school. But I did have a keen sense of wanting to go into business at a very early age. I've always been ambitious, very much so, but I don't believe there were any signs early on that I would necessarily be successful.'

His friends say he was driven as a teenager and even if he didn't necessarily show any signs of future success, he never hid the fact that he was decidedly ambitious.

'I was ambitious but I don't think you can tell if someone is going to be successful based on that. For instance, I've known Gerald Ratner since he was 13 or 14 and I think he would be the first to admit that he showed very few signs early on that he'd be successful. Charles Saatchi and Gerald and I were great friends and I'm sure that both Charles and I were far more ambitious at that stage than Gerald was. But then Gerald came from a very successful family background. He wasn't that hungry.'

Anxious to get into business, Green rejected university and a career in psychiatry. And while he might never have cared for medicine, he concedes that his impatience at that stage was a big mistake.

'It definitely was. You learn a lot at university about life. You mature and develop a broader range of interests. Now, to be successful as a violinist or a businessman, I think you need to have a single vision, you need to concentrate on one particular thing. But the trouble with concentrating on one thing is that you can become very boring. In fact, many extremely successful people happen to be extremely boring. You know the type. Unless you're speaking about their particular subject, there's no conversation because they have no other interests. So yes, I regret now not having gone to university. I think, had I gone I would have had a broader outlook. I find myself lacking in some areas of general knowledge, which is a problem in business when you're meeting all sorts of people.'

It's a problem which keeps coming back to haunt him, like recently, when he went to Japan for the first time.

'I realized that my ignorance about Japan was staggering. I blame that on the fact that I didn't have a proper education. It's my own fault. Yes, I think had I gone to university I would still today be just as successful. It would have come later, but so what. Being able to focus is essential but education teaches you to apply yourself. Nearly half of Carlton Communications is in high technology. Our video business represents 2% of total British exports to Japan. We have more science PhDs here than any other company I can think of. And I have to sit in some subsidiary boardrooms and listen to a quality of brain that I find very difficult to keep up with.'

Around Carlton's offices they claim that because Green doesn't have an Oxbridge diploma, he's overly impressed with good qualifications. Asking him about that, he nods, yes, he probably is.

'Many of the runners in our London businesses have a degree. Our errand boys have degrees. Television and the motion picture business is so attractive, people want to get into it and we have the pick of the crop. I get letters every single day from people wanting to join the company. So, yes, I do like the idea that we can hire really bright university graduates to be errand boys. I'm keen on education. I have very very few regrets but my lack of a good education is one of them.'

It must be said that Green has had other advantages. Long before he became successful, he was able to see real success close up. He married the eldest daughter of Lord Wolfson, granddaughter of Sir Isaac Wolfson, both of them legendary businessmen. And while Green and his wife have since divorced, there's no hesitation on his part when it comes to crediting his ex-father-in-law as one of the cleverest men he's ever met.

'Being married into the Wolfson family helped enormously. Not in a tangible way. But I certainly met a lot of people through them. Listening to Leonard Wolfson has been a great learning experience. I couldn't help but learn. He was extremely helpful. He never had any financial involvement with my business but it's wrong to suggest that being part of that family was not helpful.'

Leaving school at the age of 17, Green took his first job at a printer's near Euston Station. While there, he learned something about the direct mail business and three years later – having shopped around for the right opportunity – he bought a company called The Direct Mail Centre. He had very little capital, but the company came along with a building which he quickly sold at a profit. That now staked him.

He nearly lost everything during a three-month postal strike – the direct mail business is quite susceptible to such things – but he convinced his staff of 150, his bankers and his clients to hold on. They did and before long he was able to turn a small profit. He renamed the company Tangent Industries and these days uses it as his private holding company.

By 1970, anxious to flex his muscles and expand, he bought a photographic studio called Carlton. As he built it up, he realized that his clients wanted pictures that moved. Video was just beginning so he expanded in that direction. Television and film production followed in a natural sequence. In 1982, he and Nigel Wray merged Carlton with the Fleet Street Letter Group and Carlton Communications became one of the glamour stocks of the '80s.

Still it wasn't always easy gaining credibility. In 1985 he made a bid for Thames Television which was refused. Certain people thought he'd come too far too fast and wasn't yet ready for anything as important as a TV franchise. Certain people thought he was too much of an overnight success.

But after nearly 15 years of being in business for himself he didn't see himself as an overnight success. So he went about trying to change that perception of himself and his company by keeping hard at work and showing the City, at least, that he was financially responsible. Two years later, now promoted from overnight success to one of the wunderkind of the

Thatcher revolution, he bid for 20% of Central Television, holder of Britain's largest seven-day commercial franchise. And he got it because it seemed only natural that he should have it.

The following year he bought Technicolor, the US film-processing and videotape-duplicating company, for $780 million (then £459 million). It was Carlton's largest acquisition to date and the first time Green had bought an established brand name.

Established in 1915, Technicolor was the founder of the colour film-processing industry. It is today a decided world leader in both film-processing and videotape-duplicating, with 40% shares of each market. Green went into the deal because he felt the timing was right to own such a business. The growth of multiplex cinemas, averaging nine screens each, has brought increasing demand for prints of films. The deal also fitted in snugly with Green's strategy of sticking to the basics of his business. The so-called 'nuts and bolts' end.

By design, Carlton has become a major international communications company which operates at every level of television, video and film production. They make advanced digital equipment, provide a network of facilities for programme production, sound and video editing and special effects. They also transmit programmes to satellite and cable channels. Now, the company is neither the only player in its business, nor it is the leading player in any one of the fields where it competes. But making Carlton unique is the fact that it deals in more areas that any of its competitors, which gives it a much broader base.

'Products and services in our business are inextricably linked. It's all controlled by technology. For example, we have a product called the Graphic Paintbox. For me it's the most significant thing we've got in the whole company. We can scan in individual pictures, and in real time, on a high-definition television screen, without ink or paper, we can produce a four-colour separation, ready for print. An editor can sit in front of a television screen and do things that are so radically different in terms of modifying images live, that it's changed the entire pre-press business. Now, you say we're supposed to be in the television business so what are we doing back in the printing business? My answer is because the technologies are converging. We've developed this product, to some extent by accident. When you've got high-definition television you've cracked high density. When you've got high screen density it means you can play with the finished picture at fine enough quality for the printing business too. The possibilities are staggering and, as I've said, radically changing the printing business. It's funny how 24 or 25 years later, I'm back in the same business I started in.'

One of the stories that goes around about Michael Green is that by the age of 12 he already knew how to read a balance sheet.

He did.

And thirty years later, he's more keen on them than ever.

'I enjoy reading accounts. I don't want to be critical of other companies that may be great companies doing great things but some of them who appear to have huge cash mountains also have huge debts. They don't have balance sheets. In some cases what they really have is negative net worth. My company has the most old-fashioned, boring, balance sheet in terms of return on capital employed. It's in the sexiest area because every one thinks about television, video, all the new technologies. But the accounts are really old-fashioned.'

He is especially proud of Carlton's balance sheet because, he says, it is all about assets, which is what a good balance sheet should be.

'Carlton owns £100 million-worth of freehold properties, unencumbered. That means something to me. Show me another business of our size in the Footsie 100 – apart from businesses that have been going for 200 years – that has real, hard cash and no debt. Carlton is genuinely debt-free with serious cash in the bank and a serious balance sheet. That's exceptional for a fairly new business.'

Green points out that he sees his main responsibility as plotting the course the company is heading in. Carlton is in the business it's in because he's chosen to be in those businesses. Obviously he has to answer to his board and his shareholders, so Carlton is not at all a one-man band. But the board and his shareholders back him in those businesses because they agree that those are the logical ones for Carlton to be in.

'We would never buy a brick-building business just because it looks a good deal, would increase earnings per share and make us heroes in the newspapers for the next six months. But when you're talking about running a business of our size, you need to have very bright people out there. I'm fascinated with movies and television but have never put my weight behind a project just because I liked it or didn't like it. I have an opinion just like anybody else, but I'd much rather put my faith in the programme controllers of a television station when it comes time to decide what will work on television. The last thing I want to do is set myself up as something I'm not.'

Running a business capitalized at £1.5 billion, is, Green says, a lot of hard work. But then as far as he's concerned, the secret of success is hard work.

'All the rest is mythology. Most of the truly successful businessmen I've met work hard. Talent is often making things appear effortless, easy. But a lot of that is perception. The reality is you do have to read management accounts and you do have to think about them and you do have to use a calculator to check the numbers. There's no easy way round it. You have to do all the detail work.'

Many people might then assume that if making money was the end result of nothing more than hard work, anybody could do it.

Green sees if differently.

'I actually think there's a lot of myth attached to making money. Wasn't there someone at the Harvard Business School who said to his class on the first day, for those of you interested in making money, go into the property business. For those of you interested in business, come back for the second lesson. Well, I think he's right. Anybody interested in making money should go into property and odds are you'll make a lot of money. But I don't think that's very interesting or very creative. There are a few people who do some good things in property but for a lot of the people, the huge sums of money they make in property bears no relation to their talents. Yet society says they must be clever and special because they're very rich. There's something wrong about that.'

The luck element also plays a part.

Richard Avedon's coal-miner won't let him forget it.

'It's extremely important. I've been lucky and admit it. But objectively, when I've been lucky, I've then tried to use it to my best advantage. We've all known people who have been lucky and never capitalized on it. I try to capitalize on it to the hilt.'

That first trip to Japan opened his eyes to a lot of things.

'There's a country making the most enormous sums of money. Japan is leading the world in the most frightening way. It's scary. The sheer weight of money they have there. But go to the 10,000 bars they've got at night. Watch the businessmen unwind at night with two ladies on their arms. Nothing sexual about it. They sit there and tell those ladies their problems. You see that and think to yourself, hold on, there's something strange here, why have they got to do that? Why have they got such a feudal system still going on there? Why is the individual non-existent in Japan? There are no risk takers there. And yet they're the most successful people today by a mile.'

Why?

He says he's still trying to work that one out; although one answer might be that they traditionally take a long-term view.

'I did about 10 presentations there and not one person asked me about last year's figures. They wanted to know market share, strategy and where we're going. They wanted to know where we would be in five years. Yesterday's figures and even today's figures were irrelevant to them. I think if we were able to take a longer-term view, we'd be a lot richer. It also helps that the cost of money is so cheap. First they arbitrage it, then they go out and buy plants, and Columbia Pictures and Radio City. Because the cost of their capital is so low and the weight of their capital is so huge, they take a longer view. And I'm convinced that every time you can take a longer view you're going to end up winning.'

Even before he floated Carlton, in the days when he was running a private company, he operated a system of management accounts exactly like a public company and produced a glossy, full-colour annual report just like a public company. He did it because there was never any doubt in his mind that one day he would go public and one day after that somebody would go back to look at those earlier reports. When that day came, he wanted to be sure they'd see what his company was all about, that there was never any artificial accounting or funny holding companies in the Virgin Islands, that Carlton was making profits and paying taxes because that's what companies are supposed to do.

So right from the beginning, he says, he's always taken the long-term view. But when you ask him, did you know in 1985 that five years later Carlton would be the company it is today? he says no, no one could have foreseen that because there have been so many major changes in the industry.

'That's another area where the Japanese are teaching us. I've stayed in the business I know and understand. But I couldn't have told you that one day we were going to buy Technicolor. That wasn't something I knew about four years ago. It wasn't an aim or ambition of mine. I'm only now beginning to look five years, or at least a few years, ahead. Although historically we've built this business by not looking terribly far. The television business, the media, changes so fast that I've often thought the American-style five-year business plan was the biggest waste of energy and time. I do think we've got to have some plans but we've also got to keep in mind that those plans are almost certainly going to change dramatically with events. Carlton is now capitalized at £1.5 billion and running a company that size is very different to running a company capitalized at say £100 million. At £100 million you can go charging ahead whereas with £1.5 billion it's slower.'

Slower and more conservative.

'Ask any of my friends. I'm sure they'll tell you that I've always been very conservative. It used to be a joke with my friends that I was 20 going on 60. But I didn't mind that. I always felt that way.'

The coming of 1992 has been a good catalyst, forcing the rest of the world – especially the United States – to focus on Europe as a market.

It will be a more important event to some businesses than others. Included among the obvious winners are those businesses supplying equipment to television stations, like Carlton, because German and French and Spanish stations will have to put British suppliers on a tender list and give them a chance to bid. But for the most part, Europe as a single market is already happening. And satellite television is probably the most obvious example.

The right dish turned to the right satellite can bring dozens of programmes into your home from throughout Europe. Green clearly saw that coming – as did most forward-thinkers in the business – which is why he bid for a share of DBS-UK, the satellite which was to rival Rupert Murdoch's Sky.

Green lost in the auction and the franchise went to BSB.

It's a battle he still thinks about.

'I'm very upset that I lost that. I believe we put up the best package. I don't think we'd have spent £1.3 billion, which is what BSB finally ended up spending. But I believe in satellite broadcasting. I believe it will be a very important business, even more so in this country than cable. You must understand that in America, more than 50% of the country is already cabled. The costs of cabling homes here is so high that just as a television medium, when you're not cabled, it's too expensive to start from scratch. We do have a business called Cabletime. In France it's doing well. In Britain, a little bit. What you need to really make it work is an interactive cable system so that people will get lots of different kinds of information down the lines. Eventually cable will be to do with telephony. You'll get pictures from your telephone lines. And the financial driving force will be the telephone companies. Now, at the moment that's illegal. But if the government were to allow British Telecom to use their cables for transmitting into the home, then we're into a whole new business and I'm certain that will eventually happen.'

It will happen because no one can stop it from happening. And in spite of what governments now say, about how thrilled everyone claims to be that it is happening, most governments in Europe tried for as long as they could to prevent it from happening. After all, satellite presents all sorts of problems for governments where the strict regulation of broadcasting used to be their given right.

Governments always try to control the media. It is a basic belief of men in power that if they control the media they can control the flow of information sent to the people through the media. One of the things the opposition does is decry that control, at least until they come to power and then the roles are reversed.

It's a fact of life that revolutionaries traditionally feel they must capture the state radio station. Wars are fought on the airwaves, witness Radio Marti's invasion of Cuba in early 1990. Or, even better, look at how the Romanians chose the TV station as their headquarters to topple Ceaucescu.

The only totally free media in the world is in the United States where the US Constitution specifically forbids the government from having any control. When Richard Nixon and his attorney-general, John Mitchell, tried to take the *New York Times* to court for publishing the Pentagon Papers – top-secret documents stolen from the Defense Department – the Supreme Court told the governments lawyers to get lost. Arrests could be made for possession of stolen goods but the government could not, under any circumstances, stop publication of anything. The government had no right to come into the newsroom.

In nations like Britain and Canada, there are obvious controls such as D-Notices and the War Act, plus much more subtle controls, such as the appointment of directors to a broadcast authority and the award of franchises. The libel laws in Britain also keep a thumb on the press as does the government's use of 'selective leaks' of otherwise prohibited information through off-the-record briefings. They, especially, provide a huge advantage over the freedom of reporters to successfully gather sensitive information. Equally to the point, note how tightly controlled television is when broadcasting the House of Commons. What goes on there is the people's business. How that business is seen is down to the official censors.

In other countries, France, for example, the government has at times played a very heavy hand in conrolling the media. François Mitterand's ascendancy to the presidency coincided with the firing of a TV newscaster in an absolutely naked attempt by Mitterand to exert control.

Now along comes satellite television and everybody can watch everybody else's television and whatever walls have been built to limit the flow of information are tumbling down.

It's an area Green has been watching with great interest.

'There are all sorts of rules governing satellite broadcasting. In 1977 all the post offices in the world agreed that only they had the right to the space to beam down. In theory you could have porno channels and politically sensitive channels, that sort of thing. So the post offices signed an agreement to help stop that kind of stuff coming in. You can't make it illegal to have a transponder. You can't make it illegal to have a dish that receives them. But you can make it illegal to advertise on them. That's why you've got a new Broadcasting Act. That's why in France and Spain you've got more channels. That's why in Portugal they've got more channels. Satellites have meant the freeing up of television. Governments have had to say, hold it, folks, we perhaps told you a bit of nonsense in the past, in fact we can give you more channels so let's put it out to contest and everybody can have more television channels.

That's exactly what's happened. Satellites have meant more terrestrial television.'

Both the advent of satellite broadcasting and the resulting expansion of more terrestrial television has signalled a boom-time for Carlton. In addition to owning 20% of Central, they've done a lot of work for Sky Television – what Green calls 'the nuts and bolts'. They put together the schedules, some programmes and the uplinks.

It is, Green says, the safest side of satellite television, at least for the time being.

'We're not gambling whether there are two million viewers or 20 million. We just get paid for the work we do. We don't own the channels. That's our cautious side, our non-risk-taking side. When the business is matured and there's a known audience and a known advertising stream, then we might be getting involved in it. We don't have an equity participation at the moment because, as everyone knows, satellite broadcasting is a losing proposition. It's a shame. I respect Murdoch for having the courage to sink that kind of money into the business. Also for the speed with which he got four television channels going. There's a news channel on satellite where the broadcasters must know they're only talking to 200,000 people and yet they're very professional and never give you the impression that they know how few people are watching. Still, can you imagine trying to keep a business going when everyone knows that?'

With the international competition that is obviously coming, one of the most pressing problems anyone in British television has to face is whether or not their programmes can fetch an audience.

There are some people who think British television is the finest in the world and need not fear competition.

But Michael Green is not one of them.

'It's huge arrogance to say that. Listen, there are very few British television programmes sold to network television in America. By that I mean, CBS, NBC, and ABC. Most wind up on public channels, like PBS. So how come, if our television is with our formula would be to make fools of ourselves. It's so difficult these days to earn a few bob, you've really got to know the ground rules. If you don't believe me, just watch what's going to happen in 1992 when British businessmen go into Europe. For a lot of them it's going to be a disaster.'

17

Nigel Wray

He is, for the lack of a better term, a financier.

But Nigel Wray, a well-groomed, soft-spoken, good-looking man of 41, would rather be playing rugby for England.

'I would have loved to experience the feeling of walking down the tunnel and coming out to that enormous roar.'

Or cricket for England.

'I was, I say *was*, once quite a fast bowler. I used to like discomforting batsmen.'

Or both.

'I'm afraid I wasn't particularly good. Anyway, those were probably my greatest ambitions. That is, if I had any ambition at all. I certainly didn't have any ambition to make any money.'

Yet not long ago he was listed as the 114th wealthiest person in the kingdom, worth £53 million.

Not bad for a guy without much ambition.

Born and raised in north London, Wray grew up in a comfortable, middle-class home, the only son of a relatively successful printer. At the age of 18 he went off to Bristol University, originally intending to study Classics. But three weeks before he started there he reminded himself that he'd hated Latin and Greek all his life, so he changed to economics.

'It sounded like a good subject. Thank goodness no one asked me what I thought economics was because I didn't really know anything about it.'

A few years later, degree in hand, his father offered him a job. He'd worked in the family business during school holidays, so wonderful, we so rarely sell a programme to the American networks?'

Of course, at the BBC and at ITV they answer that American network television programming isn't about the kinds of high-culture programmes produced in Britain, it's about soap operas and game shows.

Green won't buy that either.

'We know that's not true. With all the television channels in America, it simply can't be true that it's all garbage and even the biggest detractors admit there are some very fine programmes. Because British television is English-speaking, the world wants to see it. But mostly the world wants to see American programming. Now, I think that's changing. We make *Inspector Morse* for Central Television and they sell it to something like 57 countries. *Paradise Club* was recently sold to Japan. You're beginning to see programmes in Britain now specifically being made with worldwide sales in mind. Because the independents are making the programmes, not just the television stations, things are changing.'

Part of the problem is the current system.

'The monopoly called ITV was once the only place you could advertise. Say I'm Procter and Gamble and I want to reach 10 million homes. If the programmes on ITV are terrible and people turn to BBC, I've actually got to spend more money advertising with ITV. In other words, the worse the programmes are, the smaller the audience will be so I've got to spend more to reach those 10 million homes. That can't be healthy. Now ITV has some competition and even if it is very small competition, things are changing. Look at the newspaper industry. Eddie Shah was the catalyst but News International are the ones who benefited. What will happen with television is much the same. Sky isn't acually taking any serious advertising money away from any of the other channels, but the mere fact of its existence means the others have got to be competitive, they must look at the programmes they're offering, they must go for good programmes otherwise they won't have the audience figures and that means they won't get the advertising revenue.'

Then there are those who say that, with competition running rampant, producers will simply allow their more basic instincts to take hold, lower the standards and go for the biggest audience.

Again Green disagrees.

'I do not believe the argument that more necessarily means less quality. That's absolute rubbish. In 1955 the BBC said exactly the same thing when ITV came on. I believe you must have a competitive environment. Deliver an audience and you'll deliver an advertiser. The end result will be more narrow casting, television channels that are going to appeal to certain audiences. There'll be a 24-hour sports channel and a 24-hour weather channel. That's fine. Ask sports fans if they get enough sports on television and they'll all say no, there's hardly ever anything on. They want to see more sports so I say given them a sports channel and they'll be happy. Some other person will tell you, I hate sports, I want movies or the opera or ballet, hence another television channel. That's good.'

He feels certain the BBC will always be the yardstick in terms of quality. As long as they produce good programmes, the BBC will maintain a share.

'It will be less than it gets now, but even if it goes from 45–8% down to 35%, it's still a gigantic share. It will still have the biggest share. There's nothing wrong with the BBC and ITV getting 70% and all the others getting 30%. If you look at America, the three main networks still get 65–70% of total advertising revenue. It's huge. And yet there are a lot of other television stations out there. It's a good business that other 30–5%. You can make a lot of money.'

All of Britain's independent TV franchises are coming up for renewal. But whether or not Carlton will ultimately bid on a television station of its own is a matter Green won't openly discuss at this time. He is, however, willing to say that it looks as though Carlton is interested in acquiring a television station. But that's all he'll say.

'The bill is going through Parliament at the moment so if we bid for a station, we won't know for some time whether or not we would want to keep or be allowed to keep our Central shares. It also depends on who we might bid for. You'll be allowed two stations but it depends which two, whether they're contiguous, do the borders touch, what size are they, there are lots of rules to be decided. The most expensive television stations are those capitalized at about £280 million so it sounds as though if we do bid we won't need a partner.'

It would be odd if Carlton didn't make a bid, and the logical target is Central TV. After all, with its 20% share, Carlton already knows the lay of the land. But as it stands, with Parliament changing the ground rules for future bids on an almost weekly basis, Green isn't convinced that the viewer will be the ultimate winner.

'There are committees meeting every week, but at the moment I don't think there's going to be very much change. It's a frightening statement. But in fact, the way it is going, I honestly don't think the average viewer will notice much difference at all. The government has so changed their original agreement. At the moment, if the highest bid is gone and they're back to insisting on religious programming, minority programming, children's programming, if they put all those requirements back in, then there's no discernible difference with the current system. And I think that's sad. I've made a representation to the Prime Minister, amongst others. It hasn't happened yet so I can't say it will happen. But at the moment I think it is looking as though there will hardly be any change. The thing I object to is the arbitrary system that the people who will win the franchises won't know why they've won and the people who lose won't know why they've lost. That can't be good. The government is backing away from their original concept. There's been a huge lobby and they're backing away fast.'

Where then does he see the future of British broadcasting?

'When I say nothing will change I mean none of the people who are now running television will change, nor will the way they run it change. What will happen is that there'll be more television, so the prognosis there is good. More is better. There will be more hours of broadcasting. The *Financial Times* says by 1995 the hours will double in Europe from what they are now. So you are talking about major increases in the number of channels and the number of hours. And that's very good news.'

Being in the business he's in, and having made such a success out of it, he's gotten to know the media on both sides of the fence.

It's an odd position for most businessmen, who find themselves the subject of stories but rarely understand what life is like for the people gathering those stories.

Unlike, say, his pal Gerald Ratner, who is always available to the press and frank on the record about what he thinks, Green has always been very cautious.

'I said before that life isn't fair. I totally accept that. But where the press is concerned it's pretty much your own choice. If you don't want to play with the big boys, then you shouldn't be in the game, or whatever that expression is supposed to be. I have had my problems with the press. I've seen things printed that I've found totally upsetting and unpleasant and, of course, untrue. But you cannot be in a major business and not accept that the press is part of your existence.'

Asked if he thinks he can fight back, he answers, yes.

But in the next breath he says, 'The question should be, can you win? It doesn't work to hit them head on. What you must continually strive for is accuracy. If you go back into the files on Carlton you'll find only one interview with me on the record. In seven or eight years, that's all. It was with Raymond Snoddy at the *Financial Times*. Because I trust him. I think he is an extremely responsible journalist. But except for that one and this one, I've never given any other on-the-record interview in my life. If you set yourself up, as some people have, and court the press and continually pontificate on how business should run and what you should be doing, then you get what you deserve.'

He finds it remarkable how often he sees comments in the press and hears them on television from businessmen telling the world how everyone else's business should be run. It's something he avoids like the plague.

'If you really think you know all about that, then you must accept that people are going to throw huge darts at you. I don't think I have such an important view that I must immediately impart to the world through the press. Therefore I talk about Carlton. I do an annual chairman's statement, which is an on-the-record thing. And yes, I've done press conferences on an acquisition because you have to. Otherwise I keep to the businesses I know about and when someone phones up and wants to do a story about me and my suit or me and my house, I say no. Anyone who goes for that deserves whatever else comes along with it.'

Anyway, he points out, 'There's a great theory that if you see a chairman's picture in the newspaper more than twice in a month, sell the shares. You know what? I think there's something to that.'

The future of Carlton, he promises, will be 'more of the same'.

Thanks to a distribution deal he recently did with Paramount, more of the same undoubtedly means a lot more. The new company – 51% Carlton, 49% Paramount – will bring Paramount into Europe and take Carlton into the States.

'We can now sell our programmes in America. That's always been tough for everyone over here to do. But when you've got Paramount selling them for you it's less tough. They've got other programmes to sell them with and a huge distribution chain. That's a very good thing for us. In return, we've become something of a back-door for Paramount to come into the EEC. It's very clever from their point of view.'

With each step, Green becomes more of a media mogul. But he says he doesn't ever see himself turning into a British version of Jack Warner.

'No. Carlton isn't a risk taker. We're a very conservative business. Sure, we're in a sexy area. But we look at it in a very unsexy way. The movie business is rated highly at the moment because they've got such enormous libraries. Income is increasing each year even if they're down at the box office. But for Carlton, our value is in our ability to deliver increased earnings each year. If you want to be a high-risk sexy company, fine, but then you're going to get a rating accordingly. One moment they make a fortune, the next year they go backwards. We don't want to be like that. We're building a company with steady growth.'

The key words there are 'steady growth'.

'It's very important. But we're not looking to do it the way, say, Hanson has done it. He's been brilliant at selling companies. That's a skill and a talent and it's to be respected, but it's not the business we're in. We don't have a bids and deals department. We don't have a corporate finance department. We have made acquisitions but not as many as you'd think.

Phone calls may come in all the time, offering deals, but he insists there has never been one that's amounted to anything.

'We've never yet done a transaction that somebody's recommended to us or brought to us. It's remarkable. We always find our own. Anyway, we buy a tiny percentage of the things we look at. If we buy one or two companies a year, that's a lot for us. In 1989 we bought two and they happened to have been very large so everybody got the impression we're very acquisitive. But frankly, if we don't buy another company for another 12 months, that wouldn't bother me at all. On the other hand, to be perfectly honest, I've said that every year and it seems every year we do buy something.'

In the end, he says, it's easy to buy a business. It's just so much harder to run it.

'I get much more satisfaction out of seeing how the managers are actually running our business than in going out and buying something. That's not the exciting part. Every company must have a boss, every good company, that is, must have a single boss. I don't believe in committees. But the ego bit is that here is this terrific company that is going places. The ego part is the fact that Carlton is growing and will be around for hundreds of years to come. The excitement for me is that Carlton is of the size that will grow, that is really strong and will definitely go on. And it will go on successfully. That's very important.'

19

Chris Beard

Christopher Donald Frederick Beard . . . who sometimes adds a final 'e' to his name to make it Bearde . . . 'just because it keeps people off guard . . .' once spent eight weeks with Elvis.

'I'm not talking about meeting him in a shopping centre in Iowa last month. When I got to know him he was still alive.'

That happened somewhere in Chapter Four of his life.

Chapter One takes place in England. Two happens in Australia. Three is Canada. Four is the States. And this is Five.

It's called 'Coming Home'.

In 1948, when Chris Beard was 12 years old – long before he ever thought of becoming Chris Bearde – his father moved the family from Shepperton, England to Sydney, Australia.

'I was very happy where I was but my father had served during the war with Australians, got surrounded with them at Tobruk, and believed them when they said Australia was the land of milk and honey. Maybe it is today but in those days it was the dark ages.'

The family set sail from Southampton on some migrant boat where the men had to stay on one side and the women had to stay on the other side.

'I have no idea why,' he shrugs. 'It took us eight weeks to get down under. We kept stopping everywhere. I loved it. The boat trip was terrific fun.'

But the fun ended once they settled into their new surroundings.

'Life out there was tough. I used to get beat up a lot because I'd been to a very smart grammar school in England and was now in a place where kids showed up for school without shoes on. In order to survive I had to learn to speak with their accent, fight back and stop wearing my shoes. That took me about six months. The next thing I had to do was break somebody's nose during a Rugby League game. After that, I was one of the boys.'

Everything changed for him again when he was 15. His parents split up and much of the burden of supporting his mother and sister now fell on his shoulders. He quit high school, got himself a day job working in an advertising agency and enrolled in art school in the evenings.

'I was a Bolshevik in those days. I read Lenin and slept with Estonian women.'

Then he discovered television.

'I was literally walking past a store and saw a little box with a frame and picture moving around inside it and said to myself, I don't know what that is but I know I don't want to be an artist. I want pictures that move. I know I want to do whatever that is.'

Banging on doors, most of which were quickly shut in his face, he was just about 17 when he finally landed his first broadcasting job.

'It was in radio. But Australian radio was very exciting. They had a lot of great performers in those days, sort of like the Australian film industry when they began. Nobody knew about it and yet it was very good. They had live programmes like *Lux Radio Theatre*. I got myself a job doing sound effects for those kinds of shows, and as soon as the people at the station saw that I always turned up on time, I got another job engineering for an early morning disc jockey. I used to sit in a little booth at 5 a.m. watching guys still in their pyjamas doing the breakfast show. Of course I used to wonder what the hell I was doing there. But it taught me a lot about timing and pacing.'

After a while it also taught him that he didn't want to get out of bed at 4.30 in the morning to play records. Although the job did have some benefits, such as being over by 9 a.m. It meant he could make the 10 o'clock film at a local cinema. Finished there by 12.30 or one, he could then catch a two o'clock movie down the block. And he might very well have continued splitting his days between working in radio and watching films, except that he heard a local TV station was having open auditions for a children's show host.

'I showed up. And so did two other guys. But one of them was a drunken Irish tenor and the other was obviously gay. I knew before anything even happened that I'd gotten the part by default. I sang 'Mares Eat Oats and Does Eat Oats', tap-danced and told a story about how I liked kids because I figured I was just an overgrown kid myself. They gave me the job on the spot.'

A few days later he was appearing on Australian television three days a week in his own half-hour show called *Smalltime*. He was then given a two-hour Saturday morning slot where he played the first mate to Captain Fortune and his imaginary houseboat.

'That guy hated me because I was getting more popular than he was. So he started making me into the villain, telling the kids on Saturday mornings, "Chris crosses the street against the light" and "Chris does everything wrong". Of course, the more he said it the more the kids liked me and my own show jumped in the ratings.'

Over the next five years, he wrote his own scripts, painted his own sets and on days when the director didn't turn up for work, he directed the show himself from in front of the camera. 'Hi boys and girls . . . take three.' But most of all, over those five years, he learned the craft of television.

'I interviewed kids and read Dr Seuss books in cadence with a three-piece jazz band I had in the studio. I was earning about £15 a week, which was a lot more than any improverished art student. In fact I was a big star, although I couldn't afford a car so I had to go home on the train. Still, it was a terrific way to learn. I could make all sorts of mistakes and nobody knew the difference. Do you know that I still get recognized by Qantas stewards. The only problem is they're all old and keep telling me they watched me when they were kids.'

At the height of his *Smalltime* days, the American talent

agency MCA came to town to produce a variety show. They walked into the TV station and asked to meet with the local writers. Nobody knew what that meant because everybody did everything, so the station manager told Chris to introduce himself as a writer. MCA believed him and together with one other fellow he scripted a show called *Revue '61*. It was so successful, they hired him the next year for *Revue '62*.

'It was a smash hit because it had American techniques and no one in Australia had ever seen anything like it. I didn't know what I was doing, except writing comedy. But that's when I started to realize that I could do more than just host a kids' show three days a week.'

MCA realized it too and the next thing he knew, they'd gotten him a deal with CTV, the first commercial channel in Canada, to write a variety show out of Toronto called *Network*.

'I moved with my family to a country where I didn't know a soul, with a 13-week contract that meant less money that I'd been earning in Australia. Looking back, it was a totally crazy thing to do. Because of the nature of the show, we had to take a piece of material from every station along the entire Canadian network. Well, when you have to accept stuff from Moose Jaw, like Enzo Stuarti standing outside in a snow-storm singing 'Arrivederci Roma', but not too far outside because the microphone cord wouldn't stretch, I knew the show wouldn't last, that I'd be out of a job and why the hell did I ever trade success and sunshine for failure and the freezing cold?'

The show did get cancelled after 13 weeks and he was out of a job. However, a few people he'd met at the CBC, the non-commercial network, soon came to him with another proposal, to do a weekly late-night show called *Nightcap*.

'The first 13 weeks were terrible. If anybody ever wanted to crawl under a rock and never be seen or heard from again, it was me. I was an English/Australian interloper into the Canadian WASP scene, doing something that was so totally against the grain in Canada – I was being funny. Now, you have to understand that in those days all Canadians retired to their basements after sundown. It just wasn't a very funny place to be. There I was doing satire on the Canadian character and, in return, getting the worst review I've ever read in my life.'

One critic went so far as to label *Nightcap* 'the worst show in the world'. Nonplussed, and in keeping with the spirit of the show, Beard reviewed that review on the next show.

'We had an English professor from Toronto University go over the thing for grammar. It was hilarious. And for some reason that changed everything for us. That night there were five or six people in the audience. The next week we had to turn people away. That one routine did it. There are watershed moments in your life when things happen and that was one of mine. Can you believe we had 200–300 people breaking down the doors to get in. It was an event. The following week, when the reviewer re-reviewed our show he asserted he'd watched the worst show in the world and that it had slipped.'

Nightcap hit the psyche of the country and every Wednesday night for the next five years, Canada simply stopped. Even Johnny Carson's *Tonight Show* couldn't compete.

Then someone called an election.

'We used to say whatever we wanted to, especially when it came to politicians. It was wild. Because it was non-commercial television and had huge ratings, the government didn't dare try to muzzle us. When Trudeau ran for office, we were having a field day with politicians, especially commenting on his sex life or lack of it, and all of a sudden they took us off the air. They thought we were too dangerous. You see, we could get people to do very strange things. We once told everybody in Canada to flush their toilets at exactly the same time and the entire country nearly ran out of water. Now with the election, the government was worried we'd somehow affect the outcome.'

Buried in a back issue of the Canadian *Hansard* is a remark from the then Secretary of State, Judy LeMarsh, telling Parliament that she'd received more mail protesting *Nightcap's* cancellation than any other single issue. A very fat woman, and the butt of frequent jokes on the program . . . 'She ought to be playing goal for the Maple Leafs because no one could put a puck past her . . .' she demanded that the programme be reinstated.

Luckily for Beard, it wasn't.

Just as Canada was losing *Nightcap* an American television producer named George Schlatter started looking for a special breed of comedy writers. He wanted guys with a track record for being funny week after week. He was planning a show which, if it worked, would eat up an enormous amount of material and probably burn out all but the hardiest writers.

He heard about Beard and offered him a job.

'While I was living in Toronto I used to go down to New York a lot. I'd rent an old car and drive down and sit in the Stage Delicatessen on the weekends, getting to know all the old comics. I'd give them one-liners and they taught me a a lot about American humour.'

Laugh In took American by storm.

Dick Rowan and Steve Martin became instant stars. So did Lily Tomlin, Goldie Hawn, Arti Johnson and a young English actress named Judy Carne.

'There I was again, packing up my family, going to a strange country where I didn't know anyone, to work on a show that could get cancelled and leave me stranded. As it turned out it was the biggest thing ever to hit American television. It was based on the idea of *Hellzapopin*, you know, unrelenting, non-sequitur humour. I stayed with the show two years, writing most of the sight-gag stuff. It was the most fun any writer could have. We were left totally alone to do whatever we wanted. And we won all the awards. We walked away with everything. It was breakthrough television. We gave the world expressions like, "Sock it to me," "Here come da judge," "Verrry interesting" and "Wanna walnetto?" We created a little bit of television history.'

With his star shooting upwards, Bearde – now more often with the added 'e' than without – started writing specials for such '60s stars as The Doors, Joan Baez and Jefferson Airplane.

That's when Elvis came along.

'He'd spent ten years in the movies getting dressed up in Hawaiian outfits and car mechanic outfits and singing all those 'Ah huh huh' songs. This was going to be his comeback to television. When we met with him the first time, he came in with a huge entourage, including the Colonel who'd sold the producers on the idea of doing 23 Christmas songs surrounded by children from the United Nations. But anybody could see this wasn't going to work. At least not for his first TV special in 10 years. We wanted him to sing 'Hound Dog' and shake his booty and be Elvis. So guess who stood up and said what had to be said?'

Beard took a deep breath, looked at Tom Parker and told him, 'Colonel, you've done a great job with Elvis and I particularly like your fried chicken.'

Parker stared at Beard not having any idea what he was talking about.

But Elvis rolled with laughter.

'I got to him. Everybody was waiting for the Colonel to throw me out but Elvis turned to me and said, "Can I talk to you guys alone?" So Elvis, a writer named Allan Blye, the two producers and I went in another room, away from the entourage and away from Colonel Parker. We shut the door and asked Elvis, 'What do you want to do?' he said, 'I don't want to be any goody-goody mechanic any more.' We told him we wanted him to sing 'Hound Dog' with a 32-piece orchestra, to wear heavy-duty clothes, wrap a guitar around his neck and go for it. And he said, "Me too."'

They walked back into the other room and told the Colonel what they'd decided. He thought about it for a moment, then said, 'I don't know about television and you guys do know about television so I'll leave it up to you.'

That 1968 Elvis Special remains one of the magic highlights of his career. It's shown on American television every year on Elvis's birthday and these days it's one of the best selling videotapes of all time.

'I'll never forget being with him when Bobby Kennedy was assassinated. We watched it on television together, then sat around until six the next morning telling each other our life's story. It moulded us together. He told me that when he got well known, people only wanted to punch him and hurt him. They wanted to affect him in some way.'

From *Laugh in*, Elvis and the other specials, Beard went on to produce the *Andy Williams Show*.

Now, until Beard came into his life, Andy Williams had always been thought of as a good-looking, very sedate ballad singer with hits like 'Moon River'. Because that's what people expected, Williams spent the first four or five weeks of the series being his usual self.

And they got clobbered in the ratings.

So one morning Beard called the writers in and warned them that everybody, including him, was going to be out of work if they didn't do something very extreme.

'I told them I wanted all of America to say, did you see what they did to Andy Williams last night? Otherwise we were going down the tubes. I convinced them we had to go for broke. The next show we had Andy coming out to sing some straight number, when, half-way through it, he stopped and said, "I don't like this set". Of course the audience didn't know this was part of the act. He threw a temper tantrum while they sat there with their mouths open. Then, all of a sudden a huge construction ball swung through the set and wrecked the entire thing. We had explosions rigged and the whole studio just blew up. Andy waited until the destruction was over, nodded thank you, and went right back into his song. From that moment on, every week, we started the show with something weird.'

One week he was singing 'Born Free' when five lions came on stage. Another week he was standing on a pier singing 'I Cover The Waterfront' when the side of an ocean liner came along, wrecked the pier and threw him into the water. Next he was singing 'I Talk To The Trees' when all the trees started moving and two guys in white coats came along and carried him off.

Then there was the bear.

Every week a man in a bear suit would knock on Williams'

front door and ask for a cookie. It was a running gag, between the cookie-begging bear and Williams who always refused to give him a cookie. What made the routine special was that Williams never knew the punchline. He'd open the door and read his lines, for the first time, off cue cards.

'Can I have a cookie?' the bear begged.

'A cookie?' Williams answered one week. 'I'm not going to give you a cookie. Not now. Not ever. I've never given you a cookie. I never will give you a cookie. I'm not going to spoil my perfect record.' He slammed the door shut.

The bear knocked on the door again, waited for Williams to open it with, 'WHAT?' and answered, 'You haven't had a perfect record since "Canadian Sunset"!'

Within a month, Beard was producing the number one show in America.

'All we did was take the Toronto stuff and the *Laugh In* stuff and put it into Andy Williams. After all, I only do what I do. I don't do anything else. But I take the chance by going for that big break.'

His reputation secured, Beard and his then partner Allan Blye were considered the whiz-kids of variety television. Offers to produce more and more shows came rolling in, from specials for Dinah Shore, Diana Ross, the Jackson Five all the way to the next series he produced, *The Sunny and Cher Comedy Hour*.

'That was an unbelievably big hit. They were hot, the yuppies of the '70s, and again we broke new ground. Technically we did things that had never been seen before on television. It stayed in the Top Ten for a long time. It was my third hit series in a row. And that's when I dropped out.'

Beard says he woke up one morning with the awful feeling in the pit of his stomach that variety wasn't going to last. Something told him the time had come to move on. Sunny and Cher were about to split up and even though he and Blye had been deveoping a new series for Gladys Knight and the Pips, a show with McLean Stevenson from *MASH*, plus a special for Burt Reynolds, Beard wanted out.

'I don't know what made me do it but I decided to stop. I

rang NBC and told them I was quitting. I sat around for the next six months doing absolutely nothing. Everybody reacted as if I'd suddenly dumped Allan Blye, that I was the bad guy. But it wasn't anything like that. I just wanted to do other things. Except I didn't know what those other things were. I only knew that variety television wasn't going to work much longer.'

That's when a very strange thing happened. Beard's phone rang one morning, literally out of the blue, and some guy he didn't know said that Bob Hope was sending a car for him that evening to bring him to the Hollywood Bowl. It sounded like some sort of joke, but sure enough, that night, a limo arrived and took Beard to Hope's show. Chris and his wife Mia were ushered into a front-row box, right next to Hope's family, without having the slightest clue why. Making the evening truly bizarre, every time Bob Hope looked down at Chris Beard, he winked.

After the show the Beards were ushered backstage to say hello to Hope. They shook hands, smiled, nodded, said nice to meet you and were then driven home. That's all there was. A limo, a front-row seat, a lot of winking and some small talk.

'Neither of us could figure out what was going on. It was just too strange.'

About three weeks later, Hope's manager rang to say they wanted him to produce Hope's Christmas Special. Beard asked why and was told, don't ask why, just say yes. So he said yes.

Again, he came up with surprises.

Hope had been working with the same producer for 22 years and was very set in his style. But his ratings were slipping. Beard says he took his life into his hands and told Hope the first thing he had to do was cut down his opening monologue.

Hope's writers couldn't believe anybody would dare tamper with perfection and even Hope himself said absolutely not.

Beard argued that by taking it down from the usual ten minutes to say, seven minutes, the show would move along faster. He reminded everyone that they were up against the *Six Million Dollar Man* and that by the time Hope would have finished a ten-minute monologue, the Six Million Dollar Man would have leapt over several buildings, destroyed the Communist Party of Romania, had his arm removed five times and made love to three women. While that was going on, there was Bob Hope, still standing in front of a microphone.

'He might have been saying the funniest things in the world, but it wasn't very visual.'

Then Beard poured salt on to the wound by suggesting Hope change the usual opening of his show.

Instead of having an announcer introduce the show, he wanted Hope and black comedian Rodd Fox to come on cold, dressed like a pair of Santa's reindeer, standing inside a stable, angry with Santa for overworking them, saying they wanted to join the Teamsters Union.

Hope personally vetoed Beard's ideas.

It's tough to teach an old dog new tricks.

Except that two days later, at the next meeting, Hope announced that his monologue would not run as long as it usually did and that they'd open the show cold in reindeer suits.

'Let me tell you, the bigger they are the better they are. Real stars are real stars because they understand who to listen to. And I've found that most of the times when you take that giant risk and go to the point of no return, it doesn't usually hit you in the face, it usually works. That is, as long as you know what you're doing. You've got to know what you're doing and they've got to know it too.'

Hope's special that year was Number One in the ratings.

And Beard was back to being flavour of the month.

Chuck Barris is a funny little man who keeps clapping his hands together whenever he laughs, which seems to be most of the time.

A television game show producer, he not only gave the world such shows as *The Dating Game* (*Blind Date* in the UK) and *The Newlywed Game*, he was also one of the first producers to understand that the secret of making real money in television is through syndication.

Simply put, when a series is made in the States, it's often sold to the major networks at a loss. NBC, CBS or ABC try to get away with paying as little for it as possible because they know that the prime-time evening exposure they can give a show will make the re-runs more valuable. Producers have traditionally gone for the networks line. Anyway, whatever they pay for the show, in a sense, underwrites some of the production costs. All the producers have to do is sustain the public's interest for five years. After that, they've got a package to sell to local stations where the series can run on daytime TV for a year, five days a week. Several hundred stations paying new money for old rope can then be worth millions of dollars. And in America, on any given day, *Happy Days* and *I Love Lucy* and *MASH* and *Hill Street Blues* and even early episodes of *Dallas* are still making fortunes for their producers.

What Barris found so lucrative was that he could short-circuit the networks and go straight into syndication.

'One night at a hockey game Chuck told me he'd been trying to sell an amateur talent show but couldn't get if off the ground because he couldn't think of anything funny to do with it. I said to him, instead of making it just another amateur talent show, why not make it the worst amateur talent show in the history of television. Let's get the worst amateur performers we can find. Let's go for bad taste. Well, having done *The Dating Game* and *The Newlywed Game*, Chuck knew a lot about bad taste.'

Beard designed a show around a celebrity panel and a huge Chinese gong. When the act was half-way decent, the panel would award points and whichever act had the most points would win a prize. But when any act was so bad that one of the celebrities couldn't stand it any longer, they'd hit the gong and that would be the end of the amateur's performance.

'I was given $20,000 to make the pilot in San Francisco. I got all the loonies I knew in LA to work for nothing and flew them up. I'm sure the stewardesses on that flight will never forget it.

We had a planeload of people with snakes wrapped around their necks and flippers on their feet. We had the strangest acts imaginable. I mean, most of the performers were from some other planet. But we literally had people rolling in the aisles. It was the funniest show I've ever seen.'

They called it *The Gong Show*.

It ran for five years, made the front page of the *Wall Street Journal* and went down into television history as one of the all-time, most legendary, wackiest programmes ever.

The Bob Hope Specials continued for three years, until Beard formed a partnership with a man named Dick Clark.

For a good part of the 1950s, Clark had fronted a teenage dance music programme out of Philadelphia called *American Bandstand*. The success of that took him to Hollywood where he has been, ever since, something of a rock and roll disc jockey/authority/friend to the stars/living legend.

Beard and Clark teamed up at the beginning of the '80s to do a string of successful shows for syndication, including *Puttin' On The Hits*. Much like *The Gong Show*, the premise was pretty simple. Believing that everybody wants to be a star and that people will do very odd things if you just give them a chance to do it in front of a television camera, Beard got amateurs to mime famous records.

And the money continued pouring in.

'But I woke up one morning and said to myself, it's time to move on. I couldn't complain about the success I'd had. I just needed something new. I wanted to travel and thought that living somewhere else for a while might be fun. I thought about Australia and Canada but couldn't convince myself. I'd already done that. So I started thinking about what was happening in Europe. You know, 1992 and the television explosion. I got to thinking that European television, and in particular British television, gets flooded with American shows. But nobody in England is making shows that go back to America. And here I was, with all this American experience and also an English passport.'

Chris Bearde Entertainment Ltd . . . Bearde with the 'e' . . . was formed in 1989 with New Zealand film producer Rob Whitehouse. Their idea was to create a bridge between British and American television.

Through an introduction to Carat, a European production company, Beard spent 1989 producing a whole series of pilots in England, like *What A Planet* starring Dan Akroyd and his brother Peter, specifically aimed at American television. Several of them have now hit the States, most notably, *Night Rap* a late-night news satire programme on Home Box Office.

All the pilots were taped at Central TV's Nottingham Studios.

Not surprisingly, Central watched Beard bringing major stars over and using their facilities, and the powers there started thinking they might somehow tie into all of this. So Central and Beard struck a deal wherein Central now owns 49% of Chris Bearde Entertainment Ltd.

Until now, no one has ever successfully produced television in England for both the UK and the US markets.

But then, until now, no one with a British passport and 25 years of American television experience has ever tried.

'The timing is absolutely perfect because television in this country has probably gone as far as it can. There are serious problems that must be remedied. For instance, the flexipool idea, where the ITV network divvies up the shows, is absolutely stultifying for the talent. There's no competition. And whenever you take competition out of the creative process, you limit the opportunities for creative people. Really creative people must compete. If there's no reason to be good, creative people will always fail.'

The proof of that, he says, is in the viewing.

'Just look at the highly rated shows in Britain today. They're not expensive costume dramas or anything to do with Georgian architecture, they're *Eastenders* and *Coronation Street* and *Neighbours*. Give me a break, the British tune in to *Neighbours* in droves to watch Australians overcoming extreme social difficulties, like bad writing.'

Then, he hastens to add, there are the sheep dog trials.

'I actually find myself rooting for the sheep.'

Next, the quiz shows.

'One very strange phenomenon of British quiz shows is that they don't give away any big prizes. People come on, make total fools of themselves and all they get is a Blankety Blank chequebook and pen. I mean, why would anyone do anything for that? In the United States the reason quiz shows are so exciting, and they really are, is because they're based on greed. You can actually win something in America. Here everybody loses, including the audience.'

As for variety shows, he says they're totally predictable, so much so that just about anyone can spot the punchlines coming from a mile away.

'People say to me, well, there's an audience out there to watch them. My answer is, the audience is there because there's nothing else to watch, there's no choice. Next they say, sure there's a choice, we have American shows here but the British prefer to watch British shows. Okay, I say, even if they do like to watch British shows better than American shows, that isn't to say that the British shows are any good. Wouldn't it be great to have really terrific British shows all the time and not just one or two great shows every few years?'

Does that mean, he's come home to change all of this?

He insists it's not quite like that.

'Change is coming anyway. As more channels come into British homes, television here will have to compete. That doesn't mean everything is going down-market, it simply means that the BBC and ITV will have to make better programmes. Rules will have to be changed because some of the rules governing television today came from radio and are way out of date. There's also too much middle management in television here. The creative people must be allowed to go straight to the money men and be told, yes or no.'

The way he's set it up, his company is here to be in the business of franchising ideas, much the way they do it at some place like Toyota. They build an engine in Japan, take it to the United States and model a car along American lines. Then they bring that same car to Europe and change it slightly for European taste. But no matter where it sells, it is still basically the same car.

'My aim is to make shows in Britain that can be hits on a network here and at the same time go directly on to the American networks. It means coming up with ideas that can cater to two different markets. And that happens to be the most difficult thing you can possibly imagine. I don't think anybody's ever successfully done it before. *The Prisoner* came close and *The Avengers* came close. But they were caricatures of the British. And anyway, that was a long time ago. International television production is a wide-open market. And the rewards will be huge for the person who gets there first. That's why I'm here. That's why I've come home.'

20

Martin Sorrell

They called a truce over dinner one Sunday night.

Martin Sorrell, the chap who was once described by the *Wall Street Journal* as the most hated man on Madison Avenue, invited the legendary David Ogilvy for a meal.

The 77-year-old Ogilvy, who likes to think of himself as the father of modern advertising, had just suffered the indignity of being subjected to a take-over battle and losing.

Sorrell was about to own the Ogilvy Group, lock, stock and barrel. He also hoped that meant David Ogilvy would come along with the deal. But first there was a score to settle.

During the heat of the take-over, albeit before the two had ever met, Ogilvy referred to Sorrell as 'that odious little jerk'.

Now Sorrell needed to qualify that.

He looked across the table and told Ogilvy, 'I can't believe you made those comments about me.'

Ogilvy looked back across the table and told Sorrell, 'Actually, what I said was much worse.'

The two have been fast friends ever since.

Odds were right from the beginning that Martin Sorrell would one day be successful.

But no one could have ever guessed that he would one day own the largest advertising and public relations conglomerate on earth.

'It's difficult to say whether or not I've always been ambitious because when you're younger and have nothing to judge it against you can't really tell. I always wanted to go into business. I read economics at Cambridge and I suppose I was thinking along those lines. I didn't want to teach or go into the Civil Service, I wanted to go into business. Whether that was because of my father, it probably was. Was I ambitious? I suppose I must have been.'

An only child, he was born and raised in London. His father ran J. & M. Stone and Broadmead, a company that was at the time the largest radio, television and electrical retail chain in the country. His parents understood the value of a good education so he was sent to Haberdashers' Aske's and from there to Cambridge.

While at Cambridge he wrote an investment column for a university paper and started a small investment club where he enticed pals to chip in six shillings a week which he then used to buy shares, most of which went down rather quickly.

His three years there were followed with two at the Harvard School of Business, a trade school notorious for not producing entrepreneurs.

'The trouble with it is that you spend two years in a hot-house. You spend two years doing case studies, answering the questions, what should the chairman do now and why. But when you come out of there you don't get a job as the chairman. You go into the financial department or the marketing department. The irony is that what you've learned over the past two years isn't very useful. That's the reason many MBAs want to get into consulting and investment banking. They find those two areas attractive because you get tremendous exposure immediately in solving problems at a senior level. The good thing about graduate school, especially Harvard, is you get a very good start with a salary. You may come out getting two or three times the salary you were making when you went in. It's probably one of the best investments you can make.'

Yet a higher education is something he will for ever be thankful for.

'I don't know if it's a good thing or a bad thing, but I do know if you go into business instead of going on to university you've got a five-year head start. People who leave school to go into business are probably, in some ways, more directed.

But I happen to think the two years I spent at Harvard were invaluable. It influenced me in what I do today, the way I think about things and the people I know. My horizons are much wider.'

He'd been to the States before attending Harvard, having covered the 1964 Democratic National Convention in Atlantic City for the Cambridge University paper. And he felt he wanted to begin his working life there, so he got himself a job in marketing consultancy at Glendenning Associates in Westport, Connecticut. And the lessons he learned there have stayed with him.

'There are hundreds of thousands of people with MBAs in America. Some are good and some are not so good, but basically you've got a tremendous pool of people there with some form of management training. I happen to think American companies are very well run and that it's therefore very difficult for a British company or a French company or a German company or a Japanese company to come along and tell an American company how to run their business better.'

He was then head-hunted by Mark McCormack, the fellow who turned financial management of sports stars into a multi-million dollar business. McCormack wanted Sorrell to open his London office. The lessons he learned there were the skill of instant decision-making and how to keep all his notes organized on index cards in his jacket pocket.

That job led him to entrepreneur James Gulliver, who hired him as his personal assistant.

'Mark McCormack was more of a classic entrepreneur. James Gulliver is an entrepreneurial manager. I'd love to have both their strengths. And none of their weaknesses.'

When the question is posed, What are your strengths? he hesitates. 'You'd have to ask someone else.' When the next question comes, Well then what are your weaknesses? he says, 'Plenty. Ask my mother.' Then he laughs, 'I wouldn't be weak enough to admit them.'

From Gulliver he joined Saatchi and Saatchi in 1976 and as finance director helped turn them into the world's largest advertising group – the very title he would ironically one day take away from them.

The Saatchi brothers were born in Iraq, Charles in 1943, Maurice three years later. Their father, a textile merchant, moved the family to London in 1947. Thirteen years later Charles left school to join a small advertising agency, while Maurice continued on with school, eventually graduating in 1966 from the LSE with a first class Honours degree. His first job was at Michael Heseltine's Haymarket Publishing.

Charles in the meantime had moved on to Benton & Bowles, a major US agency, then to a smaller creative agency and finally into a small consultancy, taking in contract work from other agencies.

The brothers joined forces in 1970.

For the next five years they went about doing what advertising agencies always do, servicing clients. Their most famous campaign in those days was the pregnant man ad they devised for the health council. Then in 1975 they acquired Garland-Compton. They hired Martin Sorrell the following year.

Now the acquisitions took on some speed.

With Sorrell guiding their finances, they made nearly 40 acquisitions, including Dorland in 1981 – which made Saatchi and Saatchi Britain's leading ad agency – and Ted Bates in America which made them the biggest agency in the world.

Charles collected art and liked to be seen with all the best people. Maurice was content to stay in the background, letting his older brother be the visible one. Yet as a team they helped bring Margaret Thatcher to Downing Street in her 1979 victory with the 'Labour Isn't Working' slogan. From that day on, they were the darlings of the British advertising world, especially among company chairmen with Conservative leanings.

However Sorrell – known as a classic workaholic – believed there should be more to life than just keeping the Saatchis happy. He'd been given part of the action of a Saatchi subsidiary but nothing much came of it. He was admired around the Saatchi offices for his financial brilliance but he was also very aggressive and that upset people, among them – so they say – the two brothers. Words got mixed and tempers were known to fly. By 1986 Sorrell realized the time had come to do something on his own.

In those days the Wire and Plastics Products Company was a factory in Kent which employed 200 people and made baskets for supermarkets. They were making a profit but there wasn't much of a future for the company unless some fresh capital came along.

Sorrell and a stockbroker friend liked the idea of using the company as a shell, bought a 27% share at 38p per for a total of £500,000, renamed it WPP and started acquiring.

His original idea was to create a marketing services company that stayed 'below the line', that is, to put together a collection of fragmented businesses that related to advertising and media – providing sales promotion, design and graphics – as opposed to 'above the line' which are ad agencies themselves. Sorrell's formula was that each company would 'earn out' the cost of the acquisition. In other words, he put some money down to buy them but the balance due was spread out over three years and tied to profits. He needed to ensure himself that the people who ran those businesses – in a real sense, the assets he was buying – were motivated enough to stay with him.

Within about 18 months he'd successfully negotiated no less than 15 take-overs, increased the group's value from £1.4 million to £135 million and seen his WPP shares rise all the way up to £11.

Now, he figured he'd see what life was like 'above the line'.

In June 1987 Sorrel astounded the advertising world by launching a £281 million bid for one of the oldest and largest American advertising groups, J. Walter Thompson.

Probably the most astounded people on Madison Avenue were JWT themselves. Martin Who? WPP what?

Undaunted, he asked JWT to respond to a request for negotiations by 4 p.m.

Still staggered by the sheer audacity of the bid, JWT's

chairman Don Johnston, managed to say, 'That's his deadline, not ours,' and promptly let it pass.

But there was method to Sorrell's supposed madness. JWT had everything self-contained that he'd need to emerge from below the line. The group included Hill and Knowlton, the world's largest public relations company, J. Walter Thompson, America's fourth-largest advertising agency, and the market research group MRB.

It was clear that JWT was having problems and was ripe for plucking. But what he didn't want was to get involved in a costly hostile bid which might lure a white knight into the game and pluck JWT away from him. So when the JWT board balked at his initial offer, he upped the stakes to £315 million 'conditional upon JWT's willingness to execute a definite merger agreement'.

Johnston responded that the board would consider the new proposal, although they still hadn't reacted to the initial bid.

It looked to outsiders as if JWT was stalling for time.

Talk on the street was of a possible management buy-out.

Sorrell turned up the heat by reminding Johnston, 'Under these circumstances, we are confident that the outside directors of your board, with independent advisers, will recognise the special responsibility placed on them in making a fair and thorough evaluation of our proposal.'

His point was obvious. He was telling Johnston, here is someone willing to pay real money for your shares, no funny paper, don't screw it up or your outside directors will have your head for it!

A week passed and more rumours circulated, including one that had JWT sharing information with a possible white knight that they had not shared with WPP. Sorrell cried foul. JWT said they would show him what he wanted to see as long as he signed an agreement of confidentiality which contained, among other restrictive clauses, one which would prohibit WPP for two years from buying JWT shares unless the JWT board agreed.

Fighting back, Sorrell claimed this unfairly hampered his bid.

Johnston now agreed to waive the two-year 'standstill' clause if Sorrell agreed not to purchase JWT shares over the next two years except as part of an 'any and all' cash offer for at least $50.50 per share – which translated to the £315 million bid. Johnston also wanted Sorrell to commit himself to certain deadline dates.

Not one to fool around like that, Sorrell marched Johnston into court to force a decision. He accused the JWT board of 'improperly' preferring a management-led group over rival bidders by providing them with access to exclusive information. If Johnston and his pals were going to bid for the company, Sorrell wanted them to do it right now, giving him a chance to see their offer and better it.

Before the month was out, it looked as if a new player might come into the game. And the rumour there was that this new player – not named – favoured a break-up of JWT. Sorrell raised the price of the game again, and at £351 million, the JWT board had no option but to give in.

Ironically, a few months later, while going through JWT's books, Sorrell discovered the company owned a building in Tokyo. The 1985 value had been written in at £30 million. He had it reassessed and found it to be worth nearly seven times as much. Had the JWT board been on the ball, they could have funded their defense against Sorrell and stayed independent with that one property.

If his bid for JWT was audacious, there's no word left in the language for Sorrell's next major move, except 'chutzpah'.

Leo Rosten, in *The Joys of Yiddish* defines it as a noun meaning, 'Gall, brazen nerve, effrontery, incredible guts, presumption plus arrogance such as no other, and no other language, can do justice to.'

'Chutzpah' is a man on a bread line asking for toast. It's a waiter who when asked, 'What time is it, please,' answers, 'Sorry, sir, not my table.' It's a New Yorker who, when asked by a Japanese tourist, 'How can I find the Statue of Liberty,' answers, 'You didn't need directions to find Pearl Harbor.'

'Chutzpah' is Martin Sorrell now bidding for the Ogilvy Group.

Throughout 1988 he had his eye on Ogilvy and Mather, the brainchild of Scots-born David Ogilvy. Author of *Confessions of an Advertising Man* – required reading in most university-level advertising and marketing courses – the grand old man of American advertising was semi-retired, living in a pink château in France. But the company bore his name and his ego has always been such that where his name is involved, so is he.

Sorrell approached the take-over with considerable stalking skills. He had reason to believe the company was in trouble. At least there were rumours of boardroom rifts. Profits were down and the overall finances were less than brilliant. For much of 1988 he dealt directly with Ogilvy's chairman Ken Roman, proposing joint ventures, while all the time quietly building a stake. In April 1989, feeling the time was right, Sorrell simply wrote a personal letter to Roman explaining that he was prepared to offer $45 a share for the entire group.

Roman's response was vitriolic.

The best defence is a strong offence, so he took the offensive. He turned down Sorrell's bid and then brought the battle to London. Roman, now joined by Ogilvy, launched an attack on Sorrell and WPP.

Although hardly pleased about being called 'an odious little jerk', Sorrell stood his ground.

Along Wall Street, Ogilvy shares started moving in hopes of a counter-bid. Leveraged buy-out specialists started circling overhead. Roman and Ogilvy were clearly worried.

Then Sorrell raised his bid to $50.

Roman and Ogilvy managed to get him up to $54.

Sorrell and Ogilvy met for dinner.

By the time dessert was cleared away, Sorrell was out of pocket £525 million. But he'd just won World War III.

He'd also charmed David Ogilvy.

The man who once expounded, 'The majority of businessmen are incapable of original thought because they are unable to escape from the tyranny of reason,' had new-found respect for 'the odious little jerk'. In fact, he was a big enough man to admit, 'The advertising business is stuffed with terribly dumb, ordinary people. And to meet someone who's neither dumb nor ordinary and is much better than I am in almost every way is very exciting.'

Sorrel responded by naming David Ogilvy Chairman of WPP.

Although the WPP headquarters staff is only 60–5 people in three offices – London, New York and Hong Kong – the entire group is now 22,000 people in 55 countries and 650 offices.

Not surprisingly, Sorrell only gets to see the tip of the iceberg.

'There are hundreds of thousands of things that go on that I don't know about. It's probably lucky that I don't. I only hear what most people want me to hear instead of some of the things I probably should know about.'

But then dealing with everything on every level is not what his job is all about.

'Our role here is, in a sense, to deal with bad news. Holding companies don't create anything, they're basically cost centres. Our role is to manage problems. When people come to me and say, there's good news and bad news, I always say, give me the bad news. No one has to manage good news. It's the bad news and the problems that we have to deal with.'

He is therefore, both in spirit and out of necessity, very hands-off.

'Hands-off on the professional side but hands-on when it comes to the financial side. I'd like to believe we run our business in the same way as Hanson or BTR. We agree a plan or a budget and people have a certain flexibility within that budget.'

There's no doubt that Sorrell is strictly a financial manager and not an advertising man. As someone once noted about him, he's spent so many years working for ad agencies but has never written a single piece of copy.

But then he helped turn Saatchi into the world's largest advertising agency group and as long as he was there they propospered. Within a few years of his leaving, they found themselves in deep trouble. It might just be coincidence. It might not. If nothing else, it's ironic that the man who helped the Saatchi brothers become number one in the world is now wearing their crown.

Sorrell himself refuses to get involved in this kind of pettiness.

'That's a media event and really has no significance in the business. It doesn't matter who's the largest.'

The question remains, however, where did Saatchi go wrong and where is Sorrell going right?

'First of all, the jury is still out on both of those. I don't know where they went wrong because I'm not there and haven't been for some time. But you've got to put Saatchi and Saatchi into some perspective. They've been around for 20 years, they've had one bad year and everybody's written them off. On the other hand, we've been around for five years, and so far so good. If I'm sitting here in 15 years' time and can say that I've only had one bad year, I'd be a very happy chap. I don't think anyone should underestimate what they've done. Whether you think size is important or not, it is quite interesting an achievement to start in 1970 with nothing and 16 years later be the largest advertising business in the world.'

Given the structure of WPP's companies, the people who are responsible for the professional development of the companies run those businesses. Sorrell agrees where he wants to get to from a financial point of view, agrees financial strategy and tactics and budgets. The managers then run the companies. Sorrell keeps all mergers and acquisitions for himself. He also stimulates companies to work closely together, as closely as they can. And that's one area he's looking at very closely because he thinks parts of his business can work together for clients in a more productive, more cost-effective way. But essentially, that's his job. It's a financial view. He's here to do the monitoring.

'We encourage parts of our business to compete. They are competing brands. Ogilvy and Thompson, for example. It's not dissimilar to other businesses, say Procter and Gamble or

Unilever. We have brands. WPP is a financial brand, those are marketing brands. But each of the brands we have, whether it be advertising or marketing research or public relations, has a unique character, a unique capability and a unique outlook. They're different. At the same time, they have certain similarities. Now, it is interesting that twice in the past ten years Ogilvy and Thompson had discussions to merge their businesses. I happen to think that's a very difficult thing to do in our industry and not in our interests. Why go and pay a considerable sum of money for brands like Ogilvy and Thompson and then go and destroy them both by merging the two. Others have done that. There have been major industry mergers. There are then personality conflicts to deal with and client conflicts to deal with and it's a nightmare.'

That's what his thinking was with Carl Byoir and Hill and Knowlton. Both well known public relations firms, Carl Byoir had been acquired by Hill and Knowlton long before WPP came along. Sorrell felt it was important to bring Carl Byoir back to life as a competitor, otherwise, what's the point, why pay a premium for an agency like Carl Byoir and then not take advantage of the brand?

With James Gulliver, Sorrell got to see a methodical approach towards acquisitions.

'Let's say he wanted to acquire a food company. We'd go over to County Bank, sit down and go through all the research files to build a long list of companies that might be for sale. We'd have five criteria and map them out. We'd hone that list of 500 down to 50. Then we'd meet with Gulliver and the others and hone it down further to four or five.'

With the Saatchis the style was very different.

'We'd begin by defining the universe and say five of us would each take 100 companies that weren't necessarily for sale and meet each week to report on our progress. It was a little like Weight Watchers in that if you didn't have anything to say each week, everyone looked askance at you. But in a way, there was a lot of method to Maurice Saatchi's madness.

When you think about it for a minute, you shouldn't be looking for a company where somebody has already said they want to sell it. When you ring someone up and they say, sure I'd be glad to sell, you've got to be worried, you have to think there must be something wrong with it. A lot of the enjoyment is in the chase. What's the expression about it being much more pleasurable to travel than to arrive? So Maurice's method was good because you built a relationship with the company you were looking to buy. And all of the best things I've been involved with have taken time. The acquisition of Dorland's took four or five years. The acquisition of Comptons took seven years.'

Sorrell's own style developed as a variation of the two, although his deals have been different in that he's acquired major listed companies, more often than not in hostile situations. 'But if you looked into the details, they all took some time.'

One of the problems with hostile bids is that they can get very nasty. It means you need a thick skin to play the game.

'You have to accept that. The issue really is, however, hostile to who? In our case, they certainly haven't been hostile to the clients or to the people who run the business. At least they haven't been hostile towards most of the people who run the business. And they've certainly not been hostile to the shareholders. The hostility is usually aimed, or at least winds up being directed, at one or two people. That's the issue. So when people describe actions as being hostile, I always say you have to examine carefully who the hostility is aimed at.'

Anyway, he insists, 'We're in the marketing services business. We're not in the deals business.'

Except that he is very acqusitive.

The difference between WPP and, say, Hanson, he says, is that there are no brick companies in his future.

'We are totally focused on marketing and will continue to be.'

Anyway, according to Sorrell, buying isn't the trick, it's managing.

'That's the most difficult. One of James Gulliver's greatest strengths as an entrepreneur was that he could manage the businesses he bought. He started Argyll from nothing in 1977 and it's now a £2 billion company.'

At the same time, men like James Hanson always warn, never get involved with people businesses. Hanson doesn't like the idea of paying for a business when the assets – people – can get up and walk out. So he sticks to buying things like brick kilns. Sorrell, on the other hand, appears to be buying people businesses. But he doesn't see it the same way that James Hanson does.

'I would argue that advertising is not as dependent on specific people as you might imagine. Now, all businesses are of course dependent on people. But J. W. Thompson has been in business 125 years. Hill and Knowlton has been in business 63 years. Ogilvy and Mather has been in business 42 years. We employ, in each of those agencies, thousands of people. Those relationships are not critically dependent on one person, either at the client level or at the agency level. The creative product is most important. But you're not talking about one or two people. You're talking about big teams of people. Relationships that Thompson has with Ford or Unilever or Nestlé or Kodak or Kraft or General Foods don't depend on one or two people. Yes, there are people who are more important and there are people who are less important. But those relationships are very broadly based, sophisticated and quite complex.'

And anyway, the only way to expand is by going into the market and buying them.

'If your objective is to build the major multinational marketing services business, and you start with a small wire-basket company, you have no alternative but to acquire. Unless you're willing to grow business from scratch which is impossible given the rapidity with which the market is changing.'

In some ways, men who build companies the way he does – men like James Hanson and Gordon White and Tiny Rowland and Gerry Ronson – seem to have a sort of collector's mentality. It could be old master paintings or art deco sculpture. In this case it's companies. Although Sorrell will only concede that may be the case with some of the others, not necessarily with him.

'We have a strategy and we're trying to execute and implement that strategy. We believe there are six critical areas in our business. One is strategic, the rest are tactical. And there are some linkages between parts of the business which will increasingly become more important and we're trying to implement that strategy.'

The six are: strategic marketing services; media advertising; public relations; market research; non-media avertising which is incentive and motivational promotions, sales promotions, audio-visual, that sort of thing; and then an area he calls specialist communications, like direct advertising, recruitment advertising and real-estate advertising.

'They're fixed but they're not written in stone because the moment you write something in stone, that's when the trouble starts.'

Martin Sorrell is a self-effacing man of 5′ 5½″ with glasses and a good honest laugh who runs a worldwide business from a tiny office in the middle of Mayfair.

He's the kind of guy who openly claims to be boring while not inwardly looking for everyone to say, no you're not.

As it happens, he isn't.

He is, however, decidedly unflashy.

He's hardly the sort of guy you'd expect to find in the world of media and advertising. He could easily blend into the background at a medium-sized firm of accountants. But that doesn't take away the fact that he's pleasant. It just means he drives an ordinary car and wears quiet ties.

Most of his office is taken up with his desk and a table covered in books that probably gets cleared off when he holds a conference – or maybe it doesn't – and lots of personal things scattered around like a rugby ball and family photos, especially one of his dad.

He's married to a schoolteacher and they have three teenaged boys. Family life is terribly important to him, which means that no matter where in the world he finds himself during the week, he always tries to get home on weekends.

But then travelling is also an important part of his life.

He doesn't necessarily enjoy it, but has to do a lot of it. The joint acquisitions of Thompson and Ogilvy made WPP a force to reckon with in many parts of the world, especially Japan, where he finds doing business exceptionally difficult.

'We have three companies in Japan. We have the Thompson agency which is the largest foreign-owned agency. We have a research business and we have a public relations business. Thompson has been doing well. It's been there for over 30 years. And we were really lucky because we came along after the initial investment was made. Ogilvy on the other hand had tried twice in Japan and not been very successful. So we're trying for a third time.'

He personally finds the Japanese welcoming and courteous and always keen. At times he even finds them anxious to explain their views. It's just so difficult transcending those cultural differences.

'I'm sure it's exactly the same in reverse for them. They find it exceptionally difficult the other way. That's why I think in our business, there will be more and more strategic alliances between Japanese agencies and agencies outside. Whereas years ago, a Japanese agency might have been able to develop outside Japan from scratch, now, because of the changes that are taking place, not only in the media but also in the Japanese economy, there will be greater pressure on them to move outside. They're already showing signs of becoming more aggressive.'

That may or may not be partially a reaction to the growing hostilities that the business world, especially in the States, is showing towards Japan.'

He mentions a book – 'I can never remember the name of it' – written sometime around 1908 by an Englishman warning about the perils of American companies buying British companies. Then, he says, there was Jean-Jacques Servan-Schreiber in France in the '60s complaining about what the Americans were going to do to the Europeans.

'Nothing changes. It's been going on like that for ever. You always get that about the foreign acquirer. So the foreign acquirer is at a disadvantage. But if you indulge in cross-border acquisitions, which is what we've done, that goes with the territory. It's totally unrealistic to believe you will be welcomed with open arms or be more attractive than a domestic buyer. The irony of that is, I think, that foreign buyers, particularly in our business, tend to be more hands-off. Foreign buyers are probably more likely to take the view that good local management knows the business and the local problems better than they do.'

Compounding the difficulties of running a global business is the speed with which business moves today.

'There's an overload of information in the world today and the critical thing is to determine which parts of it are important. Telephones, television, computers, faxes, even faxes in the car. Just look at the five quality newspapers delivered to your front door every Sunday morning. There is so much information coming at you all the time. The pace is quite incredible and I think that's the single biggest problem with doing business today. Maybe it's just unique to our particular situation because we're in a worldwide business. But so much depends on the quantity of information received, how you absorb it and what you do about it.'

On top of that, he finds the advertising business, in particular, disproportionately covered by the media.

'I don't know of any reason why it should be. It's quite extraordinary. I wonder if the newsapers think that, by covering the advertising industry, agencies are likely to place more advertising with the media. But there are advertising and media pages in the quality newspapers. In the *Wall Street Journal* it's covered every day. There's no logic in it. Believe me. This is a tiny industry and we get a lot of coverage. It's bizarre.'

So there he sits in his tiny Mayfair office, stockinged feet on the table, his chair tipped back, taking the general view of his company, making long-term decisions that only reach two years down the road.

But in an organisation so huge, can his ideas even filter down to the troops?

He admits, 'Sometimes they can, sometimes they can't. It's sometimes very frustrating. Very rarely do you have managers who don't know what they're doing. If they don't, they shouldn't be there. The problems inside our organization occur between the sharp end and the centre. That's where all the overhead is, where all the layers get built up, that's where the bureaucracy is. That's one of the things managers are paid to deal with.'

So there he sits in his tiny Mayfair office which, frankly, is too small a room for a mogul.

And he laughs, 'I must be a micro-mogul.'

21

Tony O'Reilly

Transcript of a telephone conversation between London and Hong Kong:

'You're a pretty fascinating man.'

'I can maintain that disguise at this distance.'

'Come on, both Robert Sangster and Michael Smurfit say so. That's two out of two.'

'Not since the Stalin–Hitler pact, if they agreed to that.'

'But you are a modern-day Irish hero.'

'Trust me, looks can be deceiving.'

Pittsburgh, Pennyslvania. 1873.

Three quarters of the way through the nineteenth century, most Americans ate nothing more adventurous than meat – smoked, dried or salted – bread, potatoes and the occasional plateful of root vegetables. Sometimes, usually in winter, there might also be cucumbers and pickles. But there was never salad, not even in summer. In those days, real men never ate salad.

Seriously, it was considered unmanly.

Eating habits were not very adventurous for several reasons. Commercial tinning and canning was a relatively new art form. Along with mass-market preserving came chemicals, which brought with them all sorts of new and strange digestive maladies. Then too, rail and communications networks, which would eventually link every corner of the United States, were still in their infancy. Food was not easily moved from region to region. Grapefruit was hardly known outside Florida. Tomatoes were thought of as an exotic fruit from Mexico called 'love apples'. And oranges were a rare treat, especially in the north.

Especially in the small towns of western Pennsylvania where 12-year-old Henry John Heinz first started peddling produce from the family garden in 1856.

Before long, working his way up from a pushcart to a horse and wagon, he had four acres of land and was making three weekly trips to Pittsburgh, six miles down the Allegheny River.

Sometime around 1869, at the age of 25, he joined forces with his friend L. C. Noble and their speciality was horseradish.

In those days horseradish was consumed in great quantities, not only because it helped to sharpen the appetite and give some flavour to frequently tasteless food, but also because it was said to possess wonderful medicinal qualities. It was supposedly useful for catarrh and the grippe. Even today experts insist that the very best horseradish should smell strong enough to drain your sinuses.

While learning everything anyone ever wanted to know about horseradish, Heinz and Noble discovered that it kept best if they grated it – most horseradish in those days was heavily laced with adulterants – then added vingar and put it in clear bottles.

Unfortunately grating it made their eyes water.

And anyway, their customers were used to buying horseradish in green bottles.

To better market their horseradish, they guaranteed it was the whitest variety, 100% void of leaves, wood fibre and turnip filter.

Makes you wonder just what was in the other stuff.

It took some time and a lot of determintion but Heinz and Noble Horseradish in clear bottles finally began to sell.

Almost as soon as it did, Heinz realized he'd stumbled on to a pair of very important facts of life. The first was, that a pure article of superior quality will indeed find a ready market through its intrinsic value if properly packaged and promoted. And second, housewives were willing to allow someone else to take over a share of their kitchen operations, such as bottling and preserving food.

Based on nothing more than that, Heinz and Noble were, by 1873, one of the country's leading producers of condiments. They had 100 acres of farmland along the Allegheny – 30 acres set aside just for horseradish – and a vinegar factory in St Louis. They turned out 3000 barrels of sauerkraut, 15,000 barrels of pickles and 50,000 barrels of vinegar. They were also pickling 600 acres of cucumbers.

Then they went broke.

Twickenham, England. 1970.

Anthony John Francis O'Reilly never intended on playing that day.

In fact, he hadn't appeared in an international since 1963 but less than 36 hours before the England–Ireland kick-off, W. J. Brown was declared unfit and the selectors needed someone quick.

He arrived for the match in a chauffeur-driven Rolls Royce.

His first appearance at Twickenham had been in 1956. That day he arrived on a bus. It was an icy afternoon and not one he remembers with particular fondness because he and his mates suffered a 20–0 defeat.

They were, as one critic wrote, 'Lucky to get nil'.

Fourteen years later he was back, but not merely as a star player, he'd also penned the introduction to the official match programme.

No other player in the British Isles can claim the distinction of introducing and playing in the same match.

'There they are,' he wrote, 'the entire staff, male and female of the National Health Service, the British Army from Private Rafferty to Montgomery, bean barons, hole diggers, McAlpine Fusiliers, doormen, doctors and lawyers – Irish to the core, united by the only thing that can unite all Irishmen – which is Englishmen.'

Introducing and playing in the same match was merely the last of a long string of records. In a career that now spanned 15 years, he was capped ten times as a British Lion, having played on the wing nine times and as centre once. This was his 29th cap for Ireland. He still holds the British Isles record as the most capped player on the wing. In ten international appearances between 1955–9 he still holds the record for most tries with six. In 1959, during the British Lions overseas tour he made 17 appearances against New Zealand sides and scored 16 tries. That record still stands too.

He was without any doubt one of the most glamorous stars of his era. His stride and speed made him an idol to a generation of young hopefuls. His flaming red hair, long white legs and short shorts raced the hearts of a generation of teenage girls. And some people who remember him say that he was the best wing three-quarter who ever played the game.

But now, facing England at the age of 34, the glory days were behind him.

One newspaper even previewed the game with the headline, 'Heinz Means Haz Beanz'.

The final score was England 9, Ireland 3.

The only memorable moment for O'Reilly came when he did what he'd spent most of his rugby career trying not to do – he fell on top of the ball – and a foot crashed into the side of his head.

Everything went black.

He lay on the ground unconscious for about 30 seconds. Then, slowly, the roar of the crowd came back into his ears.

He stared at the dirt trying to shake the cobwebs out of his brain, while from underneath the noise came one loud, clear Irish voice shouting, 'And kick his bloody chauffeur while you're at it'.

Wall Street. 18 September, 1873.

At exactly 12.15 p.m. the stock market crashed.

Trading was halted on the New York Stock Exchange as 37 banks and brokerage houses sank.

Over the next few days the rippling effect closed other banks across the country and completely shut down the building of several railroads. Within three months more than 5000 businesses had failed.

Heinz was one of them.

Banks had tightened their grip on credit. Heinz and Noble got caught in the squeeze. They had enough to pay for salaries and for rent and had even budgeted for an average autumn cucumber crop. Ironically, just then, a bumber crop came in. They were committed to take it all and their cash flow was shot to hell. Heinz endorsed his own life insurance as collateral on a loan, borrowed from friends and even mortgaged his home. And still the banks squeezed him.

By December 1875 there was nothing left.

Heinz and Noble filed for bankruptcy. Heinz himself personally lost everything. His house. His furniture. His self-esteem. He was reduced to begging for credit from three local grocers so that he could feed his family.

And they all turned him down.

Now, if there is one thing that people who face financial ruin seem to have in common, it's that sooner or later they discover who their real friends are. In Heinz's case, it was a man named Jacob Covode. He staked Heinz with a $3000 loan. H. J. put the company in the name of his brother John and cousin Frederick, listed himself as just another employee and went back into business.

And within a year, he was nearly broke again.

It wasn't until 1879 that the new company started to show a small profit. By then Heinz had added ketchup to the line, along with chilli sauce, mincemeat, mustard, pickled cauliflower, pickled onions, sweet pickles – he was the first to ever market those – and baked beans with tomato sauce.

Six years later he was released from bankruptcy having paid off his old debts. The following year he sailed to Europe. On 16 June 1886, as recorded in his diary, he put on his best clothes, packed seven varieties of his finest and newest goods in a Gladstone bag, left his rooms on Great Russell Street, marched down Piccadilly and went straight through the front door at Fortnum and Mason.

No tradesmen's entrance for him.

He surveyed the main hall, found a clerk and with good old-fashioned American moxie announced that he was there to see the Head of Grocery Purchasing. When a slightly bemused gentleman eventually appeared, Heinz introduced himself as 'a food merchant from Pittsburgh, in the United States of America'. He then gave his spiel and showed his wares. The British gentleman agreed to taste the horseradish, the chilli sauce and the ketchup. He then announced, 'I think, Mr Heinz, we will take them all.'

Pub lunches would never be the same again.

Two years later the company name was changed to H. J. Heinz.

Ninety-nine years after that, Anthony John Francis O'Reilly succeeded Henry J. Heinz II as chairman, the first and only person outside the Heinz family ever to hold that job.

He was born in Dublin in 1936. His father was a chief customs inspector. Educated by Jesuits at Belvedere College, he went from there to University College, Dublin where he won an Honours degree in civil law. He then earned a PhD. in agricultural marketing from the University of Bradford in England.

Tony O'Reilly has always been, to say the least, an ambitious man.

'You start with the negative. You're always ambitious to not fail. You work off that low base. I think football, obviously as a general template, was good for me. In so far as it taught me interdependency with others, collegiality, the spirit of teamwork that is essential in business. You can't get to be a significant business success unless you can rely on others, their integrity, their innovativeness, their complementary skills, etc. So football was extremely good from that point of view. But I was a pretty keen student and I sat my solicitor's exams in '57–8 and got first place in part one and third place in part two of the finals. I had a pretty decent fall-back position and could have practised as a lawyer if I'd wanted to, or taught. But I was attracted to the greater world of commerce and went off as a management trainee and a management consultancy trainee and then I moved into business.'

His first job came in 1960. The president of the English Rugby Football union rang him one day to say that he'd just met a man from an engineering company in Belfast who was looking for a managing director, and was O'Reilly interested? As a matter of fact, O'Reilly was interested enough to get in touch with that man, discover he was from Cork and not Belfast, that it was in agricultural supplies, not engineering and that the post was assistant to the chairman, not MD.

He was also interested enough to accept the job.

But his great break in the world of business came in 1962.

'At the age of 25 I was offered the position of Chief Executive of the newly formed Irish Dairy Board. I was a very young man with a completely uncharted brief which was to provide for the exportation of products from Ireland which were burgeoning at that stage. In July of '62 I took a huge gamble and launched Kerrygold.'

That became a major world brand and is today the global symbol of all Irish dairy products. O'Reilly's career was catapulted by the unbelievable success of Kerrygold. It picked up speed and reached its own momentum. And as these things so often do, the faster he moved up the ladder, the shorter he stayed in each job.

Four years at the Irish Dairy Board led to three as MD of the Irish Sugar Company and their subsidiary Erin Foods. He was, by the way, paid the then unheard of salary of £12,500. After signing a distribution agreement betwen Erin and Heinz, he was brought to England by Heinz UK where he spent two years as MD. The father of six, including triplets, he was then shipped to Heinz headquarters in Pittsburgh where he spent one year as Senior Vice-President for North America and the Pacific and one year as Executive Vice-President and Chief Operating Officer.

In 1973 he was named President.

Today, as Chairman and Chief Executive, his salary is £1.5 million, not counting stock options.

'I've been in the States over 20 years now. It's an easy place to live for an Irishman. No culture shock at all. There's been such a trail blazed on every level by the Irish in America, commercial, political and theological, that it's almost like going home. We have no difficulty at all. Something like 24% of the people in America quite proudly proclaim their Irish association, if not necessarily their Irish heritage.'

Coincidentally, O'Reilly the athlete arrived in Pittsburgh at the start of what has come to be known as 'the Golden Era of the Steelers'. The American football club there ruled the game for most of the '70s, won their divisional championships in 1972 and 1974, and the Super Bowl in 1975, 1979 and 1980.

Not surprisingly, there sat Tony O'Reilly at Three Rivers Stadium, longing to be on the field.

'I would have loved to have played American football. The year I came back from New Zealand after breaking all the try-scoring records, my friend Pete Dawkins won the Heisman Trophy as the best college football player in America. He played half-back for Army. Well, he came to Oxford and we had this great debate about the relevant merits of his game and mine. He was a pretty good wing three-quarter for Oxford while I could only dream about playing half-back for Army. I never got to do it but I would have loved it.'

Nicely enough, much of his knowledge of the game came through his friendship with the owners of the Pittsburgh Steelers, the Rooney family.

'I was very close to the Rooneys who are quintessentially Irish. So I had a very warm introduction to the game and have always been fascinated by it. American football is athletic chess. It has a drama and a theatre about it that our game doesn't. When they signal the two-minute warning, I used to think, only two minutes go? But it takes an hour to play those two minutes. I got to Pittsburgh right at the start of the Steelers' great run. So it was the perfect time to be there.'

During much of those same years the Pittsburgh Pirates baseball team was also hot. They won six divisional championships between 1970–9, two league championships and two

World Series. But, it seems, there wasn't much anybody could do to turn O'Reilly into a fully fledged baseball fan.

'Yes, the Pirates won the year I arrived but I still didn't get into baseball. Nor have I to this day. I'm totally bored by it during the year. Although I must say that when it gets to the World Series I'm riveted by it. It's curious. I'm a one-week-a-year baseball fan. But American football, well, I'll take it Monday night and Thursday night and all-day Sunday.'

As impressive as the Steeler/Pirate domination of American sports was throughout the '70s, so too was the O'Reilly record at Heinz.

In 1972 the company was turning over just about $1 billion. Today that figure is multiplied by six. When he became Chief Executive Officer in 1979, the company was valued in the market at $908 million. Today, with approximately the same number of shares on the market, the company is worth something closer to $9 billion.

'It means that for every dollar you put into Heinz shares in 1979, you'd have ten today. If you'd reinvested your dividends the rate would work out to be 1336%, or a compound figure of 31% per year.'

That, he hastens to add, is not only the best success story in the food industry today but probably one of the top five American success stories of the past 15 years.

'Certainly we're the only company, according to Valueline' – a well respected analytic forecasting group – 'that has consistently improved its margin every year since 1977. That takes into consideration all industries. They report on 4000 companies and we're the only one to do it.'

The secret of that success is, he insists, fairly simple.

'I think it all gets down to sticking to our knitting. We never lost faith in the food industry which is a fairly slow growth area. A lot of food companies went into clothing and toys. Some went into restaurant feeding, which is really a retail business, and only one or two of them did well in those. We stayed very close to the businesses we were in.'

He kept Heinz moving forward at a reasonable pace but really scored big with a business called Weight Watchers.

There's no denying that all America loves a gimmick. And in the late '70s, one of those gimmicks was gourmet frozen dinners. Considered an absolute contradiction in terms by most Frenchmen, Americans usually prefer simplicity to over-styling. What used to be known as 'TV Dinners' – an entire three-course meal in a small aluminium tray that you popped into your oven for exactly 12 minutes and which somehow managed to come out even more bland than your average airline fare – went up-market. Microwave technology meant foods could be better prepared and actually taste like something. The gourmet-style TV dinner eventually became the low-cal slimmers gourmet TV dinner. Now offering the finest gourmet recipes, with absolutely no calories and cooked in your microwave in less than 30 seconds – it had all the gimmicks rolled into one.

And America went nuts!

To be perfectly fair, many of these low-cal, frozen gourmet diet meals happen to be pretty good. They're convenient and, more often than not, tasty. But the best thing about them is that they represent, to someone like O'Reilly, a huge market. He bought Weight Watchers for Heinz in 1978 because he realized that this was the future. The added bonus was that Weight Watchers – an international organization modelled along the lines of Alcoholics Anonymous to get people to lose weight – was a well respected, highly recognizable brand name. But by the mid-1980s the competition had heated up and Stouffer Foods' Lean Cuisine was the market leader, outselling Weight Watchers three to one.

O'Reilly took that as a personal defeat and aimed to get back on top.

After doubling the number of entrées, he went into other areas, such as low-cal desserts, breakfasts and snacks. He expanded the Weight Watchers programmes, knowing that people who attend those classes accounted for 30% of his low-cal sales. He challenged Lean Cuisine head-on, and from the middle of 1988 until the end of 1989 launched no less than 100 new products in the Weight Watchers line.

He scraped back from a 7% market share to just under 17%, rivalling Lean Cuisine for first place.

'We hit a home run with Weight Watchers. That's been the great engine of growth. We were lucky to identify as early as '78–79 that calory-counting, nutrition, body-watching and diet were going to be the frontiers of success for the food industry in the next two decades and it so proved.'

At the same time, O'Reilly has been doing a pretty thorough house-cleaning at Heinz, trying to get it into shape for the '90s. He saw some of his big brands having their market share eroded. Ore-Ida frozen French fries – chips to the British – was losing ground. So was Nine Lives Pet Food.

He'd already gone the cost-cutting route. By underpaying senior executive salaries, he incentivized his management team with huge bonuses based on performance. He instituted the 'Low Cost Operator' programme, austerity measures that reaped initial rewards. But before long his own multi-million-dollar salary got in the way of the LCO programme, which was quickly nicknamed, 'Let's Compensate O'Reilly'.

Anyway, he believed, the cost-cutting exercises that had increased margins in the '80s simply weren't going to work in the '90s. To save money in the past, some factories had sped up production to the detriment of product quality. The time had come for a complete cultural change. He wanted to slow things down again and emphasize quality.

'Only 30% of our total sales are under the Heinz name. The remaining 70% of our brand names are very well known in their own right and in their own respective countries but not helped in any way by their association with Heinz. Now, if you ask, does it help to have a major brand name, the answer is, absolutely. One of the things that is distinctive about our company is that nearly 65% of our total sales are in number-one brand categories throughout the world. Wherever we are, we're not just the number-two or -three brand, we're the world leader. But because we're the brand leader, we're the one that is constantly under attack. We're the one to beat. Staying in first place means a lot of painstaking, piece by piece, day by day, attention to detail.'

One of the things O'Reilly had been so good at in the beginning was squeezing mature markets and actually making them more profitable. In the end, ketchup is ketchup – even if you spell it catsup – and Heinz has always had a major share in the world's ketchup business. Changing the product would be disastrous – ask the Coca-Cola people what happened when they tampered with perfection – so in order to expand in the ketchup market, you've got to come up with better advertising, or better still, great packaging.

That's what Heinz did, and at one point they managed to get their market share up from 25% to a whopping 54%.

Now O'Reilly wanted to repeat those kinds of successes.

His hired consultants used the phrase 'Total Quality Management'.

Thanks to TQM – as they say in Pittsburgh – the production line became the centre of attention. They wanted to get reject rates down, to increase staff for better production ratios, to better train factory workers.

'The thing I like about TQM is that it's more Socratic than surgical.'

He emphasized some very specific areas in his changing of the company's culture. He theorized that costs must continually be looked at in an effort to keep them down or, better still, cut them. At the same time, quality must be played up. Waste must be removed from the system and here he has consolidated certain services among his subsidiaries such as market research.

'Only one Bible is called for in this case.'

Next he wanted to highlight service, especially with Weight Watchers. When people come to a Weight Watchers class, he discovered, cost is not as much a factor as satisfaction. People want to lose weight and if it costs them a little more to do that, then okay.

'That's an enormous shift for us.'

Then there is something he labels 'the bile factor'.

It stems from the feeling that management wants the workers to cut costs while not necessarily intending to cut their own costs. It breeds hostilities and creates a 'them and us' attitude that is so very detrimental. He adds that by constantly firing workers to cut costs, managers breed insecurity among the work-force and that has the same effect.

The answer then, is creating small teams – notice the obvious parallel to rugby – which not only elevates the dignity of the worker but adds to his feeling of being an invaluable part of the process. It builds security.

Finally there is the future.

And here he likes to cite H. J. Heinz himself.

O'Reilly says the future has go to be about 'doing common things, uncommonly well.'

It's not who you know that counts.

It's how you can charm who you know.

And when you talk about charm, Anthony John Francis O'Reilly is in a class of his own. He counts among his friends the Bushes, the Reagans, the Kissingers, the Giscard d'Estaings, the Thatchers and the Mugabes – although in this particular case that's not Mr and Mrs, that's Robert and his mum.

In 1982 he went to Zimbabwe, hoping to get Robert Mugabe's blessings to allow Heinz to set up their first factory in that part of Africa. O'Reilly had been there in 1955, to play rugby, and was in those days greeted as a conquering hero.

This time around, Marxist Mugabe greeted him as a capitalist exploiter of the working classes.

The welcome was, needless to say, distinctly chilly.

'Initially it looked like curtains. Mugabe didn't even want to discuss the project.'

Then O'Reilly played his charm card.

He supposedly began by saying, 'We're both students of Marx. You of Karl and me of Groucho.'

When that didn't exactly win the day, he reminded Mugabe that they had a wonderful mutual friend, someone who had been important to both of them in their youth. It was a black

Jesuit priest from Mallow who'd taught Mugabe in his mission school and O'Reilly back in Ireland.

'The minute I mentioned that Jesuit he burst into smiles and called for his mother, a large lady, who took things completely in charge. She acted as intermediary in the bargaining and everything went beautifully.'

Who said Kerrygold wouldn't melt in his mouth!

Tony O'Reilly is a dual-nationality package.

There is the American-based businessman who plays tennis with George Bush and the Irish-born businessman who doesn't plan on staying at Heinz for ever.

He has been quoted as saying that he'll leave in five years and that if anyone ever asked him he wouldn't say no to a US ambassadorship or, maybe even, a cabinet post. This from the same man who turned down Jack Lynch in 1968 when the Irish PM offered him the Ministry of Agriculture. He wasn't ready for it then, he is now. Anyway, he says, if nothing else, maybe in a post like Ambassador to Japan he could help America with its trade deficit.

'I'd be ruthless with the Japanese. They can be subtle and devious and self-serving, but they do understand power.'

In case you haven't yet guessed, O'Reilly is a supreme opportunist, but very much in the nicest sense of the word.

'I'm comfortable with my Irishness and very proud of it. I see myself as a manager in the world of Heinz. But in Ireland I see myself as an innovator, a creator and a pacifier.'

He drops some Gaelic into his speech every now and then – 'just to confuse the enemy' – and is the founder of several charities, all aimed in some way at helping Ireland, the most notable of which is the American Ireland Fund, a US-based organization he started in 1976 to help problems on both sides of the Irish border.

He is chairman of Atlantic Resources, a Dublin-based oil exploration company that has not necessarily done so well, and the Independent Newspaper Group, which has.

'I'm the controlling shareholder of Independent Newspapers,

which in Ireland is a $250-million business. If you add in Australia it's a $400-million business. We're the fourth-largest newspaper group in Australia. We bought all of Rupert Murdoch's provincial press. But I have nothing to do with the day-to-day running of it. Strategically I'm a consultant on what it does. Editorially I wouldn't see the product more than twice a month. Nor do I wish to interfere in it because to interfere in it would be to assume a level of responsibility I don't want to.'

God only knows, but even if he wanted to he probably wouldn't have the time. The list of affiliations that comes with his official biography is a full page long. His board appointments include the Harvard Business School, Bankers Trust Company, Georgetown University, the *Washington Post*, the Executive Council on Foreign Diplomats, the University of Pittsburgh and the Pittsburgh Opera. His chairmanships include the Grocery Manufacturers of America and the Food Industries International Trade Council. He is a council member of New York's Rockefeller University, a member of the Congressional Award Board and a member of the National Committee of the Whitney Museum of American Art.

Then he's a partner in a firm of solicitors in Dublin and a trustee of the Committee for Economic Development. On the side he runs a small business called Fitzwilton, with a few of his pals. He is also Chairman of this Irish version of Hanson PLC, a small holding company he formed back in the 1970s because he wanted to take an interest in Irish enterprise, O'Reilly used it to buy stakes in all sorts of companies, including textiles and fertilizers.

He has recently used it to take an interest in Waterford Wedgwood. He paired Fitzwilton with Morgan Stanley to form a new entity called Investco which then took a 29.9% stake for I£79 million. The idea behind the investment is that his management skills will be able to turn the company back into a world brand-name leader.

'Management is a curious thing. I won't be managing Waterford in the sense that I manage Heinz, which is the daily perusal of costs, margins, pricing strategy, advertising strategy plus the whole logistics and financial architecture of the company. No, I won't have that sort of input. But I will be interrogating, rather than managing, the marketing strategy and how we can make the concept of great brands of the world grow. You could argue that basically the way great brands of the world will grow is by tapping into the social insecurity of the newly rich. That's a bit pejorative but it's really why some things have been so highly successful in Asia. The Moët Chandon–Louis Vuitton strategy has been quite brilliant. So strategically I will have a lot to say about that. But I won't have anything to say on the day-to-day basis.'

O'Reilly has not always enjoyed the same popularity as a businessman in Ireland that he has in the United States. His high-flying lifestyle has begat what the Irish call begrudgery.

'Small countries don't like tall poppies,' he says.

Every now and then a little salt gets poured into the wounds. Some years ago the *Irish Independent* ran a huge story on O'Reilly – they called it 'A Man For All Continents' – complete with a photo-montage of him with everybody anybody would ever want to know.

Yet O'Reilly would be a hero in Ireland even if he didn't own a newspaper that helped promote the image. Stories abound about him, ranging from his playing days as a glamour boy of Irish rugby, to the time he was asked by Hollywood to play the lead in Ben Hur (Charlton Heston eventually got the part).

One of the better stories has him getting off the Heinz jet in Dublin and saying to the steward, just one briefcase, not all eight. The explanation later came, so they say, from a crew member who claimed that as O'Reilly was about to visit eight companies, he had eight attaché cases. 'It helps to keep things tidy.'

But then he knows he's a hero, even if he doesn't care to admit it, and being a hero isn't such a bad thing, because all countries need heroes.

A few years ago, as guest speaker at Michael Smurfit's annual Chairman's Dinner – probably the biggest business event on the domestic calendar in Ireland – O'Reilly's theme was just that – a nation needs its heroes.

'I said that heroes reflect the particular appetites and needs of the time. When the State was founded in 1920, the heroes were warrior politicians, of the breed of De Valéra, Michael Collins, W. T. Cosgrave, Liem, Kevin O'Higgins, Rory Brewer and people of that particular calibre. They were superseded in the early '30s, as the State grappled with the whole business of organizing and creating job opportunities and economic momentum, by the Mandarin civil servants, like Sean Leydon and Sean Lemass and J. J. McGilligus and J. C. B. McCartney and Jerry Dempsey and others. They became the stars of their society.'

Sean Lemass was the great sponsor of that, although O'Reilly notes that when the war was over it was Lemass who then devised the more aggressive concept called the semi-state company.

We spawned a whole breed of companies like CIE and Aer Lingus and the Irish Sugar Company. These were the new state capitalists. The congruence of all these three groups of people created a platform for the Michael Smurfits and the Ben Dunns and the Tony Ryans and people of that nature. Without the work of the warrior politicians and the Mandarin civil servants and the semi-state companies there would not have been the impetus which provided us both with the capital and the sense of confidence. The entrepreneurs of today are the new Irish Elizabethans. And their notion is that the finest form of patriotism is to plant the flag of Ireland in divers countries around the globe.'

He, of course, rates high among them, very much a product of his time.

'It's an exciting society to live in today. My father was a civil servant and to him the ultimate ambition was to have a job that was permanent and pensionable. To me, the notion of permanence and pensionability are sounds from the graveyard.'

Yet he says he is in reality slightly apart from the others.

'I'm a little different in that I see myself very much as a professional manager. Ben Dunn and Larry Goodman and Michael Smurfit all started in their own family businesses and took them from local or domestic or medium-size to world-class enterprises. My task has been a different one, to compete on the stage in the United States in a very specific area, that of professional management of a large multinational corporation, to accelerate its growth and make it the best within its own particular area. At the same time I'm an investor in Ireland.'

And ever the hero.

Unlike the others, who either made their own way or took a family business and developed it, he started in the world of business as an instantly recognizable personality.

He however plays that down.

'It didn't help to be a rugby star or instantly recognizable in the sense that you think it did. Where rugby did help was in sharpening one's sense of combat. In drawing a clear correlation between reward and effort, there's nothing as obvious as a fellow who hasn't trained in the heat of battle. It also helped to learn to meet with Kipling's famous duo, triumph and disaster. You have to learn to roll with the punches. Effort brings its own reward. From the point of view of training in a discipline, football, or indeed any sport is damn good but football, be it soccer or rugby, has the added dimension that in the final analysis your excellence as a player is terribly dependent on other people. If you happen to be Bjorn Borg you can probably do it on your own. But you sure as hell can't as a rugby player. Particularly one who played where I did on the right wing or the left wing where you're at the end of a long chain of consequence. If the ball doesn't reach you in the right mode, you can end up in the local hospital.'

Then too, there are responsibilities that go along with being a hero, even if someone doesn't readily admit to being one.

'I think there is responsibility that goes along with that but I also don't think any of us should take ourselves too seriously. There's a lovely line of Sydney Smith, a great nineteenth-century English wit who said, 'The Irish and the English have defied the laws of physics. The English who are a dull lot have risen by their gravity and the Irish, a humorous crew, have sunk by their levity.' My view is that there's an important responsibility to show that you're hard-working and ambitious and can compete on the world stage. That then widens the opportunities for other Irish men and women to perform in a similar situation. But beyond that, I think, one would take oneself a little too seriously if one thought one had a kind of national obligation to be a daily talisman to everybody. You should live your life in your own individual way and enjoy it. There's a great wit called Hal Roach and he has this final line at the end of his show which goes, "Lads, live every day as though it's going to be your last and one day you're going to be right."'

22

He nearly broke his back skiing the week before and he was still in pain.

'Speed has always been a fascination for me. I've never got over it.'

At least he's come as close to breaking his back as anyone can without actually doing it.

'I guess I'm what you'd call a dangerous skier.'

He'd been racing down one of the black slopes at Courcheval – they'd just clocked him at 85 kilometres an hour – when he lost control and somersaulted three times.

'I find that when you're going down the slopes you can forget about business. If you lie in the sun there's always a phone somewhere. Skiing is different because you need such total concentration. If you don't have it, you pay a penalty. Although that's not what happened to me. I wasn't thinking about business when I crashed. I was just trying to beat someone else down the slope. And I lost. Obviously.'

He says that with some regret because when you're as competitive a man as Michael Smurfit you don't have to nearly break your back to hurt – losing is painful enough.

Case in point: a few years ago, his horse Greasepaint came in second at the Grand National.

'My son Tony and I were standing with the horse. We'd just won £50,000. I'd just got into racing and this was our first time out in the greatest steeplechase in the world. I was thrilled. But we might as well have been on bloody Mars. Nobody cared about us. Nobody cares if you come in second. First place is where the action is.'

*

Michael's father, Jefferson Smurfit, for whom the compny is named, was a tailor by trade, a good solid Protestant from the north of England who married a good solid Catholic from Belfast.

'My father and his best friend met my mother and her sister on the Isle of Man. They both got married and they both changed from Protestant to Catholic. You couldn't have more of a hodge-podge than that.'

Michael, the oldest son of eight children, was born in England in 1937, around the same time that Smurift Sr. abandoned his tailor shop to take over a small carton-manufacturer in Dublin. The family moved to Ireland after the war, not only because of the business but also because there was no food rationing so they could eat. With a Northern Irish mother, Michael Smurfit was entitled to citizenship. Although he is officially domiciled in Monte Carlo, he is today a dual national, carrying both British and Irish passports.

'My father always intended that when his sons were old enough we would quit school and come to work. He used to say, you make businessmen and you buy brains. So at 16 each of his four sons went straight into the business. There was never any discussion about university. At 16 we went to work for him. There was no argument.'

Just as an aside, Smurfit adds that he doesn't share his father's philosophy where his own sons are concerned.

'My father had the time for us because we were one factory, one company, we all lived together. We were all in the same house. We saw each other at every meal. We're now 350 companies in 15 countries. I simply can't spend the time with my sons the way my father did with us. I started at the bottom and have no regrets about it. But my sons aren't doing that. I wanted them to have college degrees. There's no reason that they should do it the way I did. They don't need to know the business from the bottom up.'

But then, it was a very different world in his father's day. And the two are very different men. Where Michael Smurfit has grown comfortably with wealth and moves easily in sophisticated society, Jefferson Smurfit was a tough, hard-drinking self-made man who had to fight his way up. In fact, Smurfit confesses he only really came to love his father later in life.

'It took me until I was in my 30s, when I could appreciate the toughness. He was nearly bankrupt twice in his life. He hit bad business cycles and really had to struggle. He came over to Ireland at a time when there was a lot of sectarian prejudice. Catholic companies wouldn't supply Protestant companies and vice versa. There were Protestant banks and there were Catholic banks, Protestant lawyers and Catholic lawyers. It's changed now dramatically for the better, thank God. But it took my dad a lot of time to be accepted into society.'

Although Smurfit wouldn't call his own childhood a difficult one, he was plagued with health problems and they most definitely altered his outlook on life.

'I think I had a very good childhood. But I was ill for a number of years. As a teenager I spent a lot of time in hospitals, weighed 15 stone, had three chins and a belly out to here. Of course it affected my life. Holding someone's hands when they die has to affect you. The general perception of me is of being very competitive. And I am competitive. I got some of that from my father. But some of it also comes from the fact that I was very young when I realized how short life can be.'

He doesn't go into detail about his illness. It's one of those things he keeps to himself. Although his health wasn't helped any by working at one of his father's paper mills. The shop where he worked was very damp and before too long he was diagnosed as suffering from a serious lung infection. At one stage he was in a cancer ward. However, it was during those long stays in hospital that he started learning about businesses.

'I was reading everything I could about business. That's how I learned about take-overs and acquisitions. I spent 24 hours a day, seven days a week lying in a hospital bed for a very long time. I had nothing else to do but that.'

An introverted boy when he went into hospital, he was even more introverted when he finally came out. So his father sent him to America, to work in a family plant there, to learn that, in business, being shy gets you nowhere.

The office was in Connecticut, in a town about an hour away from where he found lodgings. Undaunted, and without transport, he simply walked back and forth to work every day. One afternoon, in the middle of a snow-storm, the plant manager found him on the side of a road and asked, 'What happened to your car?' Smurfit said, 'What car?' The manager said, 'It's snowing and it's going to get worse. How are you getting home?' Smurfit shrugged, 'The way I always get home, I walk.' The plant manager hurried Smurfit into his car, not believing that the boss's son walked both ways every day.

'I had to walk', he now explains, 'because my father hadn't given me any money for a car. There were no buses, I was only earning $6 a week and I wouldn't ask anybody to drive me.'

When the story got back to Ireland, his dad sent him $90 to buy a car, which he did – a 1946 Chevrolet that burned more oil than gas.

'There was always a blue haze behind me. But that didn't matter because now I had a car. And of course I drove it everywhere. The greatest moment of my life was when I drove it to New York. I was staying at the YMCA because I couldn't afford a hotel, and right nearby there was the Hippodrome Parking. I'll never forget it. The fellow there gave me a ticket and as I walked away I thought to myself, they really have this country well organized. America is great. After the weekend I paid my bill at the YMCA, like $26, went back to get my car and the guy wanted $18. I said, 'What are you talking about?' He said, 'What do you mean what am I talking about. You've got to pay for your car.' I didn't know I had to do that. I genuinely thought it was free. When I was leaving America, I took a ship home and left the car right there on the dock with the keys in it. I was very naïve in those days.'

Returning from the States, Smurfit stayed with his father until 1958, until they disagreed about how the family business should be run. Needing to prove himself, Smurfit convinced his father to lend him £25,000 to buy a corrugated-box business in Wigan. He ran it for four years, until it was successful enough that he could sell it back to his father for an even £1 million. Five years after that, he took over the day-to-day running of the family business, which then had a turnover of just about £1.5 million.

'Ireland was literally held back for so many years. It was a quasi-socialistic state and very inward-looking. Until Sean Lemass came into power, we were pretty backwards. We're the product of his thrusting vision. He was the one who opened up the opportunities. We were all doing rather well behind the barrier but once he brought those barriers down it was all very simple.'

Smurfit watched those barriers coming down and clearly saw that big multinationals would soon be coming to Ireland to swamp any small Irish company that got in the way. He told his father he thought the only thing to do was merge, acquire things and go out into a wider arena.

'In Ireland we don't have critical mass and we don't have engineering backgrounds. We don't build airplanes or cars. Foundries are needing for plumbing and grates on the streets and even then someone in England can build that stuff for half the price and double the volume. So he had to begin doing things on an international scale in order to survive.'

Today, the Smurfit Group is Ireland's largest company, with gross sales approaching £4 billion.

As late as the mid-1980s, the Smurfit Group was still in the second division among the world players in paper and packaging. It wasn't until 1986 that they made it into the first division and doubled the company's size with two Stateside buys. In January, through their US-based Jefferson Smurfit Corp. – which is 79% owned by Smurfit Group of Dublin – they acquired 80% of the Publishers Paper Company, which was immediately renamed Smurfit Newsprint. In October they paid $1.24 billion for half of the Container Corporation of America (CCA) in conjunction with Morgan Stanley Leveraged Equity Fund.

The CCA deal was the largest purchase ever made by an Irish company. Included in the deal were options, which Smurfit has since exercised, to buy CCA'S interests in Holland, Spain, Italy and Latin America. He also had the option to buy Morgan Stanley's 50% by October 1990 but, with one year remaining, the partners recapitalized the deal. They each put $500 million into a new company and bought Jefferson Smurfit Corp. That meant the Dublin group wound up with $1 billion cash in its balance sheet but postponed their rights to acquire Morgan's half until 1996. Morgan Stanley, in the meantime, more than quadrupled their original stake in the matter of a couple of years.

'The deal was good for everybody and felt right to me from the very beginning. I had no trouble selling it to my board. But then my board has never said no to me on a major decision yet. On the other hand, you have to understand, we'd never bet the shop. I'm a great believer that down-side is very important, that you must always look at your worst cases first.'

Some people say that Smurfit's indisputable success since taking over from his father has as much to do with luck – being in the right place at the right time – as it has with his own ability.

In fact, Smurfit himself almost agrees.

'Napoleon once said, that new general is brilliant but he's bloody unlucky so I'm not going to have him do the job. I suspect we're all like that. You must have a certain amount of luck, no matter what the risk. If you take the right risk at the wrong time, you're dead. Or, if you get the risk factor right and the cycle wrong, you can find yourself in very serious trouble. But then, knowing when to take the right risk is one of the things I get paid for.'

As far as he's concerned, one of the best ways he knows to limit the risk factor is by building slowly, step by step. Another is by sticking to the business he knows.

'We don't buy companies the way James Hanson and Gordon White do, or the way Gerald Ronson does. I see these movers and shakers like Hanson and Maxwell and Ronson and they're buying and selling this and that, dealing all the time. I'm fascinated with what they do but I have no idea how they actually do it. When I read what these guys are doing, it's so alien to my upbringing and education, I don't know how they operate their business. Or is it a financial business they run where the numbers count and that's it. For me the numbers are a result of effort and therefore I try to direct the effort. Anyway, we're only in the paper business. We don't know anything about anything else. So when we buy something we buy it to keep it, build it and make it grow. Of course we could buy a company and sell it right away and put the money in the bank. But that's not what we do. Our job is to progress and to build businesses where we have real knowledge and unique experience.'

He says however, he is, like so many other people in this book, very much a long-term thinker. But then he doesn't have a lot of choice because his is decidedly a long-term business.

'I'm building a forest in Ireland now which won't mature for 35 years. We're spending $10 million a year on that. We've also got a 150,000-hectare operation starting in Columbia and Venezuela. That's a commitment of seven years for eucalyptus and 15–20 years for pine. So some of those programmes I'll never see as Chief Executive. They'll be for my kids and my grandchildren. But at the end of that we'll have a resource which will probably make the company $100 million a year. You see, once you get a certain land-base, you take it up and put it back. Trees are the only naturally recyclable product that exists in the world, except for food. The rest is out and gone. Oil, coal, gas, everything else disappears. This is the only one that replenishes itself.'

In becoming one of the world's largest paper and packaging companies, Smurfit says, he's had to make certain adjustments to his own style. Managing a huge conglomerate means he can't do much more than take the big picture, look at the business in a global way. It also means he's had to sacrifice some of the personal touch which used to characterize any family business.

'After a certain time you lose contact, which is a sad thing. The other morning I was in one of our factories in the West of Ireland and I realized how much I really miss being on the shop floor. That's where the action is. That's the heart of the business. I love visiting the plants. And I like going alone. I don't like to go with any of my executives. It's when I go alone that I get to hear the real story.'

His visits are almost always announced because he wants to be able to speak with as many people as he can. Another reason is because of what once happened to his father. He'd arranged to see a corrugated box plant somewhere in England but, through a diary mix-up, arrived a day early. He got there only to find everything completely shut down. When he asked at the gate why the factory was closed, the guard explained, 'We've got to paint the place because the fucking boss is showing up tomorrow.'

So Smurfit announces his visits.

'But I can tell when the factory's been cleaned, when the ladies' toilets have been done up, when everything has been put into shape just for me. I know when the machines are looking too good. I know enough to peek outback and find out what's been shipped a week earlier. I know when I'm being spoofed. I've been in this business a long time and I've got my own tricks. The worry is that they keep finding me out and I have to keep finding new ways to check on them.'

Still, he tries wherever possible to create an atmosphere of a small family firm. Smurfit's two brothers are in the company – one in the States, one in England – as are Smurfit's two older sons. What's more, everybody operates on a first-name basis.

'I'm Michael to everyone in the company. The only Mr Smurfit was my dad. I operate like that because, for me, *esprit de corps* is the single most important element. A company's culture comes from the top down. We're in a tough, competitive business and we're trail-blazing. We were the first company from Ireland to go to America. We're in the Far East,

Australia, Africa and we're one of the first Irish companies in Eastern Europe. It puts tremendous pressure on our people because we're asking them to got out and do something no one in our business has ever done before. So we need to let them feel that they can always come back into the family environment. I work hard to create an atmosphere.'

One part of the atmosphere may be team spirit. But another is a lot more basic. It's money.

'We're highly incentivized. People may not always work for money but they sure as hell never work without it. I try to find ways to share the incremental cake. Now, if there's one argument I have against trade unions, and remember I was a member of a union for four years, it's that unions block incentives. If you build incentives into a scheme, the unions see them as being automatic when negotiations come around the following year. It becomes a *de facto* result. Therefore the shop floor tends not to share in management-like rewards because they're stuck into these incremental amounts.'

Smurfit's executives are incentivized to the point where they can have bonuses of up to 50% of their salary in any year. Actually, they can earn bonuses of much more than that – the sky's the limit – but anything more than 50% is carried over into the next year.

'If you have an incentive scheme where someone does earn something like 200% of his salary, it's either a bad incentive scheme or the market went bloody mad and you didn't anticipate it so you get a one-shot deal. It happens. But when it does you have to look at it closely to make sure it doesn't happen again the following year.'

So Smurfit is all about *esprit de corps* and incentives and if that's his formula it must be the right one for him because over the past 29 years, the group's average annual growth is now 31.5%.

'It gets harder every year. But we don't compete against ourselves to move that figure up. I believe that finance resources are secondary to management resources. Again, we're managing a business that we see ourselves managing for as long as the shareholders will allow the Smurfit family to manage it. With that in mind, we're building management resources all the time. We grow, consolidate, bed in, make sure it's solid, make sure we don't have to look over our shoulders, then go to the next stage. We're not trying to run up the stairs quicker than we can bring our children and our managers with us. Our growth has been more or less steady. If the price of newsprint drops tomorrow, there's little we can do about it. We can make managers more efficient, but we're doing that in any case with working-capital controls. We charge all our plants for their working capital. We charge our managers for the use of the building so they know what their real return is. We have very sophisticated financial controls, including seven-day cash statements and monthly accounts reviewing every company in every country.'

At companies like Hanson, every expenditure over $750 has to be approved at the head office. At companies like Smurfit's they make that sound like a lot of money.

'Hanson's got me beat by $750. I take decisions on all capital expenditure. It's automatic. You can't spent any money in my company without my approval. Nor can you hire anybody in my company without my approval. Those are the two key criteria. I'm a great believer that bureaucracies don't just happen, they're created and I won't allow anyone to create a bureacracy in my company. You may think I'm crazy but to get a new employee into Smurfit, you've got to convince me that the job is necessary. And that's not easy.'

Apparently not.

When he bought CCA – doubling the size of his company – he begrudgingly accepted two extra people into the head office. And that, he adds, was only after a year of arguing with him that those two people were needed.

'I have a real fetish about that. I'd rather pay a few people well than a lot of people badly. We run a company that has £4 billion in sales with 41 people in the head office. It used to be 35, and those six people really had to fight their way in. Bloody right they did.'

Believing the old adage that money is made in the plant, not the head office, he allows replacement staff to be hired without his personal approval. But that's only recently. There was a time in the not-so-distant past when, if somebody left the company, that job had to be rationalized as well.

'Worldwide we've got about 40,000 employees. And I'm always trying to get that number down. We calculated it costs us £50,000 overhead for every employee coming through the front door. You only learn that when you let people go.'

Taking over CCA, he moved their headquarters from Chicago to St Louis and something like 80% of the CCA headquarters staff did not make the move. In most cases, they didn't want to go. In other cases, he didn't necessarily want them to go. The point is that the bulk of that office staff didn't transfer and their jobs weren't replaced.

Another area where he is quite firm in his views is in always taking the global view when buying equipment.

'One of the things we look at automatically when we purchase anything is its worldwide effectiveness. That's the only chance we have to talk to the unions about our manning levels, particularly in the UK and Ireland. We may have four men on a printing machine where the Japanese have one and we want two. Well, we know we can't get to the Japanese rate of efficiency and technology, so we tell the unions, look, the Germans or the Italians have two on the machine instead of four so we won't buy the new equipment unless you'll agree to the new manning. If they won't agree they don't get the machinery. We always look what's happening elsewhere because we have to be internationally competitive.'

Slightly less than two-thirds of Smurfit's business is now in the States. He expanded there from Ireland and the UK and now he's expanding from there into the rest of the world. But unlike so many other people, he's not rushing into Eastern Europe.

'I don't know yet how ripe Eastern Europe is. We're doing our homework now. We have a German company to worry about Germany, but I'm still trying to assess Czechoslovakia,

Romania and Hungary. All of them will need boxes. You can't sell anything today without it being well packaged. So there's going to be a tremendous need there. But where the capital base is, I don't know. One of the things we can offer those governments is understanding, because we come from a country with no capital base. We came from very lowly beginnings, which is where they are. We also know how to start a business with limited risks. We know how to build small, efficient factories. The Americans are great at building very big factories and American companies want to build even bigger factories. But I believe the biggest rivers are made of the smallest tributaries. I prefer to have 20 small units doing very well thank you, than one very big unit which, if it goes wrong, hey diddle diddle!'

Smurfit says he just can't see how what's been happening in Eastern Europe could make any meaningful contribution to his profits for, say, the next 10–15 years. After all, it takes a long time to build a mill. If he starts to design one tomorrow, it won't be up and running for four, maybe five years. It's capital-intensive, there are losses in between and there are skills to develop. Although he is keeping an eye on the Soviet Union.

'In our business you've got to plan a long time ahead. If any of the changes in Eastern Europe affect our business, it will be closer to the back end of this decade rather than the front end. Although I am now starting to factor in whether Siberian timber, which is the biggest untapped tract of timber in the world, can ever be harvested effectively to affect the programmes we do. That's one of the strategic studies we've got to do. The forests in Eastern Europe are not going to be that significant. Russia is the one to watch. They're the one that has got the trees. But even if Russia ever became like Sweden, which does a tremendous job of harvesting and redeveloping, it would take them 50 years to become a world player. The trees are very inaccessible, very difficult to get at, and there's no infrastructure. You need hydropower. A hydropower plant alone takes 10–12 years to develop. You need power and you need people.'

*

There's an expression in Lancashire, he says: 'Hogs to clogs in three generations.'

He took over from his father.

Some day his sons will take over from him.

'I'm very conscious of that expression and I hope that my sons will have the right values. I'm so proud of having made my father's business into the biggest business in Ireland and I'd like to see them continue that. I saw my father's struggles and I'm very proud that he was alive to see what I did. It was the only time I think I've ever felt egotistical.'

Like most successful entrepreneurs, Smurfit has at times taken on selected projects outside the company. He's Chairman of Irish Telecom and the Irish Racing Board. He was also once on the main board of the Irish Allied Bank. And he remains one of the few people in Ireland ever to have resigned from a major institutional board. He left the bank because he found he was devoting too much time to non-essential duties. And anyway, there was a conflict of interest as his company was suddenly branching out into banking.

'We don't as a rule move away from our core business anywhere in the world, except Ireland. That's the exception. We have in fact diversified in Ireland for a number of reasons, mainly our agreement with the government to bring back a certain amount of capital each year. We created far more than we ever anticipated and can't put that into our mainstream business so we've created new business. We hired some very able people to direct us and we're in banking and insurance and leisure and the media. We've also invested in home shopping TV with Rupert Murdoch. We are putting money into other things, but only in Ireland and anyway it's pretty Mickey Mouse when compared to our main business.'

In spite of the demands on his time, he maintains his interest in Telecom and the Racing Board. The first because he thinks he can make a difference. The second because he loves racing.

'When I took over Irish Telecom, there were 22,000 employees. I've now got it down to 14,000 and I probably really only need 11,000. We're more efficient, giving a better service at a lower cost and putting in more telephones. So what did those 22,000 people do? I found out what they did and the answer is, nothing. The guy who went in at 8.30 in the morning couldn't go out on the job because his supervisor didn't come in until 9 o'clock. And so on. There was all sorts of in-built inefficiency in the system. I just won't allow bureaucracies to happen. Now, some people ask me if I worry about all the people we let go and of course I do. I hate the thought of letting anybody go. But the alternative is that somebody will have to pay for inefficient service. And that's more incorrect in my book than keeping the person. I believe it's actually better off to have them on the dole than wrongly employed in a company.'

His attitude may be right for business but it is hardly a politically popular one.

'Of course not. But then I've never read anything that says a successful businessman makes a good politician and vice versa. Now, successful business tactics and successful political tactics can sometimes be the same. They are in the sense that I'm doing a political job by running Telecom and the Racing Board. I run them like a businessman, although I suppose you have to be a bit of a politician as well. I'm dealing with politicians all the time. We've just installed the fifth-largest cable television system in the world in Ireland. The reason cable exists is because the phone system is historically so bad and so is reception from the BBC, that we've not got several hundred thousand subscribers. But there's been tremendous political in-fighting to win this for Telecom.'

He won it because he persisted, because he knew he was right and because he eventually convinced the divers powers that he was right. And that's perhaps one of the advantages of playing at politics in a country the size of Ireland. It's manageable, at least a lot more so than, say, Great Britain. On the other hand, he says, Ireland suffers from having a limited resource of talent.

'In America you've not only got a huge pool of talent but there's a highly developed university infrastructure to feed that talent pool. There are also other great benefits in a large country, like the tax structure. Because of America's size, the tax base is 50% better than ours. That's why petrol prices in the States are so much lower. It's not that the overall revenue is so low, it's significantly higher, but there are so many people using it. We have a very small tax base and therefore have to tax very heavily. As a percentage of population, Ireland has a tremendously high cost of operation.'

While he swears that he has no political ambitions of his own, he does admit that there are times when he daydreams about politics, especially about government, and how he could change things.

'I've often fantasized about what would happen if someone came to me with a management contract to run the government. I ponder the questions, could I actually run the government as a business and how many people does the government really need. The first thing I'd do is dissect it because it's vitally important to find out what you've got. What we discovered at Telecom was that Telecom didn't know what they had. We knew we had a specific number of people, at least we thought we knew how many. But there was an inefficient system where bills went out every two months. I asked, why not monthly and they fought me on it. There's a whole host of things like that. Looking at government overall, unquestionably a lot of money could be saved. But simply having the authority to get the information and no power of implementation is no good. If I were asked to do a job, unless I'd have the power of implementation to act, I wouldn't bother. It would be a waste of time, because I know what happens to these things. I'm only interested in doing something when I know that in the end changes can be made.'

Those fantasies don't get acted out because no one yet has come along with that management contract. Yet, having encountered the waste in Telecom and having designed systems to turn that waste into savings, he's convinced that given the chance, anyone with sound business practices could tame the

Irish government's bureaucracy and take a tremendous amount out of the cost base which in turn would lower taxes.

'Taxes are very high. But our debt is so heavy per capita that we've really got Third World debt. We owe something like I£22 or I£23 or I£24 billion. Overlay that to a population of 3½ million and you're talking about a serious number. And that's an inbuilt cost we can't get away from. That has to be paid every week. The answer in large part is what we're doing now. We've stopped the proliferation of spending. We've got a government where less government is best government. We're letting the economy cure itself, don't try any radical cures. Keep government spending down and don't support any lame ducks. For the first time they've actually closed a semi-state body that was losing a fortune. The alternative is to go the way of Argentina. They're not tackling their cost problems and Ireland is. We've had tremendous growth over the last few years, confidence is back and property values are zooming up. I'm even building a country club on the basis of a new thrust for Ireland.'

On a personal basis, when he has the time, he's been putting together a collection of mainly Irish and some Swedish art.

'It's a hobby.'

So too is racing.

'If I ran my business as well as I run my stud you wouldn't be interviewing me.'

He owns outright, or in partnership with people like Robert Sangster, something like 150 horses. He says what he does each year is decide how much he can afford to spend on racing and sticks to it. He weighs his costs against the fun and the contentment he gets out of racing.

'It's sort of like owning a big boat, which I don't. What's the value of a big boat? You spend one, two or three months a year on it. You decide what it costs you and what the benefit is. I'm fortunate because I have a son who's very keen on racing and will probably want to develop the farm. But initially setting it up is very expensive. Racing has brought me moments of happiness and moments of misery. More moments of misery than happiness but I still enjoy it very much.'

'We're all the same age,' he says. 'Tony O'Reilly. Tony Ryan. Robert Sangster. Me. The glide path is all the same and we're making little bets to see who's going to touchdown first.'

Although Sangster hardly qualifies as being Irish, the four are friends and if the Irish press also paints them as fierce rivals, especially Smurfit, O'Reilly and Ryan, that's probably true as well.

A few years ago Tony O'Reilly was the guest speaker at Smurfit's annual Chairman's Dinner. He got up and told the crowd, 'Michael Smurfit and I have been friends for all of about three weeks.' They laughed. When Smurfit stood up to speak, he claimed, 'My clear view of it is all of three days.' They laughed even harder.

There is, after all, truth in humour.

Not long after that, the two met at a golf tournament in Barbados. O'Reilly supposedly showed up in a good-sized yacht. Legend has it that Smurfit showed up with two good-sized yachts, and then stayed in a hotel, just to one-up O'Reilly.

Yet, Smurfit claims that there really aren't any ego problems to get in the way of their friendship.

'I don't think I've ever had an ego, at least not that I know of. Maybe my friends might say differently. The only thing I'm really fussy about is my wine.'

That is something of an understatement.

No matter where he is, no matter who he's with, when Smurfit sits down to dinner a separate bottle is brought to the table and put in front of his place. Unlike Richard Nixon, who was known to have a separate bottle served to him when he lived in the White House because he wanted the good stuff while his guests drank the plonk, Smurfit serves the same wine to everyone.

'It's just that this way I know how much I'm drinking. You know how waiters will just keep pouring and you think you've only had a few glasses but it's really two bottles and you can't even get up from the table? I know I can drink one bottle and that I can't drink two bottles, so I have my own bottle.'

Wine notwithstanding, Smurfit, O'Reilly and Ryan are without a doubt the first of the modern-day Irish entrepreneurs. And it's not by coincidence that they happen to be the same age, that they happen to have arrived at about the same time.

'I think we're the ones that came out of our generation with the economic changes in Ireland, going from a protectionist society to an international society. Don't forget, Ireland is a new country. We had quasi-freedom from Britain in 1924 and were only recognized as a Republic in 1948. So to get the country going, all the institutions, which were British, had to revert to Irish institutions. It took a long time. There's no capital in the country, no historical fund of wealth. As far as I can remember, all wealth comes from two sources, either land or a factory. Wealth doesn't just happen, it's created. So we had to create the foundations of the state and that was created by semi-state bodies. And there were great leaders in those days. But the first thing was assistance from the state. Then fledgling industry came along. Then those industries had to be opened up to international competition. And all that took time. But hundreds upon hundreds of companies folded along the route. We own a company which was once made up of 17 subsidiaries in engineering, of which today only four survive.'

The Irish attitude towards business, is, he feels, closer to the American than it is to the British. In England, success is something that all too often is looked upon as a necessary evil just so that successful people can then be torn down to size. On the other hand, for many people in Ireland today, Smurfit, O'Reilly and Ryan are modern heroes.

'They say the closer you get to America, and we're the last outpost before you reach America, the less of a begrudger you become. We're much less so than the British because of the strong position of the British Labour Party. Whereas in Ireland, the two main parties, Fianna Fail and Fine-Gael, are both middle-class parties and have a huge chunk of something like seventy per cent of the vote.'

In Britain, as divided as the nation has become between those who do and those who want, failure can be looked upon with glee. In America, failure means at least you tried. The Irish attitude, he agrees, is more like the American.

'You know the story of the guy going down the block in a Rolls-Royce and he passes an Englishman with his son on one side of the road and an American with his son on the other. The Englishman says to his son, you see that bloody bastard there, with a car like that, it's a disgrace. The American says to his son, you see that, if you work hard you can drive a car like that too. The Irish are somewhere in the middle of the road. They don't know whether to be proud or begrudgers. Like Samuel Johnson said, "The Irish are a curious race who never speak good of one another." That's not altogether untrue, but we do admire our successes. Although there's still a part of our psyche that does become begrudgers. Once you recognize they're there, you don't worry about them.'

On the other hand, Smurfit discovered some time ago that with success comes a prying press and where he's concerned, he feels the press has at times been grossly unfair.

'I was the first one. Tony O'Reilly's divorce was never really talked about in the press. And Tony Ryan's personal situation didn't make the papers either. Mine did. They never got the hassle I got. Ryan's separation was years before mine. Maybe the press has only just grown up and they're more ready for that sort of thing now. But I certainly hit it right on the button. Mine was the first real attempt at invasion of personal privacy. I guard that very jealously. Naturally, it annoyed me, especially because I'm very low-profile. I don't deal with aircraft which is hi-tech or with newspapers and Waterford Glass. Come on, I deal with wastepaper and brown boxes. How low-profile can you get? But I'm the one who got the crap.'

The problem is that Smurfit is running the biggest company in the country and that, all by itself, makes him news. Although he's known for some time that he wouldn't hold his first place for ever.

'There are lots of very successful businessmen in Ireland.

Larry Goodman. The Dunn family. But on the international scene, Ryan has got to be the outstanding success story. I told our people nine years ago in a memorandum, there's only one comany that is going to be bigger than Smurfits and that's GPA because they're in a geometric progression.'

At least among this generation of entrepreneurs.

One of the things that he's especially proud of is that he and a few others have broken down barriers so that the next generation of Irish entrepreneurs can go even further.

'Let's say today there are ten very successful businessmen in my generation, including a few of the ones most people don't know about but who have, nevertheless, been very successful. Well, I would hope that the next generation could produce 30–50. There's no reason why not. The ground is being prepared for them. We send a lot of our young Irish employees to other countries so they can get international experience. In 1984–5, in the depths of our depression, when the company wasn't doing well and we really had to tighten our belts – we even grounded our jet for six months – one of the suggestions was that we reduce the intake of young management candidates. But I vetoed that. In fact, I increased the intake. I could see that we would eventually find calmer seas and I knew that when that happened we'd need sailors on deck. Let me tell you that there's something special about the Irish character. Look at our literary history. We have a far greater literary history than any other country our size. I don't see any reason why that next generation of Irish entrepreneurs shouldn't be expanding our reputation in the field of international business just as greatly.'

Index